WE ARE
CHILDREN-AN ORAL HISTORY OF THE NIGHTCLUB MANRAY

Shawn Driscoll

Editing and Content by
Samantha Levitre, Theodore Racicot and Mina Corpuz

Additional editing by
Riley Driscoll and Elizabeth Wahlman-White

For Louise and Charles Schauffler, Rhoda and Sedwin Chasen, and Constance and John Driscoll. My grandparents and the first historians in my life.

 For information, address Quidnet Press, 21 Oneida Ave, Worcester Massachusetts, 01606

Email Quidnet Press at quidnestpress@gmail.com

First Edition

Cover art designed by Steve Shook and used with permission.

steveshook.net

ISBN 978-0-578-95899-6

TABLE OF CONTENTS

Special Thanks

When creating a book like this, it is not a solo process. In many ways, it is culinary in nature. Many chefs, each bringing a vital component. These vital components are not only provided from the creative and editorial voices that helped to create this book. It includes a plethora of friends, family, associates, and scholars.

Shawn would like to humbly thank the following for their kindness, support, guidance: His wife Amy and his children Liam and Riley. His family and friends, all who have provided amazing support. His colleagues at the University of Massachusetts-Lowell. Special thanks to Lauren Cordiero, Mike Baker, Linda Hixon, Ted Flanagan for all the sage advice, Tess O'Leary, Grace O'Leary, Wendy Austin, Sheryl Gunapati, Elizabeth Wahlman-White, Michele Brown, and a huge thanks to all to all those who took part in interviews, discussions, and remembrances. Shawn would also like to thank his amazing team of editors, Samantha Levitre, Theodore Racicot, and Mina Corpuz for their hard work and dedication to this project.

We would also like to acknowledge Ian Tzeng, a long time ManRay attendee and resident of Boston and Provincetown, who was a generous benefactor for this project. We are extremely grateful for his support in the creation of this book.

My Editors would like to thank:

Sam Levitre would like to thank her parents, Glen and Rena, for always providing support and encouragement in everything she does, her brother, for always being there when she needs a break, and the countless friends, family, and students who continue to push her love of history and teaching.

Theodore Racicot is indebted to his parents, Rob and Diane. Growing up in the Air Force, the constant moves gave him countless opportunities to explore the country and its history. Whether it was living a stone's throw away from the spot where Paul Revere was captured or visiting Civil War battlefields on trips across the country, his parents introduced history to him at a young age. This introduction has blossomed into not only a passion, but a potential career dedicated to sharing this passion.

Mina Corpuz would like to thank her parents, Wilma and Tom, and her family for supporting her passion for reporting, writing and learning. She is grateful for their love and encouragement, even when she's chasing stories far from home.

Kickstarter Contributor-Special Thanks

Addam Rae Wolff	Jillian Venters	Niki Nevulis
Kathryn Landes	Nate Swanson	Christina Pearson
Xtine Santackas	Tim Malloy	Ahenebah Lane
Melanie Sharkey	Voravut "SpicyV" Ratanakommon	
Eric Chasen	Rick Webb	Naill Johnson
Mary Beth Doyle	Steve Chasen	Tobi Goldie
Rick Furno	Jamie DiBattista	Abigail Taylor
Jeremy Vyska	Michael Hsieh	Alaric Hartmann
Mike (Farmboy)	Jenn Sutkowski	David Winthrop
Adam Lewis	Trent Stewart	Erika Spaulding
Lisa Anne Mokaba	Shaula Clark	Deirdre Benson
Mark Chandler	Noel McKenna	Masumi Nakamura
Rob Crasco	Paul Vitagliano	Bryan Whitmore
Chris Morley	Virginia Zimmerman	
Lee and Michael Denton-Smith		David Kearney
Nicole Bartlett	"Hong Kong" Dave OHare	CF Best
Krista Siren	Maya-Bella Reeves	Diane Bono Martin
Ian Tzeng	Andrew Nelson	Scott Blinn
Cheryl Richard	Ben and Sharon Rodda	Jeremy Medicus
Joe Provo	Dave Chervenak	Roberto Caminos
Adviye Tolunay	Jess Burn	Benjamin Ledwell
Katie McGranaghan	Chris Concepcion	Liz Mellon
MJ Pullins	Michael Sprague	Eric Hoenes del Pinal
Jason Jones	Philip LaRose	Jeniphir Taylor-McIntire
Sara S. Wendell	Hannes Högni Vilhjálmsson	

Ian Tzeng Dedication

We at the book and contributor Ian Tzeng would like to dedicate this book to the life and memory of Dale Julio and Rob Morrisey. Dale and Rob were regulars at ManRay and whose hair salon, DHR Stylists, served the ManRay and Harvard Square community.

People knew them for their colored hair, rubber outfits and love for science fiction. They were open, gay, and unabashedly themselves during a challenging time. The couple was friendly and served as role models in the community.

Dale and Rob became stylists in 1985 and together opened their salon in 1990. Harvard University students and professors, businesspeople, family, and friends -- they all went to the salon for haircuts. A generation of gay people around Harvard Square went to DHR Stylists and got to know Dale and Rob, in addition to seeing them at ManRay.

DHR Stylists was a sight with colorful lights, rainbows, Star Trek and other decorations. Inside, they had a tower of pictures. On New Year's Eve, they took a picture every year with creative outfits, a time lapse of the couple throughout the years.

Dale and Rob met in 1982 and were never apart for more than 24 hours during their relationship. In 2004 when gay marriage was legalized in Massachusetts, they married at Avalon in full rubber gear. The couple lived in Boston, Cambridge and settled in Quincy.

In 2014, Rob was diagnosed with brain cancer. The couple had saved up for a trip to Italy and during the trip he started experiencing headaches. Rob died about a year later after his cancer battle. Dale died in a car crash about a year and a half later.

Photo provided and permission to use by Michele Brown

"Dale and Rob – You inspired generations with your styling, your love, and your unabashed courage as brazenly gay men. We miss you."-----Ian Kay and Eric Sage Tzeng

ManRay Manifesto
"The Art of Nightlife"

Our intentions and motives are simple:
We have built ManRay because the creative act and creative people are nocturnal. They are at their best when they are nocturnal. Those who are mired in daylight activities must content themselves to dream.
We have built ManRay because this great metropolis offers little more than the moon and a Seven Eleven after the late night news. Creative people need each other after dark.
We have built ManRay because we believe in the Art of Nightlife. We are not a nightclub in the ordinary sense. We are a new crossroads on the map of the night. All nocturnal people are welcome here. We will challenge our own creative boundaries by our contact with each other.
ManRay exists now to put people together--young and old, straight and gay. It has been built to provide a forum for new visual artists, performance artists, and those schooled in the art of revelry. It is a changing space made of color and human beings and the very best of the newest music.
It is an idea that invites us nightly to give it form.

Crafted by Bruce Jope and Francis Toohey

List of book contributors

Emily Arkin (Attendee, Musician The Operators, Shepherdess)
Wendy Austin (Attendee)
Patrick Baldwin (Attendee)
Charles Bandes (Attendee)
Koren aka DJ Punketta Doilie
Kyle Blaisdell (Attendee, Performer)
John Benshop "DJ Benny Blanco " (Attendee, DJ)
Shane Blau (Attendee)
Susanne Boitano (Attendee)
Duane Bruce (Air Personality, club DJ, Author, Actor, Producer)
Amy Butts (Attendee)
Paul Calnan (Attendee)
Russ Carter (Attendee)
Jennifer Chandler (Attendee)
Mark Clavet (Attendee)
Karla Clute (Attendee)
Jen Lucky Cole (Attendee, Employee)
Cris Concepcion (Attendee)
Hyson Concepcion (Attendee)
Rebecca Corbett (Attendee)
Gillian Cox (Attendee)
David "Daisy" Crowder (ManRay Bartender)
A. Dominy Cusraque (Attendee, Creator/Host and Promoter of Hell)
Jenny Dahling (Attendee)
Gene Dante (Attendee, musician, songwriter, actor)
Avril DePaghter (Attendee)
Guari Desai-Ackerman (Attendee)
Jamie Dibattista (Attendee)
Mark Dighton (Attendee)
Becky D (Manager/Choreographer, Fantasy Factory, Angeldustrial, Aphotica)
Eileen Dover (Performer, Door, Hostess, Lights)
Prospero Eaton (Attendee)
Chris Ewen (DJ, ManRay, Ground Zero, Xmortis, Heroes, Musician-Figures on a Beach, Magnetic Fields)
Erin Falkell (Attendee)
Chris Famulari (Attendee)

Kevin Farrington (Attendee)
Anna Feder (Attendee, Heroes Documentarian)
Eloni Feliciano "Latex Lily" (Attendee, Producer Xmortis, Creator/
Producer Miss Gothic Massachusetts)
Industrialsteve (Attendee)
Patrick Fitzgerald (Attendee, producer Xmortis)
Greg Frisbee (Attendee)
Mike (Farmboy) (Attendee, Performer, Dance Master, Fantasy Factory)
Elizabeth Galbraith (Attendee)
Liz Enthusiasm (Attendee, Vocalist- Freezepop)
Matt Gleason (Attendee, Manager)
Rebecca Griffin (Attendee)
Eartha Harris (Attendee, Musician)
Alyssa Hassan (Attendee)
Lacey Prpic Hedtke (Attendee)
Michael Hsieh (Attendee, Dancer, Performer)
Bruce Jope (Manager Campus/ Creator/Artistic Creator ManRay)
Jill Kempton (Attendee)
Julia Kilcoyne (Attendee)
Derek Kouyoumjian (Attendee, Photographer)
Julie Kramer (Attendee, DJ and Music Director of WFNX, Radio Announcer WFNX 1987-2012
Skot Kremen (Attendee, Musician and performer You Shriek, Project Sphere)
Richard LaDue (Attendee, DJ)
Liz Lamanche (Attendee)
Kathy Landes (Attendee)
Athena LasVegas (Attendee)
Tony Lee "DJ Arcanus" (DJ-ManRay, Ceremony)
Brian Legault (Attendee)
Adam Lewis (Security, Promoter)
Lucretia X Machina (Attendee, Singer/Manager Lucretia's Daggers)
Chris "DJ Wookie" Manousaridis (DJ, Front Door/Attendee)
Michael Marotta (Journalist, DJ)
Mizery McRae (Hostess, MC, Entertainer)
Noel McKenna
Gibby Miller (Attendee, DJ, Co-founder Dais Records)
Lily Moonstorm (Attendee)
Heather Morgan (Attendee)

Jennifer (Attendee, Fantasy Factory)
Norm (Attendee, Fantasy Factory)
Niki Nevulis (Attendee)
Terri Niedźwiecki (Bartendress Extraordinaire- ManRay, Ground Zero, Heroes)
Me'lissa Nin (Attendee)
ML (Bartender)
John O'Leary (Attendee, Musician, DJ)
Andrea Parros (Attendee)
Christina Pearson (Attendee)
Quang Pho (Attendee)
Rachel E. Pollock "DJ Lady Bathory" (DJ ManRay, Ceremony, Reverie)
Kathryn Pollnac (Attendee)
Marcia Post (Attendee)
MJ Pullins (Proprietor Hubba Hubba)
Corey Reeves (Bartender, ManRay)
Matt Richard (Attendee)
Nate Roman (DJ Mothra, resident ManRay DJ, Founder of Ceremony)
A. Dorian Rose (Attendee)
Tonya Sand (Attendee)
Xtine Santakas (Attendee/Hostess Heroes)
Melanie Sharkey (Attendee)
Krista Siren (Attendee)
Erika Spaulding (Attendee)
Trent Stewart (Attendee, Co-Head/Promoter Fantasy Factory)
Emily Sweeney (Attendee, Author, Journalist)
Jenn Sutkowski (Attendee)
Anastasia Taslis (Attendee)
Abigail Taylor (Attendee, Performer)
Emily Taylor (Attendee, Delicious Dancer, Performer)
Crayola Tidd (Attendee)
Constantine Valhoulis (Attendee)
Taylor Vecchio (Attendee)
Maryellen Vega (Attendee)
DJ Paul V. Vitagliano (Original ManRay DJ-1985-1987)
Kara Ward (Attendee)
Keith Ward (Attendee)
Dr Arlene Guerrero- Watanabe (Attendee)
Hideki Watanabe (Attendee)

Rick Webb (Attendee)
Sara S. Wendell (Attendee)
Jon Whitney (Attendee)
David Winthrop (Attendee, Photographer)
Addam Rae Wolff (DJ Addambombb)
Tatiana Zimkus (Attendee)

INTRODUCTION

January 1992. It was cold that night. I remember it was cold. Yet, I didn't truly mind it. The ride in from the South Shore of Massachusetts was not long. We parked in the Green Street Garage and the music (Blake Babies) abruptly shut off as the car parked. The car's denizens spilled out into the frigid Saturday evening, and we made our way to Central Square proper.

Our band of alternative/gothy brothers (and sisters) obtained more fellow attendees, friends coming in from the north, and west of the city, and we congregated at our predetermined meeting place, Burger King. As we were all not yet 21, The Middle East or T.T. the Bear's were not options.

Exiting the Mass Ave Burger King, we rounded the corner onto Brookline St. In one block's distance we stood in front of the club. Music pulsating and reverbing onto us in the cold air.

What happened that night, and this would not be clear for years, even decades, was a birth. A beginning. Births are the beginnings of trajectories. And while trajectories can be planned, they are subject to redirections.

I stood at that corner of Green St and Brookline and pondered that next step. Picturing myself walking through the gated doors, hand to be stamped, entrance fee to be paid. I heard the song, saw the decor, made eye contact with the other patrons.

What I didn't know then, was that everything was about to change. Change in weird, and wonderful ways. All I had to do was step through that door.

And I did.

SCD

Chapter 1

In the Beginning: The Years 1983-1985

"ManRay was a beautiful thing that was carefully conceived." — Corey Reeves

Situated in Central Square and owned by Don Holland, Campus opened its doors in 1983, catering to the gay community. Looking for a manager for the club, Don Holland found Bruce Jope and his partner, Francis Toohey. With Don's business acumen and the creative force of Bruce and Francis, these founders would create something truly unforgettable. Campus quickly became a club that was a destination, especially for the LGBTQ+ community that originally called it home. It was more than just your run-of-the-mill gay club, providing options. It became obvious early on that Campus had found a home in Boston-Cambridge and its clientele was broadening and demanding more and more. The three of them realized there were many communities in the Boston-Cambridge area who did not have a place of their own but wanted one desperately; the need to address a want for nightlife in multiple groups was an opportunity they would not miss. The building had a back room, which provided a unique opportunity to have two clubs in one building.

When Bruce Jope and Francis Toohey first artistically conceived the idea of ManRay, they were looking to push the boundaries of what a nightclub was and could be. They sought to provide a home for the children of the night to come together, discover, and give them a creative outlet. No one could have expected that 21 Brookline Street, which stood vacant for nearly ten years prior to its tenure as Simeone's Italian restaurant, would become what it did. It truly became "a new crossroads on the map of the night." S.L.

Corey Reeves: Cambridge has a different essence than Boston because it has this independent energy, this creativity, this liberalism. It has always been this creative field that has a different feel from Boston, which, at that time, was rugged. I felt that there was more of a cerebral thing going on with Cambridge, a lot more free thinking. To me, Central Square was urban yet safe, creative, and unique.

Chris Ewen: For me, the Central Square area was very worth exploring at the time. There was a vibrancy to Central Square. It was very vibrant. It was very artistic. Cambridge, especially Central Square, seemed to have a kind of hippie element to it that I found endearing. There were a lot of universities and it just seemed to be a lot more diverse, open, and friendlier than Boston proper.

One thing that I do love about Boston is that it's small enough that you could really tell distinct neighborhoods from each other. The North End is distinctly different from the Back Bay or Beacon Hill or Central or Davis Square. These neighborhoods and areas have a totally different vibe and it's something that I love about the city. It's great that they can all exist together.

Duane Bruce: These squares in Cambridge all had their individuality. Central Square, it was freer. Freaks let their freak flag fly more in Central Square than Lansdowne Street than they ever could because the people just demanded it that way. Cambridge is so eclectic that there's a little bit of everybody. There are ducks, there's dogs, there's cats, there's mice.

Daisy Crowder: In those days, Central Square could be kind of shady, but in an adventurous way; in a way that young people wouldn't necessarily be afraid of unless you came from an entirely sheltered upbringing. There were drugs. There was homelessness. The finer polish that you would see now was not there yet. There was no gentrification. It was a much more working-class neighborhood with families that had been around for generations.

Chris Ewen: For me, the Central Square area was very worth exploring at the time. There was a vibrancy to Central Square. It was very vibrant. It was very artistic. Cambridge, especially Central Square, seemed to have a kind of hippie element to it that I found endearing. There were a lot of universities and it just seemed to be a lot more diverse, open, and friendlier than Boston proper.

One thing that I do love about Boston is that it's small enough that you could really tell distinct neighborhoods from each other. The North

End is distinctly different from the Back Bay or Beacon Hill or Central or Davis Square. These neighborhoods and areas have a totally different vibe and it's something that I love about the city. It's great that they can all exist together.

Duane Bruce: These squares in Cambridge all had their individuality. Central Square, it was freer. Freaks let their freak flag fly more in Central Square than Lansdowne Street than they ever could because the people just demanded it that way. Cambridge is so eclectic that there's a little bit of everybody. There's ducks, there's dogs, there's cats, there's mice.

John O'Leary: Central Square wasn't really a hub for us at that point. It was a place you go past on your way to Newbury Street or Harvard Square. We started going there because you could get spiky collars. It didn't really give an impression to me until the early 90s when I started going to ManRay. I followed the scene. ManRay kind of put Central Square on the map for me and we realized it was cool.

Paul Calnan: I didn't mind Central Square, but parts of it were always a little sketchy near ManRay. One time when we came around the corner some guy just got stabbed. He was lying on the ground and actually had the knife in his back and you could hear the sirens coming, and there was another guy that said "He just got stabbed."

Wendy Austin: Central Square was definitely sketchy and Harvard? Harvard had all the punks and Skate Rats in the pit. So that was definitely a scene. I remember wanting to be a part of that. Central I think was a little grittier, and definitely more of a place where it's like, "Oh, this is what it used to be like at the time." However, I never felt it was dangerous. But I also think that I was a naive teen because I grew up in a suburb. I wasn't really that savvy or that street smart.

Mike (Farmboy): A word that was used to describe it for me was "Central Escape." The sidewalks were just the concrete sidewalks. They weren't the concrete sidewalks in the brick extension. There was a blue plywood police box where a cop would sit. At the time it was a lot of small mom and pop shops and convenience stores. It was also grungy. It was not a place where you would like to hang out on the sidewalk.

Mizery McRae: The thing about Boston nightlife in the 80s and early 90s was that there were no inhibitions. There were people doing anything and everything. They weren't doing stuff to hurt people. They were doing stuff to just enjoy the nightlife. It was like this whole family coming together and just enjoying each other. It was just a melting pot.

Julia Kilcoyne: Harvard Square was funky and fun. Central Square had an element of danger and an element of "We're not in Kansas anymore." An element of "I kind of really do need to pay attention to what I'm doing as I'm walking by myself." The square itself was almost a macrocosm of the club if you will. It was smoky. It was gritty. It was urban. The cops were always around. Somebody was always getting yelled at. There were fights.

Noel McKenna: Central Square was like going to a different country. Going to Cambridge was like going to a different country. It was a little bit rough. It has always been a very, very diverse area. There were lots of artists. Rent was a lot cheaper back then. It was absolutely adventurous to go to Central Square.

MJ Pullins: Cambridge is the best little town ever. When we moved back we lived in Cambridge for a long time.

Adam Lewis: Central Square was my place from the late 80s to the early 2000s. I stopped going to ManRay as a patron or an employee and became a concert promoter. I was doing shows at the Manor. I was doing shows at The Middle East and T.T. the Bear's Place and I was promoting bands. So, I was there all the time. I never felt uncomfortable walking around. Early on, Cambridge had those municipal lots across the street you could park in and walk across, so it's a bit of a quick dash. I don't remember it being a weird vibe in terms of being uncomfortable.

I can tell you that going to Axis on Tuesday nights because that was their dark night … God help you if the Red Sox were in town and you had to walk down Lansdowne Street in your crazy outfits and your eyeliner and [you meet] a bunch of drunk Red Sox fans ... It wasn't fun. You got called every name in the book. I don't remember that being an issue with Central Square. I always thought that Central Square was a very vibrant and diverse place. A lot of students. A lot of MIT students with a lot of creativity. Every time I would meet someone that was kind of out there, but in a fun way, they always ended up being an MIT or Harvard student. I always found that a pretty vibrant, great place.

Liz Lamanche: I had just arrived in the Boston area after college and some years of travel, and it was pretty much where I landed by chance because the rents were cheap. As I got my feet under me and started to explore, I also wound up with my first job in Bed Works. Central Square was a fun place to be. It felt like a city but manageable. There was a lot going on and it felt like a really pleasantly integrated neighborhood where people would sit on their front stoops on Western Ave and so forth, and just say hi to each other. There was the muffin store near the corner, the old people's Irish pub on Prospect, there was a Japanese grocery store, there was an Ethiopian restaurant that was sort of behind the bus station with a big yellow sign.

David Winthrop: Central Square at the time seemed very gritty. I remember first seeing where the club was off of Mass Ave. In the real early days, it didn't seem to be particularly safe. It's changed a lot since then. I remember it being pretty much a shit hole. The crowd that would gather up was a spectacle in itself because of the people getting into ManRay, The Middle East across the street, and T.T. the Bear's, and it was always like a gawk show for a lot of the non-Goths or non-fetish people, people who are just like "What is that weird club?" I just remember being so happy I was a part of that.

Prospero Eaton: Over the years I've come to know Central Square more, and I really love it. I hate to see things go. It's like this really vibrant diverse place. It's wonderful.

Gauri Desai-Ackerman: So Central Square was a lot grittier back then. There was definitely the area where Mass Ave intersected with Prospect which was definitely a little bit scarier. At that time, one of the friends I was going to the club with lived on Bigelow in a basement apartment, so you would have to walk right through that whole area to get to Brookline Ave. We definitely went as a pack or in a car. We definitely didn't want to walk in that area. She would tell stories about being chased by somebody with a knife. It was seedy and it was sketchy. There were a lot of little stores that were ethnic, like the Indian grocery stores and restaurants.

Mark Dighton: We came to really like Central Square. A lot of good restaurants. It was a little funky and a little bit dangerous, but I didn't feel it was that much more dangerous than the rest of Boston.

Derek Kouyoumjian: So, for me, up until 1986, I would never have gone to Central Square in a million years. I lived in Dorchester and Central Square was this weird anonymous station at the other end of the MBTA. But then my family moved to Arlington and I started to hang out more around the Cambridge- Arlington -Somerville -Brighton realm. Central was where I would basically get my bus to visit some friends of mine. It would prove to be a very major focus point in my life, starting from '86 because, for a while, I was living outside Central Square and felt very much a part of that community. But a lot of people seem very afraid of Central. They were afraid of it because it looked very seedy with rundown buildings. It was very unpolished. Central was a very poor neighborhood. It was kind of in between Harvard and MIT, it had a lot of different ethnicities, a lot of socio-economic demographics. It was very much a melting pot. You had a little bit of everything going on there. I never had any problems. No one ever tried to give me any problems or grief ever in Central and, back when I was a teenager, I would have looked very vulnerable. I was maybe 95 pounds. Honestly, I never felt endangered in Central ever.

Elizabeth Galbraith: Clubs, in general, I think tend to be not in the nicest of areas. There are still colleges, but it wasn't the nicest of areas to be. But they tend to be artsy.

Amy Butts: I definitely liked it. It was a little sketchier, but it was home. You go to your club all night and you walk down the street and you get some pizza and French fries at Hi-Fi in the morning.

Kevin Farrington: Because of the length of my time in the Boston area, I would say Central Square struck me as being pretty typical for a Boston neighborhood, except for the fact that there was, because of the clubs in that area, a more creative feel to it than a lot of the other urban landscapes around Boston.

Avril dePagter: I grew up in Buffalo on the west side of the city. When I came to Boston people were like, "Uh Central it's the worst, it's skeevie, you're going to get robbed," and all this stuff and I always feel like that's code for something. I remember getting off the T and popping up in Central and thinking, 'This is the best place I've ever seen.' It's one of those areas that you either absolutely adore or hate. I don't think there's an in-between. It's funny to kind of watch its evolution throughout the years.

In '99 it was like, "Wow, this place is wild and just nuts and kind of super lively." Then things changed and it got more gentrified. It's still a place where you see this amazing intersection of a couple different areas, from people that might be homeless to people that are super wealthy that live in that Cambridgeport area.

Kathryn Pollnac: One of the things that was strange to me is that we were parking in a lot behind the club and there's apartments right there, which was weird to me. But it was a nice, bright place.

Becky D: Boston was unique in that it was a small enough city that one club could have an effect, but it was also big enough to have a large enough scene for it to contribute to that effectiveness. In New York we used to go to the Batcave all the time and they have a very, very strong underground scene. It's a big city. It felt more like a club and less like a community when we would go there. It was a club; it was less like ManRay and more like this is the thing we do on the weekends.

Susanne Boitano: I'm here around '85. I worked at Strawberries Records and Tapes in Downtown Crossing. Because I knew a little bit about jazz and opera, they put me a lot on the second floor, which was nice and mellow, but I was often on the third floor where they had a spinning DJ. It was a real destination. So, I was privy to a lot of the tickets coming into town. It seemed to me that New York had more clubs and I feel like people dressed more outlandish. I remember at Black Flag no one was dancing. In New York, everybody jumped around like crazy. I remember the Boston audience being far more staid and less jumpy. I went to Avalon now and again just for dancing purposes.

Julie Kramer: Back when I was legally able to go to clubs, we just went everywhere, you could be at T.T. the Bear's Place, you could hop over to ManRay, there was something at Spit. I think Cambridge was a little more hippie-ish. I guess you could say a little freer, a little zanier. But it was different times, as you went into the 90s The Middle East and ManRay and T.T. 's sort of dominated there.

Daisy Crowder: There are, of course, many bars. There were a lot of Harvard and MIT students, and people that lived in places like Arlington and Somerville and going to Boston for them was even more that much more of a production. There was a need for it to be the right place at the right time and exactly the right setting. I don't think it would have worked in Harvard Square. I don't think it would have it couldn't have worked in Somerville at that time.

Chris Ewen: When Central Square was thought of as a kind of dangerous urban environment, we were able to make people comfortable when they were inside ManRay.

Bruce Jope: Cambridge at the time had a very different life than Boston. It was more jazz. It was more folky, almost like a coffee house. It had a little bit of rock going on. It never really fully converted from the pokey jazz way into a younger, hipper nightlife kind of way until, to be quite honest, we went there. We have kind of changed things there.

Benny Blanco: The Boston music scene was varied. You had your rock heads. I was very electronic focused. Then being at Berklee was its own bubble because there were super talented musicians there, a gazillion guitarists, just shredders that would practice all the time, and also still a bit of jazz musicianship legacy. At the time, the industrial sounds, and the electronic sounds I was into were not commonplace. I found my home with ManRay or Axis and Lansdowne Street. Just that era of music coming out in the late 80s, early 90s had tons of styles and genres that were coming out and burgeoning.

Kathryn Pollnac: I was a DJ at WRIU at the time. It was the late 80s into the mid-90s college radio, so I played some of the rotation stuff, things like Magnetic Fields. But I was also playing things like Legendary Pink Dots and Current 93 and some of the Goth stuff or industrial stuff, really an eclectic mix of things. My musical tastes are all over the place so you might hear Doris Day, Christian Death, and New Order within the same hour.

Paul Vitagliano: The gay nightlife in Boston was mainly on Lansdowne Street and Copley Square. Everybody mainly would go to Metro. There were also Buddies and Chaps. The 1270 was another place that played rock and alternative. And then there was Spit. So, you go out, you could go into the Metro, which was more disco and pop music remixes, and then Spit was more alternative and punk rock and New Wave being played. So, you really got this great kind of entry into all kinds of music just by going. We also have really great venues for live music. We had Paradise, The Channel, and T.T.'s

Paul Vitagliano: It was a time of so much newness in terms of the music and in terms of the scene that the right people gravitated to find it. MTV was a music needle; it was like an American radio station. They created massive hits and superstore artists. So, this cross pollination was going on. In '83 to '84, I was starting to get into hard rock, post-punk, like the Psychedelic Furs or Echo and the Bunnymen.

Chris Ewen: I trained as a classical pianist when I was really young. When I started going to college I also started getting into synthesizers in the late 70s, early 80s. There was all this exciting stuff happening in music and it just grabbed me. It was a whole new world that just took me and I wanted to explore. I worked in a record store too when I was a teenager. Being a DJ and still being a musician is just an extension of everything I've done my entire life.

Daisy Crowder: Boston back then had numerous gays and lesbians. The rock scene was much, much larger than it is today and live music venues were numerous, both in Cambridge and in Boston. As far as dancing went, there was Spit on Lansdowne Street, the Rat, and there were other spots. The place has a long history of both live music and nightclubs that goes back to the early 70s.

Bruce Jope: When I took over as the manager of Campus in '84 the place was in rough shape. They were only making about $1,000 a week and it was losing about $5,000 a week when I took over. Women's night was probably the thing that kept the place alive, up until ManRay. So, I was under a lot of pressure to come up with the magic plan. I had a reputation, after having been in New York, to know what everyone's doing, what the cool things are.

Don Holland and I knew each other because we had met through one of his managers, Paul Ford, who ran Campus for a while, called me up and he said, "I'm dying here, I need you to find me a manager." At the time my finances were not great so I said, "How about me?" He was surprised. I didn't really want the job; I wanted the money to be quite frank because I had no great interest in running a standard gay bar. So I said, "Well, I could do Wednesday." And I went in.

Bruce Jope: It was just me. I was just a manager. I didn't have an assistant manager until Buddies closed.

Bruce Jope: It was an Italian restaurant that had been converted into a gay bar. It's a big L on one side with the dance floor for Campus, which was in a nice shape, and a giant circular bar. There was wood paneling everywhere and stools which were very dowdy looking but workable to serve, to a certain degree, as a bar. Then they had this big room, which was like an event room that was completely desolate and empty. The upstairs office was sort of dipping down into the headspace of the room. They have a stage and they used to do drag shows. Don didn't have the budget to really bring in anyone. I guess they had tried a couple rock bands. That was the standard Cambridge model: take a dying business and throw in rock bands.

When I first went there I approached it very directly, and that was to make it gayer and make it more fun. Add some visuals. I added some color. I took all these very small steps because we had no money. The first thing I did was put these giant four by eight sheet supplies mounted and hanging down from the wall. You could rotate them in a different direction. So, you could visually change the club every night. I put a stepladder with a 1940s TV set with just static on it just to give the place an artsy kind of visual thing. The bartenders thought it was all horrible and distracting, but there was a certain group of people that came in and loved it.

Paul Vitagliano: Another thing that sets it apart is that you could change the interior. It creates conversation starters. At one point, there was a giant pink rhinoceros greeting you when you walked in and I have some photos of me sitting on it. It's like, who the hell has ever seen that before? So immediately there's an icebreaker and a conversation starter with a total stranger. I think Bruce and Francis had an understanding of that.

Mark Dighton: I was very heavily involved with the music scene and I had lots of friends who were in bands. It was through my connections that I'd heard that Campus, the gay bar in Central Square, was going to open a second dance floor that was going to be New Wave oriented, and I had kind of been playing progressive dance music shows on college radio stations for years. I had played at a couple of bars. Through various connections I ended up talking to Bruce and Francis and eventually Don about this club they were going to open and worked out a deal with them to work at the club doing security some nights and DJing other nights.

Eileen Dover: I didn't hear about ManRay at all. I only heard about Campus. It was only on Thursday nights and my curiosity was always getting the better of me and I'd be like, "Oh, well, if it's only open on Thursday night how do they make money? What do they do on the other nights?" So that's what piqued my interest. I went there with makeup on. Campus was 18 plus at one time, so that was my first. I never knew if I was going to get caught being underage, so there would be that rush of adrenaline. The first time I went there I actually didn't get in.

Daisy Crowder: That sort of feeling of community. I was a young man going mainly to queer spots, with Campus being one of them.

Paul Vitagliano: I remember bemoaning to Chris how hard it is to play for lesbians when you're a gay man. At that time, lesbian crowds were not thrilled if there was a gay man DJ, and they were very hard to please.

Terri Niedźwiecki: I would go in as a customer. Between the lights and the music and the decoration, I was immediately comfortable and, at that time, it was predominantly gay. Which I really never cared about.

Mizery McRae: You just got this feeling they were happy. They were able to be themselves.

Terri Niedźwiecki: It's not easy opening up a nightclub. It's hard.

ML Cambridge was the right place for it because it was located between those three universities — MIT, Harvard, and BU. I think the location was literally one stop on the Red Line or a short walk down the street.

Bruce Jope: I said to Don, "We've got to do something. We got a giant empty room. There's no way I can fill this thing. We just don't have what it takes." I said there was another entrance on the side. "Could we open that and do a separate deal in that room?" We took the padlock off and I opened that door into ManRay and thought, "Oh my God it's another club. We could do something really cool here." It wouldn't be a gay bar, it would be a mixed bar for the kind of people that I know in New York.

The basic question was how do we turn this big giant empty room into a cool club, not a gay bar, we had the gay bar, and it wasn't doing well. Don and I found someone willing to put in a sound system on credit. The amazing thing about ManRay was we did it with no money. Literally, I was up tearing out the ceiling panels. While I was managing Campus at night, I was next door doing construction too. So I would be walking out to check on the bartenders covered with sawdust. We stripped everything down to a black box and then we started adding turquoise, which is my favorite color. We put the DJ booth in the corner. The long bar was not there yet, it was just the bar underneath the office.

Bruce Jope: I always wanted to control the artistic vision of whatever I was doing and keep it true to what it was.

Bruce Jope: I always thought ManRay was the coolest name any artist would ever have. We wanted people to know that this bar was about more than just booze and music. It was a certain kind of a scene and we gave it a name that would exemplify that. Francis made this great logo for it. Francis, my partner, was very artistic. He went to Mass Art. He didn't have the vision, the way I did for the club business, but he certainly had the creative vision. He understood art and he was all hooked in with the art scenes and the idea of the whole Dada movement and manifestos and art being a lifestyle as opposed to just a painting or an object. It was all in his brain whirling around as being something that he understood. People were all going to art school during the day and then running out to the clubs at night and I think that he and I wanted to create a club that would sort of make that more of a seamless activity.

Bruce Jope: The inception of ManRay came about because of our view of nightlife at the time. One of the things that was always bothered me is the gay bars at the time in Boston were gay bars and they tended to play disco music and assume that all gay people love disco and all dressed a certain way. There really wasn't a place for counterculture and subculture in gay life. People knew about art and fashion. They went to museums and read books and talked about philosophy and were a little bit more intellectual. With the clubs there were only two choices in Boston. There was a ratty dive bar rock and roll joint, which was not terribly friendly towards gay people. Our idea was that there was a missing link in the club scene and that was ManRay. We had lived in New York City for three years from 1979 to 1983 and we saw those kinds of clubs there. We were publishing a New York magazine with a Boston section, but we were dealing with all the nightclubs in New York and all the nightclubs in Boston.

We looked at what was missing in nightlife in Boston and saw that people wanted a different take on going out to clubs. At that time, you had two versions of club life. One was Spit, which was kind of dark and punky and Gothy before Goth. It didn't feel like fun as much as it felt like making a scene and being cool.

Where we lived in New York, there were different kind of clubs with a mix of straight and gay people, which we found much more interesting than just a gay bar. Boston booked the place like a straight bar. They would not bring in acts or music that were different. So, we wanted something new that went straight down the middle. The differences were just in attitude and tone and maybe even in a way heightening the sexuality of the experience by making it really unique and different for straight people and unique and different for gay people because it was a mix. It was a little exciting to see a cute guy across the room and not know whether he was straight or gay. Everyone was there to have a good time. We were going to really be around like-minded people and have a good time.

Paul Vitagliano: ManRay was the alternative to the rest of the club scene in Boston because they were all kind of playing the same stuff. ManRay was the antithesis, and the alternative. If you were like me, because there were obviously thousands of people just like me, they might have gone to gay clubs because it was all you had. You dealt with the music because it was all you had. At ManRay, you could physically choose to go there because there was some music that you wanted, and it was the vibe you wanted. ManRay was mixed. It was more artsy; it was more experimental and expressive. Even the way you looked. You didn't have to look like a gay clone, you could look more individualistic than you could in the regular gay bars. As a DJ, that kind of became my calling card. I wanted to be known as a gay DJ who was playing music really opposite from what most gay DJs were playing in the gay clubs.

Bruce Jope: When we first opened, we described it as being Bauhaus in design and vibe. We had a German Dada kind of spin to the decor with the horse, the dog and a bronze man's torso sculpture. We used red and turquoise and yellow colors and were playing German surrealist clips on the video screen and weird things like Metropolis. We went with early 60s art upstairs, slightly psychedelic.

Paul Vitagliano: Don owned the building and was dealing with the money and the nuts and bolts of owning a property and Bruce and Francis were the artistic brain of what they wanted the music to sound like and what they wanted the interior to look like. They changed the interiors every six weeks or so. I was very impressed with Bruce and Francis and what they were doing because I'd never seen any bar like that in Boston.

Bruce Jope: We had originally hired a guy named Tom Lane as a DJ and he was there for about a month. I searched around and the DJ at Campus, whose name was Michael Tobin, told me about Paul Vitagliano and he asked Paul V to come see me. I liked him and he liked me. We talked about music, what he did, and what he knew. I was not a music person, so to speak. I knew what I liked. But at that point, I wasn't really turned on to most of the stuff that Paul would be playing. I kind of developed a taste for it. As a manager you really had to know how important the music was to the club.

Paul Vitagliano: I am the main weekend DJ at Celebration and I've made a pretty good name for myself. I am also working at the Boston record pool where all the local DJs would pay a small monthly fee and all the record companies would send their singles to a record pool. Each member would come in weekly and pick up their allotment of the latest promotional 12-inch singles. Working at the record pool, I got to know all the local DJs. I got to know more of the clubs. We're hearing all the dirt and all the gossip.

There was a moment of Bruce Jope finding me. By that time in '84, my reputation and status were out there. He knew he needed somebody who knew how to play the music and he chose me. I knew that I would have to basically shift all over. I did kind of a crash course of who are the bands that a ManRay crowd would want? I had to segue. My brain is kind of a Rock and roll and hard rock sensibility. I had to shift from rock to more post-punk, New Wave, electronic alternatives.

I DJ 'ed ManRay on opening night, which, if I remember, was March 30, 1985. I was a regular DJ through 1986 early 1987.

Bruce Jope: I was in my 30s, so it was really important to get a take on the club from people in their early 20s. So, I got some opinions and people loved everything we were going to do, everything we did, and everything we tried they were really into. So that made me know that I was on the right track.

Daisy Crowder: We were viewed favorably by the neighborhood and the fellow business owners and the police in Cambridge. We had a good working relationship with them all.

Paul Vitagliano: Celebration at the Station needed a DJ to do Monday and Tuesday. It was a Rock and roll 18 plus dance club, and in 1981 every main DJ was playing disco or pop. This was a club that wanted us to play AC/DC and the Rolling Stones and ZZ Top. So, I said I'd do it and they hired me. I basically had to learn on the fly how to queue up a record at the right time when one song is ending and you start the next. The DJ booth was so archaic that the turntables were probably from a radio station in the 70s. It had no pitch control where you could alter the speed, so you couldn't mix records.

I am this gay guy who loves Rock and roll. So, I'm a complete misfit. I really hated all the music at the gay clubs because it was all pop and disco. I put up with it because I wanted to be social and it was all I had. Even though the crowd at the Celebration was straight, I felt a bit of pride being a gay man playing Rock and roll. That feeling was sealed even more once I was at ManRay.

Bruce Jope: I was one of the real people that could do both — I could look at it from a business point of view and then look at it from a very artistic point of view. Not many people can do that. They are usually one of the others. I love both sides. I could bounce from one thing to the other very quickly. I could double track. I could multitask. If you're going to be successful, you have to develop those skills.

Chapter 2

The Rise of ManRay: The Years 1985-1987

"ManRay was one of many places where we grew up." — Elieen Dover

ManRay began as it intended to continue -- by setting the bar high. With performances like that of Divine, it established itself as not only a nightclub, but a venue that catered to varied and talented artists as well. The familiar faces that made the club what it was began to appear. From DJs Chris Ewen and Paul Vitagliano, the staff began to solidify and add their thoughts and ideas, growing the creativity and concept of ManRay.

Like all new things, ManRay went through its growing pains. Seeking to find its identity, the club was trying new things, from New Year's Eve parties to the very early concept of theme nights. As its manifesto said, the club sought to "challenge their own creative boundaries' and provide a space for artists of all kinds. Its first big battle came partly from the strangeness of the location. The club was walled in by residential areas and many people were unhappy living next to a boisterous club that did not seem to sleep. Fortunately, the club survived with the agreement that it would close at 1, rather than 2 a.m. While tensions remained, it was clear that ManRay was here to stay. S.L.

Bruce Jope: I'll never forget opening night. We had guys sitting at the table waiting for money to be paid. The carpet glue smelled horrible. The paint was still wet, so we were really worried about people getting paint on them if it got really busy. Well, it didn't get very busy. We didn't really have a great circle to get the word out because we weren't established with the crowd. That was going to Spit and the rock clubs. We didn't have any money to advertise, so basically we just distributed invitations to the crowd at Campus and through friends to get people there. Opening night was very slow. Maybe a couple hundred people walked in the Campus door. We had all this money we owed for the sound system and so on.

Paul Vitagliano: The first thing about a DJ booth that you need to know is most of them are way too small. ManRay's booth was the greatest DJ booth I have worked in in my entire career. It was designed by a guy named Alan Pottak who did all the sound pretty much for every gay club and for some straight clubs. When Bruce and Francis were designing the club I think Alan said to them, "You really should make it so that there are bins that DJ records can live in and stay here so that they don't have to lug their records." The booth was designed with plenty of room for the video and light person. Other people could be in the DJ booth without feeling cramped. It was truly the best I've ever been in.

Paul Vitagliano: One thing about ManRay is that they were one of the first clubs to have A VJ , and a setup so that there was somebody that was going to mix visuals with the music or try to have a video presentation on a big screen so that it was another element to the experience. Most DJ booths would have a light setup and they might have one or two decks that could play some visuals, but it was more of an afterthought.

Chris Ewen: ManRay had a dance floor with speakers' setup on corners. So, if you are on the dance floor, you'd be surrounded by sound as opposed to it being sent directly to your face, which was great.

Benny Blanco: The sound was sick at ManRay.

Chris Ewen: Everything had to be good. As far as the surrounding areas — you had The Middle East, T.T. the Bear's, businesses like Hi-Fi pizza or the Falafel Palace. They loved the fact that we had people there who wanted food late at night. ManRay wasn't just a nightclub. It was something that brought a little something extra to other businesses in the community.

Bruce Jope: When opening night happened, it was just people wandering from Campus next door. I realized one of the shortcomings was that we were so anxious, we were so hard working on building the place, that we didn't really understand how to promote the place to get a crowd on opening night. Unlike New York, there wasn't really a mailing list for the kind of people we were looking for. We didn't have the time to go out and find them so they had to find us and they found us through The Phoenix article that came out two days after we opened. Friday was a little better, but Saturday night ... my God, the place exploded. We were not prepared. We didn't have enough cash, so we were literally running up to Don's brother's pizza joint to get some. We were borrowing liquor from Latinos and T.T. the Bear's. It was just jam packed to the roof and they were just thrilled with the place. It was what they wanted.

Bruce Jope: Advertising was not a problem, promotion was not a problem, coming up with ideas was not a problem because I did that and Francis and I had help from others. So the creative element was really just the fun part for me. Our biggest problem was logistics. How do we get enough food or did we get enough ice? How do we cram people in a building that has a capacity of 800? That was basically our problem from that point on.

Paul Vitagliano: Our approach was we don't care what your zip code is or your sexuality, but when you're here these are the rules. This is how it's going to work. You make a choice to conduct yourself a certain way and add to the energy or don't come back. The wrong people wouldn't want to come back anyway.

Bruce Jope: Life magazine called and wanted to do a feature for the club. They heard it was kind of retro. I said, "Well, no, we're not really retro. We are working on a lounge downstairs that is going to be totally retro but from the 1950s Cold War perspective, not the Elvis Presley-diner-Rock and roll aesthetic." It was actually a guy named Danny Schechter who was a producer for 20/20 and Life magazine. They both called about the same time. And I thought it was perfect! Because before I had the place built, I had already sold the place in Life magazine and 20/20.

Paul Vitagliano: ManRay was really only my second DJ gig, but even just as a patron, they were doing something very unique that no one had done in Boston. I know they kind of modeled it on a club in New York which had a long, long hallway that had window displays that would be changed and the motifs would change. I think that's where they got the inspiration. There was a satellite lounge. The bomb shelter. The decor was all Mid-century. It is immediately 1950s, early 60s American style furniture and space age. People loved it because it was great to have that downstairs. If you need a break from dancing or the loudness of the dance floor, it was a great place to have a conversation. You could grab a drink and just sit down and relax.

Susanne Boitano: I was on the third floor at the counter [at Strawberries] and these two friends said there's a club in Cambridge called ManRay and

I'm thinking, "Does that have anything to do with the artist?" No. They said, "It's really cool and a bunch of us are going to go there after work." I needed more information. I needed to know how to dress, so I remember not going. Then I think about a week or two later, I'm hearing the buzz that it was super interesting. They had an article in Life magazine. Definitely time to go. I remember going and thinking this is finally like a New York club. It's got the space, it's got low lights, the music, it is tremendous. I remember just floating around and thinking this place is dark, it's full of fun people, I love the atmosphere. This is perfect. This is just what I want. Cambridge has the later opening too, so it was also open a little bit later than most clubs, which made it very appealing.

Paul Vitagliano: It didn't really take long at all for that place to be packed. It was pretty instant, so there wasn't a worry about, oh God, the numbers are down. How do we get more people? It just kept building onto itself. It was very, very crowded from the beginning and it just stayed that way just because people loved it so much. Maybe ManRay wouldn't have worked in a different town. But my gut says because of the huge college population, a place like ManRay was able to thrive and be popular from the get-go.

Chris Ewen: In the early days, ManRay being a place that wasn't burdened with having to be a mainstream top 40 club was able to create its own thing. Every DJ who worked there was able to explore that exciting and interesting part of it. Lansdowne Street aligned itself with WFNX. At ManRay we were allowed to thrive and do our things musically. I came here and was just blown away by what DJs were able to get away with. The diversity and coolness in their programming amazed me. I did not have a radio station behind what I did, so I could play Soft Cell's Sex Dwarf and stuff that wouldn't get played on the radio.

The role of a DJ is to please people but also educate them a little bit. Throw them something new and exciting. We're obviously there to entertain, but we shouldn't be there and pander. Our role isn't just to play what they want to hear. Our role is to bridge the gap between our aesthetic, which makes us who we are as a DJ, being able to speak to the people through our music and excite them and challenge them sometimes. But our role is to ultimately make everyone in there who comes to hear us very happy.

Bruce Jope: By the fall of 1985, it was kind of overkill because we had lines around the block. We actually started getting frightened at that point because of our success. God, I really had a knot in my stomach every night we were open because the lines were so long. The parking was so crazy. I was directly involved with complaints from the neighbors. We became the neighborhood pariah. We went from being the hottest, greatest thing that had happened in Cambridge since Harvard and MIT to being a pariah. We started getting some negative press about us destroying the neighborhood. So I had a neighborhood meeting. I even went into a neighbor's house and lay down on a bed because he said he couldn't sleep at night because of the music. I went over to his house at 11 o'clock and lay in his bed to see if I could hear the bass signal coming from the club. I couldn't. But I'm sure that if you are not a nightclub person, you could hear it. I told him I did hear it, even though I didn't, and I said we were working on soundproofing the club. The basic complaints were noise and parking.

There was a petition going around looking to revoke our license. It was horrible and it really ruined the whole experience for me. We tried to mitigate things with the neighborhood, but the feedback we got from the neighbors was "No, we have representation now and we were told not to talk to you."

We went to court. We had a really good lawyer. The judge actually voted to close us down and so we went to appeal immediately, which lasted for another three or four months. By March they rolled the license back to one o'clock. They also rolled T.T. the Bear's, which had gone from being a restaurant to a nightclub.

It was a better outcome than closing, but for me it was kind of a death knell because our crowd really showed up at 10 o'clock and started getting in line by 11 o'clock. And from 11 to 1 we had a line and then we had the club basically full between 1 and 2. So it was a real death knell to get rolled back to one. The club, in my mind, could not survive with a one o'clock license the way I wanted it to survive.

Chris Ewen: I know we had a couple neighbors that weren't happy with the idea that ManRay existed in their neighborhood. At that time we were on the regular Cambridge club hours which were Sunday through Wednesday till one and Thursday, Friday, and Saturday till two. A certain group of people who complained a lot about crowd noise and made it tough for the club to continue existing. It was a fairly dark time. We ended up having to close the lounge in the basement and there was a bar down there as well. We had to restructure the club entrance. It just made it more difficult for the club to exist, especially having less hours.

Noel McKenna: We all hated the fact that it was only open till one. We would stay at ManRay until one and then hightail it to Lansdowne Street to Axis.

Bruce Jope: We curated the crowd and that was one of the really important things about ManRay. The crowd was carefully selected from the hundreds of people that were waiting in line. If you didn't dress a certain way, we didn't keep you out, but we kind of let you know. How did you hear about the club? What are you expecting? We kind of used every trick in the book, without getting in trouble for discriminating, to make sure that our crowd was a good one. If we felt that you had the right kind of attitude and behavior to come into the club, you came into the club. If you were questioned or turned away, the next time you came back, you probably weren't dressed crappy. Eventually we got a crowd in there that we felt was the right crowd. I had a sense that they respected the place, they respected the people that were around them, and they kind of took care of that kind of stuff themselves. We did not have a lot of disciplinary issues in the club at all, regarding photo taking, recording, fights. The club really took care of itself. Our big problems were always logistics: having enough liquor in the club, keeping the music at a level that wasn't blowing up the neighborhood, keeping the line under control. It was all really logistics for us.

Michael Marotta: I really remember the dress code and how strictly it was enforced. I think everyone in Boston, at some point, went to ManRay with a friend who did not get it. That friend was stood up at the door and could not get in because they were fucking wearing white shoes or sneakers or a fucking windbreaker. Sometimes it was frustrating, but once you got in you appreciated those efforts and you appreciated the interest of the club to keep other people out of it and to really create a safe space where you could do whatever you wanted to do and you could be yourself. You could dress a certain way and you could look a certain way, you can act a certain way or you could just sit in the corner and do absolutely nothing and drink Terri's cocktails all night and enjoy the music.

Kathryn Pollnac: ManRay is this bar by which I judged everything else anywhere else I lived.

Chris Ewen: One of the advantages to having a nightclub in Cambridge is that your audience moves in and out. People come here for school. Sometimes they stay. Sometimes they move. Additionally, the attitudes were a lot freer, a lot more open, a lot more embracing of everybody. You could be part of the LGBTQ culture. You could be Black, you could be Asian, you could be Latino. Either way when they graduate they have taken little pieces of ManRay with them. We were able to be a part of their lives. That informs a little bit of who a lot of people are in very subtle ways, whether just their approach to what music they like or finding their life partners.

Emily Sweeney: We've always been a city filled with young people, you know, but you're talking about our glory days.

Jennifer: I feel like all those younger years I had squashed into a very small window, but I did a lot during those years.

Bruce Jope: I was managing both clubs. There was a swing door that I walked through all night long, one side to the other, keeping track of both clubs. There was a tremendous amount of work. I was getting there at 11 o'clock in the morning or noon and working till 3 in the morning. You are talking about 13-hour days. It's a tough, hard job. I loved the creative stuff, I never felt like that was work. The only work part was running two clubs.

Chris Ewen: At that time, the club was separated into two different clubs. When you walked in that was Campus and that was a gay bar and then ManRay was on the loading dock side. They were separate except on Thursdays, which was the gay night that they opened up both rooms for.

Daisy Crowder: Over time, Campus and ManRay did merge and become one thing. There were nights more popular with the gay crowd and there were certain nights more popular with the straighter crowd and there was a lot of overflow. The fear of the homophobia that initially was there at the beginning was gone.

Julia Kilcoyne: One of the things I love most about ManRay is that it was more than one club at one time.

Anna Feder: Every once in a while, if there's something I wasn't excited about, I would go into the front room and check out what's happening with the drag queens and 70s music. It was fun to be able to go between the two rooms. I don't think there's anywhere I go now where you have that opportunity. It was amazing to have a totally different change of pace. There's also places to get away if you're sort of overwhelmed. You could go to that front bar to take a break or go take a walk outside. There would always be tons of people smoking so it was an opportunity to talk to people.

Rachel E. Pollock: There was this wealth of choice for people who were patronizing it. You have two different DJs in two different spaces. If you don't like what's playing in the back, you can check out what's playing in the front room. You can sit in the lounge and talk with your friends.

Benny Blanco: It ties in perfectly with the rave world as well, where you almost always have two rooms. It allowed you to explore more. If you're in a different mood, you're not liking the song, you don't care for the DJ, then you have an alternative to go to. I really liked the chill out area if I needed a break or to shoot the breeze and mellow out. I always appreciated the multiple rooms.

Marcia Post: There were definitely lesbians in Campus, but there were fewer gay men in ManRay. We were also going on specific lesbian nights, which was Tuesday and Sunday. It would have a very different vibe, so we went just to be around the women.

Mizery McRae: When we would all go to Campus, we saw all these people come in and go straight to ManRay. I was like, "What's going on over there?" So, I just popped my head and saw people that weren't the typical gay people and thought, "Oh, this is kind of cool." So, I would go back and forth throughout the whole night.

Mizery McRae: Campus catered to the little 20 white boys and then ManRay was the older men that liked punk rock and industrial.

Kyle Blaisdell: I thought it was a perfect stomping ground because if you are in the backroom and the Goth music got a little too swirly and the Siouxsie Sioux girls start doing their twirls, you could always just step into Daisy's lounge or you could go to the front house dance floor where it was a completely different vibe. It was multiple clubs in one and you could experience it all in the same night.

Rebecca Griffin: So, I've been in many clubs as far as live show settings, but coming into ManRay was more. It was an overall feeling that I've never actually felt in a different setting. The lighting was on point. I mean, the darker the better. The sound system was killer. The fact that you have all those different rooms … It made it so harmonious because you had your space for your extroverts and you had your space for your introverts who had a quiet place to step out. You had your multi bar space with all the different bartenders. It was interesting. I think that was so appealing because I am multifaceted like that, as far as the music that I like. I had a lot of fun hopping from room to room. There was just always this air of excitement about it because you have that option to transition. There were always people playing pool in the back. Every space was utilized.

Mark Dighton: I worked security for the Divine show with Jeff Striker. Divine, she was fine. She was a little bitchy but that's kind of part of her persona. I was downstairs with her; she had the people who were doing her hair and her makeup and helping with the dress and she seemed pissed. I think she was upset about the money. I don't remember what that was, but she was kind of threatened not to go on. She worked it out with Don. I think she wanted to be paid up front and Don wouldn't pay up front. So I think he gave her half up front and half on her way out.

I will just say that Divine sweated more than any person I have ever known in my life. I can imagine when you're up on stage with bright lights on you, but downstairs, getting ready she was just soaked. It was not a very good setup for a performance venue because there was no sort of green room. There was no way to get to the stage, except through the club. We had to work our way through the crowd with a little group of security people. I was trying to tell her what to do as far as go here, go there, and she looked like we had just pulled her out of the ocean. I was looking at her makeup. What kind of makeup do you have to have to stay on someone who is sweating profusely? So, then she got up on the stage, which is basically just a glorified carpeted box and it was a high stage. That night basically Divine just kind of told stories, told jokes, played her music. Mostly they played the record and she'd sing over it, so she was on the record singing it, it wasn't like a special track for her or just the instrumental. Then sometimes she'd kind of talk and let the song keep playing. She was not much of a singer, but it kind of worked. It was just kitschy and funny.

Chris Ewen: The fact that we had Divine there totally fit in with the ManRay ethos. We're not going to have Amy Steward. We want Divine. So, in that way, it became a really historic thing. The way this show worked was the way a lot of artists would work, they would promote their shows to a primarily gay audience and they would go in and do a 20 minute to half hour show and it would just be something extra on the night. I'm just lucky we had her. I'm grateful that we did that. In the future we booked

Kiki and Herb, who were huge in the 90s and New York. I think we were always looking for ways to just bring in people to the club and having Divine there fit the whole aesthetic of ManRay and Campus to a T.

Daisy Crowder: Well, I went to its opening and, shortly thereafter, I went to see Divine who had a concert there.

Paul Vitagliano: I loved Divine. I was in charge of playing all her tracks at the right time. It was wild. It was so much fun. She was filthy and she was not in a great mood, if I remember correctly. She was kind of cussing out the crowd. But, in the in the queer underground everybody knew Divine, so it made complete sense that she would play a club like ManRay. I think it was one of the most packed nights we had.

Chapter 3

Shining a Light–LBGTQ+ Growth and Visibility

"It definitely seemed like a place where, not only could you go and be comfortably queer, but a place you could go and let your freak flag fly." — Krista Siren

For the LGBTQ+ community, the Paradise had largely been the destination gay club of the Boston-Cambridge area. When Campus opened its doors, the community suddenly found itself with more choices and options. The late 80s early 90s was an era of many serious challenges: the stifling feeling of Reagan America, the devastating AIDS crisis, and the constant stigma and discrimination faced by the LGBTQ+ population. Places like the Paradise and ManRay opened their doors wide open with welcome. For some, it was a place that was just another part of their queer identity, for others it was the only place they could be their authentic selves without ridicule and judgment, for others still it was they place they first felt safe to explore and discover their identity and feel supported by those around them. ManRay was an instrumental part in both setting the tone for and solidifying queer voices in Boston. Because of its origins as Campus, the club put in place perhaps one of its most important foundations: the no photo, no video policy that allowed patrons to feel safe and private in a world made solely for them. This legacy would continue on as ManRay opened its doors up to other populations that would equally value it and find their own home. Despite hard times, hope, and a feeling of good things to come, was on the horizon. S.L.

Marcia Post: Boston was as much, if not more, LGBTQ-friendly as New York because there was such a lesbian feminist presence here and all the schools here had women's studies and women's coalitions. We just had such a way for women, like the New Words bookstore and there was a

Women's Center. There was a vibe that was very erotic and charged and we were there to dance and listen to good music, but we are mostly there to meet women and have a place where we can be openly expressive of our sexuality. That was huge.

Russ Carter: Gay culture was already established there and nobody cared. You showed up on whatever night. A straight guy back then going to a gay night just wasn't a thing anybody else did. But we didn't care because it was all the same thing.

Marcia Post: There was baby dyke and then butch. That was all the representations of lesbian I ever had. Growing up, there was this big, bold dyke on a motorcycle and here I am playing with Barbies and liking makeup and I had no sense that I can be a lesbian if that's what being a lesbian meant. I think for me it was the turning point. I took a class at NYU for sociology called "Society and Sexual Variation" and I obviously took that class for a reason. Our assignments were to go to gay pride. An assignment was to go be a participant observer and write whole narratives on the lesbian bar. So, I went to the Cubby Hole. When we found it, it was so precious.

Krista Siren: I have a limited picture from when I was there, but it felt like it was very inclusive. Clearly, a lot of people who work there were queer, a lot of the people who were going there were queer, and there were a lot of folks who were presenting in gender non-conforming ways, whether or not they were trans. So, it definitely seemed like a place where, not only could you go and be comfortably queer, but as a place you could go and let your freak flag fly. You could be out loud. I was presenting female but was male at birth, and I would go walking in a blue latex catsuit from the Green Street garage down to ManRay down the street, and some local residents would say nice things, not any sort of scary harassing things, as one walked. Being in that outfit or something else that was comparably unusual, I felt fine. And, of course, for the folks inside this is like home base. As far as acceptance level goes it was very homey.

Greg Frisbee: It was one of these clubs that was a home for people that maybe didn't have a home.

Paul Vitagliano: I always felt like a fish out of water going into gay nightlife because I hated the music. There was nothing you could do unless you went to Spit or maybe the 1270, but the guys that I liked were not there. I had to go to the places that I didn't like the music because the kind of men I wanted to meet were there.

Mike (Farmboy): I got down there and there were half a dozen drag queens and some trans people down there and they were having their own little gathering.

Daisy Crowder: It's a place where a lot of people found it easier for them to come out. Queer clubs themselves, of course, are clear, by definition, so a lot of people who are closeted bi or trans or something might not want to make that step. A good thing that ManRay had was the whole idea of experimentation and non-traditional ways of looking at life. If you did some sort of drag or something at ManRay, nobody would blink. And if you were bisexual and dated a girl one week then dated a boy the next week, people understood that it was natural. It was always what I would call a natural place for queer people to congregate and allies as well.

Daisy Crowder: In 1985 there was a lot of stuff that needed to remain hidden. There was a glimmer of hope in the US, at that time, because kids were coming out more and more and earlier and earlier.

Jenny Dahling: I was very, very dedicated to the gay nights to the point where there was a night on Lansdowne Street, Embassy was the name of it was — it's where House of Blues is now — and I remember making "Fuck Embassy" shirts to wear to Thursday night because I was like fuck them. I want everyone to stay here.

Mark Dighton: I didn't really hang out much at Campus. If we were going to go to a gay bar in Cambridge we went to Paradise, which was down towards MIT. Campus was known for playing music videos and they mostly played very commercial pop. That was not my crowd, not my music. We never went there.

Jen Lucky Cole: I know the LGBTQ side of it sometimes gets overshadowed by the fetish and Goth side when people hear the name ManRay. They think of that crowd first. They think of all black. But I think it had a huge effect on the Cambridge LGBTQ and the greater Boston area community. It was a good place. It was a safe place before it was safe to come out of the closet. Generally speaking, Cambridge was very progressive, more so than most of the other cities. I came from such a repressive little town in Massachusetts that I didn't even know what gay people were until I was like 16. I thought they might look different. It's weird what happens when you don't get exposed to that kind of a thing. ManRay, when it came to diversity, especially on a Thursday night, you saw every kind of walk of life. Even if they weren't gay themselves, sometimes their best friend was and they wanted to be supportive, so they'd go out with them because they just came out of the closet. That would happen a lot. Here's a place that is going to protect them. They would protect the people in there from being treated like a sideshow. I got to see the people living their best lives that maybe might not have had that opportunity.

Jenn Sutkowski: There were a lot more visibly LGBTQ people there than I had seen really around. So, I felt like ManRay was doing something right. They had a night only for gay people where they definitely let the flag fly. They were gay-friendly and queer-friendly. It wasn't like but you must not mix heterosexuals!

Melanie Sharkey: I just felt like I was home just being around gay people and trans people. I would see drag queens and it was an eye-opening experience because there were so many different kinds of people. I never felt judged and I never judged the people around me. I really enjoyed being around all of those people and almost living vicariously through confidence. It's really cool to see somebody just owning every bit of themselves and being so confident and so cool and sexy and fun. I remember the early performances that Edward would do … to this day, when he gets up on stage and does Vogue, I'm such a big fan of his. I remember talking to him in the bathroom one time and just being like "Oh my God, I love you. I love you." And he was like, "Okay, weirdo." But in a friendly way. As an ally to the community, it was just a great feeling of family and camaraderie and feeling like no matter what you did you weren't going to be judged for it.

Andrea Parros: In my town there was no one who was openly gay. There were people who, later on in life, came out when they got into college, or whatever because that's where they're comfortable and that's where they know they'll be able to be accepted. But at clubs like ManRay especially, it was a safe space for all different types of sexualities and genders. Even then, gender identity wasn't as big of a movement back then. If ManRay still existed today that would absolutely be another safe space because that all kind of goes hand in hand for me. I don't know if it's just being a really sensitive kid, but for me, it was always like everybody should be accepted. No matter what type of weirdness, anything that you have that's different, you should be accepted as long as you're not hurting yourself or hurting someone else. That's something about being a really empathic person, always feeling for the underdog. A club like ManRay really allowed people who were different or who were picked on … it gave them a place where they were at home. And that's important because everybody's different.

Gillan Cox: Even before the initials of LGBTQ, ManRay was basically a space where it did not matter who you were. It didn't matter what you did. It didn't matter what you didn't do. You were there. It was safe. There was no judgment in the room. We were all one.

Emily Taylor: So, I had a lot of friends that were bisexual. There were a lot of people making out with each other and it didn't really seem to matter what their gender was or if they even had one. I had a lot of trans friends.

Jenny Dahling: There was a lot of crossovers. Some people who went on Wednesdays also went on Saturday, and so on and so forth. But Campus was a classic gay night in that they played top 40 and people would dress for a gay club. It wasn't a typical ManRay night in that it wasn't fetish or Goth bent at all, but the spirit was there. There's a spirit of ManRay. There's more of a camaraderie there then I felt at other clubs, especially being a woman at gay bars. Some of them were so meat market-like. I felt very out of place there, but everyone was super cool to me at ManRay. I felt like I was part of their group. They danced with me. There was no, "But you're a woman." It just felt like a clubhouse vibe, like this is our space. We are here to have fun.

Terri Niedzwiecki: People would be forced into conversations and walk away from the conversation thinking, "Okay, this person might be gay, that's not for me, but hey, they're very intelligent or they're very funny or they're very nice people."

Maryellen Vega: It was a lot of acceptance. I have a son, he's gay. I've grown up in a very Catholic background where that was not accepted. But having that experience at ManRay in the era that I grew up in, it's not a big deal to me. My kid, we joke about it because he's not flamboyant gay, and I'm like, "It really sucks that I can't go shopping with you." He's like "Mom I'm not that kind of gay." We joke about it.

Gene Dante: I felt that ManRay satisfied the need in these communities to have a home well before my time.

Shane Blau: I found out about ManRay because, right at the beginning of my freshman year, I attended the group for LGBTQ students on campus. At that group, as soon as the first meeting was over, one of the young women came over and said, "Hey, there's a club on Thursday nights and a big group of us are going to go this Thursday and any of you that want should come along." I am a pretty shy person and I probably wouldn't have gone, but there was another young queer person in my dorm, so that same person told her that I lived in the dorm. Within the first week of school, I had this random person knocking on my door and saying: "Hi I live in this building, we should go to this club." We became best friends, almost instantly. I followed her around for the rest of college. She brought me to ManRay, the first time. I don't even think I knew what it was called when they told me about it. I didn't know where it was. I didn't know what I was going to do. I just knew that we were all going out together that Thursday. I don't know that I had a whole lot in my head. That point, honestly, was the first time I had been around a group of out queer people, other than in Provincetown. Finding that queer group on campus was the research I did. Finding that group, connecting with them, and then connecting with my friend. Anne, after she recruited me to be her buddy, I followed her around to queer stuff from that point on. She's the one who connected us with Lesbian Avengers. She's the one who found out about some of the various different nights.

Richard LaDue: I think the Goth scene, for a hot minute, was my night because it's kind of all I knew initially. But I probably think Thursday nights, the gay night, with Brad in the front room and Chris in the back, I was like, "Oh, I can do both worlds here."

One of my biggest memories was "Who the fuck is this person?" because Mizery was super tall, braids to their ass, six foot two or six foot three, thin as a rail, gorgeous Black queen who had a black leather motorcycle jacket with the singer Jody Watley painted on the back. I was like where the fuck did this queen get this fucking jacket? I remember that vividly. This club is cool, this person's here and they have a motorcycle jacket with Jody Watley on it.

It was the 18 plus spot, so in that way, it's probably inclusive because you'd have a lot of college students there. It's probably less pretentious. Some bars would be like, we are men who wear leather, the end. We're bears and this is what we do. ManRay was young and you would really see all kinds of people. I just remember it being kind of inclusive and I think having the two styles of music fostered that spirit a little bit.

Maryellen Vega: At the height of when I was going, it was all of a sudden acceptable for bisexuality and I was very comfortable with that in my lifestyle and people being like that. So that was where I was at that time, but it was very risqué for everyone else. So ManRay was not shocking to me. There was a lot of gay and bisexuality going on there.

Gillian Cox: When I returned to Boston in the late 90s, Wednesday nights were still ManRay night. Even though I was allegedly working a responsible job that did not matter ... my eyes were held up by toothpicks Thursday morning. We would go on Thursdays because that was gay night. I was oftentimes the straight girl in the gay club because it would give me space to dance where I'm not going to be harassed.

Shane Blau: Yes, getting ready was super important. There was definitely a uniform that you wore as a dyke in Boston at the time. There was a very limited number of options you had as to what to wear. I remember people being really specifically anti-butch femme, just thinking that was oppressive and heteronormative. So, you had to dress in a way that was dykey but not butch or femme and it was really important that you hit that middle line. I'm pretty sure that I hooked into that uniform quickly and early because I didn't know what to wear yet. I didn't know how to do it yet. Even though I didn't have choices, I remember agonizing about getting ready. The only pants I had that I could wear were overalls. So really, my only choice was which t-shirt under your overalls. You were going to wear your combat boots, you were going to wear your baseball cap backwards and your brim was going to be bent perfectly, because the bend on your brim is really, really important. I remember discussing the brims on our baseball hats with people and how you got the curve right. Do you use a rubber band or do you just fold it naturally? I mean so much worry about our brims. Oh, Stussy hats. I can't believe I forgot. You wear your Stussy hat because it said I'm gay on it. Stussy was a skater brand and the original script that "Stussy' is written in looks like it says "I'm gay" in cursive. So, we used to wear Stussy stuff as another secret messaging for each other to be like I'm queer too. I hooked into that uniform early on because I was just kind of finding that piece of my identity. It was jeans or overalls, a t-shirt, a baseball hat, and combat boots. There's variation within that, but it was the range of what you wore. There were definitely people at ManRay that broke that mold. It's not like everyone there was dressed the same, but the group of people I was with were.

Kara Nemergut: My first time at ManRay was kind of funny right ... so I only really went to Campus until I started dating Keith. My most vivid memory about the first time I went to ManRay was that we walked in and there was gay porn playing on all the TV monitors. I was like 19. I think Campus wasn't necessarily always as well attended as Saturday nights because it was on Thursday. So, I remember going in there and it was pretty empty. Of course, it got a little better because I think Mizery was hosting drag shows there. So, then it kind of became more of like a typical experience of what I had previously been experiencing with clubs. I think I met Rainbow Fright which was pretty nice. She was kind of neat. I hadn't met her at any of the, I don't want to say more mainstream gay nights.

Shane Blau: When I first moved to the Bay Area I was shocked. I had no idea that you could be as out as you can be here, the idea that it could be that safe to be visibly queer. I think 1995 to 99 was a really interesting time. There was a slight change in awareness happening. If we were wearing our freedom rings, most people didn't know what they meant. A lot of people would say, "Is that something about African Unity?" You were safe if you could be invisible, you were safe if you could fly under the radar.

ManRay definitely was the first time that I was surrounded by queer women, in particular, and that's a hard community find. Even today it is still a hard community to find, there are not a lot of gathering spaces for queer women. So that was really unique and special about the backroom at ManRay. I've honestly never found another place that quite felt like that. I've never found another place where both gay men and women are in the same club and everybody's okay with each other. It was really unique for me in that way and a part of it was because I was just coming out as whatever I was at the time. It was one of my many, many coming outs.

I came out first when I was 14 and in high school and we didn't have a Gay Straight Alliance. We weren't allowed to have a Gay Straight Alliance. We were allowed to form a committee called the Diversity Acceptance Coalition and that's what we did. We made t-shirts that said,

“Love the person, not the gender” and it was a big fight about whether or not I was allowed to wear it at school and we went back and forth about stuff like that. So, when I got to college, I right away found the gay group. BU didn’t want that either. Silber was the president. He would not let sexual orientation be part of any of the anti-discrimination clauses and he did not like our group meeting. So, we got pushed back and we did a couple of marches on Silber’s house. We got push back from the college, so ManRay was the place where it was okay to be proud and it was okay to feel really good about your community. For me, that sense of pride was so important.

I don’t honestly feel that BU changed by ’99. Actually, I was turned down for a job my senior year because of how I looked and I was told that straight up. Freshman year I still had long hair and I was just starting to dress in a more gender-neutral way. I shaved my head pretty quickly and then I was very, very gender neutral and people would read me either way. I did not feel comfortable in women’s clothes so I stopped buying anything that was made for women and I started buying all men’s clothes around that time. I dressed, what for me was professional, in a button up shirt and nice pants and I went for an interview at a Boston school that I’d done my internship at and I didn’t get the job. One of the people basically came up and said, “I just wanted to let you know it’s because of how you look, we can’t let you work here like this.” So that’s when I was like, guess what, I’m moving to San Francisco, because clearly I’m not going to get a job in Boston.

Matt Richard: I ended up meeting my friend at Eros and we went out one night to Avalon in Boston. It was a great, fun night. It wasn’t my scene at the time, I was strictly a young fresh devoted heterosexual. I wanted the dark music and here I am at a gay club. If I saw a girl, she thought I was gay and didn’t want to hang out with me, so I kept to myself and just hung out with my buddy, had a couple of drinks, and that was it for the night. A couple weeks later, he brought me to ManRay with two of his friends and I walked in and was like this is my crowd. I want heterosexuals, homosexuals, who knows what sexuals, I just want everybody all in one place. I want this kind of music and just the free atmosphere of anything goes with no judgement.

Lacey Prpic Hedtke: I felt special and privileged to be in this place that was so freeing. One of the draws to ManRay was how queer it was, and that wasn’t the word that we were using then, but it was just so like the lines on everything was so blurry.

Mizery McRae: I thought ManRay was amazing. It opened my eyes to see a different spectrum of gay men and women and straight men and women that could just literally combine and not worry about each other.

Eileen Dover: It helped me to see that gender is fluid, sexuality is fluid. People have so many different facets to themselves. Some of us are 100 percent of that all of the time. Some of us compartmentalize that. And, for some of us, it's a phase.

John O'Leary: ManRay was purposefully built like a gigantic temple of a gay club and everything was acceptable and everything was great. And I think a lot of people took advantage of it.

ML: The great thing is that it didn't matter if you were LGBT or female or somewhere in between. It just didn't matter. That was nice because, in that period of time, the gay community still couldn't get married and you could lose your job, all that stuff. But walking in there … everything was based on who you were, if you were gay or a nice person or an asshole.

Noel McKenna: I guess it gave me confidence to be myself on my own terms. I think that many young gay people also had that experience at ManRay. ManRay attracted all kinds of freaks in a lot of ways. We didn't necessarily fit in in other scenes. As a young gay male, I didn't fit the stereotype. I didn't necessarily fit in at Avalon or Axis because of what I liked and how I looked. ManRay was an inclusive and welcoming space to those who may have struggled. It gave us the courage to move forward.

Russ Carter: One of the things I remember very specifically about it was, it was the 80s and 90s, so there were a lot of gender role questions. There was this time, sociologically speaking in history, where men kind of didn't know what their place was anymore. Not a bad thing. One of the ways that kind of trend coalesced into what was going on was that androgyny was a huge thing and it didn't matter if you were straight, trans, gay, whatever.

Krista Siren: Well, back when I was an undergraduate it was totally off my radar for actually thinking about going. I wasn't really up for anything club wise. By the time I was in grad school, I was interested in going out a little more. I went out to a few places with some friends and I wanted a place where I could dress up and wear stuff appropriate for the fetish nights. I'm trans and, at the time, I was supposed to be presenting male and thinking of myself as a crossdresser. I wanted a place where I could go and dress that way.

Liz Lamanche: My housemate in Somerville for the last four or five years started out as a Jersey boy with a secret crossdressing fetish. He got more into dressing up and going out to ManRay specifically and has become more comfortable with himself and more liberated and has been speaking at colleges about crossdressing. That's where I think he started to identify as transgender, just because of not fitting in the gender boundaries. That's why I always loved both the fetish nights and the gay nights. Just seeing people being happy themselves fills me with joy.

Anna Feder: ManRay is where I had my first kiss with a woman. She was 16 and I was in love. That was a place where I could figure out a lot. College was one such space and ManRay was really the other.

Richard LaDue: I remember going to a nightclub in Boston called Axis, which was on Lansdowne Street. This was in 1989 and I was in high school. I got in, it was 18 plus, and I just remember hearing all this super loud music and everyone was dancing. I don't think I ever had that immersive music experience before that moment. I was like, "Oh, this is my shit. This is what turns me on." So, from there, I just started collecting the music. When I was in college, there was a slot from 2 to 6 in the morning and I was asked, "Do you want to be on the radio?" Sure thing. I'm 20 years old, I'm a closeted gay guy, the school doesn't want me there. I'd love to. I would play all my music there and then just go out to different nightclubs and have fun. Music makes me feel connected and special. Like going through the looking glass.

Eileen Dover: There were definitely men who would dress in women's clothing. During the day they look completely different, but that was the place they felt safe going to. That was more of a sexual fetish than it was a look. They weren't as interested in how they looked, just in how they felt. I had started taking hormones for a little while. I've always looked androgynous during the day and then at night I would glamorize.

Eileen Dover: I had the gay Yellow Pages. Back then it was like the green book for gay people, and I got it at this bookstore called Glad Day on Boylston Street and ManRay was in there. It had Campus advertised and I was always determined that I was going to get in. Every club was a conquest. I was always determined that I was going to become a piece of fabric at the club because my aspiration in life was to be an entertainer. And I knew that entertainers started off in nightclubs. So, my whole life hinged on the nightclub, which, looking back, it's kind of crazy.

Eileen Dover: I was desperate for community. I was desperate for other gay people. I was desperate, not just for the gay people. I wasn't just gay. I was different. I was an artist. I was all of these different things. So ManRay kind of checked a lot of boxes off for me.

Eileen Dover: I started hanging around with transgender women and they started giving me tips to be beautiful.

Eileen Dover: ManRay patrons looked at the club demographic as more of an identity and more of a reflection of who they were. For some of those on the transgender or gender nonconforming [spectrum], that was how they felt on the inside, they were just expressing it on the outside and they were less interested in fashion or being fashionable and ManRay encouraged that and allowed people to let their freak flag fly as high as possible.

Erin Falkell: As someone who identifies as queer, I didn't have to worry about labels at ManRay. I was able to make that space for myself and I didn't worry as much about what everyone else was thinking. I was 21 years old; I had come out. People knew, but I was still getting harassed at school when I was younger. ManRay was a big part of shaping that strength that I had and really being able to be open and out. It was supportive. I could be in a room where I was seeing people like me and I wasn't getting that frequently anywhere else I was going.

Adam Lewis: ManRay was my first club. In a lot of ways, it's the late 80s, early 90s, it's a repressive time with Bush and AIDS. Not an open time. ManRay becomes the first club for so many. First gay bar for so many. I feel like people going there and seeing a world where all people are respected and welcomed. It Is the beginning of a more normal world of gay acceptance. In a way, a weird way, it's no surprise that Cambridge was the first place to have gay marriage. ManRay made a generation feel okay about being themselves and gave them a place to express themselves. And grow and start changing the world and making the world a better place.

Arlene Guerrero-Watanabe: I thought it was freeing because you could do whatever you wanted, and nobody was going to take a picture of you. It provided a sense of privacy. It respected the patrons' right to party in an environment where they weren't going to get caught or face repercussions for whatever they were doing. For example, people who are cross dressers but had jobs where this would be seen as something negative don't want people taking pictures and posting them and getting them in trouble at work. I was a grad student. I was very free to be whoever I wanted to be at the time, but for those of my friends who had jobs that were conservative, it provided a huge service to them.

One more thought about that is that in addition to protecting patrons, it created a sense of privacy or specialness to the space. If it's really private, then it's really truly your space. It gave a sense of ownership.

Eileen Dover: For some people, it was a very private chapter of their lives, where they went to do things that weren't accepted by society at the time. They compartmentalize that portion of their life, however. There were a lot of guys I know that I hooked up with that were questioning their sexuality. They are now married with children.

Christina Pearson: I mean, just like any other thing, it was possible to be LGBT and also be Goth. So, I managed to cross those paths. Everybody was definitely safe there. I do remember specifically that one of my friends was a photographer and they told her, "We can't let you take pictures in here because people who come here do so because they want to feel safe and we want to protect them." I totally respected that and it made so much sense.

Christina Pearson: I mean, just like any other thing, it was possible to be LGBT and also be Goth. So, I managed to cross those paths. Everybody was definitely safe there. I do remember specifically that one of my friends was a photographer and they told her, "We can't let you take pictures in here because people who come here do so because they want to feel safe and we want to protect them." I totally respected that and it made so much sense.

Alyssa Hassan: At ManRay I learned about being an ally, going to Campus so many nights. I could go back to my straight girl world and that whole safety thing didn't apply to me. My best friend Jimmy said he remembered once that we were sitting outside of Hi-Fi after Campus one night drunkenly eating our pizza, and some dude walked by and called everybody a bunch of fags and I started chasing them. Just learning to speak up for others. Knowing that your family is not your blood, it's the people that you come across that you find just some sort of life with.

Bruce Jope: Francis was working the door. He was one of my key people because, as a slightly a feminine gay man, he was in charge of making sure that no one who is gonna cause a problem with a gay guy would get in. We needed it, because it was a college town and everyone wanted to go there, but some people were inappropriate for the environment. When you came into ManRay, you got grilled with questions. It was sort of like a rorschach inkblot test. "Are you going to react if a gay guy grabs your ass?" That was the question my doorman asked you. Of course they would answer mostly honestly. If they said it was no big deal they were allowed in. In those days, you could get away with that a lot more, saying you can't come in. That was the way we were with our door which was not a very Boston thing to have a highly curated door.

Most clubs just let everyone in. We really curated our doors so we got the crowd that we wanted. We have very few fights. We had very few problems. We were very careful to make sure that the vibe in the club was totally fun and friendly and accepting and no one felt out of place.

Michael Marotta: It definitely gave people a safe haven. Whether or not you are straight or gay, or Goth, it kind of provided the same type of home and the same type of inclusionary space. Even now as we deal with stuff in a pandemic, it's important for people to realize that when your neighborhood bar or rock club closes, most straight people have the opportunity to go somewhere else. That's not always necessarily the case for the gay community. If a gay bar closes in a certain neighborhood, those people cannot pick up and migrate to another location. I'm a straight white male so obviously my interpretation of this is what it is ... but it felt like ManRay was a spot that was very easy to get to … and I keep going back to the word safe haven and safe spot. If you're going to Machine, you still have to battle Fenway, and you still have to get through certain areas that you know might not be particularly appealing. Whereas in Central Square, it's just anything goes.

Avril dePagter: Now I'm wondering if the reason why ManRay felt so exciting and dangerous, but also safe, was because nobody was taping me. It was kind of awesome to not have to ever think about safety. It's not something that even entered my mind. For me, if I'm observed, I start getting super uncomfortable just in general, no matter what I was doing. I think the fact that you could go there and be anonymous or be as big as you wanted to be totally specific to not being constantly recorded or filmed or observed in a way that was maybe more invasive than you want it to be.

Athena Costa: There were no pictures of the events at ManRay. It was almost like you have to be accepted into this group and the reason why you're going to be in this group is because you were an outcast. You were allowed to do whatever you wanted while you were in this group of people and, for your privacy, they didn't want it to be documented. I've only seen this once, a person with a camera went into ManRay and staff went right up to them and was like, "You cannot take pictures here, it is a strict no photos allowed event." If you had a camera, you were kicked out.

Eileen Dover: Well, I don't know if you know this, but we had meetings before the club opened every night. It was during the time when there were a lot of overdoses happening and the city was starting to crack down. They didn't want to have the same problems as other clubs, so they had a meeting at the beginning of every night, and we would all come with our concerns. I remember Terri saying once: "I think we should find a way to confirm the age of our transgender patrons." How forward thinking was she? She was like, "I think it's unfair that they have to show their male ID. So what can we do about that?" I think the solution was, "Well we'll put Eileen over at the door in drag so that they can show their ID to somebody who's in their community." That is incredibly forward thinking. They were pretty radical and pretty ahead of their time. We had discussions about photography, we had discussions about all these things and it was a democracy where we were all included. There was a spectrum of people and they all had different needs and they all had different requests. So these conversations were constantly happening. The adversity was always met with creativity. We were all in it together. People who had differences … We talked that shit through and got over it.

Noel McKenna: It was a welcoming space where you could be out as an LGBT person. I came out publicly and people would come up to me and be like, "I'm so happy for you. This is wonderful. You're awesome." ManRay, for me, was this really safe space to go through this transition, which, quite frankly, is an excruciatingly difficult transition, especially if you grew Catholic. The ManRay community was very empowering

Mizery McRae: I got kicked out of my house when I was 13. ManRay was the first club that I ever went to, so I just saw it and saw people in there and I was like "Wow, I could do that." Getting a job there pushed me into the career that I have now because it just opened so many doors for me. The fact that I could feel safe where I was and not be scared of who I was and what I was and not having anybody to help me figure all that out when I was young … ManRay was there and it taught me so much about about life in general about the gay world, about the straight world. It just taught me so much.

Krista Siren: We didn't get marriage equality until about '03 here. I know that Cambridge was one of the first communities and cities to do some trans civil rights protections a number of years before the state. It certainly has changed a lot since then. The way that we talk about these things has changed a lot since then too. Certainly, in regards gender identities, the language has changed a whole bunch since 20 years ago. The way that the broader awareness of BDSM and folks actually knowing what the heck that means and what safe word means is sort of pop culture now, when you never hear those outsides of the context of somebody who was in the kink scene during the late 90s, early 2000s. But now it pops up and everybody knows what they're talking about when somebody mentions it.

Jen Lucky Cole: The gay community definitely worked with a promoter, they definitely helped set us up with a lot of record release things we would do for more popular divas and popular gay artists that cater to the gay community. For instance, we would do a Whitney Houston record release in Boston once, which was a big deal and we would hire drag queens, such as Mizery, and we would do it all up. If you were a charity and you wanted to say set up for, say, the Gay Action Committee or Aids Action Committee of Boston, that was free. We're always letting them have fishbowls on the table full of condoms and lube and paperwork about where to get tested and how to go for counseling and things like that. And we did Pride every year. We had a float in the parade every year and that money went to things like Bagley and stuff like that in Boston. We did one year in 2000, for instance, which was a really big year because it was 2000, and we had a float that year with a singer that did a hit song in the early 80s called "Coming Out of Hiding." Don's just very respectful and he saw as a cab driver back in in the 70s in Boston, he saw a lot of shitty thing happening to gay performers when they leave clubs and he saw a need for that and he developed a soft spot.

Adam Lewis: There was a mutually beneficial relationship. The police would always come by and park out in front of the club, basically roll down the window and check in or ask if Don is here. Don would often stand out on the sidewalk and see what was going on. If the cops came by, then they would chat. They definitely had a connection and a good rapport. We never got screwed by the cops. Which again, think about early 90s views of gays and fetish people. I never saw any real major problems with the police. We always had good relationships. They were always checking in and they were friendly.

Emily Taylor: The cops would come in sometimes. They never did anything weird, but we noticed their presence. I feel bad for any city that didn't have a ManRay, because it means that the kids who were off the spectrum a little bit had no place to go. All the subculture kids came to this one place. It was like a meeting ground. I know people who met their spouses there, who had children and were pregnant there. I know people who went there and are dead now. It was like a family, and it changed nightlife.

Mizery McRae: I am friends with very, very few. Most of them have moved away or have passed. Around the 80s, that whole HIV thing took a lot of our good people away and took a lot of our friends away.

Eileen Dover: In the 90s, especially if you're a queen, it was bitchy because all these gay people that are hurt by society land in the clubs. I hate to say this, but AIDS and drugs took a lot of those people from us. If it didn't hurt so much that there were these people that weren't there anymore, I would question my own sanity. I was like, "Was it really that fun or was I just high?"

Eileen Dover: I got bored at the gay nights.

Mizery McRae: I had a few romantic happenings in and out of the club. But for most of them, either I was a fetish for them — I was the pretty Black girl — or there was the drag fetish. That really sucks because it kind of fucked with your self-esteem, a little bit. I really want to be in a relationship, but you can't deal with me and you don't like me if I'm just a boy, I have to be in drag, or I have to have a wig on.

Eileen Dover: It was the 90s. I think there was a lot more intensity to it. Everybody was sick of AIDS. Everybody was burying a friend on Sunday, then we'd go to dance and get high. I was trying to drown it out, you know, just get through it. But in all that darkness, there was a lot of light in the scene.

Chris Ewen: It was interesting in the sense that I was a male DJ for a women's club night and the DJ before me was a woman. So, there was a little bit of pushback from a certain few members of the crowd. They used to go there and hang out in the more alternative room. I sort of won them over. It's like, "Okay, so he's got good music days, and he will play our requests." So that was good and then let me see.

Chris Ewen: I'd say, part of the reason that we survived was because we did a gay night and Cambridge is a very liberal and open and inclusive.

Chris Ewen: Being able to prove, beyond a point, that you could play music that wasn't necessarily thought of as the stereotypical gay bar music and draw in an even a wider crowd and add even more diversity to the gay scene was really valuable.

Rebecca Corbett: So, when I was 19, I hung out with my friend Tina, and she was a high school friend. She went on gay night, which was Thursday nights. So that's when I first started going with Maura, Tina, my friend Scott. There was a whole group of us that went. That's how I first heard of it and started going. I have to say, being a 19-year-old from a really small town, there was no minorities and I never really saw anyone gay except for my friend Tina and Scott, who wasn't even out at the time. It's the first time I got any exposure to anything like that. I remember the male dancers wearing little leather underwear. First time I ever saw two men kissing. I loved every second of it. I had a blast.

Erin Falkell: I went there every Thursday night. I didn't just stay with Thursdays, although that was kind of my foundation, obviously, because I'm queer. I felt more comfortable on that night. I felt like that was my night. Not that I exclusively owned it.

Eileen Dover: Don would introduce me because I was so outrageous looking and glamorous. He would always introduce me to people and he would chuckle and say "She's" — he used the right pronouns — "She's from the projects of South Boston" and he got a kick out of that. I wasn't from the projects; I grew up just outside. He really got a kick out of the fact that the blue collar, rough, dangerous, homophobic neighborhood could produce something like me. He wasn't saying she's from the projects of South Boston to insult me, it was more like pride. He had an inside thing with everybody that went there. He was fascinated with the duality of people who found safety in his club.

Chapter 4

The Call of Nightlife

"I would definitely be impressed. It almost looks like something out of a movie from the 80s where ... the misfit kids go to a club." — Keith Ward

To all the nocturnal people, the lovers of music, and the tireless dancers' nightclubs provide spaces to follow all those pursuits. For some ManRay was their first club experience, for others it was just one in the long history of being a creature of the night. Although it may not have been New York, Boston provided many choices for its revelry followers — another night down at The Channel, the top 40s style of Narcissus, the seediness of the Rat, or catching a show in The Middle East. ManRay became another face on the scene.

Perhaps it was an ad in The Phoenix, a poster as you walked out of a show, a friend convinced you to go, or that unique man with the wide brim feathered hat handed you a pamphlet that first put ManRay in your awareness. Maybe you knew it as that strange ominous building on Brookline Avenue, maybe it had been described to you as a strange place to be avoided, or maybe you went in totally blind. For some, they walked through the doors, looked, turned around and walked back out never to return. For others, that dark brick building became a major center of their lives. Each new patron had to make the decision for themselves whether ManRay was worth their time. S.L.

Bruce Jope: To me, nightlife is about youth and exuberance and getting together in a space with like-minded people and enjoying music, art, a way of dressing, a way of seeing yourself, a way of expressing yourself.

Susanne Boitano: I really feel like I was in the gem of nightlife, which would be New York City. I spent more time in clubs than I did in homeroom, I hate to say, and I had the pick of the litter. I had the Danceteria, I had the Limelight, I had CBGBs, Max's Kansas City, the Peppermint Lounge. We have places in the Bowery, A7. It was all about just getting dressed, just taking anything, you could find, vintage stuff, your mother's slip, and turning it into outfits and slathering on the makeup. You didn't get there before 11. It was just my whole world. It was just so fun. It was just fashion and music and it was alive and anything went. It was just a wonderful escape from the suburbs. I grew up in New Jersey, so it was a quick half hour away and far too much temptation. I don't feel like it was a wasted youth. I'm glad I had fun when there was fun to be had. The 80s was New Wave, then punk and all of that coming out. I got the best of it and I made up for lost time.

Amy Butts: Originally I'm from Long Island and I kind of grew up with the New York City club scene. I had very understanding and liberal parents who understood that, with my love of music and just the way my life was kind of heading, that I was going to go into the city regardless if I had their blessing or not. So, they decided, "Tell us where you're going, tell us who you're going with, that way we can find you if something happens." I went to Hofstra University in Hempstead, so I spent my college years going to the Bank, Pyramid Club, and Batcave. I was accustomed to a certain type of nightclub growing up in the New York City area.

John O'Leary: There were places like Avalon on Lansdowne and they were just concert venues. You didn't go there on just any night. Nobody knew you at the door. Nobody cared about you, you would see your friends there and you felt like you're at an assembly at school or something.

Norm: I got to ManRay later than a lot of people at the time. I was close to 30 by the time I started going there. I had been to a number of alternative clubs already at that point, mainly on the West Coast. A few in New York. I went to chill dance clubs, more than other clubs, a lot of New Wave and a lot of the more alternative lifestyle, was definitely what I liked.

I was living in Portsmouth, but I was going down regularly to music events in Boston. I didn't really have the heavy familiarity with the big nightlife scene down there. I went to Spit and the Channel because that's where you went to see bands. So it was interesting to be led to such a place in Boston.

Skot Kremen: I was 16 and you were supposed to be 18, but they didn't care. I remember walking up to the door and going into Limelight, and there was nothing like it. It was like a gigantic universe of culture and depravity. The music was amazing. I ended up getting to go to all these very cool parties where I got to meet New Order, Siouxsie Sioux, Debbie Harry, The Ramones, Johnny Marr. It was really cool.

Gibby Miller: I had very little nightclub experience. I would go to nights at bars where I was a promoter or DJ and would host an evening at a bar.

Erin Falkell: I had gone to a club before ManRay, and I think I had bumped into somebody dancing. I was probably drunk and spinning around. Whoever I bumped into was getting really pissed off and being like, "What the fuck?" I remember the same thing happening at ManRay, and the people kind of responded in a positive way there. They were like, "Yeah, we love that you're spraying us with your beer."

Wendy Austin: [Venus and Avalon] That was the Eurotrash version of Boston.

Emily Arkin: I don't think I did a lot. I went to college in kind of a rural place and there was one gay bar called Risky Business, which in retrospect was kind of an unfortunate name. I went to a couple other dance clubs near my college. There's a huge Goth scene in Ithaca, so I did go to some Goth nights there, so that was probably my gateway drug into ManRay.

Brian Legault: The alt clubs in Montreal were not as big. They really went from the alternative scene and really just focused on the college kids.

Julia Kilcoyne: As I got a little bit older and moved to Boston in the early 90s, there were all kinds of bands playing. I saw Siouxsies and the Banshees and Screaming Trees. Venus de Milo was a club that I went to just to dance with my boyfriend. I really wanted something much more like the Rat. Something much darker, grittier, more like something you'd see in London or New York. I really crave the darkness and the dirt and the grungy bathrooms. So, what I wanted wasn't always what I got.

Matt Richard: My nightclub experience was, shall we say, sheltered. When I was 17, I enlisted in the Army and shipped out before I was 18 so I didn't go night clubbing. When I was 18, I ended up in Washington D.C. and I went to this club, Tracks, with some friends. It was a dark venue and they had techno, an industrial room, and some gay clientele; it was like a melting pot of everybody on the dance floor. Later I went to college in Vermont and we went downtown to the 135 Pearl. It was a gay club and everything inside painted black. It was a great welcoming and fun place as a nightclub, but they're playing top 40 music and I want that unique techno or that unique industrial stuff that I've been playing in college. I was looking for Thrill Kill or Misery, I didn't need to listen to the new Mariah Carey Remix.

Anastasia Taslis: I kind of grew up in nightclubs honestly. My father is a group musician and he was always in nightclubs, so I was always in nightclubs as a kid. It was a different style of old school nightclubs with candles on the tables. I grew up going to those kinds of nightclubs and I was always wondering why I was the only child there. Later on I went to a few, like the Palace back when I was like 15 or 16. Terrible, I hated it and after that I was just not into nightclubs at all. It's like that's not my scene, hanging around a bunch of stoners and smoking weed, it was the 90s. Then finally when I went to college, I was really not into going to nightclubs and then my friend Amy, who I met in college, said, "I think you might like this one," because I was wearing all black and had the look anyway.

Heather Morgan: When I was growing up, I started trying to crash into clubs in my later high school years. I went to the Pyramid club in the Village and felt super real. Then I went to some little divy hardcore clubs in Jersey City, places that high school kids could go, but my parents were pretty strict. I had some older kids bring me to a couple of drag nights at Copacabana. Those kinds of things were like an adventure, and I was this wide-eyed kid taking it all in. It was kind of a mind blower as a first experience. There are these crazy worlds out there, but I felt like I was just visiting those times as a high school student trying to get into club nights. Not knowing people and not having much of a social life and just being this kind of weird kid, I didn't feel at home. When I started going to ManRay, it just felt like home. I'm no longer on this weird underground music safari peeping in from somewhere else. I was like, "I have arrived somewhere that I can just hang out now."

Paul Calnan: I'm a musician and I played in rock bands most of my life, so, up until ManRay, I would say the majority of time that I spent in bars and nightclubs were probably more rock bars or rock clubs or dive bars. If I did go to dance clubs, they had a tendency to be more top 40 or Eurotrash. We used to go to Axis, Avalon, Bill's Bar, the Rat.

Eileen Dover: I went to a Catholic high school. The bus drove to the Combat Zone and all that neon was really glamorous. I'd seen movies with different pieces and bits of nightclubs in them, like Desperately Seeking Susan, but I didn't have much context for it.

Corey Reeves: I was really a club kid. I started going to clubs before I turned 21. I used to sneak into a lot of the gay clubs, Fritz and Chaps. When I turned 21, I started to go to a badass club called the Haymarket which was in the Combat Zone. Then I started working at Chaps in 1990 until 96. I was let go because I was in a contest with the lady named Lolly who I thought should have been promoted, but the general manager said no. A manager by the name of Rice had hired me, who I was acquainted with, and he asked me to work at ManRay. I also received work as a day bartender at Ramrod and I also received a bartender position at Avalon on Sundays. I was kind of working the scene.

It was Halloween of 1987 [when I first heard about ManRay]. My boyfriend, who was a badass at the time, had said that the Halloween party going on and Dead or Alive was supposed to show up there. I was like, "Wow, that sounds pretty exciting." We didn't go, though. Then we went on Campus nights later on and the music was great. I love the whole aspect of it. I was underage and wasn't able to get in at the time, but I was excited about the whole thing. We were gonna throw costumes together but decided not to do it. It was exciting.

Keith Ward: I was more into the hardcore metal scene at that point, going to shows at The Rat or The Channel. So that was my introduction. Everything before that was crappy dance clubs that very rarely ever played music that I really liked.

Heather Morgan: I had already started hanging out at Axis on Friday nights and I met some people there, who were like, "Yeah, this is alright, but you really have to go to ManRay." I was friends with the boys in the You Shriek band. Razi knew Chris. He's like, "Oh this guy, he was in Figures on a Beach. He's a brilliant DJ. It's a big place and it's great music with a couple of rooms and this is where we gotta go." I was really excited about it.

Greg Frisbee: ManRay was my first nightclub experience, so it was all new, and it wasn't a huge club. You see these huge dance clubs on TV and films where there are these huge discotheque dance clubs and ManRay was a very small, very intimate club. You would show up there for the night, and maybe you had a few people waiting in front of you, but there was never a line to really get in.

ML: Well, I first heard about it for Sunday nights. Traditionally, the gay community would go out on Sundays, because a good Catholic wouldn't be out on Sunday night. I heard about it at lunch from friends who were like, "Let's go to Campus."

Eloni Feliciano: I actually heard about it in New York because I was a kid in a nearby city. Somebody was like "Oh yeah I heard it's a really cool club, but it's really crazy like it's way more fetish and people have sex in bathrooms and all this type of stuff." So I know I went to college a bit young. I was 17 and I knew the clubs in Boston-Cambridge were 19 plus at the time. So, I really tried to squeak through and get in. It was on Saturday night. So it wasn't that crazy, but it was beautiful.

Hyson Concepcion: It starts at Axis on a Friday night, early because that was when you could get in free. I was at Brandeis and I didn't have a car and public transportation closed before the clubs did, so it was always kind of the plan to get to the club early on. We were upstairs and there weren't a lot of people. We met this group of Goth kids, one of whom was Skot Kremen. It was his 21st birthday, March of 1995. We were hanging out and they said, "Hey, we're going to ManRay tomorrow. Why don't you guys meet us?" So we made a plan to meet at Scott's house to pregame a little and then go to ManRay. I remember being excited that I was going to go to this place I'd sort of heard of and finally have a Goth experience. I remember the anxiety of getting dressed for it and worrying that I was going to do it wrong somehow.

Arlene Guerrero-Watanabe: I was living in Providence, Rhode Island at the time, attending graduate school at Brown and I would go to regular Goth nights which were pretty small. They weren't the best goth nights. A couple of people from the Boston scene happened to go down to one of them. So, I befriended them and all of a sudden, they're like, "You need to come up to this night we have called ManRay." And I was like, "When. What's the best time to go?" and they're like "You have to come on a Friday." So, shortly after hearing about it, I got a couple of my girlfriends and we started doing the pilgrimage. It was like coming home. We would go every weekend. We would do the hour drive.

Amy Butts: Goth clubs were where I maybe felt most comfortable and really enjoyed the music and the subculture and the people. I always found Goth clubs to be way more accepting and way more inviting than any other type of subculture. I heard about ManRay from a bunch of my older goth friends who used to go to Boston. It was this far away Gothic Wonderland that I couldn't wait to go to someday, but I was too young.

Krista Siren: It was an evolving process. When I was an undergrad, I heard a little bit about ManRay because I was in Cambridge. I knew some big thing about there being some kinky events going on in the early 90s. When I was in grad school, in the mid-90s, I'd been following some Goth newsgroups and some folks who were regular attendees or who had been to events were participants in these groups. I think Cusraque and DJ Lady Bathory were participants in some of the Goth forums online and mentioned it.

Michael Hsieh: I don't think anybody described it to me. I was in town for work and I opened up The Phoenix. I was looking at club reviews and just looking for the words Goth and industrial. I think there was a flyer or review about ManRay. I decided to check it out. That's what I do in every city.

Gene Dante: I was hanging out at the Rocky Horror Picture Show in Harvard Square and someone said there was a really cool nightclub that we should all check out. We were all young and adventurous and it seemed like something we might want to do. It intrigued me that it was supposed to be wild and cool and you can express yourself. I would mostly go to rock clubs. So I went to The Middle East and clubs on Lansdowne Street and The Rat and Axis. ManRay was heavier than anything I'd been in before and I thought that was intriguing. You usually see those movies and they try to emulate a nightclub element, but it's way more brightly lit then ManRay actually was. So that was my first impression. I am a big fan of great lighting being the passivity to a great experience.

Sara S. Wendell: The first time I heard of it was from one of my friends at Rocky Horror who said, "Oh, we have to check out this club. It's doing all this crazy stuff on Friday nights like fetish stuff and leather and let's go check it out next week." And I said, "Sure. Okay, that sounds interesting."

Nate Roman: In the late 80s, early 90s, I really wasn't thinking about clubs.

All people used to talk about were raves back then. I did go to a couple of raves, but you can't really call those nightclubs. The first one I ever went to was the Paradise Cafe right down the street from ManRay. I was a metal head when I was in high school that discovered electronic music and a very good friend of mine introduced me to industrial music. He told me to check out ManRay.

Eartha Harris: I grew up in the Berkshires, the rural area in the mountains along the Massachusetts-New York border. When I was 15, I had a couple of older friends who introduced me to the local Berkshire punk and Goth subculture. As a "small town" pretty much all of the alternative subcultures just grouped together into one since there were so few of us. I heard many mythical tales of "Batcave," "Limelight," and "ManRay." One driver's license, one summer job, one teen heartbreak, one year of high school, and a year of college later, I was sitting in a computer lab chatting on IRC #goth when I received an invite from a kind yet mysterious stranger named Cusraque to dance on stage in a performance for a night at ManRay called "Hell", and the rest is history.

Wendy Austin: When I was in college I started reading The Phoenix and all the club listings. I'm pretty sure that's where I initially heard of ManRay. I knew it was one that was going to be on my list that I wanted to check out.

Tatiana Zimkus: I learned about ManRay in more detail through Ceremony. I was actually introduced to Ceremony first, I think it's sometimes the other way around. I happened to meet someone who worked at the art store across from ManRay. He must have seen me decked out in black and said, "Hey, do you go to ManRay? Do you want to go to Ceremony?"

Christina Pearson: It would have been '91 when I was attending Massasoit. I made friends with someone, Jimmy Reject, a punk rock guy. I had told him I was looking for a Goth club to go to because I had attended one in the past in Phoenix. When I moved to Massachusetts, I really missed it. We talked about music a lot. We had a lot of musical tastes in common and I had told him that I didn't care for the sort of regular mainstream things that were offered on Lansdowne. Not my scene. And he said, "You want to go to ManRay." He knew exactly what I was looking for.

Jamie DiBattista: The first time I heard of ManRay was when my friend,

Christina Pearson, told me about it. I don't think she had been there before, but I do remember her saying, and I quote, "They play oldies, you know, 80s music."

Chris Famulari: So, I'm pretty sure I was told about it, possibly by Christina Pearson and Jamie DiBatistta. I don't know how I got there, but I was there. It was not on Saturday night, but people were like, "You've got to come back on Saturday." I was told that it was just this unbelievable club. They play great music. I was told about the different types of nights they had and the people there. It was very-gay friendly and I was like "Okay, I don't have an issue with that." It was very inclusive. A lot of folks on certain nights were walking around with chains and leather.

Julia Kilcoyne: My older brother was living in Somerville for years before I ever moved to Boston. He said we were going to go to this fun club that is really artsy. He's like, "I know that it would appeal to your aesthetic." A couple years went by and he said, "Oh, some drag queen friends of mine are going to ManRay. Do you want to come up?" I think I was sick and I couldn't go. I had been really excited and I had bought a cute outfit at Hubba Hubba.

Abigail Taylor: It was probably my friend Aaron White who I met at Mass Art. He was like a little boy. He said, "Abby you are really going to love this place, we gotta go." So, we ended up going to Ceremony when it was at Fenway. When I was there, I heard people talking about ManRay, but I was 17 at the time and it was a 19 plus club, so it sort of remained a little bit of a mystery at first; it was the place where the older people could go. Then I met Trent Stewart, who was sort of the head of this performance art group called Fantasy Factory and he was like, "I can get you a job at ManRay. Want to go?" So, we were able to go there a little bit earlier than we should have. They didn't even ever ask what my age was. I never had to fill out a form or anything.

Liz Enthusiasm: I remember it being mentioned in some of my classes in art school. Since we were so new, we didn't really know where to go in town, so we always ended up on Lansdowne Street, just because that was what they advertised. We would go to Venus de Milo on Fridays, which was always pretty cheesy and the music was not really what we liked. So hearing about this new place we're just like, "Yeah, let's go check it out."

Emily Sweeney: The Phoenix and the Dig did a really good job of covering Boston nightlife. I remember in high school just tearing through looking at all the band names and nightclubs even though I was too young to get in. It was such a huge influence.

Emily Taylor: The first time I ever heard about ManRay, I had started going to Ceremony, back when it was in Fenway. My sister Abby was going to Mass Art and she was like, "I think I found your people!" And I was like, "What?" And she was like "Goths!" as I was pretty much the only Goth at my high school.

She took me to Ceremony, and the first night I was dancing a guy named Trent Stewart approached me and said "You're a really good dancer. Have you ever been to ManRay?" And I was like, "I don't know what ManRay is. This is my first time here at Ceremony." I'm clueless because I was still like 17 at the time. He was like, "I want you to come to ManRay. Here's the address. Here's my phone number. Come on Wednesday and show up and I'll tell you all about it. We have these dancers and it's a club night and you'll be like a Go-Go Dancer and dance on a box." And I was like, "Cool! That sounds awesome!" Is this a dream come true? I go to a club and then someone wants me to be a dancer? So, I showed up and that was my first time at ManRay. I'd never heard of this place. I didn't know it was a club. I had never been to a nightclub like that before. I went there before it was open and it was Friday's Fantasy Factory.

Emily Arkin: I think I had high school friends — I went to Cambridge Rindge and Latin — who grew up and were more adventurous about clubbing. The places they would go, if they were sophisticated enough to figure out how to get in, were ManRay and The Middle East. It was a place where people serve drinks, where it's slightly more grown up than what we were doing as teenagers. I think I waited until I was 18 to start going to see what this nightlife that Cambridge has to offer is, and that was pretty much it.

Andrea Parros: I really don't remember, but I definitely felt drawn to it; there was a buzz about it. It's definitely possible that I could have heard about it somehow through classmates. Maybe it was just from being involved in nightlife. I used to go to The Middle East a lot to go to shows, so I must have gone to shows at least two nights a week during college and ManRay was right around the corner. So, I definitely think it could be possible that maybe there was some night that I was at a show and then I kind of saw the line around the corner and thought like, "What is this place?" I also might have seen a flyer at Newbury Comics.

Chris Manasouridies: I guess my buddies had gone to the club, and he said, "You have got to check this place out. We're going to go on a Saturday night." He didn't really say much, just that it was a great time and it was kind of 80s, but there's a lot of dark aspects to it. Me being from the South Shore, we didn't hear anything about that, especially where we lived growing up. People didn't talk about it, so it was all new to me as far as that goes. It was just a club in Boston that I had to go check out.

Taylor Vecchio: I was obsessed every week with getting The Phoenix. I would look to see the nightlife and what was happening, so I might have heard about it from that. I'm from a small town so I was always looking for the cool spots. But I think it was also just hanging out in Central Square. Sometimes, I feel like we would make fun of people who went to ManRay. You'd see somebody looking Gothic and say, "Oh, go back to ManRay" or something.

Melanie Sharkey: I first heard about ManRay in the mid-90s. I was a pit kid in Harvard Square and I hung out with a lot of older people. They would tell me about this amazing club where the clothes were amazing, the music was amazing and there's just this great vibe of dancing, having fun, drinking, and going crazy. I was 15 so I couldn't go, but I kept hearing about it. I was kind of in a punk phase and had surpassed the Gothy music phase, so I wasn't quite sure if I would even enjoy it.

Later on, I was in a relationship and I would hang out with my ex's brother's wife. One day she's like, "Hey, did you ever go to ManRay back in the day?" and I said, "No I didn't but I heard all about it". She was like, "Dude, you have been missing out. We need to get you there. Do you like to dance?" And I was like, "I'm really self-conscious. I don't think I would like it but like I've heard it's a really good time." She convinced me to try it.

Steve Friedrich: I first found it when my friend and I went to see Nine Inch Nails in April of '94. We parked in the back lot and then we went to the concert and after the concert we went to the club.

Tonya Sand: The first time I heard about ManRay was actually the first day I ever went. I went to a Nine Inch Nails concert at The Boston Garden with my boyfriend. When we were leaving, we got a flyer for an after party at ManRay and thought it looked cool.

Becky D: It was through a friend of mine who I met in college. He didn't go to the same school, but we ended up meeting and becoming close friends. One day he came over to the dorms to visit and he was dressed up in his fishnets and all that stuff. I was like, "Where are you going?" and he said he was going to ManRay. He explained a little bit about what it was about and it sounded intriguing to me. But it was also intriguing because it sounded different. It wasn't your standard Lansdowne Street club. It sounded unusual, so it kind of piqued my interest.

Lucretia X Machina: WFNX was my favorite radio station and I was friends with a bunch of pagans and witches. I worked at a synthesizer company, and I was hanging out with people who worked there who are also pagans and witches. I was getting a whole new worldview of many things. We were actually going to Axis very regularly. I met somebody co-incidentally on Boston Common who looked like a freak and I took note of that. I didn't talk to him. I was just like, "Well, that was an interesting looking person." We went from Axis to ManRay, it was probably a Wednesday night, and there was that same guy. I took that as a sign.

Lilly Moon: Well, this is back before I had a computer and internet. My best friend at the time was living in Boston going to art school. She had a crush on a guy that she met at this club called ManRay. She had written me a letter, old fashioned mail, with drawings and things about her night there and meeting people and it sounded nice.

Maryellen Vega: I was hanging out in Holbrook at Jillian's with Darren Goldman, Chris Famulari, and our friend Jim. I am at Green Day on the Esplanade and they were like, "Oh, come to ManRay with us on Saturday night. It's a club in Boston." That was all they told me, and I was like, "All right, I'll go."

Karla Clute: I was a part of the Rocky Horror Picture Show at Harvard Square for 10 years. A lot of the Rocky folks talked about going to the Goth night, dancing, and having a good time. When I turned 18, a few of them took me to Ceremony which introduced me to the scene. I loved it. I was a very shy young person, so I was extremely anxious, extremely nervous, but everybody there was very friendly. I had a great time.

Gillian Cox: I first heard of ManRay thanks to a friend of mine in my English class my sophomore year of college in 1989. She'd been going to

Ground Zero and I heard of ManRay from her. She said, "Yeah, maybe we should go ahead and explore that one." And I said, "Is it 21 plus?" She said, "I really don't know. But I've been to ManRay a couple of times." "Well, how is it there?" And she said, "It's really cool. I think you'll like it. It's much better than Axis."

Rick Webb: The first time I went to ManRay is a little bit hazy. I know it was fall 1990. I went to the Consolidated show there. I remember going to dance nights pretty quickly after that. Ironically, I kind of thought of it as a live venue only at first.

Koren Bernardi: I went to school in the area around '96 and I was interested in industrial music. I was weird in high school. I think I first heard about it from folks that were part of the Rocky Horror Picture Show. They did that and also went to ManRay. There was a Goth night on some nights and it was gay night on other nights, and that kind of was the perfect mismatch of what what Rocky Horror folks were. It looked kind of interesting because, on the outside, it was just brick walls and a little door on a tiny side and every other club had posters and you could see in the windows. So I was like "Oh, what's in there?" There was always a line out the door.

Jenny Dahling: The very first time I ever heard of ManRay, believe it or not, was from my art teacher in high school. I went to Burlington High School and the teacher had a daughter who was a few years older than me. I'm not sure how or why exactly this teacher knew that I would be into this club, but she picked up on something. I was kind of a weirdo in high school. I glued rhinestones to my face. I wore spray glitter a lot. So I suppose she picked up on something about me and she thought I'd be into this club. I asked her what it was all about. She didn't really give me any gory details. She said, "Well, it's in Cambridge and your type of people go there," which I was kind of confused by, but I thought, "All right, I guess I'll look into this more." From there, I asked a few friends about it. They had a website up but it didn't really tell you a whole lot about it. I had zero experience in nightlife, so I didn't understand what fetish was or even that I liked New Wave music. I was really kind of a babe in the woods going in, but I remember going and having a blast.

Guari Desai-Ackerman: To put it in perspective, I come from an Indian background, so going out to a club was a little bit, how can I put it ... it was frowned upon. My parents were not super keen on me going, but they also didn't want to hold me back with my social activities, so they very reluctantly said that I could go as long as I was in a group of people. I hadn't really gone to a club before then. I was probably about 18 at the time and I had a job in Harvard Square as a square deal girl handing out flyers. The group of people I worked with were very much into that scene and considered themselves punks. At the time I was very homesick for England. I liked Stone Roses Charlatans, Happy Mondays, that sort of thing and that was the kind of music I was looking for. So that's kind of what my first initial pull into ManRay was because you had sort of old school punk Goth and then the alternative floor.

Elizabeth Galbraith: I started going out with some of my friends to punk shows, maybe at the Rat, and I started getting into the rave culture that was still around at that time. ManRay probably totally blew my head off in terms of it being a nightclub. I was used to some night culture, but it was just a little different because I always liked music that might be a little darker.

I used to hang out with kids down in Harvard Square. It was always kind of interesting because it was such a mix of different people from different areas and different classes and different situations, but we're all kind of together and we had our little group and culture going on down there at the time. Some of us would be more Goth-ish and I started just finding myself wearing dark clothing and feeling like that was me as a way of forming an expression and I started dyeing my hair different colors. I think it was probably there that I started hearing about ManRay, because I maybe saw Cusraque or someone else would say hey there's this night at ManRay.

Alyssa Hassan: I first learned about ManRay through grad school friends. I went to Tufts and we were a small department so that led to us getting to know each other really well. My friend, Dan, who was a Massachusetts native and involved with bands, had suggested that some of us go to ManRay, probably 80s night.

Kevin Farrington: I was older than a great many of the people that were regular attendees during the years that I was going there, so, for me, it was kind of a return to any kind of nightlife scene. I had been away from it for a good long while, I had raised the family, I had been working out of UMass with crazy hours, an hour commuting in both directions.

I think that my first knowledge of it probably came, not through word of mouth, but probably from The Phoenix. I still remember seeing advertisements for it. If I'd stumbled upon ManRay at the age of 18, because it was a different time and place and country when I was 18, I probably wouldn't have been as alert to what it seemed to offer or as interested in what it did offer. As I get older, your personality emerges and your interests become more complex and developed. I think that the concept of being an alternative club, kind of on the edge of a lot of things that had attracted me, but I hadn't necessarily fully developed or hadn't fully investigated. Anticipation and expectation would be the best words to describe how I thought of the club before I even set foot inside.

Athena Costa: I grew up here, so I always read The Phoenix and knew things. But when I started college in 1995, these kids in my dorm came up to me and they were like, "You need to go to this club with us. You need to go dancing. They have an 80s night." I couldn't go because I was very broke, so what I would do instead is dress them up. One of the girls in my dorm had no hair because she was going through cancer treatments, so she had me draw these elaborate tattoo-like things on her head that people thought were real, and she was super excited about it. She'd be like, "I want this today," so that would be part of her thing when she went out. After they would go gallivanting off to the club, I would literally go into another roommate's room with this other kid who also couldn't go and we would watch Depeche Mode videos on repeat every Saturday.

Cris Concepcion: I was born in the Philippines in '74. My family moved to Canada in the late 80s. I was in high school during the early 90s and I came to Boston for college. I'd heard about industrial music and I was quite aware of Goth music in the early 90s. I had an older sister who knew about the scene, but I didn't go out very often. My sister and I would sometimes go into the city to go see a concert. She didn't really want to go out to clubs. But I remember seeing a Phoenix ad for a show at ManRay. For some reason, the fact that a club like that was hosting a show, that really stuck in my mind. But I was in a small business school called Babson where there weren't a lot of other sub-cultural alternative kids. I was kind of shy and I didn't really want to go all by myself. Finally, when I was a junior, I was with a group that went to a party at MIT which had gotten busted, so one of them proposed the idea "Oh it's Saturday. We're in Cambridge. Might as well go to ManRay." And that was the first time I ever went. I was really eager to have a sort of opportunity to go with other people that I was friends with.

Patrick Baldwin: There was a midnight premiere of Interview with a Vampire that I went to with some friends. Afterwards, there were some random folks talking outside and there was this little redhead Goth girl that I found particularly striking that I struck up a conversation with. My friends and I ended up going with her and her friends to breakfast afterwards. While at breakfast, she mentioned ManRay and was like, "Hey, I'm going to this club. Would you like to go?" I hadn't heard anything about it at all, but she was interested so I went. My only experience was metal clubs. So when I first went to ManRay with her that Wednesday, I had no idea what I was walking into at all. It was something else. It was like something out of a movie. I remember that chain spider web, in particular, when I walked in someone was attached to it and it was just one of those moments of "What the ...?"

Liz Lamanche: It was a part of the landscape and it was a place that people were going. It was sort of my neighborhood place because I lived like two blocks away. I wound up meeting up with friends or just going because I heard about the different nights, the Goth nights, the fetish nights, and the Thursday gay night. As a young woman, I could dance unmolested, and the music and people were really good.

Mark Clavet: The first thing I noticed was a billboard or a poster advertisement at a different club and the description promoting one of the nights. I think it was probably Saturday New Wave night and I thought, "Hey, this looks interesting. I'll check it out." So I made a mental note of it and then I saw a couple more stickers and posters here and there going to different concerts and events. I began looking online and asked a couple of people about it and it sounded quite interesting. What I think piqued my interest was that there were different themed nights and I thought it was interesting.

Xtine Santakas: I first heard of ManRay as a nightclub when I was too young to get in. I was told it was an alternative club. It was very Goth industrial and you had to wear black in order to get in and it was where the weirdos went. I couldn't wait to be old enough to get in the door. My godfather used to hang out there when I was a little kid and he would come over and read my sister and I a bedtime story and then teach us the latest dance move, which was kind of counterproductive. Then he would get dressed in whatever costume he was going to ManRay in. At that point I was terrified. As a little kid this is very, very frightening. What's funny is, as I got older he asked me where we were going and we said ManRay. And he said, "Yeah, it was just a matter of time for you."

Gibby Miller: My first exposure, before I went to ManRay, was a flyer which was either given to me by Cusraque or by somebody else. It was definitely one of his flyers- the long, crazy wordy descriptions and the Shakespearean borders.

Derek Kouyoumjian: I would have been hanging out on Harvard Square. I didn't really fit in very well in Arlington, which was very conservative, very townie. I wasn't from there and, even if I did look more conventional, which I did, I would not have been welcome. But I spent a lot of time in the Square and there's a lot of people out there that were talking about checking out ManRay. "It's really cool. They play loud music and you'll love it." I remember feeling like I was in this sort of sci-fi world with all the flashing lights.

Anna Feder: I had only turned 18 three weeks before I went to ManRay, so I had not really been to clubs. That may even have been my first club. So, going to clubs in general is a totally new world.

A. Dominy Cusraque: (Overheard while waiting in line) "Dude, I heard there are vampire chicks in there."

Julie Kramer: Dark, loud, and packed with people.

Gibby Miller: My impression of that place was that it was probably over my head. You have to be 19 to get in, which was different because these other places are 18 plus or 21 plus. I remember being kind of intimidated or afraid and I felt like I didn't have the cool clothes to go.

Jenn Sutkowski: I'm pretty sure I heard about it from this guy Chris, who was in my psychology class freshman year. He was kind of Goth and I was kind of Goth, and he told me about this club. I don't remember everything that he said, but I remember that it sounded like it was right up my alley. It was definitely a unique experience the first time.

Charles Bandes: I went to a club with a friend in New York called The

Bank, probably in '93. I came home to Cambridge and was telling my friends about what a good time I had there and they said that club sounds kind of like ManRay. The moment you walk in the door it's smoky and it's loud. Those are probably the two key experiential things immediately. I have never been a smoker; I don't like cigarette smoke, so that was always a little bit of a turn off coming in the door, though, is usually more sort of clove cigarettes, which I find less offensive.

Adam Wolff: My first experience there was experiencing it as a Goth club tourist, if that makes sense. I was familiar with the scene elsewhere but I thought it was really cool to see what it was like in Boston.

Michael Marotta: A friend of mine, DJ Ken, wanted a fresh start and moved up to Boston in '97 and started the Pill. I would come up to Boston and visit and see the kind of community that they have. I graduated school in the spring of 2000 and offered to have me move in. At the time, there were so many nights, so many dance parties, so many club nights in the early 2000s, but ManRay was the only spot that reminded me of those old New York City clubs. It was a true nightclub in the city. Here, in this strange little enclave in Central Square off of the hustle and bustle of Mass Ave, you had this dark, dank venue that was just unlike anywhere else.

Paul Clanan: I think I went into it with a kind of a fairly open mind. I don't really think I knew what to expect to be honest, but I knew it was going to be something a little bit different than what I was accustomed to. I believe, if I remember correctly, the person that first invited me to ManRay had already been going there for a while. He was actually a former band mate of mine, and he was the first person that thought to mention it to me and tell me to go and check it out.

Jon Whitney: Well, it kind of reminded me of the sort of more intimate clubs in New York that I was going to. They had a crowd who were primarily dressed in black, and it had a theme, and it was very intimate. I think it was cozy compared to a lot of the New York places which was good. You can really get lost at some of those bigger New York venues. It was intimate, it wasn't boring, the music wasn't boring. You could just hang out with people in the lounge and just talk, or you didn't have to.

Skot Kremen: When I first walked into ManRay, I was unimpressed because I always went to the Limelight. I thought the whole place smelled like fucking stale beer. The carpets are disgusting. But I felt like nobody tried as hard as they did and that was interesting. Everybody was super friendly and I met people that I remained friends with until the club closed.

Adam Wolff: It was great. I went back to New York and I was like, "They have strobe lights on the floor, dude." That was terrific. It's very different from the New York scene which had these super clubs.

Nate Roman: I was given almost no warning. I walk through the door and I'm greeted with Brad spinning in the front room and Chris spinning in the back room and I've never seen anything like it. Of course, it's Fantasy Factory. I was newly acquainted with the music, but I remember feeling familiar with it. It wasn't just the music. It was the way people were interacting.

Erin Falkell: I think I definitely had the impression that it was a place where you could be yourself and also that the boundaries were a little bit less clear about what happened there. It was like an amusement park but it was also this kind of home.

Matt Richard: I was in college at Saint Michael's in Vermont, and I got into Goth-industrial DJing. I was looking around New England for resources and ManRay came up in my internet searches. I'd heard about ManRay online, and then eventually I met a friend who was working at Eros Boutique and he said he was going to ManRay, that mythical place that I had heard about or seen online as a Goth slash industrial slash fetish venue, and I was like, "Oh, great. Well, that's the stuff that I spin, my kind of music, so I can't wait to see what it's going to be like inside." When I get there, it is an alternative and fetishized kind of nightclub or Goth place, not your stereotypical techno pop music kind of place. I was looking forward to actually getting in there and seeing it. I knew it wasn't going to be your run of the mill top 40 place and it was more like the Pit from The Crow.

Crayola Tidd: So, before ManRay, I always hung out at punk rock clubs. Mostly The Rat and The Channel. A group of friends one night was like, "Oh, we're going to do something a bit different. There's this goth night at this place called ManRay." We went and had a great time. And I was like, "Oh, this is very different." Cusraque seemed to be everywhere that I was. I'd go to a party and there was a beautiful flyer.

Derek Kouyoumjian: First and foremost was smoke. There was a lot of cigarette smoke and there was a lot of dry ice. There's also the smell of alcohol and drugs. It felt like I was in a different world with all these creatures just dancing and riding in these different rooms and I loved it. It was where I really, as a nightclub photographer, developed a sense of aesthetic as to watching people dance and how it looked, what looked good and didn't look good. There was a big sense of freedom there. People just simply were who they were, they went in there as whatever they wanted to be.

Emily Arkin: I did feel curious about it. I remember thinking it seemed more grown up that people were like, "Oh, yes, I've been to the places you get carded to get into." … I thought everything was boring, even things that I hadn't done yet. Just because I was like a surly teen. I would say that I cultivated, like many teenagers, a super jaded attitude towards everything.

Brian Legault: So I'll preface this by saying I was working a travel job. I was using Montreal as a home base and flying out every Monday morning to wherever I had a gig and flying back Thursday or Friday night. I found myself with an eight-week contract in Boston and I was staying at the Marriott in Kendall Square and I had met Tony Lee at a Goth festival before. He was from Boston and all of a sudden I found myself in Boston for a three-month period. I reached out to him and he said, "Oh, you're in Cambridge. You know tomorrow night is the Goth night at ManRay." I was staying in Kendall Square so I literally just walked over to ManRay, and lo and behold, there is the most amazing club that I've seen. It was a very different club from what I was used to in Montreal.

Abigail Taylor: The first time I walked in, it was full of smoke because cigarettes were a thing still and they also had the smoke machines and the lights and everything. There was a very specific ManRay smell that you got right away as soon as you walked in the doors, like a combination of years of spilled drinks on old carpet, much like musky undertones of sewage and cigarettes. The aroma got worse when they banned smoking. Then just feeling as if I was in a room with the coolest people in the world ... in the most exciting place I have ever been to in my life. So that was my initial feeling, like, oh my God, I've made it. These are my people. I will become them.

Julia Kilcoyne: I've only had two panic attacks in my life. This is corny, but my first thought is "Jesus, how are we going to get out of here in case of a fire?" But then I was mostly taken by the black with splashes of color. There were pockets or enclaves that had little conversations happening. "Who are these people and what are their lives really like?" Those are the things that I wondered immediately. I didn't feel like a fish out of water. I felt like we were all these fish that had jumped into this pond from other water, if that makes sense. I felt that it was dark, but it was bright. It was beautiful and ugly, and yet wonderfully pure at the same time. It was everything I was looking for.

Hideki Watanabe: My college roommate said, "There's two of us going to an 80s night, would you like to join us?" And I wasn't really into 80s music at the time. But we went and it was okay. Didn't know what to expect and then shortly thereafter another friend, he had never been to a club ever in his life. And I said, "Would you like to go to ManRay?" And he's like, "Okay, sure."

So, we show up and they ask for ID and it was 18 plus back then. But they asked for ID. And so, they're like, "Yeah, what's going on?" It's a special night. But we're like, okay, and we walk in and right away we see someone on their hands and knees crawling on a chain. And the person who has never been to a club before is like, "Whoa, are all clubs like this?" and we're like, "No, we've never seen this before."

Wendy Austin: When I first started going to clubs I was impressed because it's like, "Oh, finally, I can see the lifestyle that I imagined for myself." So, I'm sure that I was impressed. But then it just wasn't my scene. I don't have any regrets, but I did not enjoy it. Very soon after I would go with friends and I was like, "Do we have to fucking come here?" I don't know, it just wasn't my place. I mean, it wasn't a place I ever felt like, "Oh yeah … this place." I'm glad it existed for other people, but it just wasn't for me.

David Winthrop: My idea of nightlife was just crowded dance floors and just a lot of beautiful people doing beautiful things. My first trip to ManRay was on a Wednesday night, and I was still in high school. It was very dark and there were some really interesting characters and I remember just people watching. I was too young to drink, so we went in and got the x's on the hands.

Trent Stewart: I loved the layout. It had more than one primary dance floor and several bars and a lounge. The first thing I noticed, because I love to dance, was that people were dancing, but they were dancing by themselves. That struck me as incredibly interesting. It wasn't just one or two people. No one seemed to have a dance partner. Coming from a traditional club scene, when you hear a song you want to dance you actually have to find someone to dance with. By the time you get to the dance floor the song is nearly over. If nobody wants to dance with you at that time you're just out of luck. So, this struck me as gold. And just as I started dancing. It stopped and I was confused but then they had a performance. It was like a vignette with light BDSM. It was explained to me later that people actually have different nights.

Heather Morgan: The first time I went to ManRay I was with Raziel and Jason, the two original Shriek's. Jason was driving his giant white boat kind of car, like an Oldsmobile. It had the You Shriek symbol painted on the side so it's just the Shriekmobile. It was so funny because almost nobody in town had cars and I was a freshman, but I was hanging out with boys who lived over on Hemingway Street on Fenway. It was not necessary to drive from there, but because we had the You-Shriek-mobile we drove over there. We're kind of front loading on the way and I had the world's worst fake ID, which I just used to get into clubs on Lansdowne Street. Most of the time they would spot it, but they would let me in if I wouldn't take a bracelet. But when I got to the front door of ManRay, they wouldn't let me in because they were still 21 plus on Saturday. So the boys disappeared in the side and I was standing outside. I had this bottle of hootch and I just went over and sat by the car and got totally hammered on the sidewalk. But, in a way, that made it even more intriguing.

Kyle Blaisdell: I grew up about 90 minutes from the area and, when I visited Boston, I'd just be casually in stores and someone who saw my look and saw that I was into a scene would just come up to me randomly and say, "You have to check out ManRay." But I didn't really live locally at the time, so it's always just in the back of my mind somewhere that I'm gonna have to check it out. Once I relocated to Boston in '93, I started attending. I remember the very first time was in the middle of a massive snowstorm, so only about two dozen people wandered the building all night. It was me with a couple of friends. We all walked in blind, not knowing what to expect, so it was kind of nice having a small crowd. We could really take in the bones of the place and the atmosphere.

Jill Kempton: I remember I was at the Emerald Square Mall and I was walking around and this guy came up to me and, oddly enough I had never seen him at ManRay and never really saw him again, but he came up to me and said, "Hey, do you go to ManRay? You'd like, ManRay. Do you want to go there?" And I was like, "No, what is it?" I was just going to concerts, starting to get my feet wet with going out. My friend and I took a drive out there.

I remembered finally thinking "These are my people". I first went to the right room, but it wasn't really my area, that was too techno or rave. I didn't know about the back room yet, it was just like when I first went to Limelight in New York. I didn't know about the overly cool room yet. I'm stuck in this other room going, "I guess it's okay. But this isn't a big deal." Then some girl comes up to me and says, "Mo, no you want to be in this room" and I went, "Whoa," and I never left that room.

Gibby Miller: I remember feeling extremely nervous. I hadn't really found my niche in terms of who I was or what my look was. I was a nomad, kind of a subculture nomad, but I do remember the room. You walk in, you walk through that hallway and it's kind of like you're walking through a gauntlet.

ML: The techno room off to the right, which is where I used to work for the longest time, had Spiderman on the wall. They had one of the rooms, the lounge area set up like a church with the pews and everything in these things would alternate as time went by and it had an industrial goth feel about it, then you just didn't see anywhere else, not in Boston.

Chapter 5

On the Stage: Artists and Bands at ManRay

"Going there for a show is always something special. It was a different type of venue. Everybody at a ManRay show was there because they wanted to be."
— Jon Whitney

Central Square provided a vibrant place for the local Boston-Cambridge music scene to thrive. From Axis and Avalon to T.T. the Bear's Place and Middle East, the area catered to music, bands, and DJs looking to showcase their crafts. ManRay doubled as both a dance club and a concert venue, proving itself versatile. Probably the two most infamous shows to grace the stage of ManRay was Nirvana's second ever visit to Massachusetts and the night the crowd listening to KMFDM broke the dance floor. Bands from across the country and overseas hit the stage, including acts like Consolidated, Skinny Puppy, VNV Nation, and Wolfsheim. ManRay also showcased and provided opportunities to local Boston bands You Shriek, DDT, Sleep Chamber, O Positive and many more. Central Square was a place for people to gather, see shows, and fall in love with new bands or show their devotion to those they already loved.

ManRay also made the stage so much more than just a venue for bands. From Hell to Fantasy Factory and everything in between countless performances took to the boards. For the viewers, it seemed like the most amazing, effortless visual art, but these performances took incredible time and dedication. Deciding on a theme, choreography, weeks of rehearsal, getting the outfits picked out, setting up the stage and props, wriggling into latex or corsets, getting make-up just right, all of this had to happen before the performances graced the stage. Once it began, the cogs moved seamlessly and perfectly. Whether you enjoyed the performance or not you left ManRay that night a changed person. S.L.

Jon Whitney: Going there for a show is always something special. It was a different type of venue, like everybody at a ManRay show was there because they wanted to be there. People were at The Middle East shows and T.T. the Bear's shows because they were the backpack crowd. I did go there with the backpacks because they're supposed to like this band. You go to a show at The Middle East upstairs or T.T. the Bear's or Bill's Bar or any of the other places and there's a lot of talk, cash registers and beer drinking, but when you went to ManRay everybody was there fixated on the band because it wasn't it wasn't a common thing. Nobody was there taking notes on bands. People were there because they wanted to pay attention and enjoy the band, give them their attention. It was a venue that was a community, it was a place that they trusted.

Patrick Baldwin: I loved ManRay as a venue. The fact that you can have a show going on in the back room right, but there was that space and the central room where you could still go and have a conversation with your friends, if you needed a break, or if the act that happened to be on right now wasn't doing it for you. And there was often still dancing in the side room. You had a lot of options and that's really nice. It meant that if you were a little unsure of the bands that night it didn't matter, because if you didn't dig them you could still have a good night.

I saw a lot of shows that are some of my favorite shows. There was this band called One of Us, a local Boston band, and they did a show at ManRay that was really astonishing. I saw You Shriek there and their live show was super, super fun. One of my favorite shows I've ever been to, in my top five, certainly, I saw D&B Nation and Covenant and Apoc there and that was amazing. It was the only time I saw the entire club dancing. There were none of the Goths holding up the walls. It was amazing.

John O'Leary: It was the late 80s, early 90s. It was a great time. I remember seeing Nine Inch Nails at Axis. But I think what sets ManRay apart, was that it had that feel of a tiny venue, but it was huge. It was big.

Chris Manasouridies: It was a very strange venue to see shows at because you already had that conception of the dance club and it sort of didn't translate to me very well because people were still dancing, as if the show really wasn't going on, except for Amber, but the other shows like Faith in the Muse and everything. What a lot of people don't know is ManRay had a lot of connections to Ramrod and Machine. There were different owners, but they were very close, kind of like CVO. Of course, Ramrod was a leather bar and ManRay on Thursday nights was a gay bar. We did a whole group show with Black Tape For Bue Girl and it was for charity. And again, it was very strange to look at a concert at a dance club. That whole vibe kind of changes where you're just like, it's still a dance club. It's still ManRay.

Chris Manasouridies: Axis was the same way for me. A lot of us who worked at ManRay. I can't remember the guy's name now, but he owned Merlin Security that did a lot of the shows down. So he would hire us for free. We would go for no pay and bounce for the shows. But we got to see the shows, so that was kind of like our pay was to get to be right up close right in front of the stage and kind of enjoy the show, while we worked. That was our pay which was fine by me. I mean, I've seen some killer shows.

Noel McKenna: Chris was always very supportive of DDT. He actually produced a couple of songs for us. And one of our most popular songs, which I thought got a bit of recognition, we covered Madonna's Vogue.

Chris Ewen: There was another band called DDT that I met through Ground Zero around the corner and we became friends. They formed and we loved to give bands like that a platform to play. We would book bands that might not have full access to the full rock and roll clubs. Having a place to meet and socialize and collaborate was a really valuable thing at the time. You couldn't dash off an email or do zoom calls.

Noel McKenna: During those years when DDT was really going strong, we put a lot of effort into writing new music and learning to play. We put a lot of work into learning how to present the music in a live situation. Often after ManRay, we would just go and work on music.

Skot Kremen: When DDT did their cover of Vogue. That was everything.

Keith Ward: It was definitely more hardcore shows. Just more going to different shows and stuff. I think I got more into live music and going to ManRay all the time.

John O'Leary: Providence was the best kept secret because you could see the same band you're going to see in Boston the next night.

Noel McKenna: We played at The Rat. We played in Providence and then we got offered an opening slot for Catholic Guilt at ManRay in the summer of '91. That first year that we started playing we opened for Sleep Chamber. ManRay offered us an opening slot for the band Fetus, an influential industrial band. Oh my God. So we were able to open for Fetus to a huge crowd. ManRay offered us a lot of really good opening slots for really established bands, like Alien Sex Fiend. Those shows were really important for us because it allowed us to reach a bigger audience than just the regulars who went to ManRay.

It was interesting being a purely electronic band in Boston because Boston is a very traditional Rock and Roll city. We were playing rock clubs and nobody knew what to do with us. The sound engineers had no idea what to do with us. So, it was like that was not a struggle. It was kind of fun, actually. We really stood out. We got a lot of press and we became very popular in Boston in a very short period of time. DDT happened in Boston at the perfect time because Boston did not have an electronic scene.

Elizabeth Galbraith: There were definitely performances I saw there that were pretty good. I remember seeing Ogre and Skinny Puppy. That was a good performance. Switchblade Symphony played there quite a few times. There were definitely some interesting performances there that I saw that were new to me at the time.

John O'Leary: In the 90s I was in a Goth industrial darkwave band called You Shriek, who played ManRay a bunch of times with a ton of other bands. It was our home away from home.

Richard LaDue: I remember seeing this band called Consolidated in the early 90s and they were industrial. I remember they would do a Q&A during the show or afterwards. I swear to God. It was funny. I remember thinking Consolidated was cool. Do you remember Pete Burns from Dead or Alive? He performed there in '93 maybe. So, I was like, "Oh wow they book cool bands." I don't know if I realized it then, but looking back, that kind of intimacy, you're in a room with 300 people watching a show. Smaller venues are a lot sexier. I don't love being in the House of Blues with 2,500 people. I feel like I'm at Home Depot. There's something about that kind of intimate small setting that I like more.

Terri Niedzwiecki: Oh, dear God. Pete Burns from Dead or Alive had to be everybody's nightmare. In the deal he had to get picked up at the airport. I grabbed another friend of mine, Adam Lewis who was like,

"Sure, I'll go to the airport, but I don't have a car." And I'm like, "I'm sure Don will let you borrow his," which he did. Adam had his little sign and Pete Burns came off with his manager. Still to this day I don't know whether the manager was a female or male or transitioning, but they definitely were stoned out of their gourd, which made Adam nervous and he set the car alarm off. He couldn't figure out how to shut it off. So, we get this emergency phone call. "Terri. Terri. This is really, really awful. I want to run away." I tell Adam how to shut the alarm off. Pete Burns is in the background bitching. It was just horrible. Bitch, complain and, at one point, Don came up to me and said, "You know, I can't take this. Can we just throw him out?" And I'm like, "Well, we can do anything we want. But we have to pay." He was almost willing to do it, that's how evil Pete Burns is. That evil queen.

John O'Leary: The Crow came out in '94. We would see Marilyn Manson at ManRay whenever they would play. I remember them coming to ManRay one time after they played The Middle East around maybe '95 or '96. There was a center bar that was never used and they came in and were standing there and they didn't know there was no bartender. Someone was like "You guys go in there, go to Terri."

Kathryn Pollnac: I think the first time I went to ManRay I saw Alien Sex Friend there. It was a show. I want to say that I actually won tickets to see the Cure, it was the Wish tour, that night randomly. I think it was probably a few months before I went back to ManRay after going to the show there.

Jon Whitney: You open up *The Phoenix* and you'd see all the shows that were playing and my thing was always live music and live shows. I went to ManRay probably because of a live show and I'm guessing it was Alien Sex Fiend. That's my best memory, I could be wrong, but I know that it was shows that drove me there in the first place, and then I got to learn more about it.

Rick Webb: Well, they had a good person running sound on live shows. It sounded good there. That Pigface show sounded awesome. The Consolidated shows were great. Even towards the end, stuff like Switchblade Symphony, that just sounded fine.

Chris Ewen: We did some things with Joyce Linehan like the Lemonheads. Joyce probably brought an element that ManRay hadn't really had with this indie rock scene and that was great.

Skot Kremen: I joined a band that I was roading for because the bass player didn't show up. It was called Planet Mosquito. I was doing music with Model Behavior, which is straight up synthpop. It was never supposed to be something we played live. We would road test our songs because you don't know how it's gonna sound on big club speakers. It sounds different. So, we would always road test our songs at ManRay. We'd go to the DJ booth and ask Chris to play it and that was how we would check our masters.

Skot Kremen: We finally got to the point where, if we wanted to play a show, I just had to ask, which had never happened before.

Becky D: I'll be honest, I don't remember the first performances. It was absolutely at Hell because those are some of the first nights that I went to. It absolutely was an acoustic performance that I saw, but I don't remember what one. I just remember being excited at the idea of performances. One of the first bands that I saw there was Cruxshadows. So that was really cool. Yeah, again, it goes back to the idea that there was this safe haven for creative and quirky people to be able to do artistic and creative stuff.

John O'Leary: When a big show like Wolfsheim would come to town, ManRay was going to be 1,000 people instead of 500.

Terri Niedzwiecki: They would wait for someone else to go when you told them about. I have this friend, Harry, who I met through DDT. I think he might have done something for them. He could fix anything.

Rachel E. Pollock: They had to cordon off the dungeon space to have a VIP area for Marilyn Manson and actual people that worked in the club weren't allowed to go in the VIP area. That turns that into, I gather, a big headache on behalf of the security team. It was not a good venue for somebody who was that famous.

Terri Niedzwiecki: Well, the traditional dance nights … God knows it's easier because, when you deal with bands, you have to be there so early to be ready. And then they get Prima Donnas. It's hard working with bands. I don't know how people do it on a regular basis.

Rachel E. Pollock: Chris and Terri would refer a lot of bands that came to us at Ceremony because they knew they were not gonna bring enough people to ManRay. One of the frequent complaints was that there was no dedicated backstage space. So they had to either hide in their van or socialize with the crowd, which I mean, get over it dudes. You're dealing with egos where it's like, look, you're in this club because you can't draw enough people for a club that has a real backstage.

Terri Niedzwiecki: Well, I think you have a completely different mindset when you're working already at the place and they're coming in. Don't get me wrong, I wouldn't pass out if Peter Murphy ever played there. But for the most part I liked the people that played there. But, they had their job to do and I had mine to do. For the most part, for the people you didn't expect to be nice.

Rachel E. Pollock: While working at Ceremony, we would actually be the ones that booked a lot of the smaller Goth bands, because they couldn't draw enough of a crowd to play ManRay. They could really maybe only bring out 200 people and that's a shitload in for Ceremony when they're in some tiny basement bar.

Liz Enthusiasm: So we started in '99 and it was just kind of this thing, like so. My friends and I had a record label already. So, we put out some stuff by local artists, so we kind of were like, "Oh, hey, we can put out CDs? And we can just kind of keep doing this." The instrumentation was so limited like we didn't have to book studio time or whatever. So, you know, it was all kind of done in our basements and then I was like, "All right, let's put out CDs and let's do this. Let's do that. Let's make a website. Let's make a video. Let's, you know, do all that stuff." It was exciting but at the same time, like we had no idea that it was going to kind of get as big as it was getting. So that was sort of a huge surprise.

It was basically like in the early days, we got put on a lot of bills with other Goth bands and stuff. Just because there were so few other bands doing you know like synth pop kind of stuff. Boston at the time was very rock oriented. And so the bookers didn't really know what to do with us and just put us on bills with, you know, various other Goth bands.

We didn't tour that much. We would maybe go out for like two weeks at a time or something like that. One of the things that I learned from just being on the road and like going to all these other nights and stuff was like Chris is such a good DJ. We were like, "We're so lucky to have Chris." And like, a lot of times we would play a show and then afterwards, it would turn into a dance night.

Emily Taylor: ManRay was a place where musicians would come through and tour. Marilyn Manson came through after his tour one night and we all hung out with him. I mean Nirvana played there.

Duane Bruce: There's only a one-word answer for that and that's fate. Radio Free Boston was the show that I did for a couple of years overnight on FNX, Monday through Friday. Through an outside source, I found out about Nirvana and then through an inside source, I found out about Nirvana almost at the same time so I started playing them. We didn't add them officially onto the station's rotation. I played them overnight because I had the ability in the free format to do it. But they were not being played.

Duane Bruce: I showed up that night with Kurt St. Thomas and we decided we wanted to go downstairs and meet with the band and clear the MC with them. So I went down the stairs to that smoky sort of room with the pool table and the three of them are sitting on the couch. It's not Dave Grohl. It's Chad Channing at that point.

Duane Bruce: They were talking about the fact that it was so big. I remember them saying, "My God, this is a huge, huge place" when they walked in, they weren't even sure what room they were playing in. I think they really liked the club. I know that they enjoyed the show and had a great time. Even though it was sparsely attended, that was still quite a bit for them coming from the West Coast to the East Coast for only their second show. They doubled the attendance, more or less, from the first show. I'm sure that was a blessing in their eyes.

Duane Bruce: I ascertained that I could, in fact, bring them on stage. They were so cool and happy with the fact that. I had only read the intro once and how it stuck in my head is beyond me, but I didn't fuck it up at the time. It was great I said "Please welcome fudge packing, crack smoking, Satan worshipping mother fuckers. Sub Pop recording artist: Nirvana." There's a bootleg that's got 90,000 viral hits and that's how it opens with me saying those words and then the band kicks into "School" and it just goes crazy. Their set was about maybe 50 to 55 minutes. Kurt wiped out the drums at the end by diving into them. That was exactly the type of thing that you expected after a rocket set like that. The guy could scream; he had a really good way of singing very beautifully and then breaking out that raspy smoker screaming screeching thing that he was known for. That drew you in and emoted all his pain. Even back then off the Bleach album some of those songs were guttural. And that's kind of what that performance was. If I had to define it in one term, it would be guttural and it just progressed that way, all through the show, until finally he just dove through the drum set at the end.

Duane Bruce: I know a lot of people claim they were there. I'm not saying anybody's fibbing, but I would say there were about 80 people in that club that night.

Chris Ewen: I was at the Nirvana show. While it wasn't necessarily my cup of tea at that time musically, I found them really engaging and really great and the show did really well. It was really lively. It's one of those things where I didn't realize just how special it was going to turn out to be. I basically hung out in the DJ booth and watched the show from that vantage point, so I was very, very close. It was very, very loud. It was great. I know Kurt Cobain was in a very loose and funny kind of mood. He kind of broke into a little bit of acapella between songs. While he was probably being a little sarcastic, I found it quite endearing. It kind of became a moment from that show that people seem to remember really well.

Duane Bruce: I may have very well contributed to the explosion of the knowledge of the 1990 Nirvana show at ManRay. I had sitting on my shelf a cassette of that show. It was bootleg from the audience, but it was still pretty good, a seven out of ten-quality bootleg. That was on my shelf for twenty years and one day I went like, "Shit, man. You know what, when I die that's just going to wind up on the curb and that doesn't deserve that." So, I dumped it down to an MP3 and I posted it on my Facebook page through SoundCloud. Michael Murata from Vanyaland graciously picked up that story and then it just went viral. To this day, it has 90,000 plays on my page. That's an amazing feat. I can track it on SoundCloud and see where it's been downloaded thousands of times and I can see the breakdown of the countries and cities. It's in Guyana, Africa. It's in Mother Russia. It's in Beijing, it's in San Juan. It's in Monte Carlo. It's everywhere that American Express goes.

Emily Arkin: I was in high school with Mona, Elliot, and Megan. They were an awesome band. Mona went on to be in Victory at Sea. I had been a classical musician most of my life. I've been a violinist and I went away to college and I came to be a college radio DJ in the 90's so I got very, very into indie rock and also metal.

Musicians play a ton of different instruments. I'd never taken lessons. In my mid-20s, which is pretty late picking up guitar, I was self-taught and started just playing stuff after some of my favorite bands. I was very influenced by 4AD, and a little bit spilled into ManRay, actually, like Cocteau twins and then very much the Boston 4AD, Breeders, Throwing Muses, and stuff.

I formed a band. Our first show was in 1999 called the Operators and our first gig was at a Riot Girl showcase and right away that was really influential for me. I remember we played with trans women and we played with gender nonbinary people of all races. I really feel like I have to keep paying this forward, the spirit of just trying to lift up other bands and other performers at the start of their career. We also had kind of a naive sort of jangly indie rock sound, so at times we would self-deprecatingly be like we're a little like The Shaggs, we're kind of shambolic and people would be like, "Oh, it's like The Raincoats and other bands, but sort of like drumming that is a little like herky jerky."

I did that for ten years and then one of my bandmates moved out of town or moved to another state. From then, I started playing with Hilken Mancini who'd been a rock fixture for a long time. She was in a band called Fuzzy. She and I started out playing really quiet shows together. I actually brought back my violin, which I hadn't played since college, and we would play acoustic guitar and violin at people's outdoor gigs and then we added in a drummer and bassist who were great and suddenly, over time we just became louder and louder and more rock. There was no violin after a while, it was just a huge guitar feedback and super loud drums. I have been doing that for, I think a little over ten years, although we have not played since the pandemic obviously.

Christina Pearson: I know that the band Sleep Chamber, I saw there a few times and I don't think I would have gotten into them. I mean, I don't think I would have found them. They were all turned into they were goth that they were like that they were really like that sort of alt-sex stuff going on that. I don't know what I would have found, and I really did enjoy it like I love those albums.

ML: Now we really saw a lot of people coming through, who were really good and maybe didn't achieve. The notoriety, but it was a good place.

And I also saw different things like DJs and competitions and we'd work strange special nights that they come in on a Sunday, and you go in with, you know, the three of us would pretend to be at the bar and work this special event. With me it was like you have a shot. If you were booked there or your last hurrah if you're on your way down.

ML: There were a lot of performances at ManRay that are now famous. Like Tiny Tim there, he did one right before he died.

Adam Lewis: The problem with doing shows at ManRay was there was no sound system in the house. So you had to rent every time. You have to rent sound and lights. All you had was a PA and disco lights there. That means you've got an added expense right off the bat that you don't have in The Middle East or what not. So it makes it a little harder but not impossible. And you would have to take off. You know, if you were facing the stage, the stage wasn't big enough.

Adam Lewis: I know that we had Dead or Alive at ManRay. I remember that show very, very well because the lead singer was a terror. I mean if you remember, he transitioned. And so now looking back at all kind of makes sense because I don't think he was particularly happy and I think he was pretty drugged up or something at the time.

Jen Lucky Cole: The first show that I got into was Death in June, and I think it was in 96. That blew my mind too. I couldn't believe I was seeing that band on a stage in front of me. All the other bands I had already seen … I still was like, wow, because they were so controversial. A lot of times their shows would get canceled before they could play and it's not their fault. It's the fault of a lot of fucking dumb people that don't understand their ideology. ManRay was a home to them. The last band that ever played at ManRay in 2005, their last show, was Death in June. They were kind of like a haven for bands that were misunderstood by mainstream culture.

Jen Lucky Cole: Yes, putting those together. As somebody who actually was the person who organized New Year's for a couple of years in a row. 2000 and 2001 actually I took it to be a serious one, too. So, from 2000 to 2001, I'm like all right 2000 was a crazy good year. By that point I had worked there for a year so I had more clout over a lot of things. I had been booking shows and everything had been going well. In late October they started having me look for a performer for New Year's Eve and I got really excited about that. So, I started hitting up all my contacts and I wound up getting Joan Jett. Right, she had done pride that year in Boston and she was really popular. She had just come out of the closet. She looked the lesbian look [with] the short bleached blonde hair that summer and everybody wanted her and I got her for a really good price. Unreal, you know, cause she was a sellout, you're guaranteed it would sell out.

Don took the Green Line for some reason and he ran into John from Sleep Chamber who's driving the friggin 'Green Line train. So, Don comes into work like hey forget what you're doing. I got our act for New Year's Eve - Sleep Chamber. And I was like, "Are you serious?" I couldn't even laugh, it was like a knife in my heart. I was like, "No." And he's like, yeah, and his price was considerably less. Yeah, and I got vetoed. I tried. I was kind of pissed because it made me kind of look bad to the company that Joan Jett went through when I was trying to build up a lot of really good contacts. That didn't sit well with those people. Well, it did not sell out. Let's put it that way.

Adam Lewis: We heard a loud bang. And we didn't know what it was. It was breaking, the floor broke. So we had to have everyone, we had to pause the show and make everyone step back. Just had to make an announcement and basically had to step back and no one could jump up and down. Vinny, the manager, and my roommate had found a beam to put under it. I feel like we got another beam from T.T. the Bear's, but I could be wrong on that. But we were able to put some wood underneath paired up to support it. And then resume the show. It ended up not being a big deal. Like it ended up being okay they were able to deal with the situation, but it was scary for a moment. It was definitely like I mean it was scary for us only in that you want the show to go on. You don't want to have to send people home unhappy. No one could believe it was kind of happening. I mean, in retrospect, ManRay wasn't in great shape. So looking back, I'm not surprised that that could possibly happen. I mean ManRay was great in the dark. You know, you never wanted to see it in the daytime, or, you know, with the lights on.

Heather Morgan: I don't remember that much about KMFDM except for the stomping. I think that's what caused the floor to collapse, there was just so much stomping. You Shriek opened for them. That was a really exciting night for me because those were my best friends there and they were fucking opening for KMFDM. So, the kind of highlight, for me personally, had already passed by the time that happened. I wasn't as into KMFDM as I was into Neubauten, so after You Shriek went on I was kind of popping in and out. I remember hanging out with my friend Bobby in the front room. We were just talking for 40 minutes about Strategies Against Architecture and what a great album it is and standing outside smoking and talking. I remember somebody, either from the band or the audience, climbing on a pole on the ceiling and scaling it across. I do remember that there was a lot of "STOP IT!" over the PA. It was pretty out of control.

Terri Niedzwiecki: There were over 700 people there and everyone naturally gathered near the stage. All of a sudden Harry comes running up and he's like, "Oh my God, you're not gonna believe this." I told them to go find the manager or find somebody. I mean, what am I supposed to do? So, I've got a little freaked out and Harry thinks he can fix this. "What do you think?" and I'm like, "Well, unless you want everyone to end up in the basement, let's see what happens." But in the meantime, we had to get people off the dance floor. So, Harry is up on the stage going "Okay everybody backup. Don't move," with the fishnets, no less. It's one of the funniest things I've ever witnessed. Nobody died, the floor never caved in. The building department was there the next day. It was fixed in 24 hours. Harry actually did a very good job.

Skot Kremen: They stopped the show and the manager, Vinny, got on stage and went, "You guys gotta chill out for a second. The floor broke." Basically, they had to go into the basement and prop up the floor.

Mizery McRae: ManRay was the epitome of anything and everything that can happen.

Constantine Valhouli: Overheard at ManRay, at some point: "You could probably extract DNA samples from the most brilliant and mischievous people at MIT and Harvard just by taking a core sample of the couch and running it through a centrifuge."

Michael Hsieh: Okay next month is sci-fi or strange forbidden planet or something. Is it okay if we get bitten by a planet? We would go to somebody's house to make dinner and just brainstorm. What can we put on for this performance? We want aliens to be robots. We've done that before. Maybe there's a *Star Wars* movie coming out. Maybe we would like to do something like that.

We just got the concept down and then said, "Okay, what do you want? How many people are doing it? What props do we need? What about this music? We can do choreography for it." Another day we would get together at somebody's house again and go through the choreography. Me and Becky used a big mirror. "Okay, how about this? That doesn't work. Let's try this." We would probably have a couple sessions working out choreography and then we get the people who are in it. We would find another space, or go to the club early before it opened, and practice over and over and over.

The night of Fantasy Factory we would get there an hour early to do one last run through and then put it on and that was pretty exciting. Then we do it all again the next month. We had sort of a rotating cast of Go-Go dancers. Most always just stayed for a good long time. People moved out of the area or stopped coming because they had other scenes and other things to be doing, but it seems we had a pretty steady core. And we meet new people.

You're paid to dance up there on the block for two, three, four hours and just kind of be scenery. That's what it felt like. It was really a privilege to be part of this constant creative team and have this constant responsibility. Most people don't get to do that.

Trent Stewart: We made sure that we had an art director because we would decorate the club the night before and we were responsible for breaking everything down at the end. The performance would have to be based on whatever the theme was for that night. If you were scheduled to do a performance, you had to actually have it in writing. I had to have everything a month ahead of time, including the rehearsal schedule. You couldn't just fake it. There's a lot of moving pieces that you're not seeing and it's our job to make sure you don't see them.

Becky D: I met Trent through my friend six months of me going to ManRay. I used to spend time at the side cage watching people dance and learning how to dance. Eventually I got confident enough that I moved to the actual dance floor. Soon after that I got a call from the person who was in charge of the dancers, and she said that she and Trent wanted me to be one of the Delicious Dancers for Fantasy Factory.

My confidence and feeling like a part of a community was what really tied into being a part of the Delicious Dancers. Once I started doing those, that was really the performance bug and the itch that got scratched. Being on stage, entertaining, but also kind of navigating working with people on stage — that relationship you have with another performer. But also, the energy that you feed off of each other and the energy you feed off from the audience. There's a connection there between your co-performer, but also the audience that you're performing for and that energy is like a high for me. I love it. So, I would say that's what really drew me in and made me fall in love with it. It ended up being the reason why I spent so many years doing it.

I definitely was one of the staple dancers for those last five years. I was also doing a lot of performances, and I did them differently. Most Fantasy Factory performances were you take a song, and you kind of act campy or sexy or whatever plot and you kind of tell a story and it's kind of miming and kind of acting through the song. It was very choreographed. I would pick a song or two for performance, I would have an idea and a plot of what I want, and then I would literally choreograph the whole thing out. So, there wasn't a lot of ad lib. Because it was so structured, for six weeks on average I was meeting with the group that I had in the performance probably twice a week and teaching them the choreography. Some of it was just blocking, but a lot of it was actual dance. We would spend an hour and a half each of those nights after working through the choreography and figuring that out. The last couple of years Michael was kind of my go to help with that. I would turn to him and be like, "I'm going to do a performance for this night. Can you help me block and figure out choreography?" and he would. We would try out different things and figure out the choreography. He would help me teach the people that we wanted in the performance. So it was a very intense process. I didn't pay anybody, we got no money. I may have covered the cost of materials and costumes. These people would spend a lot of time learning this stuff and they loved it too, but it was a lot of work. The end result was we all put on fantastic performances and we even got invited to different cities to redo the performances. We performed in New York and we went down to Providence. Once we actually were supposed to perform up in Montreal, but we didn't get past the border. It was different from the normal Fantasy Factory stuff because it was more intense. So a lot of more effort was put into that stuff.

I would be really picky about who I asked for performances. In the beginning it was mostly my close friends that love dancing. We had this passion and love for dancing itself. So there was a love that they had for that. And I'm sure they hate it, that I made them do all the work. But I think that they had a creative streak and artistic streak. They loved dancing and they loved the end result. Because it's a volunteer thing there's got to be an intrinsic kind of commitment to it that they have and then also a commitment to you as a friend or producer, I guess you could say.

Trent Stewart: A quick anecdote about Chris ... So, I was in charge of the dancers for Fantasy Factory. We had Go-Go dancers for the atmosphere because you never want to leave the dance floor empty. We all got to choose two songs on a request sheet we filled out when we got to the club that would go up to Chris. Chris would be sitting at Terri's bar, he would light up a cigarette, and study that list and have a pen and make notes. Sure enough, he would seamlessly fit those requests into a night. Not missing a beat. Nothing seemed awkward. He made me really snobbish as far as DJing.

Abigail Taylor: I was basically a Go-Go dancer, it was called the Fantasy Factory dancers basically. I was hired to do performances and to dance on a box in nipple tape and a G-string.

Jennifer: Just kind of happened. They're like, "Do you want to dance tonight?" The next thing you know you're in everything. From then on, you were a dancer. I had a badge and I was official.

They were always looking for people to be in performances, so if you're willing to do that it was pretty easy to get into Fantasy Factory. You didn't have any obligation that you had to commit to X amount hours or anything. Most of the time, your only responsibility was that you signed up to dance. Some nights there were specific people assigned to dance. If you wanted to be in a performance that was totally up to you. They were always looking for people to write new performances, so I wrote some. Depending on how involved your performance was (that) determined how many rehearsals. There were some people that were capable of throwing together a great performance by the night before. Then there were some people that needed weeks and weeks of rehearsals.

We do have a lot of good stories from over the years and rehearsals and dancing and getting to know people. People were very dear to me and are still some of my best friends. It was definitely a huge part of my life and it helped mold me to who I am.

Emily Taylor: I would go to ManRay early for rehearsal for whatever the performance was on Friday. Sometimes I would rehearse for two different performances that night, and then I usually stuck around for what was basically the Goth night and danced and hung out. Thursday's work was on Campus. Sometimes we'd have rehearsal beforehand. Sometimes I would stay for a little bit, but I didn't often stay at Campus because Thursdays were my night off from partying.

Eileen Dover: I would show up in drag in a dominatrix costume. I would say that I was pretty boyish. I did like drag, but I had the same outfit over and over. I would look around and see what the people in New York were wearing and that's where I drew my inspiration from that. I stole a book called *The Drag Queens of New York* from the bookstore and cracked that open and picked a couple queens that I really thought were phenomenal and I started to build a look. At first it was a sloppy process. I didn't really know how and the queens corrected me really quickly.

Daisy Crowder: Well, I think it was around that time that I really began to truly see the difference between drag and trans. Certainly, a lot of gay men, like myself, didn't really fully understand even though I grew up around friends. Somehow they always got blocked and sort of shunted into that drag category. That was something that really came into my consciousness — seeing obvious differences between individuals who wanted to change gender versus individuals who have fun.

That led me into doing a night on Saturday along with Chris. I wanted to do it all, by which I mean I wanted something that was drag heavy, entertaining, and anything goes. Around midnight the music would stop, lights come up, and I'd introduce two or three, known or unknown, drag talents and they would do their thing. We'd give out prizes to audience members and ask a couple of trivia questions. We would have some ridiculous contests, like who can dance the fastest, just as an excuse for us to give away some of the promotional items that we had. Then everyone got to choose their favorite performer and whoever won got like $50 or $100.

Eileen Dover: Drag queens, there were only about ten of us in any given city, and now there's like 50,000 and everybody wants to be a queen. But we were a rarity back then and we got paid what we were worth. You had to have talent, you had to get your look together, and you had to be fearless. If somebody was half assed, if you weren't willing to put in the time and effort and you didn't have the talent for drag, you would be ignored. When

I was in my awkward phase I got ignored. You always have to bring it up to the next level.

ML: I remember these shows because they were well put together. I would get to see a lot of the drag shows though. That was fun.

Chris Ewen: Drag queens played in shocks. They weren't really part of the mainstream club experience.

Anastasia Taslis: I loved the drag queens in the front. That was my first experience with drag queens.

Rebecca Griffin: I used to love it when Rainbow Fright would come in and have her show in the front.

Mizery McRae: Filene's basement. I would go down there and go into the woman's rack and they would be so funny because the workers would be like, "Oh my God, you're buying for your girlfriend?" And I'll be like, "Show to do tonight." Dorothy's was the place to go for drag shoes, makeup, and wigs.

Mizery McRae: Unless I booked them or Rainbow Fright booked them, they didn't understand it. They thought ManRay was an S&M bar. They thought it was kink or fetish. And they were like, "Oh, we don't do that." And I'm like, "Girl. It's not like that, just come." Then everybody that I brought was like, "Oh, this is different." I was like, "Exactly." Once they get there, they're like, "Okay, I can do this weekend Kiki."

Steve Friedrich: One of my favorite memories, I brought one of my co-workers and he's watching Glam Boy Dance and says, "She's so hot." And I say, "Do you want to meet him?" Then he's like, "There's no way that's a guy." That was something he'd never experienced and I hadn't either really.

Constantine Valhouli: I remember one performance vividly. It was a single dancer dressed in a romantic gothic 80s pre-Raphaelite look (hush, all three of those Venn circles overlap), a single spotlight, and the familiar opening notes of Dead Can Dance's "Rakim" began to play. She did the undulating belly dance with arms raised; the dais became the dance floor and she stood in for us. She was joined by someone dressed as a street punk from Harvard Square, who did the punching-in-the-air dance moves. A stanza later, they were joined by a couple of shirtless men in biker vests and police hats, like a Tom of Finland image. And every stanza, another subculture was added. It was an amusing microcosm of the club itself, and the performance ended with the crowd up on the stage, dancing with these archetypal figures.

Michael Hsieh: We all had day jobs, but we just kind of made it work.

Michael Hsieh: Well, they all seem to be getting a lot of applause. We would see a huge crowd around and a lot of enthusiasm for us. I'm sure some people would just kind of be annoyed because we took over the stage on the dance floor and they couldn't dance anymore. Some people just aren't into performances. But I think it was something kind of special.

Norm: At the end of the day, ManRay was a dance club. It wasn't a performance club. It was a dance club. No matter what it felt like when you were performing, there were enough times I'm absolutely sure that people would say "Oh my God, I just want to dance. Here comes another fucking performance what's wrong with these people."

Eartha Harris: Well, I had grown up doing theater, so somehow I felt totally comfortable dancing on stage in fishnets, a thong, a corset, and knee high black chunky heeled boots, pretending to cast spells while dropping dry ice chunks into cups as an entire packed club of people I had never met before watched me with arched eyebrows and most likely wondered who the hell I was.

Rachel E. Pollock: There was definitely something grotesquely sexy about the performances. What was compelling was that it made you feel gross that you thought it was sexy. I was like, "This is fucking awesome. This is really disturbing and people are going to freak out."

Karla Clute: I was introduced to Cusraque, who then said he would get me into his Friday nights. After watching people dance and just trying it out for myself, Trent invited me to be one of the Fantasy Factory dancers when I turned nineteen. He kind of took me under the wing. I mostly learned how to dance by watching everybody else. I liked being able to go early and get ready down in the basement with everybody else. You would play your outfits off of each other, especially if it was a theme. Cons, you are kind of always expected to be by the box, which I think for most people was fine, especially for me. I didn't socialize a lot outside of the dancers, so

I was rarely very far from the box. I don't know, I can't really think of any cons. I loved dancing at Fantasy Factory.

Karla Clute: The bouncer was great at just spotting people that didn't belong or that looked a little bit like "What the hell are you about to do? Don't fucking do it." Then Trent was great for paying attention to when things start to get shady. It kind of trickles down to the rest of the dancers. Norman was the same way, they were all very protective and had eyes on everybody, making sure that everybody was safe.

Mizery McRae: One thing that I liked about the security guards at ManRay is that they watched everything, but they didn't get involved unless you needed it or unless they saw something that somebody was taken advantage of, which was rare.

David Winthrop: A lot of the really great pictures that I loved taking were mostly in the dressing room downstairs. It would be people getting ready and the dancers before the performances. Trying to get a good angle on the performances was always tough because the people that had been waiting up front didn't want to give up their spots.

Norm: I'm involved with the creative side of it, whether that was the artistic side, whether it became somebody who became a DJ, or somebody who ended up doing some of the paintings on the walls.

Norm: Toward the mid to late 90s, it felt like all of a sudden there were these people running around in and out of dressing rooms and bathrooms and telling them where they could dance and not dance. I have heard from a number of people that there was friction between the people who were performing there. It got more and more formalized as things went on. There was definitely friction sometimes and definitely a sense of prima donna-ism.

Emily Taylor: We had these cool performances. I remember maybe a couple years after I started working at ManRay there was a club on Lansdowne Street that was trying to do something like what we were doing. So, they would have dancers and stuff, and they had us come dance and it just wasn't as cool. It was Lansdowne Street so it fucking sucked.

Jen Lucky Cole: On a night we weren't open, Don would hire entertainment. He likes to hire drag queens and the performer Ryan

Landry. He would do the Christmas party and he would write custom gags, like "'Twas the Night Before Christmas," but he did it to ManRay and he included all of the employees that year in it. He would hire entertainment and pay them. He'd get a bunch of food and it would be an open bar. You could bring a couple people and everybody that was an employee could come. He would give little gifts, he was really a generous person. That was something I definitely looked forward to every year and it was great to be able to help plan it with him. Consequently, in the summertime he had a summertime pool party every year for his employees with a cookout.

Tatiana Zimkus: I'd say within six months, I was occasionally doing performances. I wasn't part of Fantasy Factory, but I did become part of Latex Lily. A couple times Cusraque had asked me to be in various performances. I saw a number of the performances early on and I was like, "Wow, this is really awesome. I haven't really seen anything like this." And I wanted to be involved. Once Latex Lily came about and the fashion shows were happening, then I got more involved with that sort of thing. It was exhilarating. When the Miss Gothic Massachusetts pageant came about, some friends encouraged me to be a part of it.

Becky D: I would see someone on the dance floor and be like, I want that in my next performance.

Emily Taylor: On Thursdays and Tuesdays I would take the night off because Mondays were Ceremony, which I religiously went to. Tuesdays were like I don't know what's going on, Wednesdays were always at ManRay. Thursday was usually sometimes at ManRay. Then Friday I would show up early and get things ready for a performance. It was always a clusterfuck trying to get the set ready and the costumes and one last rehearsal and everything else, because oftentimes we throw these things together with no idea. Sometimes we'd do a photoshoot for whatever flyer we were going to have for theme night. I'd be there pretty much until close on Fridays. That was just a regular club night, but we were also working. I would spend a lot of time dancing, especially after performances because I'd be really hyped up. Then Saturdays were Heroes. I liked it because it was different music, and I would just go and enjoy dancing to different music. On Sundays, I don't think we did anything at ManRay.

Kyle Blaisdell: I did my very last performance in '99. I got a bunch of my roommates together, good friends, and we just decided we were all getting too old for it and this was going to be the last time I did it. So, we made a little show of it. We didn't make a big announcement. We just knew, up on stage, that this was the last time we were really going to do that. We went out with a bang. We built a giant rubber seven-foot vagina and, instead of killing off the character, I decided to unbirth him and had three of my roommates and myself burst out of the vagina and pull me back in so I'm unbirthing myself, rather than killing off the character. We had blood pumps. We had green slime being sprayed through air hoses and we were known for making quite a mess. I was a big fan of the Grand Guignol theater out of Paris, a good theater that specialized in shock and gore. I wanted to bring that into the mix. That's exactly what I did. We had literally buckets of blood, at times we used fake pig entrails, real pig entrails. It was insane.

Chapter 6

Beat of the Music: DJs and Music

"From the second I was on the decks, I could feel the beats and I could feel the music and what to play next." — Chris Manousaridis

Music is the common element that anyone who attended ManRay, or any night club, can relate to and connect with. With its different theme nights and numerous events, ManRay provided a musical draw for many different cultures. Over its twenty-year history, Wednesday nights often catered to the Goth crowd, Thursdays the LGBTQ+ community, Friday alternated between Hell and Fantasy Factory, and Saturdays brought life back to New Wave. Any night guaranteed hearing old favorites, discovering new songs and bands, waiting in line to make a request at the phone booth, and bringing life to the dance floor. Whether a patron dedicated themselves to one night or circulated them all, music is something that united all who walked through the doors of ManRay. As important as the music itself was, one cannot forget the many gifted DJs who spun the atmosphere of ManRay into a frenzy. These masterminds set the tone, created the atmosphere, analyzed the crowd, and brought life to the club. S.L.

David Winthrop: Music was just the backbone of that club, for sure.

Abigail Taylor: Having a club like ManRay in Cambridge ... it was one of the only places that you can go to hear that music.

Jennifer Chandler: I remember being able to hear the music before I even made it through the door, and it was dark and it was loud and it was lively. The music just would overtake you. You could just feel like being transported back into your favorite time.

Paul Vitagliano: To me, what makes an alternative club is not that every single track you play is by an alternative band. It's that there's such a breadth of diversity in what you're playing and how you put it together. That's what makes an alternative club alternative. Amongst all these British alternative bands and hits that we were playing at the time this big pop hit would not only get requested but people would also run to that dance floor like there was no tomorrow. I feel like that really sums up how cool ManRay was.

Eloni Feliciano: The music was very different on certain nights. Campus had very different music from Hell, but you still heard stuff that you were familiar with.

Paul Vitagliano: I have always been a huge fan of music. Even growing up. We had WRKO radio in Boston. I was the youngest in my family, so it was often me and my mom and her car, her Galaxie 500. I just love music. In those days you were listening to pop music, R&B, Rock, and roll. I just absorbed it all.

Tony Lee: Honestly, there's always been a good amount of freedom at ManRay as long as the floor was reasonably full. Requests were always up to whoever was DJing. I've generally been a very requested friendly DJ. There were more requests than any of us could possibly play. We could have just played a night where every single song was a request, and we went through all of them. It was just completely nuts.

The thing that changed the most about the DJ booth upstairs was the equipment and sometimes the lighting console. And obviously the music. You continue to incorporate newer music, so there would be more and more CDs. Chris also kept some other CDs in the little hallway area.

Paul Vitagliano: A typical playlist from 1986:

The Clash -- "Rock the Casbah"
The B-52s -- "Private Idaho"
The Cure -- "Let's Go To Bed"
Sting -- "Set Them Free"
Aretha Franklin -- "Freeway of Love"
The Smiths -- "Barbarism Begins At Home"
The Buzzcocks -- "What Do I Get?"
Tones on Tail -- "Twist"

Violent Femmes -- "Gone Daddy Gone"
Modern English -- "I Melt With You"
The Bongos -- "Barbarella"
Art of Noise -- "Close to the Edit"
Sam and Dave -- "Hold On, I'm Coming"
Stevie Wonder -- "Superstition"

We played what we liked to play and what we thought was cool. That's the way that I became a DJ at ManRay and shaped who I was and how I began to define my DJ career. From that moment on, it was always how I DJ 'ed. I looked at it like I'm gonna play the best music from every decade.

I am not going to be afraid of cool, fun. Another DJ felt like if he played Jackson Five's "I Want You Back" at an alternative club everyone's gonna leave the floor pissed off. No, no. They're gonna love it. I have always said that what makes a great alternative DJ or club is not that every song is alternative or post punk. What makes it alternative is that you would literally go from James Brown into Tones on Tail. You would find the connective bridge between James Brown and Love and Rockets to Ball of Confusion, which is a cover of a Motown song. You are able to go from the past to the present. So that's always been my take about being an alternative DJ. It's the way that you would look at an iPod. Your iPod is loaded with incredible music from every decade, every genre because you probably like more than one style of music. Yeah, so I looked at it like I can be somebody's favorite iPod, but I'm just going to put it together way more creatively and way more interestingly, then you've got in your shuffle. If the DJ is amazing, you walk out of the club and think you had the fucking best night of your life. If the DJ is completely the opposite, playing crappy music, or they might be playing good music but they just don't have the right way to put it together, then that person is not going to walk out and say, "Oh, I didn't like the bartender. I didn't like how bright the club was. That DJ sucked. I'm not coming back." Yeah. So you really are the Pied Piper and you either figure out how to keep people following you with honey or you turn them away with vinegar.

Rachel E. Pollock: ManRay was very much, from a DJ perspective, about keeping the floor full. As somebody who DJed at both ManRay and Ceremony, I felt like I had more creative freedom at Ceremony because I could have fifty people on the dance floor and it looked slammed. If I had the same at ManRay, Don would be screaming down my neck. Not without justification. Once Marilyn Manson started getting radio play like, I'm sorry, but he filled the floor. So, you were still going to hear that at ManRay because it's a huge club. It's a huge dance floor, you need to put in 300 people or that floor looks dead. So if I'm going to play Cake and Sodomy and that means 300 people are definitely out there. I do not care if he's mainstream.

Nate Roman: One of my favorite memories of all time was probably in '96, '97 playing Hell to a very packed crowd. I remember I played "Beautiful People" by Marilyn Manson and everyone's just bouncing up and down. Everyone's just totally wrapped up and it was exactly the right moment to play that song to that crowd. I played "March of the Pigs" by Nine Inch Nails right after. The crowd just exploded. I remember that you couldn't see the boundaries of the dance floor, all you could see was a depression and the crowd. Every square inch was full of people bouncing up and down and there was sweat pouring down. Don bursts into the DJ booth and screams at me. He says, "What are you doing? These goddamn kids are gonna tear my club down!" I looked at him and I was like, "Don. That's the nicest thing anyone's ever said to me." He just stormed out. It felt like such an achievement.

Rachel E. Pollock: My floor stayed packed from 10 to 2:30. I never had a dead floor, except in that window from 9 p.m. at opening. The policy for that, as I understood it, was to put on a mixed CD from 9 to however long it takes to play out and then you start DJing. As soon as it went from the CD to my first song people flooded the floor and it stayed full and that's why I got asked to DJ and why I did it there as long as I did.

Julie Kramer: You need to know your audience. I used to spin upstairs at X night, and the people who are there are there to dance to the 80s. But you have to get a feel for it because you can't just throw out anything and you're taking requests and you see what people are dancing to. If they're dancing to more stuff like New Order and that sort of genre, then you kind of go with it. If you're spinning a Goth night then you're pretty much sticking to that kind of realm. You might sweep out a little bit, but you're not going to go into something completely different. People are there to have that experience.

Tony Lee: I was absolutely blown away and honored that I was asked to spin at ManRay. This is amazing. Of course, I would like to DJ here. This was around the time when they moved the DJ booth from the downstairs to the upstairs. People weren't supposed to be upstairs anymore. The Thursday before this release party was when they installed the phone booth. I DJ and that Friday, which I believe was at Hell. So, I'm nervous as hell. This is my first time ever DJing in public. I was just sweating the entire night. I was shaking. There was one point, early in the night, when I accidentally hit stop on the CD player, but luckily I hit play again really quickly. I was like, "Oh my God, I can't believe I made a mistake early on." Thankfully, that was during the first hour where there weren't as many people there. As the place filled up everyone was just calling that phone and there was no way to turn the ringer off, you could just make it less loud.

Mark Dighton: It's very black, very dark. There was a kind of perfunctory light system that I hardly ever messed with, which they were very angry with me about. They were like, "You gotta do the lights." I'm like, "I don't give a shit about the lights, I'm here playing music." Then we had the big screen and the projector in front of the DJ booth. I was very much into cult movies, so I was just throwing VHS cassettes of *Orgy of the Dead* or *Barbarella* or *Vegas in Space* in. To me, that was the visuals that went with music. I didn't care about strobe lights or the disco ball or anything like that.

One thing I'll say that was weird about DJing there compared to other places was that because the big screen was in front of you, you didn't get a lot of interaction with the crowd. Sometimes people didn't even know there was a DJ there. I remember the place stunk, but that was mostly after we closed. I realized later on that that was just what bars smell like: industrial cleaners and cigarettes smoking and alcohol.

Nate Roman: I can tell you that the DJ booths tended to smell much worse.

John O'Leary: Chris was always a musician. It's his job, to be a DJ, but it also really helps you be a good musician. Chris was great at that. I learned a lot of that from Chris.

Chris Ewen: Keeping the dance floor happy is a fine line. It's why I'm not a wedding DJ, for example, because I can't go play everyone's top 40 favorites and make them be thrilled. So, I've always tried to walk that tightrope of making people happy and also trying to turn them on to new and exciting things. I don't plan playlists. I always do it kind of live. You have to play off the people that are there. So even if you do plan things out, it never turns out the way that you want it to, or that you were thinking it was going to be. It's an ongoing philosophy in how I've approached DJing.

Adam Wolff: One of the things that Chris is great at … his pacing is fantastic. He understands what's going on the floor. He watches the people. You recognize who they are and how they dance and what their tastes are as a dancer. You try to put them on the dance floor by playing stuff that you know that they'll dance to because if you put them on the floor everybody else will go dance.

Gibby Miller: Chris was a really good DJ technically, as well as conceptually with the tracks that he pulled and picked. He was extremely well liked in town and was able to create a night that felt like you were attending somebody's party.

Paul Vitagliano: The mark of a great DJ is to give the people what they want. If you think you're too fucking cool to play something that people are dying to hear then you suck. Your job is to entertain and to make people happy and make them leave the club in a better mood than when they arrived. You also have to understand that nobody's music tastes are only one thing. There's too many DJs that get too caught up in thinking that they know everything, and they don't. They think they're too cool to play a more mainstream or predictable track. I mean, there are limits. I've gotten requests for something that I would never ever play in a million years. I think Chris really understands this. That's why he's a great DJ.

Richard LaDue: ManRay was my first gig where I was getting paid money to play music for people. I remember just feeling like I had arrived. The experience of doing it was stressful as fuck because I'm here, there are people dancing. "What do I play next? Should I keep this going? I don't want to do something that's too Chris Ewen, but I don't want to do something dance-y, because this is ManRay." There's a lot of dance floor profiling I do as a DJ. "All right, these people like this, so I'm going to guess the next one they might like is this. There are some alternative kids and they're dancing to this kind of dance remix of an alternative group. Let's stay in that vein, or let's push a little bit." There's a lot of like who's dancing and how do I keep this going and how do I attract more people?

I remember the ManRay booth was a little bit hot. You have a weird way to get in. The front room was a little bit of a walk. I remember that the turntables were sitting in rubber bins to keep them from skipping. I remember being very stressed out. That room was super square and you had the speakers in the corners, the bar in the back, and then this sort of drink rail around it. I just remember being nervous and stressed. It was never easy, but when it was done you went, "Okay." I'm not celebrating while I'm working. I'm trying to make sure every minute is good and people are happy.

You want to get a reputation for doing a certain kind of thing. I think for me, I probably got a little better at it when I gave up more control. I'd be like, "Hey, what do you want to hear?" I became more approachable and less like this is a gallery and for the next three hours I will be presenting my work. I think that's probably how I started at ManRay: "These are the songs I've decided are cool. Do you like them?" Now that I'm older, and with the technology, I'm kind of like "What do you want?" I'm a little less dramatic.

Rachel E. Pollock: I felt like it was always very important for me to take the temperature of the room, "How can I make song selections in such a way that I don't ever lose my dance floor entirely?" You really had to tap into the crowd energy in a very primal sort of way and you really had to be attuned to where people were, when they ready for the tempo to change so that they could stay on the dance floor, but not have a heart attack. You had to maintain the balance of people going to the bar and people coming out on the dance floor.

Michael Hsieh: In the late 90s, synth pop came in and that changed the tenor of it, which was great. We get to talk about how Goth music has changed. Just being able to connect with all those experiences and all the people who were involved with the club. It was a creative outlet for everybody. You just get to talk about everything that you're interested in. Most clubs, with their layout, had one dance floor. So it was just a Goth vibe or industrial or disco and 80s.

Tony Lee: At least in this scene, people are pretty generous and pretty encouraging when it comes to new DJs. People are willing to give a listen.

Jen Lucky Cole: Lady Bathory was leaving Boston and we needed somebody pretty quickly to fill in those Wednesday night gaps. We didn't want them to be playing the exact same music Chris plays. I hired Brad and I paid it back because he was my first DJ that I went to a Goth night back in '95 to '96. So then three, four years later, I'm working at the club. That was my dream. I'm in the position where they asked me if I knew anybody? It was a pain in the ass for him to drive up there, but he would do it and he's a phenomenal DJ. It wasn't the same as what Chris was playing on a Wednesday.

Rachel E. Pollock: I think that I sort of fell into it from a fan's perspective. When I went off to college there was an alternative club that played the Smiths and KMFDM and non-mainstream music and I would go there five nights a week from the time they opened and danced till the time they closed. The guy who was the main DJ for that club got approved to study abroad so he asked me if I would take over DJing and promoting the club and take over his radio show while he was gone for a year. It wound up being a really good thing, just luck and circumstances coming together. The slot at the radio station was a specialty show that was Goth-industrial music. Anything that didn't go into rotation they gave to the DJ, so I wound up getting all this super cutting edge new release stuff through the radio station that helped me build my reputation as a DJ to where I then began receiving promos from bands. When I moved to Boston, I started at Ceremony and then I got the offer at ManRay shortly thereafter.

Nate Roman: Right around 2000, from my personal experience, my musical voice as a DJ changed tremendously. It did get a lot more electronic

Benny Blanco: Music was probably always pulling me, even when I started going there. Music was crossing over in '89 as styles were changing. Each year it probably became greater because of the electronic, techno, rave, and House music. The electronic rave explosion took my interest. The New Wave and Dark Wave stuff that was coming out was less interesting to me. It was becoming too cheesy or too trance-y. Stylistically, the newer material from some of the existing bands just didn't catch my ear as much as the other electronic sounds from the US and Europe.

Duane Bruce: This may be a bold statement, but music snobbery is a good thing because it allows you to form something inside you that nobody else can touch; it's your take, and for you to decide if you like it or not. The great tree of Rock and roll has many branches, and that is the beauty of it all — same backbone, different ribs. For example, I'm a huge Beatles fan. That's my number one band. John Lennon is my guy. When you said, "Let It Be," I was kind of shocked that you didn't say the White Album. Everybody has their own taste, but so long as you understand the Beatles and you love them … God bless you, man. That's the basic shit, that's almost the litmus test right there.

Norm: We imprint our own ideas of what is good music and bad music at that time. I spent most of my time in Chris' room. I did not go to the front rooms quite so much. You had two complimentary music styles going on. I hadn't thought about it until I said it, but it was very unique to almost any club.

Chris Manousaridis: Music. It always comes back around. No matter what it does, it is a cycle. There was a point for a while where ManRay was really slow then it slowed down for a little bit and then it started to build back up again. I think a lot of that was due to popular music at that time. You had your Marilyn Manson, White Zombie, or Rammstein that started coming out in these movies and more people were being introduced to it. So you had movies with killer soundtracks. Strange Days was one and the other one was Hideaway. All of a sudden it's becoming mainstream even though it's not.

Tony Lee: At that time, we had a good number of nights covered in Boston: Ceremony on Monday, Crypt on Wednesday, Friday's Hell and fetish nights, and Hexx on Saturday. So, there was a lot to choose from. A year into the Ceremony, we started having DJs spin the first hour so it gave a lot more people the opportunity to play pretty much whatever style of music they wanted. It provided more opportunities for people to try their hand at DJing.

Koren Bernardi: I started DJing at Machine actually and then just kind of filled in. I asked Nate Roman, who I'd known from Ceremony, if I could open when he was there on Wednesdays. So, I'd go on from 9 to 10 when nobody was in the club, but I got in for free and I got to have a set list. Once you get that list you can publish them, and at the time I probably put them on Live Journal or Myspace. It was a way to build people's interest.

I did a lot of industrial stuff rather than Goth stuff. I'd fill in for people. I really liked doing it. Even though I was making less money or no money or getting a free drink or whatever for DJing, that was something that was exciting enough or rewarding enough in itself to keep going, as opposed to going to do the lights.

That was at the beginning where I had lots of energy. Eventually, as they got more and more into DJing and did more extensive sets and got into promoting events ... It's weird how your hobby, once it seems like work, becomes less fun than it was when it was your hobby.

Chris Manousaridis: I started in the clubs in North Carolina. I was 17 and I worked at a country western bar. I knew the owners and I always loved music, so they hired me seven days a week to do karaoke and DJ. I was transitioning music back and forth to the big club down the street. The owner had come in a few times and heard me and he heard my transitions with just two home players and a PA system. He's like, "Why don't you come work for a big club?" So, he brought me over there with turntables and there was another DJ there and I started watching him and learning from him and it came natural to me. It was almost as if I was built for doing it. From the second I was on the decks, I could feel the beats and I could feel the music and what to play next, so I did really well there.

When I moved back to Boston, I started doing weddings and corporate events for a big agency. This guy, Rosco Cigna, was on Kiss 108 back in the 70s and 80s who made a big name for himself. He had a multimillion-dollar company and, next thing you know, I'm doing weddings galore left and right. So, at that point, as things progressed there, I would take nights off from ManRay here and there so I could do a wedding or a function. I was like "Can I do some guest spots over in the Campus role?" He's like, "Sure, go ahead." Nate, Lady Bathory, and Chris were in the main room, they were doing more of the high energy stuff, so I would do a set here and there and that continued probably for the last year I was there. I started doing Ceremony as well on Monday nights. So that's just sort of how it kind of transitions with that.

Chris Ewen: I thought it would be really good to hire a WFNX DJ to come in and do something in ManRay. Why don't we bring in an extra night DJ and give these people what they want. So, I think that Duane Bruce was brought in to do that. I wouldn't fault him at all.

The crowd was so offended that they actually staged a sit in on the dance floor because I was not spinning the music. I think that was a pivotal thing, simply because it showed Don that what Terri and I were doing had produced loyalty in our crowd. People weren't coming because they were walking down the street and saw a club, they were coming for specific things. It showed that we were offering something good.

Adam Wolff: Chris was the sound of ManRay. Like anything else that happened there was incidental if that makes sense. Like it didn't really matter what was played in the front room. Chris was the tastemaker. To play on Chris's dance floor, you had to understand Chris's taste, and he was really, really particular. There's only a couple of us that could be the guest DJ at ManRay for Chris. He hated having to take a night off. You had to be able to deliver the expectation of ManRay.

Koren Bernardi: I was pretty involved in music and I have heard a lot of the bands. I was a radio DJ instead of a club DJ, even when I was a patron, so I was pretty knowledgeable. However, I did love having new DJs that would do guest nights. There's music and then there's music together in a set. Once you really get familiar with a DJ, sometimes you can be like, "Oh, I bet he's going to go from this song to that song," and you're kind of familiar with the groups they like. When there's a new person that shows up from a different city because different cities have different greatest hits, there's certain songs that maybe do not fit perfectly into the genre in Boston, that get played, almost like an inside joke, but everybody loved it. It's "We know you like this music, but there's this other song that's really good that I like that you all will like, so I'm gonna play it anyway." I think that's the power of the DJ, knowing when to bring that in.

Chris Ewen: The powers that be at ManRay were very traditional in their sense of what they expected from a DJ. Our house DJ and our techno DJ played vinyl. It took maybe a little bit of arm twisting to say, "Hey I need to embrace this technology." I kind of had to fight to get CDs in there.

Richard LaDue: I was doing this Saturday gig that closed at one o'clock, two in the morning. I would DJ at this radio station that I worked at and one of the nightclub promoters is like, "Oh, you should really work at the gay club down the street, the Paradise in Cambridge." So, I was like, "Now I'm gonna get fired and I like this ManRay gig and they told me I can't work anywhere else." He's like, "Well, change your name." So, I was Rich LaDue on Saturday nights and then I was Richie Rich on Thursdays at Paradise. I think Don found out and it was no Bueno. So, it's a wrap for me. He's like you've got to go and I got fired from the thing I love.

Tony Lee: When I came back from my second year at BU, I began a position as a program director. I was in the DJ booth a lot at ManRay asking Chris questions about. He was going out of town and he knew I had been DJ at the radio station at BU and he asked if I would do Saturday night. It was for *The Doom Generation*, a release party. The movie came out in October of '95.

I was chain smoking and just freaking out up there. Eventually, most of the way through, I finally just ripped the phone off the wall and threw it down that little hallway up there because I couldn't stand it ringing behind me anymore because I was so nervous. Near the end of the night, I was just like, "Oh my God, they're never going to want me back and everyone is going to kick my ass." I went downstairs and I was just a mess. Friends came up to give me hugs and we're like, "It's okay." And I was like, "No, it's not. I'm having such a terrible time." When it is all over I went downstairs and people are like, "That was really great. Oh my God. You played all these songs that I always want to hear. Thank you for playing this request." People were really, really encouraging. They did not care that I had a couple of mistakes. It was all in my head. I just wanted to be perfect. I was asked if I wanted to do this again. I was like, "No, I absolutely do not want to DJ at a club again. That was so nerve wracking."

Eventually, enough time had passed where there wasn't so much pain or anxiety that I was willing to try this again. That next experience wasn't as terrible for my anxiety about performing in front of people and making mistakes. And it's not like I didn't make mistakes at the radio station, it's just that nobody was in front of me. Chris kept asking me back periodically and I said yes more and more and more.

Terri Niedzwiecki: I think that Chris paid attention to what was coming out on the air. The first time he actually worked at night as a demo, I was like blown away.

Chris Ewen: There was a creative explosion musically with a lot of bands. So having lots of music helped, you didn't just have to play The Cure to a full Goth night. You could throw some Skinny Puppy in. I think, especially in the Boston area, there was an explosion of this stuff because of ManRay. People realized that this stuff could work. This was a viable thing. Boston, because of all the universities, brought in people from all over the country and all over the world who came here for school. Many came from their own subcultures and were looking for places to go.

Hideki Watanabe: The musical tastes that I was pursuing at the time were all techno. I was never looking to buy Goth music which I thought was a little weird being a Goth, but I was never listening to it at home. At ManRay I would hear everything that would be new at some point for me. There was a period of time at ManRay where I had a few friends that felt the music was the same and the nights were getting repetitive. I never felt that personally, but I do remember thinking that I wanted to try to push Chris to play things that he wouldn't normally play. There were a few songs that he would play for me, which I really appreciated. Songs he wouldn't necessarily play all the time.

Jenn Sutkowski: To me, the similarity in the nights is that flavor of Chris Ewen's musical choices. I always appreciated it. He kind of couldn't do any wrong in my book, musically.

Eartha Harris: Tons, of course! As an electronic music producer, my time at ManRay was hugely influential to my career. I give so much thanks to the inspiration I drew from the Boston bands You Shriek and One of Us, and to the Angeldustrial crew that brought all the incredible industrial synth pop acts of that era to the venue, of whom I would often host at my house or at least throw the afterparty for. I got to meet and befriend Eskil Simonsson from Covenant, Martin Atkins from PIL, Ministry, Pigface, NIN, Killing Joke, Daniel Myer from Haujobb, Ronan from VNV Nation, the list goes on. Many of whom I am still connected to today.

Norm: It was a dance club, so the music changed a lot of the culture. The coming of the industrial age … Michael and I are perfect examples. Michael and I were definitely Goth kids, but there was a lot of industrial influence that came into ManRay as time went on. It really morphed and changed the music and changed how things were done with things like performances.

Tatiana Zimkus: I've been listening to that genre of music, at least the old school post punk and Goth from when I was thirteen. Industrial music, believe it or not, I really didn't know any of those bands. I wasn't exposed to any of that. I grew to like those bands and become familiar with them. I would still dance to songs I didn't know as long as I felt like something that moved me, which is why I love being introduced to new music.

Skot Kremen: There was tons of new music that we would hear. Things that I never heard at Goth clubs and stuff that I wasn't really exposed to. There was interesting industrial music that I just would have never really heard. There were a couple of ManRay staples, but Chris would also play local band music. ManRay probably felt so good because they played the music that I already owned and that would never be played in clubs.

Xtine Santakas: Well, the first song that I ever heard at ManRay that made me go "Wow" was Ladytron's Seventeen, which is still one of my absolute favorites and Chris knows that. And he plays it for me all the time, especially on my birthday. I would also request a lot of The Cure, a lot of disease. Depeche Mode was another band that I heard for the first time at ManRay.

Michael Hsieh: That's where I first heard Wolfsheim and all the synth pop stuff when New Wave came in and smaller bands like Hungry Lucy, which was one of my favorite small bands. Having the stage and being able to see live bands too.

Skot Kremen: I've always been involved with music in some way, as if it was just one of those things. It was something that just called to me. There was nothing that could keep me away from it. If there was a room with a piano I was there, even if there were one hundred people in the room.

Becky D: Music was definitely a big part of the experience for sure because I was relatively new to the scene. I learned a lot about my music tastes based on what Chris or whomever was playing. The club is how I learned about Goth music and then from there I would kind of explore on my own. I'd be like, "This band is really cool, I'm going to go see if I can find other ones like them." There was a group that I hung out with that was more into the EDM industrial side. Chris definitely played that stuff, but I got introduced to that music more by hanging out with that group of people. I kind of explored it much more. Then synth pop, especially early in the 2000s when it really kind of hit a peak in the U.S. I wouldn't have heard any of that music if I wasn't going to ManRay.

Guari Desi-Ackerman: I mean, so many. I grew up listening to The Cure just from being from England, but I wasn't really into them. They just played in the charts. You know what I mean. At ManRay, I really got introduced to their music and really got into them. At that point, I appreciated that music a lot more. The main thing I remember from that period was KLF, Thrill Kill Kult. Then a lot of the Wax Trax! industrial stuff. Ministry. Nine Inch Nails. That was huge for me.

Karla Clute: Chris played a lot of songs like Delirium and Peter Gabriel, which I had never heard before and loved. I heard a few remixes from bands I had already listened to, which was great to hear. As far as the front room, they played a lot of really fast, not techno but industrial, which I was a little more familiar with anyways.

Eileen Dover: I remember "Don't Cry for Me, Argentina," was released. Madonna released that and I wanted to pull out my ears. They played it so much everywhere.

Jen Lucky Cole: Peter Schilling Major Tom. Such a great song. It wasn't Saturday night till they played that and everybody was fighting to get onto the stage.

Andrea Parros: The other dance nights I felt had a little more of a poppy type thing, whereas ManRay was more dark, more chill. People weren't trying to dance super-fast or to be super poppy and peppy and happy. It was more like the opposite, like people dancing at half speed and it was more about ambience and the vibe than it was about dancing as fast as you could or anything like that.

Abigail Taylor: I remember this one specific night — I don't remember who was DJ — but someone was spinning "Rebel Rebel" by David Bowie and I was the only one on the dance floor. I had my eyes closed, and I was just channeling my Bowie. I was just in. I was like, "I am a Rebel Rebel."

Jill Kempton: My first few times there I wasn't comfortable dancing. I remember I had to go to Club Hell in Rhode Island. Being a smaller place, they didn't look as cool, not to knock them, but that's where I felt comfortable starting to learn how to dance. So, I dropped out of ManRay for a couple months. I cut my hair. I got some better clothes. I came in, they didn't even know that I was the girl that was just there a few months ago with the long hair. I didn't feel cool enough and I had to get cool over at Club Hell first.

Adam Wolff: There's no place in the world where people dance like they danced at ManRay. Boston has a style of dance that is so unique that I can literally spot people when I'm on tour. I've gone up to people and been like, "So when were you at ManRay, what years were you in Boston?" And they're like, "How did you know?" You lift your feet on the two beats, this thing that we do that we all picked up. No idea where it got started. There are these little ways that you can tell when somebody was a regular at ManRay, because we all picked up dance moves from each other.

Chris Manousaridis: Anytime I go to a club or listen to a DJ, my main focus is listening to their transitions and their style. You always take something away from each DJ that you listen to. My first few times, especially on a Wednesday, I was dancing a lot. It got to a point where that was really driving a bigger guy who normally wouldn't dance and not feel bad about it or not feel ashamed about it. So it was real. It was safe.

Julie Kramer: Well, music is and always will be part of my life. I first got into music when a camp counselor turned me on to Hunky Dory, from then on I was hooked. My mom took me to a Bowie show in the 70s at the Boston Garden and music was always in my house. My mother's a musician, both my sisters are musicians and I got into radio because I have no musical talent whatsoever. So was the only way I could sort of fit in.

Mike (Farmboy): The music was a bit overwhelming. I was part of the alternative college radio station, so I went in expecting to hear pretty much what I would hear me and my friends spin on the radio. I'm trying everything and I'm like, "Can I dance to this?" because it's my first time. I'm super awkward and not terribly comfortable with my body. It's a lot of new music I just have never listened to before.

Russ Carter: I'm from Blackstone, Massachusetts. So I was the first born American in the family, even my brothers and sisters, who are 10 years older than me, were all born in England. I kind of grew up half in England, and the only reason I mentioned that is because it had a profound impact on me as far as post punk when it was happening. Even at a very young age, because I had brothers and sisters who were like 10 to 12 years older than me, every time we got out of school in America we would go back to England for the summer. So, I just ran around South London with my older brothers and sisters who were buying up records and playing Joy Division for me in '83, when I was like nine.

Eileen Dover: I remember there were record release parties like Mariah Carey or Madonna or Whitney Houston — a lot of the big divas. Warner Brothers would send us CD singles and promotional posters and the first X amount of people that got there and all the employees got to have a copy. The DJ got the music before the release.

Rebecca Griffin: Music was my outlet. I didn't grow up in a safe environment and that's why I think I gravitated towards the punk scene because that was the "Angsty Teen Outlet." It was a community where we could get together and have mosh pits and that's how we would get our frustrations out. I was exposed via ManRay to a bigger, broader spectrum of music than where I was.

Andrea Parros: I never would have been exposed to something like this in my tiny town of Hanson, Massachusetts. My high school alone needed two towns to basically make up one school because there just wasn't enough kids in either town. I decided to go to school in Boston. I thought, "Oh, wow, wouldn't it be cool to go to school in a big city that's kind of near where I grew up and I could still visit my parents."

Basically, the four years of college were an awakening. You're leaving your parents' home and you're becoming an independent young adult. You're learning something at school that's going to then get you into a career, basically transitioning you into adulthood. Similarly, the nightlife of Boston was huge in transitioning me to growing up and exposing me to all kinds of cultures and different types of people. ManRay though, was like that to the extreme. I was going to shows and I wouldn't see some of the diversity or some of the different walks of life that I would see at ManRay, and I think that was part of the appeal. Here you are in this kind of little cave where it's like, "What is going on here? What is all this? I've never seen anything like this."

A lot of the music there was different from what I'd been listening to. I knew Joy Division and The Smiths a little bit, then this whole explosion of different genres of music hit me. As a music industry major, I realized there's this whole sub-genre that I don't know about and I need to learn about every single one of these bands. So that's definitely how I got into music.

Koren Bernardi: I came from kind of a punk background, I guess hardcore. I came from the country, so a lot of Rock and roll. My parents were very classic rock. So I hadn't really heard a lot of electronic based music, stuff that didn't have a typical on the radio kind of aesthetic.

Lucretia X Machina: Going to ManRay would have been the bulk of my musical connections. It was all new to me. Nine Inch Nails, Sister of Mercy. I saw bands at ManRay like Envy and the local band You Shriek.

Arelene Watanabe: I had been a lifestyle goth and an aesthetic Goth. Music has never been my primary drive. My drive has always been aesthetic. But I learned so much about music from Chris because I love to dance. If I was at ManRay I was either at the bar drinking, flirting with someone, or dancing.

Crayola Tidd: For new music, I think I learned about Sisters of Mercy from ManRay, and Cruxshadows. They had a nice show there. I really learned about industrial and Goth, whereas before I mostly just heard punk.

Heather Morgan: When I came to Boston I was really into The Cure, The Smiths, Echo and the Bunnymen, Joy Division, Bauhaus. The Cure was really my favorite while I was in high school. When I started going to ManRay that's when The Cure really started to decline in quality, then ManRay was there to fill in all this other stuff. I feel like it introduced me to the hard stuff. I got really into Nick Cave, Blixa Bargeld, and Skinny Puppy. I felt like it just got darker. I enjoy it, it's totally liberating, totally theatrical and all about the performance of identity. Fabulous. Fantastic. So much fun. What could be more fun than something out there as the Legendary Pink Dots?

Wendy Austin: The problem is … The Cure isn't dancing music.

Emily Arkin: I got a much better appreciation for this kind of British music, like the whole of Manchester and also The Cure and The Smiths. There was just something about it. As part of my high school "things to decide about yourself" I decided that I liked American guitar bands. I don't like all this British synth music, and so I'd never really gone very deep. I think I got a second bite at the apple. I discovered stuff that I really liked and appreciated and associated with ManRay. For the newer stuff, it was more like I just built up a tolerance for dumb techno. There's a lot of things that would just wash over you. Now there are songs that aren't a gourmet experience, but it's a song that's so good to dance to.

Paul Calnan: That was probably the first time I was exposed to KMFDM, Lords of Acid, Sisters of Mercy, stuff that was more Goth. I grew up listening to a lot of rock music. One of the things about ManRay, it really broadens your horizon in general, with music and just different things.

Shane Blau: It was very influential music for me in that it is now the music that I will always associate with being young and queer and coming out. It's still most of the music I know. There were a couple of songs in particular that my friends liked to embarrass me with and pull me out onto the dance floor. There was a song from *Romeo and Juliet*, the movie, the "I would die for you" one, they really liked to embarrass me with that song for some reason. They would pull me out into the middle of the floor and grind on me. Anne Z had a dance that she loved called the percolator and it involved her getting down on the ground and humping the floor. So that was always a hit at ManRay. It's not easy to get enough floor space to do the percolator, but she would make it work. I still have a lot of affection for all of that music, even the songs that I hated at the time, like "I'm Blue." I hated that song, but I still have associations with it because it's one of my ManRay songs. I remember how everybody would dance to Cotton Eye Joe. And I also remember that the place went crazy when "Raining Men" came on, which is very funny because we were in the dyke room, but the place just lost it when Raining Men came on.

Emily Taylor: ManRay was where I heard pretty much all of my new music, whether it was because the Dj was playing it or because of people I met there. Chris was always good at spinning things that were sort of borderline Goth or borderline industrial music. He just would be like "It's a song by Madonna that's kind of Goth-y." I don't know any other Goth clubs that would play Madonna. He was really good at genre bending. I never would have heard Nick Cave or Covenant. MTV was way less relevant. They weren't playing good, weird, shit anymore. I didn't buy a lot of CDs because I listened to so much music when I was at ManRay that I didn't really listen to stuff at home very much. I don't know why, but I got all the music that I needed at the club.

Matt Richard: I was a college radio DJ in Fremont, that's how I started my musical journey. Basically, I learned about Nine Inch Nails and then The Crow soundtrack. I did not know what was played at nightclubs, so when I finally went to ManRay, for the most part, it was a lot of music that I didn't know but that I kind of wanted to know. The one song that caught me the most was "O Fortuna," it just brought me to the dance floor and I had two or three people and we'd all kind of meet on the dance floor. I found out from one of the DJs what it was and then I tried to track it down. I remember the DJ saying I'd never find it. I did my research and found it was on this compilation that was taken off the market because it was this illegal song, they didn't get the rights to use the sample. It was one of those CD compilations that you couldn't find anywhere, so I kind of gave that up. Eventually, when eBay was starting up, I searched for it. It was my first purchase on eBay and I bought the two song CD for like $33 and that's where I got it. I still have it and I still play it every now and then when I DJ.

Benny Blanco: The bug hit me when my cousin, who was into New Wave and Goth, introduced me to the B-52s. He had a Sony Walkman and I heard the first opening tones of "Planet Claire." I was mesmerized and blown away. What is this world?

DJing started when I was buying more vinyl. I would listen to radio shows, and Boston was great because of all the college radio stations and WFNX. There was a fantastic show that was super cutting edge called Moods for Moderns that had this DJ named Diego Martinez playing, just the coolest upfront music on the commercial side of the airwaves. I would see his playlist in *The Phoenix*. I was getting publications at the time, going to Tower Records on Newbury Street, and sourcing the magazines. You would read through the alternative charts and the dance charts and see interviews. It was pre-internet where you couldn't just go to Google and Instagram and follow your friends, that didn't exist. You still had to do the legwork and you did everything you could through print medium.

Melanie Sharkey: I listened to a very eclectic mix. But I remember often being like, "Who is this? What is this? I've never heard of this before, but this is amazing." Back in the day, I had pretty limited Internet access. Nowadays, I can just Google a couple of lyrics and it immediately comes up. I was really into Depeche Mode and Duran Duran and Madonna, obviously. But I heard a lot of one hit wonders that I wasn't really familiar with.

Sara S. Wendell: It was what first turned me on to Sisters of Mercy. I didn't actually know them very well before then. Depeche Mode, I knew the stuff that had been played on the radio, but that was it. Same thing with The Cure. I definitely fell into, became a fan of, and started chasing stuff down and buying it simply because I'd heard them there and loved the song.

Abigail Taylor: I would be the girl that would be calling him on the phone going "Chris, what was that song? What was it? Tell me what it was!" I always wanted to know. We had a bunch of used CD shops on the South Shore that I used to frequent and just go through and find so much music.

Lilly Moon: A huge reason why I went to ManRay was to talk to the DJ and ask them what they're playing. If I fell in love with a song, I needed to know what it was. I needed to know right away. Sometimes if the DJ wasn't available to tell me, I would just start asking random people.

Eloni Feliciano: It was harder to find music back in the day because you'd have to ask somebody next to you who you don't even recognize. You didn't have those little phone apps. One of the things that I found was the best, and that's where the sense of community comes in, was that people will just make mixtapes and let you borrow them if you were kind of curious about the music.

Gibby Miller: My music … I guess the short answer is that, at a young age, music was the thing that made me feel part of something or made me feel it was a source of escapism. We were lucky that we had cable in the house and I was able to get MTV, seeing early videos from Blondie and Michael Jackson and Billy Idol and Duran Duran. I had a little radio on my bedside table and I would just listen to the classic rock station when I went to bed at night. The biggest breakthrough that occurred to me is that there was a girl named Christine that worked at Second Coming Records on Mass Ave and, when I was 17 years old, she gave me a mixtape that totally blew my mind and opened doors. So it was very much through peers and friends that I was being exposed to music and then later it was through Newbury Comics.

Jennifer: Well, there's a lot to say about music. You know what night you are at based on the music. I was like a music virgin when I went to ManRay. I knew some of the 80s music. Once I started hearing it, it was like a whole new realm for me to start exploring — everything from Ultra GFI to Lords of Acid to some of the techno stuff. I was all over it. I would go to Newbury Comics and a few more record-CD type stores in Cambridge. I didn't know who sang a lot of the music, so I always relied on the people in ManRay who used to make mixtapes. I got a lot of music that way. It wasn't until much later than I knew who's singing most of the stuff that I liked. It's crazy, because you hear the songs come on the radio or on your Spotify, and it reminds you of different times in ManRay and that time of my life.

Julia Kilcoyne: Well, this was the age of Napster, so I would make a CD based on the songs that I had heard at ManRay.

Prospero Eaton: Newbury comics. That was definitely a big one for finding stuff. Back then, Newbury comics used to have a pretty good stock of music that was maybe a little underground.

Lilly Moon: Tower Records in Boston is where I would get my music. In the early 2000s, Bull Moose in Portsmouth started a Goth collection. It was started by a friend of mine that worked there.

Steve Friedrich: I ended up getting the nickname "Industrial Steve" because that's what I would go dance to. But the music … if we didn't know a song, we couldn't just research stuff on the internet. We would have to find it in magazines and compilations. I had never even heard of Sisters of Mercy before I was going there.

Emily Arkin: Mystery Train was the big one for me. I worked there along with everyone. It's funny … there were definitely jobs you can have that went with a subculture. You'd be someone who works at the Garment District or Pearl Art.

Liz Lamanche: Strangely enough I'm a very visual oriented person and music isn't really a large part of my life, so I don't really independently go out and buy it. I love the total environment of the club: the dark, the lights, the people, the music, the beats, getting lost in dancing, and that group social/physical body thing. So, I'm an uneducated consumer of music. I like something with a beat that I can follow, and other than that anything's good. I was just happy to be there. Happy to take it in. Which is why noise and industrial and whatnot doesn't get me because I lose the beat and it becomes inaccessible.

Constantine Valhouli: In the days long before Spotify, Shazam, YouTube, or even Napster, there was a phone line in the telephone box that went directly up to the DJ booth. Chris Ewen patiently answered all my excited, slightly drunk questions about "What song is this?" But seriously, I owe much of my musical education and development to Chris Ewen. The challenge was then to decipher the drunken scrawl on a napkin shoved into the pocket of one's leather trousers the next day.

Jenny Dahling: A lot of bands I like now are thanks to Chris because he educated me about it. I've also gone to a lot of concerts because of him and the ticket giveaways. ManRay really and truly colored a big portion of what I would say was a cultural awakening, or cultural awareness in my adult years that I'm not sure I would have had I not gone.

Jamie DiBattista: It was the first time I heard Lords of Acid. I didn't know much about music. I acted like I did, and I definitely knew a little bit more than some people, but I don't think I heard Sisters of Mercy until I went there. A lot of Goth bands. My only alternative music was watching MTV's 120 minutes, which is a good starter for if you were a kid. But 120 minutes was like a 101 course. This is more of your master's course in music.

Adam Wolff: One of the things that was so great when I first went to ManRay was that they played everything. It was much more diverse. In New York, for example, Batcave was Goth and nothing else. But ManRay had Goth plus all this great other stuff. Chris Ewen and Ian Ford, they have very different styles, but they have very similarly excellent taste. Both can play a great diversity and bring things in from different places. So that was one of the things that was really great initially, hearing all these favorites that were in my own record collection and then hearing all the other stuff that I liked, but I never thought of at the club.

Corey Reeves: The music would inflame emotion and radiance because it really set the tone. ManRay had it going on as far as the music. If you don't have great music then the people won't show.

Constantine Valhouli: I remember evenings when Chris Ewen literally spun the crowd into a frenzy. Rather than mixing peaks and valleys of emotion, Chris kept bringing the crowd higher, and ended the night on an incredibly high note. In my mind, it was something incongruous, like Journey's "Don't Stop Believing"' But people on the dance floor had their arms in the air, they were spinning each other, and were doing impromptu pole dances. The Addams Family meets Dirty Dancing.

Heather Morgan: The last forty-five minutes of ManRay was always really intense music, really intense dancing because Chris knew how to end the night and he totally engineered it that way. It was a real blast at the end, the night didn't just peter out, that would have sucked. People always want one more song and he would always be like, "Okay, but this is the last one." You knew it was the last song. He often would have a period of time where the last song for a few weeks was the BiGod 20 cover of "Like a Prayer." You knew it was the end of the night, so you were hounding that last drink and you were totally spinning around like a maniac and then rushing to get your stuff. I would grab my stuff, but I would always be drenched in sweat because I danced like a freak. I will never forget the last three songs of the night at ManRay.

Chris Ewen: Back then, I think being a DJ was considered something almost godlike in a way. DJs had access to tons of music that the regular customer couldn't get. The mystique of being a DJ has been altered. It's been changed by the fact that there are computer programs that can mix your records for you. Spotify and iTunes. I think DJs run the risk of being thought of as basically a Spotify playlist. Crowds just want to hear their own personal playlist and that's not our role. Our role is to play to lots of people and make lots of people happy. So, there are some challenges. In the last few years, being a successful DJ now relies on that person's taste more than anything because anyone can mix just by hitting a button. So, it's a matter of what that DJ brings to the table in terms of their aesthetic, what songs they pick and how they put them together. Our craft is more challenging.

Chapter 7

Working for the Weekend

"What I actually took away from him is that when you get in a position to have employees, treat them well. Treat them like family. Treat them like humans." — Jen Lucky Cole

The sights. The sounds. The taste. Behind every successful nightclub is the staff who made it all possible. The security met you at the door, becoming the first faces you saw each night. They checked you over, welcomed you in, and kept the club a safe space. The bartenders poured your usual before you even made it across the room. The DJs spun the music that spilled out onto the streets enticing people in. They set the tone for each unique night, where you were guaranteed new hits and old favorites. The lights, bands, artists and performers caught your eye and created unforgettable shows and memorable moments. The staff were the true faces of the club. These nocturnal nighttime and weekend Heroes made ManRay everything that it was. S.L.

Chris Ewen: ManRay, throughout its entire existence, was a drawing point for creative people. No matter if they were artists or craftsmen who built the cage or the artists who did the graphic designs on the walls. What we delivered over the course of all the years of its existence was the sum of all the creative people who worked with and for ManRay. We always try to play off the tagline: The Art of Nightlife. We were always about promoting the artistry and artistic leanings of people from all different areas.

Paul Vitagliano: The people, the DJ, the bartenders, and the door staff are kind of the foot soldiers of the club. They are in the trenches and they're hearing from patrons and they're witnessing everything, so that input is very, very important.

ML: When I was working there I heard how "scary" ManRay was. I was like, "Oh, please."

Bruce Jope: I remember Jared Hoffman who worked the door. It was funny … I always thought of him as a nice Jewish boy because he had such a Jewish name and we used to joke about it: "What's a nice Jewish boy like you doing in a place like this?" He was a really positive energy at the door. He was very sweet.

The first vibe you get about a club is the door and the first feeling you get can almost tell what a club is going to be like on the inside. So, when I created the door staff for ManRay I took all the things I hated from my own experience out and what was left was nice people who explained what the experience of being in ManRay was and tested them to make sure that they were cool with that.

Chris Manousaridis: I worked the door from 9:30 until midnight and then I walked in and I handled the inside. I would look for any reason not to let tourists in, right from the get-go. I would use the dress code as my biggest. I'd say, "Well, you're not wearing all black or creative attire", but he's like, "Well, this is creative. Who decides what's creative?" and I said, "Me." I was using that sort of as "You ain't getting past me." I even told one guy, I'll never forget, I said, "If you really want to come in then you want to go down the street and buy black trash bags and wrap yourself and come in as a piece of trash, you're more than welcome. But if you take it off inside, you're going out the door. Otherwise, you ain't coming in. I don't care who you are." I had it with a radio DJ. I wouldn't let him on the first night. I told them absolutely not. It's all black or creative attire. He was like "Do you know who I am? I work for the radio station." I said, "You can be God himself and you ain't coming in" and then he finally wore all black, came in, was obnoxious the next time he came in and I threw him out.

Chris Ewen: It was part of his philosophy of how he ran his business, he was very hands on. Don wanted to know what was going on even with the outside promoters.

Chris Ewen: It started through my friendship with Paul V. We were friends outside of the club, but I also spent time going to the club and just hanging out. About '86 Campus was a five day a week club. They did a gay night on Thursdays and something on Sundays for gay women. The DJ who was doing Sunday night left. So, the spot became open and Paul, knowing that I did stuff more on the alternative and rock side of music, asked me if I wanted to apply for the job. I borrowed a reel to reel, went into the club and made a demo tape. I spun music for a couple hours and got hired and started doing Sunday nights on the recommendation of Paul.

Terri Niedzwiecki: Well, I think it was a discussion about whether or not I wanted to be a bartender. I'm assuming that's what happens. It's like that was 100 years ago. I was trained by David Bailey, who was the head bartender, and all was going well and good, until he saw a cute person across the room and then he just left me to sink or swim.

Terri Niedzwiecki: I started to look at it more when I was working at the bar there. We're going to look at the potential to make more money. I'm a company girl. I worked at every bar there until I found my home in the back with Chris.

ML: I think ManRay was unique because, for most clubs, people who worked in them didn't stay for over a decade like we did. People used to ask us, "How do I get a job here?" and I was completely honest, "You have to kill one of us. We're not going anywhere."

Daisy Crowder: There was not a high turnover. There's always a certain amount that will come and go, either because they wanted it to be temporary or they didn't work out or it was not what they had in mind. So, there's always a revolving door of people, but there's also a somewhat larger core group that always worked.

ML: I would work every Thursday night. In general, Thursdays start off slow with everyone coming in looking fabulous and the boys were fabulous and we had a fair amount of girls as well. It's just a different energy

Adam Wolff: The story of how I ended up at ManRay is kind of funny. I was making chain mail jewelry and selling it to some of the boutiques around Cambridge and Salem. I was at Hubba Hubba one day hanging out with Susie and her co-manager, Christine, said, "You should talk to Cusraque over at ManRay about vending at Hell because his brother used to make chain mail and he'd probably be interested." I hadn't been there in a couple of years at that point, but I showed up at ManRay one night with my bag of jewelry and I found Cusraque and showed him my stuff and he booked me in for Hell. And so, I started vending at those.

A little sidebar on that story … that first night I showed up there to talk to Cusraque, I ended up giving him and his girlfriend at the time, DJ Lady Bathory who played in the front room on Wednesday nights, a ride home that night.

Later on, I was there early one night and their lighting director called out sick. They didn't have anybody to run lights in the front room, so I said I run lights. They opened the door on the DJ booth and pointed at the lighting controls there and it was just crazy. I figured it out pretty quick. I did the lights that night and they hired me at the end of that night. They were like, "Hey, you know that was pretty great, would you do it again?" And I said, "Sure." They put me on the payroll and I started doing lights in the front room on Wednesday nights for DJ Lady Bathory.

I did that for a few months with her when she showed up one night and said, "Hey, you're a DJ right?" And I said, "Yeah." And she was like, "Do you have your music with you?" I said, "Yes, in my car." She told me to go grab it. I went out to the car, got my music, and I started spinning in the front room there that night.

Koren Bernardi: I started doing lights there in the mid-2000s. I had a day job and I did lights because it was an easy $75. The guy that was originally doing lights had gone on, I think, to do Rise, so he had already programmed all the lights. I just had to press the buttons and do the levers. Eventually you kind of learn which buttons and levers do which.

I did not like working Thursday, Friday, and Saturday from 10 to 2 and also working on the show. I wasn't a very good employee. I wasn't 100 percent in it like I should have been. I was just kind of doing a bunch of stuff. So, I called out sick once and they were pretty much like "You can't do that." So, I got fired. I feel like I'm a very responsible person now, but it took me a while to get there. At first I was like "Well, I didn't need the job anyway. It's fine, fire me. I was kind of sick of doing it anyway." A while later, I changed my hair and I was there one day when they didn't have lights for the night. I told them I could do lights. I think it was just convenience, like, "Oh, well, if you're here and you already know how to do them, I guess. Sure, whatever." So I did them for a little bit longer. This time I actually gave notice when I was not gonna be able to do it anymore, but I just thought it was funny.

Mizery McRae: This is how I started in most of all the clubs that I've worked at. I was a tender young child using my brother's ID to get into these bars and I got up on a box and I just started dancing. I had long braids down to the crack of my ass and I was dancing and flinging. This older man comes up to me and says, "Who the fuck are you?" I looked at him, I said, "I'm Mizery." And he was like, "You want a job. Go dance and fucking look amazing." I said, "Okay, how much are you giving me?" He was like, "I'm gonna give you 50 bucks and you can drink all you want." I said, "Okay, I'll see you next week." And that was my introduction.

I was always a really pretty boy, very young. I would go in there and I would look very androgynous to some people and they couldn't quite put it together. My thing was I was just a dancer and I just loved to enjoy myself. People saw me enjoying myself being up there, letting loose, not caring who was watching me. I was just enjoying myself and I think that's why he hired me.

Nate Roman: My friend Ben was studying graphic design for computers and he got a job at ManRay doing flyer designs and working in the office. Because he was an employee, I ended up hanging out with Cusraque. They were the ones that basically taught me.

My first night DJing in a nightclub was the back end on a Friday night with Ben. DJing wasn't really a big part of his thing. We had very little idea what we were doing. We screwed up a lot. Somehow, enough people had fun that they allowed me to continue. It was just like a comedy of errors in technical stuff. We lost sound at one point and the manager ran up to the booth. We had four songs playing at once. But whatever, we had fun. Everyone had fun and the comment that I got about that night was that I had played stuff that no one had ever heard there before.

Gene Dante: Terri is a personality larger than most, she's wonderful and she is definitely a mama bear when it comes to the kids from the club. I would love to go to Terri's bar early in the night because it was always mobbed. She was very popular. When I started bartending there, we definitely bonded pretty closely. I gotta say, Terri and Daisy were somewhat like maternal or paternal fingers for me.

Daisy Crowder: We were all very close at that time. It was a very family-like atmosphere. At the end of the night, we're all counting out and unwinding. We would share all of our secrets and dirt. We would discuss politics, TV, movies, whatever, but we would also care about each other.

Paul Vitagliano: If I remember correctly, I was spinning ManRay, but also

Spit simultaneously for maybe six months, and then I think I eventually just completely left and worked at other clubs for a year. At Spit, and eventually Axis, I felt a little like a smaller cog in a bigger wheel than I did in ManRay. ManRay felt more like a family and a smaller entity, whereas working on Landsdowne you were thrust into this much larger group of people and politics and personalities. I then moved to LA in 1988.

Chris Manasourides: Well, I approached Don because I started getting to know people at the front door, especially James. I had talked to James every time I was at the front door and kind of hung out with him and I went to Don and I said, "Hey you need a bouncer, James says you need a bouncer, I'll do it. I've done it before." He's like, "Fine you start Wednesday." I did the paperwork and it was a done deal. Literally next thing you know I am working the front door checking IDs with James. I'll tell you it was family from the get-go, from the moment I went downstairs and got my walkie talkie. It didn't feel like a job. It was all of a sudden, boom, you're family. The first time I put that walkie talkie on my belt and the speaker mic on my shoulder it was like a cop getting a badge for the first time. I'm now a part of the building.

My first night of course I'm nervous as far as doing my job, making sure fights don't break out, checking IDs, and making sure everyone is wearing the correct attire. But it didn't take long for me to get comfortable in that position. It was because the staff there was just welcoming from day one. It was just, boom, now I'm a part of the building. It was fantastic getting to know the people coming in, especially on the other nights. At that time I had a steel cage memory. I can remember faces, names, IDs, everything. So it was great because I was like, "He's good. He's good. He's good. He's good." It got to that point where the people coming in were family.

For bouncers it was me, James, Nick and Ray. Ray, at the time, was sort of head of security. James and I liked to give him a hard time on the microphones all the time. We'd be up until midnight so we'd get on the microphone like "Ray, I think he can hear you" and he would be like, "Oh God, not again". We had a great time with it. I've worked a lot of jobs and I can't tell you this one here was something that shaped me in every possible way. I was a bouncer from the end of '94 until 2001.

Matt Gleason: We didn't, as far as outlets for advertising. At the time, we weren't doing radio. We used to do radio for Saturday. Don had a full-page ad in a newsweekly which was for the most part, the gay publication in town. It was kind of like I always thought it was like the gay Phoenix. It was a cool newspaper. I mean, you know, I liked it. Other than that, we were pretty much word of mouth and flyers and posters. We're definitely a step ahead in tech. We had email lists going before. I mean, this is all pre-Facebook. We had email lists. And, you know, ways to contact customers. So, you know, I think we did pretty well in that category. We had a lot of help with that which was something I really tried to put a lot of effort into. Like we had a website, but it wasn't really truly interactive.

Rachel E. Pollock: While I was a DJ, Amanda Palmer was the Bride in Harvard Square and she would take the train to the Ceremony. She asked if she could store her wedding dress and all that rig in the DJ booth while at the club.

Rachel E. Pollock: A part of being there because I was the front room DJ on Goth night and I was a public face, a staff member, I would just talk to people because they are a patron and they are interested in things like the music I'm about to play or they just wanted to talk.

ML: There was a certain point where I trained all the bartenders when they came in. Eventually, it was Daisy because I was like, "I really don't want to do this."

Daisy Crowder: There were managers there at times that I could easily say did not quite get along with the employees as much as other managers did. But some of those managers that I saw at ManRay were dynamite people. Excellent. And they went out of their way to help. I think everyone that was there understood the difficulties of being there on the job and I think we all tried to help each other.

Adam Lewis: It's a little weird because I've kind of been my own boss. When you're on the road you're your own guy, you're kind of in charge. But now you're working for minimum wage and being told what to do by the manager. It wasn't the easiest for me. There wasn't a lot of structure or management. I'd say there wasn't a hell of a lot of training, either. You are either a security or door person. Outside was dealing with IDs and customers, keeping order, and having people line up. Or you could be right inside the door making sure people weren't walking out with a drink, being another set of eyes on the cash register, and protecting that area. Or you could be the roamer, looking for any problems that could possibly happen. You had a route that you were walking continually to keep an eye on everything. That was basically the job right there.

It wasn't a particularly long shift. The club opened at nine, but no one got there till quarter till 10, and it was open till 1. So, it's a four hour shift toward the end of the day. I will say it wasn't a place where we had a lot of scuffles. There was a pretty calm chill crowd for the most part. Every once in a while you have someone that would get a little too drunk and maybe there'd be a little bit of drama, but it wasn't real violence. That also had to do with who we were letting in. We were definitely trying to do a little bit of the Studio 54 mentality of not letting just any people walk in. They weren't going to be happy when they got in so you were doing it for their own good more than anything, although they would be pissed at you for saying no. The crowd that's coming straight from the office and still wearing a collared shirt … I tell them not to come and deny them. No sneakers, no baseball caps, no blue jeans, stuff like that. You would push people away.

Rachel E. Pollock: Well, I actually quit ManRay twice. I only remember this because I found my resignation letter on an old computer recently. I resigned in protest, because the guy who was managing ManRay at the time was a townie, yahoo type. He always sort of took a lot of pride in the position that he had the power. He decided to throw his weight around and try to intimidate me. He told me that I had shirked my duties as a DJ by putting on a mix CD at the beginning of the night, even though that was the policy and Chris did it too. As punishment for shirking my duties, I was not going to work the next Wednesday and that I should think about my transgressions. So I wrote this big resignation letter that I sent to everybody that worked at ManRay because I wanted them to understand that I wasn't abandoning the club, that I wasn't giving everybody a big middle finger

Corey Reeves: I worked Saturdays and Wednesdays. I think the whole thing was looking for a certain way, presenting a certain product. By my bar, I had the gummy savers, the candy, the fruit with the grapes. Thursday night, I would be at that small little bar that's lit up with UV light. So, for me, because I'm really hard on myself, it was all about presentation. I wasn't in competition with anybody. I wanted to make sure that people had the best experience possible. My teacher was Lolly Mason, who was one of the best bartenders in Boston. She was tremendous. She taught me a lot of things. So I had my core value that I was to entertain these people. I brought in a whole bunch of stuff and I introduced them to a whole lot of drinks. So, it was more of a personal thing. It was not just the look of what I was giving but also the drinks that I was making. I never wanted to repeat myself. People really enjoyed it. I never felt uncomfortable at ManRay because we were all treated like family and people really cared. The struggle for me personally was to keep reinventing myself over and over and over. For Friday nights and Wednesday nights I would go thrift store shopping and I would wear nail polish, I had mohawk spiked hair, leopard print pants, just crazy and fun. I just kept wanting to exemplify originality and make my own voice.

Gene Dante: I began as a patron. Then I became a performance artist. Then I went away for a while. I walked in and I just basically called everyone I knew and said I needed work. "Has anyone got anything for me?" and Matt, the manager at ManRay, offered me a fill in shift as a bartender. I actually tended the bar on the very last night we were open.

ML: I remember working on Halloween night. I said, "I don't care if I know you here, if I've slept with you, here are the lines here. You better know you drink because it was just deep at the bar. I don't have time for anything else."

Trent Stewart: The person who hired me, Jenny, was doing her job promoting her night. She asked me what I thought of it and I gave her a thumbs up, but also honest criticism and she smiled and said, "Do you think you could do better?" I said, "Why, yes, I think I can." So, she says, "Okay, I'll keep that in mind." She asked me about doing a fashion show that they had coming up and I started working. That signaled to a lot of people outside of that group that I was safe. I was here to stay.

Jen Lucky Cole: It has become my standard by which I judged every club I went to and Don taught me how to judge every club. I swear I have like a little switch that I can put on in my head where it turned on, like ManRay brain. I look around and I start critiquing stuff like the way the lights are set up, the way they have a stage, how the acoustics are, how the speakers are set up.

I knew that to be able to pull something like that off, because I mean he could guarantee a regular crowd for each of the nights, like he pretty much knew what the numbers were going to be every single night. You could not do that with other places like that. It was people who would try to steal his ideas, even when it came down to the advertising. It sounds silly, but I handle all the advertising and we had a lot that would go into different kinds of print media.

Every week we'd have to have fresh stuff and it was weird because I would change the way something would look and then two weeks later, a bunch of the ads for the other clubs would look almost identical. I was really flattered, which was cool, but it also gave me a lot of pressure because I'm like "Oh cool, now I'm in charge of the way all the gay ads look in Boston," you know. So it was a weird thing to notice, that people had that tendency, and I didn't understand how clubs were like that. But he made me understand it better. I knew I was dealing with something cool because when ManRay was still open, and it was relevant, it didn't matter where I went in the country people knew about it.

Jennifer: I literally would work without sleeping, and then I would have to pull my car over on the side of the road and just crash every now and then, because I just couldn't keep my eyes open anymore.

Jen Lucky Cole: Because I was a female employee, if they ever needed somebody to go into the ladies' room because something was happening I'd be there with one of the male security guards. One night was a crazy night. I don't remember the name of the professional wrestler, but one of those WWE mega slam things was in town. One of the wrestlers apparently had brought a lady downstairs to have a fun time in the bathroom. We didn't know who was messing around in the bathroom. Me and just one security guy went down and I knocked on the door. He wasn't very happy. He was very rude about the words he was choosing to use and he slammed the door shut and told me to "Mind you own F-ing business, you dumb dyke." So, I walked away and they called for all of the security to go down there. They actually had to pull the friggin door off. The guy got crazy with them and it took all of the male security that night to remove this guy.

Mark Dighton: I was somewhat sympathetic, especially once I moved to New York and lived next to a club for a while. That really does suck. I get it. That was probably one of the most memorable things about security. The hardest part of the job was at the end of the night, when people were drunk and having a good time and loud and rowdy, we had to stand out there and go, "Shhh shhh neighbors neighbors."

Mark Dighton: I wanted to turn people on to what I thought was cool music. The trouble was the crowd didn't want to be pushed, I guess, as much as I was prone to pushing people. It was 50/50, people will come up and say, "What is this crap you're playing? Play something I know." Others were like, "Wow, that was great. That was so cool." It got to the point where the management started to complain, mostly Don. I think Bruce and Francis both had a vision and they knew what I was doing, even if it wasn't their taste. It was cutting edge. Don was giving me a hassle and I walked out, told him I wasn't gonna take music advice from somebody who didn't know anything about music and probably used a couple expletives in the process. When I came back the next week they had replaced me and they claimed I had quit. I still think I was pretty much fired and they used the fact that I had walked out one night as an excuse.

Corey Reeves: One Thursday night I came in with my friend Frank and I was setting up, then I was told by Cheryl to meet up with Matt Gleason at the office, so I went downstairs. He told me he was going to be putting David Bryson on the square bar tomorrow night for the big event. I felt really slighted that I wasn't asked, that David Cafferty, who's head of security, had actually pushed Matt to put David on that bar. There was nothing that I had done that was warranted. It wasn't a monetary thing. I was usurped and I felt really hurt and disappointed because I loved Matt and I didn't understand where this was coming from. I was fuming, so I went upstairs. I looked around. I put away all my little gummy savers and I grabbed Frank and then I went to Cheryl and I said, "Just tell your father it was great working for him" and I walked out the door. Donald senior was not happy with me walking out the door, and I believe that, on that next Friday night, the general manager of Avalon came in and Donald had words with him about me and he was very, very angry. Then Sunday night rolled around and I walked into Avalon and, the manager would not do this, but the head bartender came up to me and he said, "We're letting you go, you can't work." I was fired at Avalon for walking out there on that Thursday night from ManRay.

Rachel E. Pollock: In 2003 I recognized that I was growing farther and farther apart from innovative new music that would have an appeal for ManRay. I really got sucked into other kinds of alternative music. My musical tastes were changing and I recognized that they were changing in ways that would not fly at ManRay. Ultimately I need to give up this big room to somebody who is going to find the next Wolfsheim.

Paul Vitagliano: If you do it right, and the crowd understands that the people running the club or playing the music envision why it works, and they may not know the machinations of exactly why, but when they're there they know that it's right. If you have that something when you do a club event you're gold. If the crowd has trust in the DJ, the promoters, the managers and the venue they will keep coming. You have the comfort level and the welcoming energy. The idea that when you walk in, you fit.

Daisy Crowder: ManRay was one of the greatest jobs I ever had and it was something I'll never forget. They are memories that will carry with me till the day I die. Some terrible, some awesome, but most of them are pretty good.

Chapter 8

Roots, Growth, and Options: The Years 1992-1994

"I think '92 to '96 were very important because a lot of things changed. A whole new generation came around." — Patrick Fitzgerald

By the late 80s, it became clear that ManRay was setting down roots. There was no longer a question of will it or won't it survive? The clear answer was that it was now firmly entrenched in Central Square. Having lived through the initial growing pains, ManRay turned its eyes towards making a name for itself. The 90s also marked the beginnings of new crowds and horizons that ManRay was eager to embrace. Hell would begin to take shape, Goth culture was seeking itself a home, and New Wave was becoming a legitimate listening option. So, the club began experimenting with ideas of different nights that showcased different types of music and aesthetics, drawing in a wider variety of patrons. These early nights would solidify into one of the characteristics ManRay was best known for.

The inspiration for this may have come from the duality of ManRay and Ground Zero, which were both owned by Don Holland. Ground Zero had a darker industrial Gothic atmosphere that was more on the edge as compared to ManRay's beginning and growth as Campus. It was here that Terri Niedzwiecki, bartendress extraordinaire, was working when she would meet DJ Chris Ewen. Like Terri and Chris, Ground Zero and ManRay seemed to play off of each other in a way that encouraged each to change and grow. ManRay had officially hit its stride. S.L.

Chris Ewen: The owner of ManRay, Don, opened up another small nightclub around the corner from on Mass Ave that was called Ground Zero. The idea behind that was to be even more underground than ManRay and to be more punk. They started using the words industrial and

Goth. It was a bit rougher and tumble and the interior was designed to look almost like an apocalyptic fallout shelter.

Susanne Boitano: For a while there was Ground Zero and you could just wobble your little self over around the corner and I was like this is completely perfect. It was small, it was intimate, it was right around the corner.

Terri Niedzwiecki: By the time I moved to Ground Zero, I already knew what I was doing.

Chris Ewen: Diego decided to retire from the club world, and he did Thursdays and Saturdays, so they were looking for a DJ for Ground Zero, which was managed by Terri. She was also the bartender there. So, at that time, Ground Zero was her domain.

I remember sitting in one night after ManRay had closed and Terri had come back over from Ground Zero. We were talking about what to do and I said I'd be willing to take over the DJ slot that Diego was vacating. Terri burst out laughing in my face because she knew me only as a ManRay DJ — a little too fluffy for the hard-hitting stuff that Ground Zero was doing. Cooler heads prevailed and I was given a try out doing Thursdays and Saturdays there. I DJed there for a couple of years until Ground Zero closed. That's actually how Terri and I developed our friendship.

ManRay was maybe more of an accessible side of alternative music. We did play a little bit of industrial stuff, but also a lot of new beat stuff. It was kind of left of the dial musically. Then Ground Zero tended to be more punk stuff and hardcore industrial and Goth stuff. Maybe more rock oriented. It was a bit harsher. I actually enjoyed the duality of it. The challenge was to make each night different and exciting, not just doing the same thing four nights a week. So DJing that Thursday and Saturday at Ground Zero I could explore more things and go deeper. You could be more interesting and harsher and a lot more underground. I loved doing both.

Chris Ewen: Ground Zero had a Friday live concert series. We brought in a lot of really underground bands. We brought in My Life with The Thrill Kill Kult. Nick Fiend had an art show there. They weren't going to get booked on Lansdowne. I don't think there was ever a time musically that we could initially bring those bands to ManRay. We had a much larger capacity than Ground Zero. Eventually we started working with some New

York promoters and live booker's who offered us bands. So, we just started randomly booking things while still being a dance club.

Adam Lewis: I grew up in Lexington, Massachusetts and was going to school in southern New Hampshire, so I was coming down on weekends and special events to shows at Ground Zero. Then that kind of bled into ManRay. So, I kind of did it the other way around. A lot of people were going to ManRay and then hanging out at Ground Zero because Ground Zero was open an hour later. Ground Zero was my introduction, and then I started knowing about ManRay. I was a tour manager for Alien Sex Fiend, and the last date on that tour was in the summer of '92, so that's when I started going back to ManRay again and got hired.

It's funny because, again, I was coming from the Ground Zero perspective and my college radio station, so I was very much tied into underground music. Ground Zero was doing a lot of shows and it was the same owner. My introduction to ManRay was negative because ManRay closed at one and Ground Zero closed to two, so all the staff would just be like "Oh no they are all coming here." ManRay was kind of the slightly softer version, the slightly softer edgy place.

Chris Ewen: The way that ManRay developed came, I think, as a direct result of Ground Zero closing. Terri and I really loved the divide that we had going at Ground Zero. One of the things I talked to her about and then had to convince Don about was that we both thought that there was a growing audience or a growing culture for what we were doing at Ground Zero. I thought it would have been beneficial to the club to bring that atmosphere and music into ManRay. On Wednesday I was trying to bring that atmosphere and people over and give them another place to go. Since Ground Zero closed, there really was no other place in town for that culture to exist.

Terri was behind the bar and managing so if she was going to be brought to ManRay then it made sense that we brought the rest of the Ground Zero package too, musically and so on. I think both Terri and I were able to convince Don that maybe we should try going down this slightly darker path with the music. As long as people were willing to show up for it, I think he was happy.

Chris Ewen: We wanted to bring Nick Fiend over for an art show initially right after Ground Zero closed. We knew that a lot of people were going to come to it, so we were going to do it at ManRay but we did it as "Ground

Zero present at ManRay." We were able to convince Don.

Noel McKenna: I first found out about ManRay because I used to go to Ground Zero around the corner and it was owned by the same person. Chris was the primary DJ, Terri was the bartender and then a couple of other people worked at Ground Zero and also worked at ManRay. The last night Ground Zero was open there was a girl passing out ManRay flyers. Ground Zero definitely had a little bit of a tougher edgier crowd then ManRay at that time. Our goal was to infiltrate ManRay and change it from the inside.

Adam Lewis: Ground Zero was very different because it was one floor, one long narrow space, leather, and industrial, dark and loud and abrasive music. Then walking into ManRay....

Chris Ewen: We had to place the expensive ads in *The Phoenix* just to let people know that we existed. We didn't have this giant infrastructure that was willing to promote us for free. It was pretty much word of mouth. We had the strike against us, of having to close an hour early and compete with Lansdowne Street for people who wanted something a lot more alternative. We were constantly trying to make things better and cooler and have a concept that would be easy to explain to outsiders. We spent a lot of time trying to define what different nights were going to get people to come back. We started coming up with different themes. "The Art of Nightlife" being the ManRay tagline gave us the opportunity to kind of expand and contract and explore. I think the challenge was always to keep ManRay interesting on all the different nights.

Chris Ewen: When we were retooling the club, at one point we realized that we could have these themes on Saturday night. They were kind of alternative enough yet all-encompassing enough where we could actually bring in two distinctly different crowds. That was a magic formula. I think it started as maybe a once-a-month kind of thing because it was untested. If it fails miserably we can move on. If it does something, then let's do it next month and see how that goes. Why don't we lock these themes in and make a night that people know they can come to every week? We had to dig a little deeper and do some things that nobody else was doing.

Bruce Jope: The club lasted so long by using young attendees as promoters, having the people from within the club promote the club and come up with the themes.

Daisy Crowder: Don and everyone who worked at ManRay all definitely had different fields. Some were more fetish oriented. It had a manic kind of sexuality; the atmosphere was bristling with sexuality. Campus also on Thursdays did too. Other times, there was a different kind of energy. Saturdays used to be just a good drunken hoedown.

Michael Hsieh: Each night definitely had its own character. Wednesday Crypt nights were definitely just wonderfully Goth. I don't think I ever made it to any of the gay nights on Thursday, which I'm kind of bummed about because I heard it was just a great party. Then there was Fantasy Factory and Hell and the 80s Heroes.

A. Dominy Cusraque: I went on Wednesdays and Fridays, maybe sometime on Saturdays. But I was told, probably by Vinny, to go back there on Wednesday.

Terri Niedzwiecki: Dance nights are definitely easier and, to be honest with you, I think you make more money.

Abigail Taylor: I usually went on Wednesdays and Fridays. I also sometimes would go on Saturdays because the 80s night was super fun. I was absorbing a lot of music at the time, learning about all these genres. I worked Wednesdays and Fridays Go Go dancing. Wednesday nights were full on Goth, so there was a lot of The Cure and Siouxie and what you'd expect from a Goth place, but Chris would also spin really cool weird stuff like music from Cirque du Soleil and The Chameleons and even Velvet Underground. That night was definitely one of the nights that I learned a lot about music because it wasn't as crazy and hectic as Friday nights. There's more mingling and socializing. Fridays were more like fetish and Fantasy Factory nights, so things got a little crazy and way more packed. There was a little more pressure and tension in the air. Saturday I would normally just go to have fun and dance all night.

Patrick Fitzgerald: Taking a step back and looking at the scene as a whole, I think '92 to '96 were very important because a lot of things changed. A whole new generation came around that time. My generation is the people who are in their early to mid-40s now, and they were kind of the old guard that was very entrenched at that time. We were fairly resistant to the younger kids coming in who listened to Marilyn Manson and Nine Inch Nails and wearing their silly makeup.

Skot Kremen: Right around '92 there was still a combination of the rave scene and there was also the industrial scene. There wasn't a huge Goth scene in Boston at that time. ManRay was not as pretentious and it wouldn't get that pretentious until around 1994 to 95.

Greg Frisbee: I think I spent so much time in that club that I can close my eyes and I can picture the entire club exactly how it was when I was there in the 90s.

Jon Whitney: I think 1990 was the first time I had gone to ManRay, but I had been to T.T. the Bear's, and a couple Middle East shows in 1990. Central Square was a place that you don't want to go to. It was filthy and there was a lot of crime. It wasn't really gang violence, but there was definitely violence. You didn't want to be walking there alone when a show gets out at two in the morning, and I think that's why a lot of people gravitated to Hi-Fi pizza because you could go there and grab a mushroom slice and see some people that you just saw at the show and you're around people. I went to a lot of shows alone, so if I was getting out at like two in the morning I would stop over at Hi-Fi and have a slice of pizza and make sure that everything's okay.

Chris Ewen: The way Central Square is developing and changing, ManRay, as well as T.T. the Bear's was looked on as a golden age by some people. I'm sure that ManRay helped bring a lot of business into Central Square. Just like T.T.'s and The Middle East, in terms of bringing people from all over. It just brought a vibrance.

John O'Leary: Chris was still downstairs, and we would just hang out and then your friends would show up one by one by one and you would get to dance almost by yourself. You would go and you just relax.

Me'lissa Nin: I think after a while people get used to it. Back in the early to mid-90s, Goth wasn't quite as mainstream as it became later on. If somebody saw a guy in black eyeliner and a skirt on … you get this horrible mentality. But thankfully that isn't so much the case now, at least not in bigger cities. It's not as weird as it used to be. Even just a lip piercing … people thought, "Oh my god, that's so weird." But now, everybody has a nose piercing or lip piercing like it's not a big deal anymore.

Athena Costa: Through some lip gloss on and eyeliner for lip gloss — things you were tormented for on a regular basis in the normal world, you were ridiculed and screamed at and made fun of and bullied and picked on and they didn't accept you. So when you met another person that was into the same thing, it was kind of like a holy shit moment. When I've got black tights on and black shorts I'm feeling okay with myself. But when you went outside you knew that there was probably a 95 percent chance that you were going to be like shit on. It was terrible. I got yelled at out of the car windows. That still occasionally happens, but then at some point in the 2010s, it suddenly was super normalized, so you get ridiculed less. There was a lot of bullying, even from family. It was extremely terrible because they didn't get it.

Susanne Boitano: Fashion took a little harder edge too. I think a lot of this stuff that had been percolating underground came up from couture, like Jean Paul Gaultier. Maybe a little bit de rigueur, the black leather and the chains and a lot of things became just a tad riskier, a little darker. I think maybe we're leaving behind the bubble gum New Wave and that sort of B-52s everything's kind of swell. Techno started to come in with more Ministry. Things got a bit windier and the music became a little darker. There was just some shift in sociology. People became harder.

The 80s were hard to sustain because you had to be rich too. It is all Reagan and go, go, go and lifestyles of this and that. That's unsustainable and I think people just hit some kind of weird ass wall. A kind of a hardness set in, more of an armor set in. I think a lot of the people from the 80s weren't getting what they wanted. People were tired of greed and so forth.

It was more nightlife, but I think it was also more produced. I think a lot of it used to be a little more independent. I remember there'd be larger shows and larger venues that, before, didn't exist. It was just these three bands playing on this night and then things became more packaged.

Richard LaDue: I think I was working at Rise at that time on Sunday nights going into Monday mornings. After '91 to '92, a lot of my going out would almost be research related — what are the kids listening to, what's responding, what's working well, what's not? Rise, during this time period, was an afterhours club scene. It was just kind of removed from the

ManRay world. I would go to New York City and chase music and go to nightclubs and do the Satellite Record routine. I was probably on that tip and not really looking at young kids and that vibe anymore.

Arlene Guerrero-Watanabe: It just felt like, in the 90s, the people that I met at ManRay we're all educated and interesting and smart. We were successful people doing interesting things in our own rights.

A. Dominy Cusraque: As an entity, ManRay was fully formed when I first started going in. When I first went in there I was sort of poking around, as I do whenever I go into a club. I looked at how many rooms there were and approximately how big the place was. I noticed how many bars there were, looking at it from a business perspective, but also from a personal perspective. I was feeling out the place and trying to figure out who else went there because I was among the first people who were in the door that night.

There was a promoter named Mistress Diana who did all the prizes for a living. At the time, I was working and trying to start Ratchet Designs as a company with my brother, so when I went to ManRay I was looking for a place to market what we were doing. I had no idea that there was an overriding culture at all, or subculture as it were.

Susanne Boitano: Terri's Red Death. There's a marvelous horror movie called Red Death and, whenever I see that, I think of her. She was great. I don't know whether she could just remember everybody but whenever she said "Hey, how are you doing, honey?" you just felt like she remembered you. A great club will be as great as the bartenders. If you get some jerk who doesn't want to serve you, or could care less, it makes a difference. It really brings a place down.

John O'Leary: I've worked in a lot of clubs and been to a lot of clubs and ManRay had that great feeling. I would walk in and I would go straight through the front door. Brad would be DJing in the front there. I wave. Maybe Daisy will be at the front bar in the lounge. Depending on the time of year, you go down to the coat check. We'd run downstairs immediately and go into the ladies' room to fix our eyeliner and make-up, because you don't want to be in the men's room. Then I would go straight to Terri's bar.

Kyle Blaisdell: Everybody had respect for Mama T, everybody loved Terri, she ran the bar. She was the queen of the alien hive, as I have referred to her before. I saw it as the mothership. She would be the alien queen receiving all our progress reports before sending us back out into society. She made the meanest Red Death's right up until she cut you off.

Me'lissa Nin: I loved every bartender. Daisy was one of my favorites, but, because I hung out in the Goth room, I was pretty much always at Terri's bar.

Wendy Austin: I think it was something fruity and super sweet, like a Fuzzy Navel. I remember Grape Crushes at ManRay and this was before I had an attitude about getting my drinks in plastic cups.

Chris Manousaridis: Absolutely Mama. Mama would make my Grape Crushes. Mama always knew that was my drink. Especially at the end of the night, we would have a shift drink. She would always make my Grape Crush and have it ready for me.

Anna Feder: I remember Daisy now that we have connected around the documentary, but at the time, Terri was the only bartender that made an impression on me because she was just always so dour looking. I was just like "She hates me." She has a resting Goth face for sure. It wasn't a favorite bartender for bartending skills or anything. I remember Terri because she made an impression.

Becky D: So, I didn't have a bartender or a drink like some of the regulars did. Terri was the first bartender that I met there and the Red Death was her signature drink, so I got to know that in the beginning really well, but my taste changed. Sometimes I'd drink White Russians. Sometimes I would have a shot of good vodka. Sometimes I would have a vodka tonic. As we got into the late 90s, early 2000s I loved going to chat with some of the other bartenders. I'd go into the front room and talk to Daisy for a bit and get a drink from him. I didn't really have a place at a bar that was mine.

Jon Whitney: I would go there on Campus night or Heroes night. I'd feel alone sometimes, and maybe I'd be at the bar and there's Terri and she and I are talking about that and she'll nudge me to say go say hi to somebody.

Emily Sweeney: I think Daisy introduced me to try Skinny Black Bitch, which is basically just vodka and Diet Coke.

Mizery McRae: I have never paid for a cocktail since I started working. I tip very well.

Eloni Feliciano: It was usually a Long Island Iced Tea or a Bombay gin and tonic, but she would switch it around. We used to have our own sign language from across the bar. You put your finger to your head and that meant Bombay. A margarita was a check mark in the air. A mind eraser was a finger to your ear.

Julia Kilcoyne: During my time at ManRay was when Red Bull first came out, and all I could smell on the kids was Red Bull and vodka. I don't ever need to smell that again. But the Grape Crush was happy land.

Eartha Harris: Well Terri, of course. And especially Daisy. He would always bring a smile to my face and make me feel so special. I grew up the lonely outcast kid in school (as most of us attending ManRay probably did) and Daisy would always greet me with "Well if it isn't the queen of the scene!" and smile when I would approach his bar at the start of the night. It was the first time in my life when I really felt special, like a queen, and to this little misfit girl it was a big deal.

Tatiana Zimkus: Terri!!! I was scared of her at first. She was intimidating and she's not always the friendliest if you don't know her.

Jennifer: I didn't really start making friends until I used to hang out in Mama's corner. Once you were in her corner you were accepted. Then you just start becoming more connected with people who work there. If you were cool enough to be doing Mind erasers in the corner., then you were okay in everyone else's book.

Rick Webb: Terri!!!! She made my first legal drink. I made the mistake of telling her it was my 21st birthday, and she looked at me and she's like, "You fucker," because I had a fake ID from BU before that. But, yeah, I went to Terri pretty much from then on.

Xtine Santakas: Actually, my first drink at ManRay was, of course, Terri's Red Death. If you don't have one of Terri's Red Deaths are you really at ManRay?

Taylor Vecchio: I really would only drink Miller High Life. I did not like IPAs. I only liked PBR and Miller High Life and it was super cheap. I couldn't drink liquor out even to this day. I can't take shots or I was too broke for mixed drinks. So I would only drink beer and it would probably be whatever was the cheapest thing.

Adam Lewis: Terri was my bartender and my drink, at least in the early years, was a White Russian. I didn't know what I was doing. All of a sudden, I'm in a bar, I don't know what to order. In later years, I was doing vodka tonics. Terri knew how I liked it and she was generous because I was a regular.

A. Dorian Rose: Terri's Red Death girl. Then it became a screwdriver. She would have one ready for me. She's that kind of an artist.

Terri Niedzwiecki: Do I think that there was a certain amount of respect involved in the squeal on each other. I mean, if someone under the age of 21 no one would have a problem coming up and telling me that because they've been want to lose the night they you know they didn't want to lose the places they enjoyed because one person's get stupid.

Amy Butts: Terri. My mama. I did have a drink for years. Oh my gosh, what the heck was it? It was a particular beer. They stopped making it over a decade ago and Terri knew that I loved it. As soon as I would come up to the bar, she would hand it to me. They stopped making that beer and she saved a few for me which was so sweet. I got the last couple.

Russ Carter: Daisy and Terri. Terri had this drink, everybody knows it. It was the Red Death and the Red Death literally tasted like Kool Aid to me. It was great. You can pound that stuff because of the liquor was tasteless, which was fucking dangerous because you had like five of them and realized you just drank the equivalent of five Long Island Ice teas. Shit got weird.

Heather Morgan: One night, before I turned 21, I got hit in the head during a mosh pit when Chris was playing "Jesus Built My Hotrod" by Ministry. Everybody was slam dancing and I got hit in the head with a spike from someone's bracelet. It didn't really hurt, but I went to walk toward the stage, I felt really hot, like I was sweating, but it wasn't sweat. I looked at my hand and it was just covered in blood, pouring down my face like Carrie, because your scalp bleeds a lot. It looks worse than it is. My friend Chris brought me over to the bar, I wasn't 21 yet, so I was just like,

"Come on, Terri haven't I earned a drink?" She's like, "No, but here's some napkins." She did not fuck around.

Matt Richard: When I first started going there, there was a bartender named Kelly at the bar by the steps that went down to the coach check. I would get a Bacardi Lime and Sprite. I'd go to her on my way to the coat check and that became a little ceremony for me. Then I started getting into rums like Captain and Coke. I ended up going to Daisy to get drinks when he was in the lounge room. My girlfriend at the time was a friend of ML's, so I became a regular at ML's bar too. It was at the point where I could walk into that room and, if ML saw me, she would pour my drink by the time I got to the bar. She got me on to the Captain Morgan private stock which was a nice vanilla hinted rum. There was one time that I needed to get water and I ran into the room and she was pouring my rum drink for me. I was like, "No, I need water."

Jenny Dahling: I think I had just turned 21 and I was very ignorant of how you absolutely do not buy underage people drinks. I learned my lesson. I brought my underage friend and thought it would be no big deal if I put it there and then you pick it up. You know, very, very slick. Mike the bouncer, who was a big guy with glasses, threw me out, and rightfully so. But I became very indignant. And I said, "Sure, just give me my money back" I had been here 10 minutes, so it was obviously an absurd request. But I said, "Fine, I'm calling the police on you." I called Cambridge Police and a few minutes later a cruiser showed up. Meanwhile, my underage friends say "You actually called them?!" and she grabbed my hand and said, "We gotta get out of here." So that was that night. I went back a week or two later and who was working the door but Mike. Mike said to me, "Are you going to behave yourself?" And I said, "Are you going to be a douchebag again?" and Mike thought it was hilarious. He let me in and after that we were best buddies.

Crayola Tidd: Well, Daisy, definitely. We loved Terri too, but Daisy is our favorite bartender. Me and Frankie would do Mind Erasers together. When I first started going there, I was always a Bacardi woman. I loved rum. One night, they had these promotional people come in with t-shirts and this new kind of rum called Sailor Jerry Navy rum. They gave me a t-shirt with a girl on the front like the logo. I tried it and I was like, "Oh my God, this is the best drink I have ever had!" After that, that was my drink.

Keith Ward: I'm not sure if I should admit this or not, but there were times at the end of the night where I just dropped whatever I had in my pocket on the bar and was like, "Can I get one more drink?" and they just made me one more drink.

Brian Legault: I was working as a consultant and I always had to be on point the next day, so I didn't drink a lot at ManRay. I'd have one or two drinks. That was never the big draw for me. However, when I did drink, it was gin and tonics.

Jamie DiBattista: My drink was a gin and tonic because, and this tells you how sophisticated I was as a young person, there were so many fucking black lights in that place that you looked like you were drinking something cool because it was glowing. But, let me tell you, gin and tonics are fucking disgusting.

Christina Pearson: I got to be more of a gin and tonic person because you look so cool when you're drinking one and there's black lights. Before I would go in I would always drink Southern Comfort and Coke so I'd get that good buzz that I didn't have to pay for. Those were standards.

Sara S. Wendell: When I first started going I was into the Tequila Sunrise and Paul, at the mid bar, would make them the way that I loved them, which was two thirds tequila, a little bit of orange juice, and literally a drop of grenadine. You could practically hear the Bugs Bunny sound effect when he made it. I used to walk in the door and, by the time I came up from checking my coat, my drink would be sitting on the edge of the bar.

Chris Famurali: I would always go to the back bar with Terri. One day I said to her, "Well, what kind of drink will get me drunk?" And she said, because I was probably having a particularly bad night, "Hold on a second." She turned around and filled a cup with a bunch of different stuff. I drank it down and she was like "Holy shit." I asked her what it was and she's like, "I call it the Red Death." From that point on, every time I went in she would make it.

Jenn Sutkowski: Yeah, Terri. She made strong drinks, but I was underage. My friends would get me an Amaretto Sour. I got kicked out once for drinking underage there.

Avril dePagter: Vodka tonic and it was always Terri. I thought her personality was perfect for ManRay. She always appeared stoic but was kind. ManRay always felt like there was sort of a collision of a binary of either/or. Terri, she appeared one way, but she's actually such a mixture.

Paul Vitagliano: That night that we met started Chris' trajectory towards working at the club. We became really good friends and I told him you should try to get a gig.

Avril dePagter: Chris Ewen was my first experience of a DJ who I never felt objectified by or who talked down to me or my friends. I remember Roberto, my best friend, was really into Britney Spears. We would request Brittany's "Toxic", "Hey Yeah" by Outkast, and then my favorite, Ladytron's "Seventeen." We would request those songs every single Thursday. What's amazing is that he would play them and he never batted an eye about it. He wasn't judgmental. He was just kind of like "Yeah sure," and when he played them everybody danced. When we were in Provincetown, maybe two years ago, I requested Ladytron's "Seventeen" and the DJ looked at me and was like, "Uh, look around the room. If I play that I'm going to get booed out of here" and I looked around and I was like "Oh."

Patrick Baldwin: Chris Ewen really was the soundtrack to my life for a good long time and still kind of is. I look at my Spotify playlist and I see his playlist basically.

Gibby Miller: Chris knew his shit, he wasn't some kid playing the 80s compilations. He would mix in punk and post-punk with New Wave. He would always prop up his friends' bands if they had a track that was hot. He was just warm and kind and it was the perfect convergence. It was all the concentric circles. It was the Goths and the punks, and the jocks and the Campus crowd. It was like concentric circles.

Rick Webb: Chris is a phenomenal DJ. He can beat a match in his sleep. I worked on Lansdowne Street and I saw a lot of those big DJs up close, and Chris is just as good as them. It's crazy.

Noel McKenna: Chris has always been really open to requests, he has never been the type of DJ to turn his nose up at requests. He has a great love for his audience and a deep, deep love for music.

Kyle Blaisdell: Chris was really gifted at being able to bring the ebb and flow of the dance crowd from a Goth swirl right into an industrial stomp. I really loved the sound we used to get from the dressing room when it was located under the stage. All you got was the feet bouncing on the floor above your head in rhythm with whatever Chris was playing. Most of the time the song itself would be drowned out, but you can almost tell what track was playing by the rhythm of the feet above your head. If they had that industrial stuff going on, you can look up and see the ceiling moving. We would have the whole dance floor right down there with us. The whole room would vibrate with the tempo. It wasn't very reassuring to see they had brought in makeshift support beams in areas they had concerns about.

John O'Leary: Chris knew everybody on the dance floor. You can look out there and he knew exactly what the next song was to play to make everybody happy. He always knew when to put a new thing in just at the right time, so it wouldn't kill a dance floor.

Jen Lucky Cole: I was in charge of all the media and the website. People wanted to get his setlist, you know, because it was really popular for a DJ to freely give up their setlist all the time. Chris kept that secret to himself. I never thought to sit there one night and write down every song because I respected him so much. It was just one of those things that I would be like, "Oh, hey, by the way, people want to know your setlist. What do you think about doing that?" It wasn't like he was trying to keep it from people, he just likes to force people to have to go there to find out.

Chapter 9

New Horizons: The Years 1994-1997

"A club like ManRay, which offered so many different things, was a crucial link for people." — ML

When ManRay began working directly with promoters who had visions of what nightlife could be, it was a match made in heaven…..or hell, as it were. People began approaching the club with ideas about events and themes, making it obvious there were populations of people who wanted the experience of nightlife but never had the opportunity. In particular, the kink and BDSM communities had long been hidden away and denied access. ManRay stepped up and provided groups that have always been around, but never had the chance, to build their own destinations and voices. Because of its origins as a gay club, ManRay was used to providing an atmosphere of safety for it's patrons, which perfectly fit in with these new nights. For many who lived their conservative lives most of the week, Fridays became a moment of freedom, a place where they could safely explore themselves and be exactly who they wanted to be.

Around the same time, Rhino Records began releasing cassettes and CD's called Just Can't Get Enough: New Wave Hits of the 80s. Suddenly the 80s were back with a vengeance and New Wave kept turning up wherever you looked. While the club was originally leery of the genre, DJ Chris Ewen managed to convince ManRay to give it a try. Chris' New Wave Party was born. Despite initial fears and doubts, the New Wave night quickly gained a following, fast becoming insanely popular. It's more relaxed dress code and atmosphere, coupled with a diverse variety of music, made it a great introduction night for people cautious of ManRay's reputation. It saw the greatest mix of people from every night ManRay had to offer - from Hell and Fantasy Factory to Goth and gay night patrons. All felt welcomed and comfortable.

For patrons, these new nights provided a chance to find an aesthetic that really fit their wants and needs. What they might not realize is the huge amount of work putting together such nights entailed. Whether it was a flyer as you walked into Newbury Comics or out of a show at Avalon, word of mouth from your friends, or perhaps you were fortunate enough to see Cusraque himself — the broad brimmed hat with the feather unforgettable — as he invited you to a new experience. Promoters came up with the ideas, created the flyers and advertisements, walked the streets, figured out the logistics of time, space, food, performances and made sure everything ran smoothly, all during a period before the true era of digital media. If they were willing to put in the immense amounts of work to make a success of their idea, ManRay would provide promoters with the opportunity to create something unforgettable and bring their own contributions to the "Art of Nightlife." S.L.

Chris Ewen: Initially it was a tough sell to convince Don that this was something viable at that time. Let's say the 80s and New Wave wasn't looked upon fondly. There were doubts that I could do something with that. Like I mentioned earlier, ManRay was constantly evolving and changing and trying to find the right elements. I thought of New Wave because it was something different that we weren't doing and nobody else was doing it.

Jennifer Chandler: So, it was from a group of kids that I went to college with. They would go there on Friday nights and on the weekends. They would tell me all about it, that there was a New Wave dance club that played our kind of 80s music that we liked and that it was a really cool place to go. So, I found a group of friends to hang out with at Massasoit.

Abigail Taylor: Chris was and still is, so influential. He introduced me to an endless list of music. I was listening to a lot of Depeche Mode in high school. He really made me a Depeche Mode fan, like, I wanted to see Depeche Mode after the songs that he would play. He also kind of turned me on to New Wave. I knew a little bit of 80s music, the typical things but he'd play New Order and some different Duran Duran songs like Rio or Joy Division and all this British rock and pop, I guess I obtained a broader appreciation of music in general. He would also play a lot of new music from older artists.

Gibby Miller: On a Saturday in the front room there would be a little bit more of a potential for newer tracks being played on the electronic side of things. Chris would weave in new tracks that are exciting to hear and fun to hear. Sometimes he would sneak in the track of his own. Chris' New Wave party was by nature or by concept, sort of an nostalgic night. It was a night to play the older music, but he would also drop new tracks. There were bands that were going at the time. Chris would play older tracks that I didn't know and I would hop on the phone and say, "What is this?" To my horror, one time it was "Telephone" by Blondie, something that I should have known. Why didn't I know that?

John O'Leary: It was that excitement. I've only felt for a few clubs and you would park your car, wherever you got to go or you take tea and you feel that kind of thing. As you're getting to the door. You see it. Oh, there it is. It opens the doors right there. And you see the gates, the cage kind of gates open at the pride. And whoever we would be working the door and they would just wave us in and you get in and I forget the name, who used to work at the door, Sue. I think I remember the black hair and she would just like stamp our hand and immediately you were just in.

Eileen Dover: Chris' variety of music that came out of the New Wave period, it was like re-learning amazing songs I've heard before but never really got to figure out. He would go from Marilyn Manson to Culture Club to Madonna to Morrissey. It was so varied and he really knows how to read a room.

Kathy Landes: I was a metal head in high school, so I was into the Guns and Roses, and all that stuff. I guess this was the music of when I was a kid, all the early 80s New Wave stuff. I remember listening and writing down lyrics when I was a kid. So I felt like it was more reinvigorating. I really didn't hear anything new. I would say it was much more the reinvigorating of that type of music and being like "Oh, like this is this is the music when I was a kid.

Chris Famulari: Since it was New Wave night it was all music from the 80s. I was born in '73, so I was 10 in '83 and I only listened to the radio and MTV. A band like Flock of Seagulls, everyone obviously knows I Ran. But then there is "Space Age Love Song" ... I didn't know that song. I had never heard of it until going to ManRay. It made me go back and look at a lot of these bands that I remembered from my childhood that had more than one song, even though the radio only played one song. I discovered a lot of side songs that way. It was the feeling of your early 20s and being alive and free to do what you want but harkening back to when you were a child with New Wave music and when you were as a kid without responsibilities or bills and whatever other hell society puts on top of you. You could just forget about it for that period of time. That was what was important with the music for me. It just made me feel good because it made me remember those good times. I got to share that feeling too. There were certain songs and certain people I would dance to whenever they played. "You Spin Me Right Round" was a song Christine and I would dance to. She would specifically come over and grab me if I wasn't paying attention. I think everybody kind of had those songs.

Keith Ward: It got me into bands like The Fame and Goldfrapp. Between ManRay and the people I was hanging out with, it got me into that whole electronic scene and electronic bands that were definitely influenced by New Wave bands. I think it also has to do with DJ Chris branching out and starting to play more stuff like that, not just playing 80s, 90s New Wave alternative dancy stuff, but branching out and being like, "Alright, I'm gonna play "Ooh La La" from Goldfrapp and I'm going to play stuff from The Fame. I'm going to play and mix them in with stuff from New Wave and stuff from the 90s."

Becky D: I wasn't confident enough yet to go by myself because I didn't know anybody other than me and the random people that my boyfriend would introduce me to while we were there. I'd say after the first year I started going pretty regularly. I started going to Chris probably every other week, if not every week, and then definitely Hell. I had started to build my own group of friends and was pretty much a regular at Crypt and Hell and that crew was like, "Hey, let's go to New Wave" and that was probably the first time that I went.

Susanne Boitano: Crest of the New Wave was a radio station out of Princeton, and the first thing I heard was "Warm Leatherette" by The Normal. I was like, "What is happening to my ears? Tune that in!" Then it was this cascade of amazing early Depeche Mode, early Human League, Kraftwerk, The Fall. It just all opened up and then you could see the [kids] starting to have funny hair and the safety pins exploded. Madonna and Cyndi Lauper sort of contribute to this anything goes fashion. I was a big fashionista. I went to Trash and Board Bill, Andy's Cheapies, I had Manic Panic all over me. It was just the center of my planet and it was great.

Hideki Watanabe: I think I remember Saturday having techno in the front room. That was a big feature for me to be able to say, "Oh, let's check out the other room and go back and forth." There are so many clubs these days, just in Boston at least, where you don't have space. So having two rooms is kind of novel here. I felt it was a big draw for ManRay.

Kathy Landes: I don't think I had been to too many clubs. To be honest with you at the time, I really didn't go clubbing at all the other places in Boston. So, when I walked into this place, I just assumed this is what all clubs are like. It's really dark. So, I'm going in there and I'm just like "Where are we?" and we had stood in line before and you know you see all the characters that were outside. I'm like, "Where are you taking me?" And I mean, the characters outside were just like, you know, all the people in the leather and the chains and like not just normal leather and chains for, like, you know, 80s, early 90s. It was much more like we're talking fetish type chains and leather. It was like "Wait what's going on?" This is not like usual clubs like this can't be right. I just felt like I belonged there. It was just like this feeling of like I was a little nervous walking in. And when I walked in, we got there pretty early. It wasn't really crowded. It was really up and I was like okay this is like relaxing to me. You'd go in there and the music's playing and it's like the 80s. I don't remember what was playing, but you know, you hear, whatever. Sounds like the new wave of 80s music and I was just like, "This is wonderful. I'm like this is so cool. Let's do it."

Anna Feder: I was definitely exposed to a lot of stuff, it was maybe not new, as in it had just come out, but new to me. I feel like I had a very limited experience of New Wave music, I mean my sister was a great source for music when I was growing up. She's four years older. I'm in middle school and she's in high school and she turned me on to REM and the Cure and Depeche Mode and Siouxsie, so I feel like I got much deeper into that whole sound through going to Chris's New Wave. For me, Turn It Up was a big place in Northampton to find used cassettes or CDs. Tower Records in Harvard Square, when I would go to Boston, and Newbury Comics. Those were sort of the places that you went to get CDs.

Anna Feder: Even with Chris' New Wave party I was dressing Goth. I wasn't wearing an over-the-top costume, but I'd be wearing black and fishnet nets and boots or Mary Jane's. I'm the kind of goth that I feel like I could still go somewhere else and not totally stick out. I didn't commit fully. I fit in in the club, but I could also go somewhere else and not totally stick out. It informs your style at some point.

Keith Ward: I mean the music, definitely. The two different rooms. There was more New Wave or New Wave derivative music in the far room and then the front room was a mix of techno disco, stuff like that.

Gillian Cox: Saturdays were definitely a favorite because they gave me old New Wave music or, for that matter, what I referred to as the music from MTV when it was good, when MTV was new.

Niki Nevulis: I recall hearing about ManRay while I was going to Massasoit with my friends. I had a group of friends that used to hang out in the lounge and we met a new group of friends that I think we all really melded together because our commonality was really that we were all, I don't want to say misfits that's really just such the wrong word, but we weren't the cookie cutter mold. I'm really not too sure who said, "Hey, did you know about this club called ManRay? But I'm pretty sure that somebody probably says it's 80s night, you should come with us" and I probably said, "Sounds like fun" and followed the crowd because I really loved 80s music. I felt really comfortable with our group of friends and I trusted them. I thought we were all cool as shit because we weren't part of the mold. I was up to the adventure.

When we would go on 80s night there was that combination of light, pop-y stuff that you would hear, like Kids in America. I really loved a lot of the quirkiness of the music, the fact that there's this section of music that didn't take things overly seriously. Then there was stuff that was a little bit more, like Bauhaus and Joy Division. Joy Division is really one of the bands ManRay turned me on to the most. Joy Division, New Order, Siouxsie and the Banshees. A lot of other stuff I really listened to outside of ManRay already. Listening to a lot of music, for me, was always really important. I love music. I love listening to it. It was my escape from the hell of growing up. So, I had a pretty broad taste in music that I listen to.

Kathy Landes: I definitely was there for Saturday nights. Mostly because of school and work anyways. But also because of the 80s music. So that was my thing. I love the anthem and the New Wave and like the one room, and then the 80s going like it was fantastic. So that, to me for some reason I always went for anything, but I definitely had gone to all the other nights.

Wendy Austin: The music?? Not by choice, and not my preference. I can't stand that 80s, early 80s Euro sound.

Christina Pearson: I had different periods of time that I would go there. When I also had my work schedule and schools, getting all changed around, I would go there for all of them and I liked them all. I think that by the end of the New Wave nights, which for my memory wasn't every single week. It might have gotten to be that way. But I remember it seemed like I had to wait for them to come around like once or twice a month. And those were definitely my favorite. By the end, but I would go whenever I got a chance. And then like as a bisexual, there's like during their certain piece of it that ... I was dating a woman, Danny. We would always go to the to the gay night because we weren't you know, we felt comfortable with that sort of thing, so that you could feel comfortable anyway there at any point, but that was sort of like the girl with the Simmons girls. We were all hanging out and would all want to go. So I think I probably attended that night, more than others, but not because I liked it more just because that ended up in rotation when I was dating Danny.

Jamie DiBattista: It was great. And I loved it. We also used to go to what became Heroes. The 80s night, but I mean, originally this was the front room. They used to play. Techno then later kind of played like I remember there was a drag queen kind of and they used to kind of more play like queer club hits, but that was also fun. It was fun to kind of have two different kinds of scenes going on. You'd have the kind of the weirdo kids in the back dance in the New Wave night. And then the other weirdo club kids dancing to, I don't know, whatever, whatever, like a lot of like Madonna remixes and Cher remixes and like Britney remakes. If you have enough gin and tonics in you, man, anything is fun.

Shane Blau: I remember the front room being all dance music with a really strong dance beat and everybody just kind of grooving to that. Packed in gay boys and I never felt unwelcome in that room at all. The backroom was all 80s music — Duran Duran and "Tainted Love" by Soft Cell. I was actually an extremely non-cultured non-musical kid. I didn't grow up listening to music, other than musicals. I had almost no pop culture knowledge. I was a little young for 18 years. I just had very little knowledge going into it. So actually, all of my knowledge of 80s music comes from ManRay. I didn't know it before ManRay necessarily.

Marcia Post: I remember WFNX started in 1980 because my friend Kim kept winning all these tickets to things because they were the first station to play New Wave. I had already been introduced to that by some friends at school. That was why I went to ManRay, the music was the draw and the fact that it was women's night is even better. ManRay was the first place that my love of New Wave and The Village scene met the lesbian scene. I remember this bar called the Cubby Hole. I thought it was like the most exciting place to be because all the lesbians were there, but I stood out in my punk attire there. The typical dress for early 90s or late 80s was the Doc Martin, roll jeans, t-shirt lesbian look. But ManRay was the first place I can picture myself being kind of punk-New Wave-lesbian and being amongst others.

Maryellen Vega: I went on Saturday night, and we were in the back room. My friends wanted to take me to the 80s night. I wasn't particularly into the 80s, but I grew up listening to all that music so it just kind of brought me back, like nostalgia, and I knew all the music. I was like, oh, I kind of like this. I started going with them faithfully every Saturday.

There was one person I remember from ManRay vividly to this day. I think it was a guy dressed up like Amadeus and he always would be off dancing in the corner. I was in line one time and I'm like, "Hey, I always see you here." I'm like, "You're the Amadeus girl" and he's like "Guy"! Every Saturday this guy was there and he had the collar with the ruff, the jacket, the waistcoat, in the knickers, in the knee socks. He looked like he just came out of the 1800s from England. It was every Saturday night he was there in the 80s room. It was so funny like it was so normal. But I was like, well, I see you every Saturday.

Trent Stewart: I really liked New Wave. It lets me pretend that I'm a junior again. That was just a fun night and one had an older audience. Saturday nights were just so laid back and so relaxing. So chill. Plus, we had DJ Chris who I just adore.

Kyle Blaisdell: I became a regular almost right off the bat. We started showing up for most events and every goth night, we'd show up for New Wave and before we knew it were approached by Cusraque about Hell. My first impression of him was as just a silly little man, just a black leather musketeer in a plumed hat coming at me with flyers. That's how he made his statements. I don't think anybody walked around Boston in the 90s without a Hell flyer in their pockets. Other times we'd put on whole little parades, all dressed up, the goth crew just marching down Newbury Street, a block long just flyering every store up and down the street.

I had a friend, Brett the Unholy, who did some promotion and stuff around Boston as well. He did drag shows and worked with ManRay at the time I was showing up. He needed someone to fill in a spot for his deviant theater, so I just stepped in to fill a role for him one night. Not a big role, just man on a rack or something like that, and I guess I caught Cusraque's eye and that's when he approached me. I didn't realize you were interested, had the exhibitionism in you to get up there and entertain. We spent a lot of time together, discussing what we thought it would be. He let me run with it. I was going to develop a character — the best and worst of my ideas and egos, all magnified and just amplified out there and I would wind it up and let it go and see what happened.

Mike (Farmboy): Eventually, the second Convergence was held at ManRay.

Rachel E. Pollock: The first time I went to ManRay was probably for Convergence, the festival. I was there as somebody who was a patron, but who is a part of the event that's going on and needs to view it from a professional perspective as well as a recreational perspective. You need to worry about sightlines from two different heights and traffic to the bar on the left side and I was paying attention to the space in a very architectural sense that was tied to what I was there to do.

Tony Lee: And so, we had an entire festival planned out for basically a concert and two days, Friday and Saturday and only DJ on Sunday. We had both the front and back rooms open through the entire weekend that also coincided with ManRay going to 19 plus a couple of weeks before Convergence. So, a whole bunch of the people who came and they were 18, sort of got screwed out of being able to get in. I think some of them got it anyway, one way or another. It was pretty amazing to host. We had somebody who was actually in town from Scotland.

Tony Lee: Convergence is a North American music annual music festival that started in 1995. The idea was to throw a festival and basically get people from like alt Gothic to show up so that we can all hang out and actually meet each other in person and there'd be bands and DJ, and a whole lot of drinking. I knew a whole bunch of the people who were on the committee, so I just was like, "I will go to this thing and anything you guys want to do anything that you need for me, I will help you."

Tony Lee: It was a pretty amazing experience. I was able to meet a lot of people I was already friends with online. Got to see a lot of great bands here like great DJs and when I came back to Boston in the fall, I don't know if it was decided before or after Convergence that it would travel from city to city, but there was a bidding process and Cusraque was interested in hosting it in Boston. There have been varying degrees of success over the years, but Boston ended up winning by vote from people from alt Gothic.

Tony Lee: So, after all the tallies, Boston won the privilege of putting on the second one. The second Convergence was the one in Boston on August 9 through 11th in 1996. After winning the bid, we had a committee to put everything together. It was held at ManRay, and we booked a bunch of DJ and bands and organized, kind of a city tour. We had a program book, a shopping guide. We had a fashion show that year. I think we were the first ones to have a fashion show.

Tony Lee: Over the years a lot of the people have been to many a Convergence and whether they started at the very beginning, or somewhere in the middle, everyone's gotten older so these are things that we had to think about when we put on Convergence 25. Issues like wheelchair accessibility or, you know, if they have any sort of disability. We definitely made sure that people could get into all of the venues that we had events and that they were thought of and taken care of. We tried very hard to Involve the local New England scene as much as possible. We really wanted to bring a lot of people together for conversions. I mean, it's in the name, you know, so it was important for us to make sure that we weren't just representing our own interest, but we were kind of presenting New England, and specifically Boston in particular. We also wanted to attract younger people as well. There's been a long perception that a lot of people who go to Convergence are older and that is, to an extent, true. Yet whenever I've gone, I have always seen younger people there and we made sure that between the bands and DJ and activities there was something for everybody. Whether you were young or old, or if you like industrial music or Goth music, there was a reason for you to show up every single day and night.

Tony Lee: November 11, 1995

Doom Generation soundtrack release party at Man Ray
DJ Arcanus
Cure - Plainsong
This Mortal Coil - Another Day
Lestat - Baptism
Spiritualized - These Blues
The Wake - Christine
Mephisto Walz - Painted Black
The Mission - Wasteland
Sister Machine Gun - Crackhead!
Psychopomps - Godshit
Leæther Strip - Adrenalin Rush
X-Marks the Pedwalk - I See You
Virgin Prunes - Pagan Love Song
Einstürzende Neubauten - Feurio!
Sex Gang Children - Maurita Mayer
Skinny Puppy - K-9
Cyberaktif - Brain Dead Decision
Nine Inch Nails - Dead Souls
The Sisters of Mercy - Walk Away
Delerium - Resurrection
Coil - Love's Secret Domain
The Cure - Primary
Bauhaus - Spirit
Death in June - Runes and Men
Current '93 - Happy Birthday Pigface Christus
Rosetta Stone - Subterfuge
My Life with the Thrill Kill Kult - Kooler Than Jesus
Nine Inch Nails - Wish (Remixed by J.G. Thirlwell)
Machines of Loving Grace - Butterfly Wings
Sunshine Blind - Crescent and the Star
The Machine In The Garden - A Touch of Heaven
The Mission - Severina
Dead Can Dance - Summoning of the Muse
Fields of Nephilim - Psychonaut Lib 111
The Wake - Masked
Front 242 - Gripped by Fear

Klute - Desert Storm (Remix)
Babyland - Kill Bugs
KMFDM - A Hole in the Wall
Skinny Puppy - Worlock (ed)
Informatik - Peril Eyes
The Sisters of Mercy - Lucretia My Reflection
Psychic TV - GodStar '94
Christian Death - Romeo's Desire
Nick Cave & the Bad Seeds - Where the Wild Roses Grow
The Chameleons - Swamp Thing
Curve - On the Wheel
Strange Boutique - Hills Like White Elephants
Death in June - The Accidental Protege

Chris Ewen: We were approached by a fetish group who wanted to do something in a nightclub on a Friday night where they could have their members actually meet up in person because they just dealt with stuff online. That evolved into a fetish Friday night. The BDSM demographic hadn't really been touched upon by nightclubs. No one was really doing anything for these people so it was something new that no one else was doing and it was interesting because a lot of these people weren't really club goers per se. They did their own private parties and that sort of thing. It was interesting to work with a whole new social dynamic. When Cusraque approached us, the idea of bringing in different promoters to bring some new life into different things really began. We began doing stage performances very geared toward that community. We set up a dungeon. That brought on the idea that we could have these wonderful stage performers do things to break up the night.

Norm: It was Cusraques' personality and a lot of his creativity that drew a lot of people in the first place. His flyers, for example, are idiosyncratic, to the point of absurdity in a good way.

Chris Ewen: As far as the whole a fetish scene, we made it a point to really know what we could do and what we can get away with. Sometimes we pushed it a little bit, but never too much.

Chris Ewen: In Cusraque, we had a great promoter. He had a vision and delivered it. He and his brother were their own street team and they wanted to make something work and they did. Cusraque was really, really smart in setting up his persona with the hat and the feather and his outfit. He became a very identifiable creature of the night. Cusraque brought a complete package to ManRay with his vendors and the performances and his whole bread and fruit buffet thing and his flyers and himself. He brought a unique and dynamic atmosphere to what ManRay did.

Terri Niedzwiecki: Cusraque is, I gotta say, probably one of the best promoters. I mean, he was on the streets everywhere. And anyone who walked the path got a flyer.

Constantine Valhouli: Cusraque was an absolute genius, and we were so lucky to have him curating the music and scene of those decades in Boston. A wonderful storyteller, a pied piper, an artist, and ManRay was his palette. The theme nights and the performances were brilliant. I was in NYC at the time, and there was very little going on there to compare with what Cusraque was doing every week in Boston.

Koren Bernardi: I may have heard about ManRay through Cusraque from, you know, wandering around Harvard Square, the Pit and just seeing this very unique character in full kind of pirate theme. The brimmed hat. He was just such a character. He had these flyers for Hell and they were in this very delicate script and it was very aesthetic DIY but very different from what I've seen, so that could very well have been the first time I actually kind of connected that place and physical space with this idea that was on the flyer.

Daisy Crowder: There was an energy to his vibe that I didn't really find elsewhere.

Norm: Year two and year three for me there I worked in the dungeon. I actually ran the dungeon twice. ManRay as a BDSM club incarnation is very important to its identity and very important to understand who it was earlier on.

Rebecca Griffin: I would say most relatable for me was Friday into Saturday, but I went every night. As soon as I started going there I was there every night. My first experience on a Friday walking in was when they had the dungeons and I was like a little girl in a candy shop. Mimi was the dungeon master. Mistress Mimi, I was just enamored with her and she was just amazing.

Krista Siren: I had gone looking for clothing that would be appropriate for a fetish night. There is a shop in South End called Eros Boutique, around where they used to hold the fetish flea market in the summers, and the first time I went Mistress Mimi was working there. She helped me find suitable attire and also mentioned that she would be there on Friday night. So, I made a point of checking in with her again. She was sort of my safety person to go to like "I know this person here." I was into some kinks stuff too. So, I went ahead and engaged and hung out there for a bit with her. She was not only friendly and helpful for stuff that was outside of the scene, but there was another trans woman there about my age and she pointed me to her as being a person who might have comparable experiences with me.

Eloni Feliciano: It was extremely glamorous to me, the people on stage. There were certain people that stood out. I remember one woman had these crazy outfits with huge hair pieces. I think there were some guys picking her up and lifting her up through the entire club. They just walked her through and then they set up at a mini station in the pool room area. She did a little theatrical kind of BDSM playtime thing. I just was like, "Oh my God, she is the most beautiful woman I've ever seen."

Anna Feder: It was very exciting. I felt like, "Oh, this is Studio 54 for a bunch of different cultures" and it was just a window into a whole world that I was just able to start exploring. I had only moved out of my parents' house a couple of months before, so it was this exciting adult world where people got to do what they wanted to do, be who they wanted to be, dress how they wanted to dress, and, for me, it was a space of liberation. This was a space of exploration. This was a space where I could see what was possible in terms of how people live their lives.

Derek Kouyoumjian: Cusraque wanted me to photograph Sin performers. That's what I was allowed to photograph. Sometimes I would photograph down in the basement in the green room. As silly as it sounds, I felt it was a very appealing site to have done. It was trust given to me and I really was very humbled by that.

Norm: It started with Hell, being my regular. But that obviously changed very quickly when Fantasy Factory became more a part of what I was doing. I did a bunch of performances with Cusraque early on. It's not hard to convince me to get up on stage. I have no stage fright whatsoever. There was no such thing as rehearsal with Cusraque or it was just like we're doing this thing. I need you to do this and that, and that's it. Which was one of the things that eventually got me into Fantasy Factory.

Becky D: I met Cusraque through my friend Tim and he asked me to do a performance. I think it was based on *The Pirates of Penzance* for one of the Hells. So that was my first performance ever. I fell in love with it.

Jennifer: If you ever saw a Hell performance, which was probably the first performance I was ever in, they were just thrown together the night of and they pulled random people out of the audience. I think that's why I was in the first Hell performance. Fantasy Factory and some of the other Friday nights ended up putting a lot more time and energy into the performances. If there was a big ball coming, which was the most stressful but the most fun, then they required a lot of rehearsal.

Gibby Miller: I think it was Cusraque's helmet flyer. That dude and his hat. The velvet pants. I mean, it was like a medieval minstrel and he was the greatest.

Jen Lucky Cole: Wednesdays were really good because that's when you got the people that were regulars. It's more of a Cheers kind of atmosphere, in a sense. You know fetish things would get kind of old. I'll be quite honest, if I was paying to get in I liked Hell because it had themes. I didn't really care so much if I missed any of the other ones.

Mizery McRae: They started doing a lot of promotions for Hell and for all those other nights. They were doing a lot of photo shoots because I was in a few of them and it was amazing. It brought in more people.

Eileen Dover: On the BDSM night on Friday, it was hardcore. But everyone was respected, you know, if you were an onlooker or if you didn't want to participate you were respected. We had a good time.

Jennifer Chandler: I accidentally went on a S&M night a couple times by accident.

Kathryn Pollnac: I really liked Hell. I was actually living in Brighton with a friend or Allston when this other woman and I did a performance when they had Hell. Hell was neat. Sometimes I'd watch the performances. A lot of the time I'm just coming here to dance. And it was like, "Oh, neat." Okay, there are performances. Because it was a fetish crowd, it was a bit different but everybody I knew went too so it was sort of a nice to have that event. I would look forward to Hell because there were always themes and themes were interesting.

Chris Ewen: With Hell I was able to expand on the whole Goth industrial thing that I've been doing just to a larger crowd.

Matt Gleason: At night we used to put the security on the street and make it safe for people as much as we could. Local police were very familiar with us. A lot of them actually liked to go there sometimes. They enjoyed it. They just say like well you know there's no fights here and you know it's a little different than what they are into, but they like it because the people are good. They're dealing with people who a lot of them aren't in the right frame of mind or they're just having a bad day, but everybody at ManRay was pretty cool. You know, so they were open to it. I even and I'm not going to name any names, but I remember patrolmen even dress up and come on Fridays.

Kyle Blaisdell: If it was an event, especially if I was doing a show, it would take a whole lot more planning as far as outfit. For an event night there were often times when the groups of us would get together, there would be a theme for the night, so we kind of worked along that theme.

Rachel E. Pollock: The legal capacity was 750 people. On a regular Saturday or Friday night, there would be more than 750 people. From Cusraque's perspective, he cared about how many people because he's getting paid per person on the door.

Emily Sweeney: Yeah, I mean the nights where there was some overlap but not really. I mean, all the nights are pretty different. The two nights that are probably attended the most on a regular basis were the Wednesday night Goth nights and the Thursday night Campus nights. The monthly Friday night, you know, a big one. Usually Cusraque's nights and on Campus, I was there a lot

Emily Arkin: Hell definitely had much harder partying than Wednesday nights, which was more laid back. I think that I did not typically go on Saturday. I think I've been to Wednesdays, Thursdays, and Fridays. But I think it's Friday that I'm thinking of having the biggest "This room may have been moping in the corner and this room is grinding on each other in the cage."

Eloni Feliciano: Friday had bread and fruit and cheese on the pool table and I remember always taking little nips of it throughout the night.

Wendy Austin: Well, I think it was a great place for people who felt that it was their home. We all have bars or places that we're like "This is my second home." It was a great place for those people who really were tuned to it. I was always fascinated by the S&M aspect because I was always interested or curious about that, but seeing the one Hell I went to, I was unimpressed.

Anna Feder: I definitely gravitate towards Chris' night. I maybe went to Crypt a couple times. It was one of those things I couldn't really get to because it was during the week because I was in Western Mass. I definitely went to a few Friday nights. I feel like in Western Mass the only place to go is the Goth night. There weren't really any other options. I was going to Haven.

I would definitely come in on Fridays. I didn't really understand Hell so much, but I definitely went to see what it was. But I was uncomfortable because I didn't get it. I didn't understand. It was interesting to watch, but it felt weird watching. I'm not sure if people wanted voyeurism. I felt like, if I'm here I should be involved or participating. You don't want to feel entirely like a tourist. I get it much more now then at the time, but then I wasn't comfortable with sex. Coming from a religious background, I was entirely uncomfortable, but at the same time, I felt out of place so that wasn't really my night.

Tonya Sand: So, there was a lot of that like going to after parties and things. There was kind of like more of the hardcore kind of fetish people who were probably there that were very voyeuristic. So, there's people in the dungeon and there's people upstairs. You come downstairs and you could just sit there and be an audience, basically. You can see what's going on and have a drink. It was really cool, though it was never creepy. It wasn't a creepy vibe. It was definitely people who kind of knew what they were getting into. It was a very safe community, and people would always look out for each other.

Erika Spaulding: It just seemed more industrial on Wednesdays and more traditional Goth or maybe more romantic Goth on Fridays. Regarding music, I didn't really notice a difference because I would mostly dance in the front room. In terms of production stuff, a lot more seems to be going on on Fridays, of course, just because there's more availability.

Adam Lewis: Hell was obviously, very, very different, you know. And you had people coming in that you didn't see on other nights or or whatnot. I mean, it was the only night of the week where I would you know could potentially have you know a woman walking her husband on all fours and tell him to come up and lick my boots clean, you know, which was fine.

Crayola Tidd: My parents are pretty liberal. I'd always go to a fetish night at ManRay so they're used to hearing about ManRay. Once my father came to visit so I took him around the city. He said, "I just want to hang out with you whatever you do, day to day that's what I want to do." Then Friday came he's like "Let's go to that place you go to." I'm like, "I don't think it's appropriate." But he's like, "No, no, no. I want to go. Sounds fun." I love ManRay but you can't take a parent with you.

We got there and I told Daisy "Please don't give him hard liquor. He gets crazy. Give him beer." We're hanging out and he sees somebody across the way, and he says to one of my friends, "Wow, that woman is beautiful." My friend takes him aside and says "Listen. See that woman. She looks more beautiful than any woman you've ever seen. That's a drag queen." And my father says "Oh wow, this is cool. I love it here." I was like, "Okay, we're having too much fun." I didn't know how the night would go but he liked it.

Another time I brought my younger sister who loves 80s music and dancing, but she's much more conservative than me. I thought she's going to have so much fun but she was miserable.

Patrick Fitzgerald: Well, I mean Fridays were the big show. Hell was the big show. At that point, by the time I was 22 I would just kind of skip those for a while. One night when we were kind of seeing each other we had to leave because there were so many people in there that the humidity was so bad. There used to be like 1,500 people, you know, 800 to 1,500 people would show up during the late 90s, early 2000s. So probably '98 to 2002 were sort of a peak era or at least it was kind of reaching critical mass really before it started kind of winding down, which it did.

Patrick Fitzgerald: Cusraque put a lot of effort into it, especially back then. He was always hanging in there for like sometime in the morning until the next morning. Yeah, either decorating or taking decorations down. Hanging and stuff from the ceilings all over the walls everywhere.

A. Dominy Cusraque: Yeah, because for me, it was talking to patrons, you know, at that point and sort of because the models are just people that we knew who wore chain mail and sort of worked the crowd. And then when I started doing Hell and I was down there more regularly. I was vending my best on Fridays, and I sort of looked around and I thought, you know, this promoter isn't doing this as you were doing that. I thought of it from another customer's perspective. I mean, so I went to Vinny and I said and I basically wrote the first held flier out on the back of both other fliers and it said "Hell- In light of decadent pleasures, performances to include" and I said, "Can I do this on a Friday?" So he sort of probably begrudgingly gave me the chance. And the other promoter wasn't very into the idea because, you know, that's taking a lot of money out of their pocket.

A. Dominy Cusraque: It's possibly because Fridays were very established. You know, they had been doing what they did on Fridays for quite a while. I told him, on Wednesdays you have the Goth crowd and on Fridays you have the fetish crowd. But whereas what I was proposing hinged on decadence, you know, so both the Wednesday crowd and the Friday crowd would come on Friday and he was intrigued by that idea. So, I fliered for it a lot more aggressively than the other promoter did. You know I went up to every single person that I saw and made sure that I talked to them personally and let them know that it was a new night? And I was very excited about it.

A. Dominy Cusraque: I had one of the first laser printers that was only black and white. I had an artist who worked for me doing his end of the company called Insidious Images. OK, so Rooted Design was the umbrella for Hideous Garb and Insidious Images. I had him basically draw me instead of it being a font. And then for the rest of it, I did it in a bond called Black Chancery.

A. Dominy Cusraque: Vinny had put himself on the line for this. His job, as was on the line with Don because Don was like, Jesus Christ, or we're going to fuck with what we already have. And, you know, and they were probably getting only like 300 people, I guess something like that. So, the first thing I know, I got it set up, I had my piece of bread and fruit. I had the vendors set up. I had people in the dressing room for the performances. I don't remember what the performances were like at that time. And we walked around nine o'clock. There's going to be two people, three people in the place, 10 o'clock like five people, six people in the place, and Vinny is giving me the side eye. Looks like, "Oh shit, yeah, you're fucked." And then at 10, 30, people started to come in and more people came in and more people came in. We realized that there was a line down the block and around the corner. And eventually around 500 people showed up.

A. Dominy Cusraque: That's the first night which was, you know, they were doing probably 300 as a regular thing. And it was all because of my personal wiring. You know what I mean? Because I saw specific people that I know that I had asked them to go, you know? And I went up to each one of them as I saw them, like, thank you so much for coming. You know, wait for the performances and see the vendors and eat the bread and fruit.

A. Dominy Cusraque: I did the whole night craziness with performances going on and everything. And then at the end of the night, Vinny pulls me over and we go into the I'll for the steps to go up to Chris's booth. And he gives me a large amount of money, and I counted it. You know what I mean? And I was just, you know, adrenaline, pure adrenaline. Seeing this big stack of cash come, you know, and I counted it and then I went out and I ran into Vinny again. And mind you, it's bedlam in the place because everybody has never seen it.

A. Dominy Cusraque: I got to Vinny, and this at the end of the night. They already called last call, and it's almost one. And I said, "Hey, Vinny, I'm going to do this again." And he says, "Oh, you're going to do it again?" So, I went from every Friday to, I think, the last Friday of the month. And then eventually it was the second Friday and the month, and I started the second Friday night for the whole run. I did an anniversary in June or July, and I was on the fifth Friday. So, it ended up being 13 held. But it got sort of tiring really quick. I mean, so I started feeling the night. So, it was decorated differently, and it was also decorated in the theme. So, it was like "Hell freezes over in January" or "To Hell with February." I also had a floater night that I may, or may not, do over again.

A. Dominy Cusraque: I what they decorated with banners with congee on them, like on off, oh, I'm like going up. Well, anything written, but specifically one like on a kimono. And then I filled in the rest with fake cherry blossoms. So, you walked into a big room and it was beautiful, you know? And how about the gardens of the whole ones where I went around to every single class that I could find and follow up on if they were going to throw away because it was in full bloom, right? And then I suspended them from the ceiling of the net. So, you walked into the big room at ManRay and there were like five or six nets full of laurels. And I actually made the club smell good, which is the weirdest thing.

A. Dominy Cusraque: Sometimes the ideas come really quick and you're like, "Okay, I'm going to put them on the back burner for a while." And then there's other ones like, "I don't know what I'm going to do next". And luckily, it was a monthly incentive for weekly ideas.

A. Dominy Cusraque: I've decorated the club with borrowed mirrors and also little, tiny mirrors that I got from pearl art and all the angles, so you can look into that pad and see someone across the room. Well, yeah, but people who had like whole collections of big, huge mirrors that let me borrow them for the night, you know, which was a good testament to this, so I was regarded in the scene.

Jamie DiBattista: I remember going to the Heroes nights a couple times, maybe three or four times and then my friend, Christina and I and Christina's friend who later became my friend. I think 16 at the time had a fake ID and she flew up from Phoenix, and she was visiting and we went to the very first Hell. Wow, talk about a goddamn eye opener. Because Hell was a BDSM, and this is again, you're talking about a until recently raised Christian kid just in this environment. It was like there were no rules. We went and saw two bands playing. The first was a performance art type thing called "Women of the SS." It's just these women dressed in like skimpy Nazi outfit. By the way, not gonna play in 2020, but then it was performance and performance art obviously very dark. Like yeah, the women just kind of performing this group that was just I mean, they were very beautiful, very scantily clad I remember one of them like had a rose and some guy tried to take it from her and she was like "No, no," and she gave it to me specifically, and I felt like I belonged. And then Sleep Chamber played and they were a local industrial band. And yeah, it was just that first Hell was just crazy.

Crayola Tidd: I always went to every Friday that was fetish. And then once a month Hell night now was a total blast and that one was more really dressing up. I bought so many clothes for that night. You know, every Hell night everybody bought new clothes. It was nice to see everyone really, I think, put a lot of effort into wearing something very unique.

A. Dominy Cusraque: But I've also had people come to the door. In black, except they have a white stripe on their shoes. Yeah, OK. And I had to go and find a Sharpie and include color in the kids, probably in one-hundred-and-fifty-dollar basketball shoes. Because if they turn him away, his three or four friends that came with him are going to leave too. So, it's going to cost me X amount of money If there's one kid who can't get in because he's got a white stripe on his shoe. In the end, I was so pissed off because the people didn't understand what their dress code was supposed to be. It would be like flying and then turning away anyone not wearing black.

A. Dominy Cusraque: I had a vision that just wouldn't quit. I had this picture in my head of what I wanted a night in the club to look like. It's just that I didn't get exactly there because in my head, we are fully developed freaky. The example I always use is if someone comes through the door and is wearing a banana yellow zoot suit with the hat and for me … I want that guy in my club

Cris Concepcion: I was definitely a big fan of Wednesday nights, the main goth night. I liked going on Saturdays. And I definitely identified, both as a Goth kid as a raver as just a general like an indie kid. Yeah, I definitely liked Saturdays to be able to go to both places. Certainly, after a year after '96 when I graduated, this is always just like, there's a lot of other things and I compete for it. But I definitely went all the time on Wednesday nights. I liked fantasy factories. I liked Hell.

Paul Calnan: I would say the two nights that we frequent the most were Hell and then Wednesday's Crypt. Overall, we just really liked the vibe on those nights, we loved the spectacle of it all. You know I became fairly friendly with Cusraque, back then. We all knew him, he knew all of us. We'd see him out at shows, and so it just became more like a family environment. You'd walk in and everybody knows you.

A. Dominy Cusraque: The team was basically the person who drove me around. Because the first couple of Hell's, it was me driving. But in June of 94, I had some health problems, and it made me not able to drive. And so the day of, someone drove me around and drove me to the place where I got wholesale fruit from. I went there for the whole run of Hell. So 10 years of going to this place for fruit and another place for bread.

A. Dominy Cusraque: Ooze was basically built around a particular performance and that was the main thing, you went for the performance. I would help them promote When you go into the big room, they had boxes right there and the dancers would stand on the boxes in costume.

A. Dominy Cusraque: OK, so you got to get them. And not only that, but if they get on a flier for your monthly night a month in advance, when you want to remind them to go, they don't want to hear from the guy. We already got a flier for that, but then they won't show up, you know, I mean, because they forgot about it. So what you do for a month and night, I say start two weeks in advance. So, I would give you a flier two weeks in advance. You would remember and show up in two weeks and get the next flier for the next one.

A. Dominy Cusraque: Promotion is the main thing and I make no bones about it.

Greg Frisbee: As far as the cultures go, whether it was the LGBT community, or the Goth kids, or the industrial kids, or the New Wave kids, or the grunge kids, all these people who didn't necessarily feel like they had a club, or a home, or a place to hang out, or go dancing was due to the fear of not being accepted ... ManRay was that place. I'm going to go here to the place of no judgment where I can be me.

Niki Nevulis: Between 1991 and 1997, I think we were in a really good place in time. A lot of times I'm kind of jealous that we weren't part of the post punk era, but at the same time we were at that transition point into grunge music and we had listened to glam metal. I think we had the best of all the world. I think we were the last real generation to appreciate going out and kind of having those experiences. I think the generation within the 10-year period before us probably spent more time in The Rat and in The Middle East. We also get to experience The Middle East and The Rat towards the sad end. I would say we got to experience the best of the Boston clubs. It makes me sad that these clubs just don't exist now.

Chapter 10

A Night on the Town: Preparation, Dress, and the Door

"Clothes were the ritual." — Emily Arkin

A carefully crafted outfit is laid out on the bed, pieces courtesy of Hubba Hubba or the Garment District. Siouxsie is playing in the background as elbows are thrown for mirror space. The ride will be a fair distance with three stops to pick up more friends, so everything needs to be done right. The wait in line on the street will hopefully provide some good inspiration for a future visit from the other excited club goers and their styles.

The ritual of getting ready for a night out at any club is key, maybe even one of the most important parts of the whole experience. For ManRay that was even truer. Whether it was an all-black, head-to-toe ensemble or an elaborate costume that you had spent weeks shopping for and creating, ManRay provided a space for people to explore and be themselves. It became a home for many subcultures that may not have had a space to call their own otherwise, such as the LGBTQ+ community, the fetish community, Goths, punks, New Wavers, and everyone in between. Its numerous theme nights and concert events created an even wider space for people to become whoever they wanted to be and find acceptance with a community of like-minded people. S.L.

Keith Ward: Going to Boston was a big thing. Growing up and being in college became less and less of a big thing and more of just I'm going out with my friends, but you were opened up to so much more in regard to cultures and subcultures. I'm sure you remember the first time you ever walked into Hubba Hubba and we're like, "What is this? This is a real thing?"

Me'lissa Nin: You'd start getting ready at two or three in the afternoon, maybe five o'clock if you were working. You take your shower and then you'd do your hair and your makeup, and you'd spend forever trying to figure out what the hell to wear? For me, it was not a lot of planning, it was more on the fly. I was going through 80 billion different outfit combinations and then finally realized, "Oh my God, look at the time! I better throw something together!" There were times that I didn't have a lot of money. I was scrounging, like so many others, so I had to get creative. We didn't have ready-made Goth clothes. It was just DIY. One of my favorite outfits consisted of this skirt that I made out of this black oval or oblong shaped tablecloth. I can't even tell you how many compliments I got on that damn tablecloth skirt. Nobody believed me.

Mizery McRae: The level of creativity. The ability to create how you're going to look tonight back then you could use anything and make it into an outfit. You could tear up a t- shirt. You can literally take a pair of scissors and cut the neck out and a half shoulder and it would be a dress. A shirt could be used as a skirt. I think people have forgotten that creativity. I think the DIY aesthetic is important. If you're going to Avalon or Venus de Milo, maybe brands are important. If you didn't have Vivienne Westwood or any kind of designer, you would be looked down upon.

Rebecca Corbett: I did a lot of sewing. I would either make my own patterns and create my clothes or I would go to thrift stores and find something really cool looking and alter it for ManRay. That was a big, big part of getting ready clothing-wise. It was way before the days of Hot Topic. I had black corsets. I would buy fishnet and tear it, or I'd buy tulle to create skirts to wear underneath my corsets. A lot of my makeup was, because I was a poor college student, 99 cent black lipstick. I found a foundation that was white, and black eyeliner and mascara. I would take black eye shadow and put it almost like blush to create contouring.

Crayola Tidd: I have a ritual. My friend Frankie and I went together to all of the nights. We were going to all the same places so he would ring me up and we would always talk about what we were going to wear, which seems hilarious now because I would dress like a schoolgirl and he was in what I call Gothic loungewear.

Athena Costa: Even though I'm a goth person I have a wide eclectic taste in music. So, before I go out dancing and also when I'm driving home, I listen to rap music. I usually have an idea of what I want to wear, depending on the night, and I would cycle through like four different outfits and be like, "I don't know. I don't know." Once I put it on and I had a drawer of tights and I went through like 15 pairs. Then it comes together. I never really had a lot of accessories. I only had like one purse, which was mainly to hold my gigantic Nokia phone.

Amy Butts: I probably planned my outfits the day before or the day of. I was always very particular about not wearing the same thing for a while, but I also had favorite outfits and it was hard not to wear your favorite outfit all the time. Those first four years I went to ManRay with a lot of my best friends that I lived with in a dorm. We would all get ready together but separately in our rooms, constantly running back and forth asking if this looked okay or should I wear this or that? It was really fun to get together with everybody. It was like a nice social experience. Then we all descended upon the club. I remember parking in the parking garage and the walk from the to the club and you just get so excited.

Erika Spaulding: I was a pretty easy dresser. I've never been too complicated. Fortunately, with the dress code being all black, everything matches easily.

Eloni Feliciano: I used to have these little tips and tricks to get myself into things. I figured out how to lace up my own corsets and also create quick releases just in case. You want to be able to release that immediately.

Julia Kilcoyne: I always felt like I am not pretty enough for certain clubs. I'm not fashionable enough for this place. But at ManRay, I felt like I can own this, and I felt like the belle of the ball 90 percent of the time. That was a pretty new experience for me. All my shoes literally made me taller. If you're six foot two you kind of take over a room and people are going to come to you. It was pretty neat to feel that way.

Jenny Dahling: Typically for the fetish nights, I planned those well in advance. I remember I literally just wore nipple clamps as my top as no one told me that you're not supposed to leave them on for over an hour. Oh my God when I took them off … They were sore for about a week. As a girl you're supposed to really glam it up, so you kind of need to decide whether you're going to go by 8 o'clock or so. Keep in mind, I live about 20 minutes away and I had to figure that in as well. From bath to out the door it took me three hours between shaving legs, blow drying hair, and putting on makeup.

Eloni Feliciano: I think the different nights have different levels of prep work to them. For Hell and Crypt on Wednesdays you could just come up with something pretty fancy on the fly. Maybe the day before you kind of get a general idea for it. It would still take as long to get ready, but it was something that you didn't need some super concept for. The fetish nights, Fantasy Factory specifically, usually took a lot more prep work. Anything that was latex obviously had to be thought about way in advance because you have to prepare for that and get the lube and make sure that it's not broken when you put it on. The different themes needed thought too.

Russ Carter: For some people, it was the pageantry, if you will. Some of us felt like jaded old school elitist douchebags. This was a way of life for us every fucking day. We got up on Monday morning, put your fucking hair up, put your stupid fucking thing on. We just made clothes. Most of us are from that area, we weren't college kids. We weren't paying for clothes. We were kind of like derelicts and so we didn't really have any fucking money. So, we often made our own clothes.

Chris Manousaridis: When I first started going it was very simple. It was black t-shirt and black pants or a black button down with black pants. That was my go-to. As I progressed, I started to take little shopping trips here at Hot Topic or Hubba Hubba and picking up things little by little. A really good friend of mine, Ashton, made leather work. I was getting some pieces from him, so it built up. At the same time, I was also doing marketing, so I would incorporate some of that. I had poet shirts and leather jackets. My mother said I was always such a mortician because I was in all black. Being a ManRay patron kind of changed a little bit of my style. So, I was wearing the trip pants with the chains. I was wearing black T-shirts with mesh underneath.

Anastasia Taslis: One of my favorite parts actually was getting ready. Most of the time I'd sew and make a lot of my own stuff. I'm a plus sized person so, especially back then, there was no plus size clothes and club wear. You couldn't just go on the Internet. I remember going shopping at Frederick's of Hollywood to get corsets. Because we went to college up in Beverly, we would go to the Salvation Army on Route 1 and go hunting. I found a really great dress I wore like a million times to ManRay, a black and white striped dress. I've always been a huge makeup person, so I loved being able to wear all the black eyeliner and all the eye shadow. I would spend a good hour and a half, two hours getting ready listening to music. It wasn't Goth, I would save it for the club. I would listen to funk and Stevie Wonder and upbeat music, like disco. I'd never drink while I was getting ready because I had to concentrate on my eye makeup. When it was fully done and ready to go, I would have my first drink.

Shane Blau: I remember agonizing about getting ready. We were freshmen. I was in a dorm. I had a roommate. There was no mirror in my room. So, you had to go all the way down the hallway to the common area to find a full-length mirror. I remember running back and forth from my room to the full-length mirror.

Paul Calnan: My wife and I used to probably fight each other for the mirror in the bathroom getting ready to go to ManRay. We spent a lot of time. I myself had long hair and it was dyed all kinds of crazy colors, so I blow dried, I flat ironed, I'd spike it up. Lots of makeup. Clothes wise, Allston Beat was one place I would shop. Then there was Hubba Hubba and there was another place in the Garage in Harvard Square, Hootenanny. We definitely bought a few things from Hot Topic. Serious Clothing and Lip Service were two of the brands that we bought a lot of. We would always pre-game, having a few drinks while people were showing up. We would be listening to Ministry and various electronic dance and industrial music.

Benny Blanco: For me, the fashion was pretty simple, it was a t-shirt, jeans, and Docs. While getting ready we would make dinner and put on a mixtape. At the time it was more of the rave stuff, the newer music that was coming out versus the old. There was the prep of the girls that I hung out with. They would get dressed up and I would just hang out, listen to music, and cook food. There's definitely a "You're going out tonight" energy. Even though you're doing this week after week after week, there's still excitement for going out and doing what you love. It was just part of the lifestyle.

One of my old roommates, Hoss, was a miracle worker because he would go pick up people from all over town and get everyone to ManRay and then drive everyone home or to the IHOP in Brighton. Hoss was integral to getting people there. This one girl, Casey, lived in Providence and he would drive there, sleep for an hour and half at his mom's place, and go to work. We did road trips to go to parties. We would calculate "Oh, it's one and a half mixtapes" to get there and a typical mixtape would be 90 minutes, 45 minutes each side.

Mizery McRae: When I was outside, I saw people literally changing in their cars, putting their tight pants on and their shirts on. At the end of the night, you would see them go back in the car and do exactly the same thing but change back into their regular clothes.

Gibby Miller: For me, I'd put on Sisters of Mercy or whatever you were listening to that night. I love the ritual of getting ready to go out. Typically, my friend would come over and we would crack open a beer, start listening to records, and pregame. At the time, I was in art school and the indie rock scene was huge, so my outfits were less loud, a little bit more integrated. I'd wear a leather jacket or black jean jacket and a t-shirt with rips in it with a pair of black Levi's and black boots.

Gene Dante: It would have taken at least an hour to get ready. As a performance artist you got to the club super early to get ready there.

Nate Roman: It was clear that in this scene it was important you find a way to be unique and express yourself. There's an authenticity to Goth stuff and it's not about that you have a cool outfit. I've spent a lot of time putting together outfits. I'd go to the hardware store and get hose clamps, bicycle chains, stuff like that. My hair was like a vertical thorn bush. Prep was different because I felt like I was there to be contributing to it. I definitely had a look, and it became my signature.

Greg Frisbee: I didn't have a huge process to get ready in terms of what I wore. I never got decked out wearing all black or getting myself too made up. I guess we all kind of had a style of how we were dressing in the 90s. Maybe it was an alternative kind of flannel shirt with baggy shorts or pants. I have to at least wear black or they're not gonna let me in, I can't show up in jeans, because that's a definite no no. So, there was a certain dress code in terms of if I'm going to either wear my alternative-y clothing with really baggy oversized shorts or pants and a baggy shirt.

Emily Taylor: I remember in the early, early days, my friend Aaron would make mixtapes all the time. He had bands like Pig Face and Twitch, and more industrial stuff. I had CDs like Nine Inch Nails, The Cure, Nick Cave,

Dead Can Dance, that kind of stuff. I would be driving down the highway doing my makeup. I was really blessed with perfect skin growing up. so, I would really just throw on eyeliner and lipstick and that would be good enough.

The first couple times I went to Ceremony and ManRay I got ready in my sister's dorm room at Mass Art and we would paint elaborate eyeliner all over my face, which was really fun. Those are precious times. Then later on my friend Jillian lived up the street from ManRay, so I would go over to her house and we would hang out for a while, probably eat dinner, and then we would start getting ready for the club. We would put on some music, things like Chicks on Speed and Le Tigre and other girl power music. She would lace my corset. She was always wearing latex. I wasn't really super into latex, but I would help her get into the latex. I remember her downstairs neighbor finally complained because we were clomping around in our high heels too much for him around 9:30 to 10 on a Friday night. He'd be like, "Arghh! I hate these women in their high heels!" And I was like, "Dude, you have to understand. You gotta put your shoes on before your corset because once that corset is on, you can't put shoes on." Then we would tromp down to ManRay.

Jen Lucky Cole: I worked at Tower Records and I bought this fancy lamp that had three different colored light bulbs and a black light, and I had this fancy mirror in my room. I would be listening to some Christian Death and I would see how my makeup looked between each of the different colored lights because I wanted a high look in the club lighting. It didn't matter what I looked like in my bathroom lights, what matters is what it looked like in the club lights. I'd turn all of the lights on and stood there and just started swirling around in the mirror.

Hyson Concepcion: I had a friend Rebecca who'd recently moved to the area and recently discovered ManRay. We met through a mutual friend and she was very striking. She was tall and had this amazing head of curly strawberry blonde hair and she was beautifully statuesque. We were just hanging out and it was probably a Wednesday, maybe Hell night, I don't know, but we decided to go to ManRay. But I was totally not dressed for it. I borrowed something from her and we really weren't the same size. I ended up borrowing a pair of her fishnets and I was already wearing black shoes. I borrowed a dress except it actually wasn't a dress, it was a slip. It was backless. It was part of a two-piece outfit. It was supposed to go under this lace overlay, and it was a little bit different. I was really, really, really skinny in those days, like scrawny and I was wearing this black slip that wasn't even really a dress. This friend always had all these interesting pens and markers that were invisible but would glow under black light, and she drew all over my back. There were a lot of black lights and apparently, as I walked through the club, it would sort of appear and disappear. Total strangers, not all of them sober, were grabbing me by the arm and asking me very intensely "What is on your back?" I only got the reaction. I never actually saw it.

Rick Webb: We would prep together. Megan would come over and we would all dress up together. Jessie would put a ton of effort into getting ready because she had giant hair. I had white short hair and I just wore black. I still have my awesome leather jacket from Hubba Hubba. I bought a lot of good shoes there too, but mainly I was just wearing black. We got ready at the house and we would all drink a little bit beforehand. Jessie didn't drink and Megan had a car, which was great, because Jessie would drive Megan's car. We lived in Allston, and we'd sing this weird stupid song, just a nonsense song about bacon.

Anna Feder: I would definitely start listening to the music that might be playing. I was one of the people who, even if I was going to hear that song later that night, it didn't matter. It was about building excitement and there was a lot of attention paid to makeup and hair accessories. My boyfriend at the time had a uniform he would always wear, sort of black jeans and combat boots and some kind of band t-shirt. His look was pretty simple. He would do eyeliner for sure and sometimes nail polish. I didn't have lots of money for some of the things I'd see people wearing. I was not a leather person or corset person. I definitely had big clunky Doc Martin Mary Jane's and never wore pants. I was always in skirts and dresses, which is funny because at Hasidic school I had to wear those. For a while I rebelled and every time, I left I would put on jeans or pants. In college I didn't enjoy wearing pants, so I was always in skirts and dresses. I experimented by dyeing my hair black … that did not stay very long. It takes a long time to grow out my hair and there is the awkward in-between stage. I was playing with lots of different things.

A. Dorian Rose: While getting ready, I was always playing CDs. Sisters of Mercy is just such a go to for me in so many ways. I did the white face thing. I went through stages where it was more caked on, but I really wanted too just be more pale. I successfully made my image pretty. Sometimes I didn't have a good sense of blending, so there's some things that I could have done a bit better. I had shaved sides of my hair at the time. I'd let my mohawk grow out and it was orange.

Brian Legault: I'm a biotech consultant and I had to dress for a day job. Colored shirts, dress pants, and then I swapped out. Most of my wardrobe was black, but I wasn't strict about it. I'm living out of my suitcase at this time too, so there's only so much room. I was mixing and matching a little bit most of the time. I'm actually more of an industrialist so I've always got band T-shirts. In my quick dressing down, as I take off the dress shirt, I've got an industrial or metal shirt underneath.

Xtine Santakas: I would get home from work and make myself a quick dinner. I'd have a pre drink. I would put on The Cure or Depeche Mode. For Christmas, Chris would give out CDs and mixes that he created, and I would put one of those on. Getting ready was a ritual. It wasn't just throwing yourself together. I started picking out my outfits on Monday for both Wednesday and Friday. Then Sunday was always laundry day. I made sure all my Goth clothes were ready for the week. My Goth clothes are more important than my work ones.

Jennifer: The times I put the most effort into my outfits was definitely when I was working for Fantasy Factory. There was a lot more pressure to look a certain way. You had to deal with themes every night. We were always last-minute scrambling for costumes. The night before we'd all be together at someone's house putting together and sewing stuff and seeing what bits and pieces, we can borrow from each other to make whatever the next night's scene come to life.

Kathy Landes: I didn't put a ton of thought into my outfits because I just wore black. If I really had to get something good, like tights or fishnet, I would try to visit Hubba Hubba and see what I could get every now and then. For the most part I wore my little black dress or some fishnet tights or other tights with black shorts and some sort of top depended on how cold it was. I never wanted to wear a coat.

Jenn Sutkowski: My hair was very short at the time, so I didn't really have much to do. All of the black liquid eyeliner. I had two different Revlon BlackBerry lipsticks and there was also this matte eggplant. That was like the darkest lipstick without it being black that you could find. And then clothes. Lots of black tights or fishnets. Big boots, the higher the platform the better. I remember I had this pair that had like three huge Velcro straps. Then the rest of the pregame. We would get ready for Wednesday's in our dorm at BU. Then we would go to my friend's on campus housing and watch Beverly Hills 90210 and Melrose Place.

Rebecca Griffin: I didn't have an iPod or anything. I had a lot of punk CDs so I would just throw in something like that. It doesn't take me too much to get amped to go to ManRay, that's for sure.

Kara Nemergut: I don't know that I would necessarily plan my outfits in advance, but I had kind of a section of my wardrobe that was more what I would wear to clubs. A lot of it was crop tops and leather pants. I lived with a drag queen one summer, towards the end of 2004, so I used to get him to do my makeup when I was going because I'm not necessarily super great at makeup.

Matt Richard: I was regular on Friday nights. There were a bunch of us that would come down from Salem. I would get out of work for my second job at 11 o'clock, which was a liquor store in Salem. I would close the grate, get changed into my black pants. In 2004 I think I started wearing kilts or black PVC pants. I'd get changed in the liquor store and I jumped in the car and drove to Boston. I'd either pick up two people on the way, or it would be arranged that I would take three people home who wanted to stay all night at the club till the end.

Melanie Sharkey: So, my friend Mary Beth and I would hang out in the bathroom blasting Depeche Mode because that was her favorite band. I feel like we also did a little bit of Duran Duran and Madonna. So, we would listen to music while we were getting ready. I have a lot of great memories of just eyeliner and jockeying for position in the mirror. She wore more basic black fishnets while I often wore raver-like pants and a tank top. I really liked tank tops for dancing.

Guari Desi-Ackerman: I definitely had more of a homemade look, but my homemade look looked good because I used a lot of my Indian clothes. I definitely mixed and matched a lot of the skirts and jewelry that I had with cut out stockings and corsets and stuff like that. I had a certain look that I always went for. I also had a couple of pieces that I picked up when I was in London that I would sort of repurpose for going out clubbing. It was a lot of mix and matching, a lot of patchwork.

Lucretia X Machina: I'm a planner and I needed a theme to decide what I was going to wear. Mostly 90 percent black. I'm cheap so I would go to thrift stores or Goodwill. Then I started looking at Hubba Hubba, which was in Central Square at the time.

In the beginning, I was listening to the radio. I had WFNX on until it didn't exist. I would leave by nine so I can get there at 9:30 when it opens. I would get the discount if there was one and I would stay until almost the end. I never drove. I am a non-driver for life. I was dependent on the number 70 bus and, luckily, it's direct to Central Square. I would have to leave an hour or two before the last bus left.

Jamie DiBattista: I bought these green Doc Martens from Allston Beat, which no longer exists. Allston Beat was like Hot Topic before Hot Topic. Hot Topic is like the mainstream version of Allston Beat. My outfit was the green Doc Martens and fishnet stockings. I had this black and white checkered skirt that I got from the Garment District. Then the choker with The Cure hair. Then eyeshadow the eyeliner.

I would get ready at my house. When I was getting ready, I would listen to a local Stonehill College station. On Friday nights they would play electronic and industrial music. Our friend would pick us up and we would go to her place and pregame, which pretty much just meant drinking a lot. We had a friend, Jimmy Reject, who was 21. The rest of us were like 19, 20. He would just buy us shitty booze and we would just get really drunk. We would drive into Cambridge and then get more drunk in the parking lot before we would head in, usually about 11 to 11:30.

Hyson Concepcion: My go-to album to listen to when getting ready for a night out was not a very ManRay sort of album but I stand by its excellence: Fear of Music by Talking Heads. I lived in Boston during the academic year, which meant the chances were, if I was going out to a club, it would be cold. So, there was always the challenge of how to wear sexy skimpy club clothes … and bear in mind that coat checks charged by the item. Even if you're wearing your boots with fishnets it can be pretty cold, considering how far you have to walk. Once I changed my clothes in the bathroom of a store.

Cris Concepcion: I was a pretty low maintenance person when it came to getting dressed. I went to a lot of boarding religious schools when I was younger, so I was very much used to a uniform. Going to ManRay, I was very much a black jean, band t-shirt, leather jacket kind of Goth person. I certainly shopped a lot at Newbury Comics. I never got tattoos. I didn't really push along those particular boundaries, but I love being in a space where other people were really pushing beyond and flaunting a whole bunch of other ideas about fashion. Being able to be a part of that was really great. You had people who borrowed fashion from both genders. I had a lot of respect for somebody who just knew enough about themselves. This is who I am. This is who I want to be. Take it or leave it.

Hideki Watanabe: I would often spend an hour and a half to get prepared and I would pick my outfits that day. I would see what I had in the closet and what I wanted. Near the earlier times, I lived with some people at Berklee School of Music, and I wasn't quite comfortable wearing a skirt in public. I wouldn't want to walk out in front of them, so I had like this trench coat that I would wear to hide from them.

My makeup was very simple, just black lipstick or eyeliner. It was more about trying to figure out some outfit that didn't look like a repeat.

Arlene Guerrero-Watanabe: The ritual of getting ready for ManRay involved a few drinks, preferably with friends. In the early days, with my grad school friends who are Goths, we did our outfits at home and then we would go to each other's apartments and have a few drinks and do our makeup, which took like an hour at least. Really good makeup. I guess we were listening to stuff like Sisters of Mercy, Bauhaus, and Gary Numan. We had skulls and candles, black curtains, and spider webs. This is our whole entire way of living and it was very aesthetic.

Gillian Cox: I had this particular little basket of mixed tapes. I've got to be able to sing to Sisters Mercy. Or ,if it was for a Saturday, I'd have to be listening to New Wave: David Bowie or Joy Division.

Chris Famulari: Every ManRay night would consist of me usually listening to music that I didn't think I was going to hear. For example, if it was Saturday night and it's mostly New Wave, I'd listen to Nine Inch Nails. I would usually get some sort of Gatorade or fruit punch, drink half of it, and fill it up with something like Southern Comfort or vodka. Then I got picked up and, whoever wasn't driving, would start drinking the whole way.

Oh clothes, I went through a lot of different things. I wasn't always comfortable with my weight or the way that I looked, so I would wear baggy things and usually a black button shirt. I had a pair of black pants that were really comfortable, and I wore my dad's dancing shoes. Occasionally, I would wear a full-length pantyhose underneath my clothes without any underwear so that I would feel a little loosey goosey. One day I got something in the mail that said, "Do you want to try our free plus size women's pantyhose?" and I ordered a pair. I got it specifically to wear to ManRay. I remember the first night I did it, I felt a little weird, but then I was doing it all the time and nobody knew the difference.

Heather Morgan: I did a lot of shopping and a lot of collecting clothes during my free time, so I would always have a ton of things laying around in my room. I would spend an hour cranking my stereo, Tones on Tail and Bauhaus. I was dyeing my hair at the same time as I was trying on clothes. I put everything in my hair: Elmer's glue, gelatin, Aqua Net and then I graduated to this big yellow can, It. My friend Russ showed me how you could spray your hair with It into one massive spike and then break it down like straw, then we all had hair like Nick Fiend for a while.

Niki Nevulis: I had some stuff in my closet, but I'd never been to the Garment District. I had such a limited budget that I just made do with what I had and I would just make it work. I didn't feel like I had to be anything different than myself so more of my preparation was around makeup and hair. Heavy black eyeliner. My hair was a little bit shorter at the time, so I really had the Winona Ryder/Lydia look going.

It was more musical prep for me. I had a bunch of tapes and CDs, all the different bests of the 80s and New Wave. I always love to hear things like Kids in America, ABC, Human League, Soft Cell. I'd listened to a little bit of Joy Division and then New Order and Siouxsie, what they probably called Dark Wave now. Coming from the South Shore, it probably took us an hour to get in so you had all that time to listen to stuff. I still get excited when the Safety Dance comes on. A Flock of Seagulls, Don't You Forget About Me, it would always be some of that stuff that we would listen to and play on rotation.

Liz Lamanche: I'm more of a visual person so my preparation is more about getting dressed in front of the mirror than about listening to music. There were a couple of standout times when a friend and I would, either at my house or her house, go through the wardrobe and try things on and get dressed and do our makeup to make sure we look good. Getting ready was more important for the Goth and fetish nights, because the other nights I felt like I could just put something on that looks good and go out. Whereas costuming was quite central to the Goth and fetish nights.

David Winthrop: My nights would usually wind up waiting for the girls I was going with. A lot of makeup time, a lot of hair time. I was a pretty simple ManRay dresser for the most part. There were times where I got creative with rubber outfits. These are the days before you can just order everything off the Internet, so you would be going to Hubba Hubba or something like Hootenanny.

Susanne Boitano: It would start with putting together my outfit, going around town to different vintage places and places like Hubba Hubba. To me, part of the sensory and fun of it was to dress up, the art of it. The fishnet and the lipstick and running around that afternoon. Saturday was a whole day of putting yourself together for Saturday night to go to ManRay. You get up around 2 and then you might go down the street and get pizza and those big malt liquors because you are poor. Then pregame by playing all the music you're going to want to hear. I went all over, but definitely Depeche Mode, Human League, Kraftwerk. On the industrial side, Throbbing Gristle and SDK. I loved the local band Think Tree. I thought they really had a great sound to them. When it started to get dark, when it was appropriate to go out, I'd go to the subway because I wouldn't want to drive all dressed up. There's always a challenge to how much you can cover up. So there's a wonderful balance. Later in life I had money for a cab which seemed like a godsend.

Adam Wolff: Are you kidding? We spent all week thinking about what we're going to wear next week. We would go around to all the places. As a promoter, I was putting out flyers for ManRay for my own events, so I'd be all over and I'd run down Newbury Street and hit all the little places down there. There used to be all these great shops. Now it's all just fucking generic brand name mall stores. It used to be all these little record stores and fucking great little clothing stores and Newbury Comics.

Elizabeth Galbraith: For me, I've never really been someone that takes forever putting on makeup. I'm slightly low maintenance for being in the Goth category. I've always had shorter hair. I did go out and get my hair braided one year, I think I sat for three or four hours getting that done.

Maryellen Vega: It wasn't intense. I used to have a bob haircut parted in the middle. I used to wear liquid eyeliner and I would have it on all day. I would change my clothes and it was usually a PVC skirt or something funky and some sort of Docs. I had all different color Docs: white ones, velvet ones, black ones.

Karla Clute: Getting ready for Ceremony, especially in the early days, was a two-hour event. I listened to a lot of industrial music, Skinny Puppy, and a lot of Nine Inch Nails. I would try everything on in my closet and see what I liked most, which was probably a good 45 minutes.

Marcia Post: Fashion-wise I was into some weird punk-lesbian-mix fashion. I wasn't really dressing any differently to go to classes or to ManRay. For me to come out as lesbian, my path was through punk because it was punk music and New York City punk scene that let me kind of find space. Punk was like the anti-establishment safe space if you don't want to be a conforming nice girl. Being a lesbian, there was a uniform you were supposed to have, and I was not that. I tried to do a flannel shirt, but I was always feminine, so I did not feel like that aesthetic was me. So, I would go to get dressed in my office in skirts that I ripped up with fishnets in kind of like a Cyndi Lauper meets Pat Benatar look.

Adam Lewis: I was shit at putting on makeup. I'm six foot six so you do not get a lot of fashion stuff that's going to fit you. I have got to improvise. So, I was just wearing a lot of black and doing the best I could. I remember buying a ridiculous pair of boots at Allston Beat. They had kind of like creeper shoes that had skulls. Just ridiculous. I also bought a ridiculous pair of boots that were right out of Mad Max. They had metal shin guards and were almost up to your knee. People would notice them walking down the street. I even wore them around college.

Emily Arkin: Clothes were the ritual. I don't think I pre-gamed with music or alcohol or anything, but I would get ready in the mirror with friends where I would be like, "Is this enough black eyeliner?" "No, you need much more black eyeliner." We would shop for clothes and we would pick things out where you'd be like, this is too low cut for real life, but it's perfect for ManRay. We would go to Gypsy Moon, which is more in a velvet sort of hippie vein. Dollar a Pound and just the regular Garment District with all their vintage clothes. It's kind of amazing that two of those three places are still around, which is really nuts.

Chris Ewen: The connection was Susie Phelps, the owner of Hubba Hubba. It just seemed like a marriage made in heaven. She wanted to dress the people that came to our place and we wanted to have her do that. It was a time when you could do mail order, but you just couldn't go online and order your cool outfits. She made a point of catering to lifestyles that ManRay represented on different nights. There have been a couple other stores in the Boston area along those lines, but I think Susie's sensibility fit the ManRay people the best. That was part of Susie's punk rock sensibility: "We're here to make you look great and feel good." You could go there, and you were never questioned on your sexual tastes or preferences or what you wanted to do with any of this stuff. It was like "We will make you feel good and look good. You're here to be beautiful and we are going to meet you." Hubba Hubba and ManRay had a symbiotic relationship and that continues to this day.

MJ Pullins: One of the reasons Hubba Hubba exists today is because of ManRay. Of course, it started off as a punk rock store. It was the first place in Boston to carry Doc Martens and various other brands. One of the keys to longevity is its ability to move with the markets and the communities. We've been very open and attuned to transgender and nonbinary and things like that because that's where things are moving. We must be nimble and be able to change and reflect the community and serve the community's needs. In the end, it is a community store. I have a sign in there: It's your community store, you need to tell me what you need. Because that's what happened with ManRay. As ManRay opened around the corner people would come in and say, "Hey, I need this. We need this clothing." And, as ManRay got more BDSM, it became "Hey, we need these toys" so the store pivoted into more of that.

MJ Pullins: Susie always said, "go forth and be fabulous." I mean, that's exactly right. Go forth and go to ManRay. Go forth, take what I am giving you, what I have helped you put together and go be fabulous. Her job was giving you the tools to help you be the best you could, to go live your life, to go live your dreams.

ML: Hubba Hubba was a big place to go because they had a lot of diverse stuff. There was a secondhand store that we used to hit on Newbury Street. They used to have some fun stuff.

Abigail Taylor: There was a store in Marshfield for a while that was tucked away near where town hall was. There was this little thrift store that had all kinds of things. I got cool necklaces and scarves and this Victorian era skirt petticoat that I wore all the time. Lots of old band T-shirts. When I was getting ready I would normally go to a friend's house to front load. We would drink wine and put on makeup and figure out our outfits. Sometimes we'd like to swap clothes.

Abigail Taylor: If it was a Friday night, and there was a theme, I would try to figure out some kind of theme. But if I was just going on a Wednesday, I would frequent a lot of thrift stores, trying to find cool flowing black clothes or fishnets. I would go to the Garment District all the time. In fact, I worked for the Garment District for several years.

Emily Taylor: As time went on, I would put a lot less effort into my outfits. Also, I would get ready at ManRay because I would be in the dressing room. I would show up in street clothes and I would be making costumes for the people there, cutting up black cloth and wrapping it around them or making outfits out of Saran wrap or electrical tape or caution tape or latex or whatever was around just taping these kinds of outfits together for the dancers, which is fun. Sometimes, if I really wanted to treat myself and I had extra money, I would go to Hubba Hubba. I loved those days because I was like, "I'm gonna look really hot. I'm going to have a new outfit and everybody's gonna be like 'Your outfit is so cool!'" I would go in, try out a bunch of shit and find something new and probably drop like $200 to $300 on it, which at that point in my life was a lot of money.

Jen Lucky Cole: I hate to pretend I didn't get stuff from Hot Topic, but....

Rachel E. Pollock: We were involved in a lot of online arguments about if it was okay to buy clothes at Hot Topic and wear them to ManRay and other Goth clubs.

Prospero Eaton: I didn't necessarily go to the Boston/Cambridge area to fulfill the need for clothes that often. I did a lot of my shopping just at Hot Topic. They had some nice stuff back then. As far as how I prepared, I did plan out ahead of time. I can envision times where I was putting nail polish on my fingers. Eventually, I started to get glitter to put on. So that would be part of my preparation.

Xtine Santakas: The Garment District is for an off-theme item that I knew Susie wouldn't really have anything for, like maybe it's an apocalyptic theme. Also, if I wanted to tear something up and sew it back together, like Frankenstein, I wouldn't pay top dollar for a beautiful outfit. I found my very first pair of boots in the Garment District.

Steve Friedrich: All sorts of places because they didn't have things like Hot Topic. Even Marshalls, you could always find some weird stuff. A fishnet top thing I had gotten at Garment District. When I'd worn that my dad started going to church every day of the week.

Gibby Miller: Hubba Hubba. You would get your skinny suspenders, your boots, your leather pants and your bondage belt.

Taylor Vecchio: If I knew I was going to ManRay I would hit Tellos because it was so cheap. They always had black stuff or weirdly sexy stuff that you could make work. I could get off the T, go there, grab something cute, and then go home and hang out for a little bit. I wasn't like, "Oh, let me listen to this ManRay type music" but I would have been like drinking Miller highlife.

Emily Arkin: Amazing Tellos moment that I witnessed — I had the window rolled down and it was like new Somerville and old Somerville encountered each other on a street. It was two women who were pretty townie and one woman who was wearing a multi-tiered skirt. One was like, "Oh my god, I love your skirt, where did it come from?" And it's just one that I saw at Anthropologie or Free People or something. She's like "I have one that's exactly like that, but I got it at Tellos."

Anna Feder: Well, I was always adapting new outfits with things I would find something out in my travels. I was probably working at the Mercantile at the time, which was a great place for jewelry, lots of stone, and that stuff for Goth attire and sterling silver. I remember going to the Army-Navy store in Hadley, the Drop Zone, which also had horrible racist bumper stickers. I started going to the Northampton one that opened up so I didn't have to go to the one in Hadley.

Tonya Sand: I liked to have a unique kind of appearance. I would wear corsets or dresses. I used to wear a black satin ribbon almost like a choker in style. I would go to the fabric store and get all kinds of different ribbons. Satin ribbons. Silk ribbons. Whatever outfit I was wearing, I would have that. I would buy it at Hubba Hubba in Cambridge. Fishnet stockings that you can get anywhere. Honestly, I would get them at Hot Topic because that's when Hot Topic first started really becoming a thing. I remember some people, who are kind of more hardcore be like, "Oh, I would never get Hot Topic, that's poser." But if it was going to go get tights, why am I going to pay extra?

Jennifer: I definitely shopped at Hubba Hubba, like a lot of people back then. I'm embarrassed to admit this now, but I did get some stuff from Hot Topic. Occasionally, there would be vendors in ManRay that I buy stuff from. It's easy when you're a girl. You don't need a whole lot.

Sara S. Wendell: My standard outfit for ManRay was a corset and a skirt. Over time I amassed quite a corset collection. Most of the ones that I bought came from the Fetish Flea market. There was a particular vendor who would come up from New Hope, Pennsylvania, called Le Chateau Exotic and they had the best deal on the best corsets. So generally, for me picking out an outfit was just "Which corset am I going to wear and what skirt goes with it?" I had two or three pairs of boots that just rotated.

Christina Pearson: My pregame would start three hours before. I might take a bath and shave, really do the pampering style. I would always know what I was going to wear a good week or two before. I couldn't really afford to go to some of the novelty shops and Hubba Hubba could be very outside of my price range. So, I was often going to thrift stores to try to piece together ManRay outfits.

Hyson Concepcion: You could get clothes at The Gap You could get a flowing black velvet shirt because velvet was in during the 90s. I had a really nice silk shirt from The Gap. It had buttons and I used to wear it open over something and it was nicer than Goth clothes.

Lilly Moon: It was a magical time for me as far as clothes go. This was before Hot Topic. The boutiques had expensive Goth clothes. Sometimes Betsey Johnson had some cool stuff, but it was not accessible for me. So I made my own stuff.

Gillian Cox: Hubba Hubba. I loved that store, particularly when there was a sale going on because I could never afford anything in there at full price. Sometimes they let me be an in-store model for half the day on Saturday.

That's how I'd be able to bring home the outfit that I was wearing.

Jill Kempton: I had no idea where to shop, really. So, I'm just putting together anything I can. I went to Rainbow where you could find cheap, plasticky vinyl. You could probably only wear it at once and then it broke. You had to really be overly creative with what you wore because it was incredibly hard to find stuff to buy and I don't have money to be buying a ton of stuff. Frederick's of Hollywood, I bought all my corsets there. I'm not the most creative person, I'm not a sewer, but I can glue things. So, I used to go to Joann Fabrics and buy tulle to make some bustles, secretly I'm hiding my butt which I didn't think was good in those pants. I added a feather boa to everything that I ordered off Oriental Trading because we don't have internet. I added them to little pocketbooks, I added them to hats. I remember I had this long zebra robe that somebody gave me, and I added a whole trim of boa and then I felt like an idiot wearing it because it was just a little too much like, who do I think I am? But I only wore it like once or twice. I still have it.

Of course, it took me like two hours to get ready. I had great skin. I don't know why my makeup would take that long, my makeup took longer to do back then than it does now, but I would just all go: Perfect, perfect, perfect. I would stay in the bath for like an hour. My hair just looked high maintenance. It really wasn't. It was just nice and sleek. I worked in a salon, so that's part of the prep too. Sometimes my hair looked unbelievable because I worked in a salon. Maybe when I'm 21, 22 I put black lipstick on, but I got out of that. We don't need to wear black lipstick. I like red, red looks really good.

Alyssa Hassan: H&M, sometimes I got sparkly clothes from Filenes. I didn't accessorize and my friends were gay boys who wore jeans and t shirts and baseball caps. We weren't obsessed with getting ready. We wanted to feel kind of good, but it wasn't the most important thing. But I wanted to sparkle. I went through a phase where I wore candy necklaces.

Michael Marotta: First of all, I would say that the art of getting ready to go to a nightclub is completely fucking dead. The ritual of it. I feel like there are some people that keep that spirit alive because they still get done up and they still have a presentation when they go, but I feel the art of getting ready to be seen and to present yourself in a nightclub is kind of over. It's kind of sad. I just don't think people give a shit. I think people care less about how they look than they did back then. In terms of me personally,

I've always worn black. I've always kind of looked the part. I always kind of just looked the way that I looked. Maybe that's why I always leaned into that subculture. I don't consider myself Goth, but my next-door neighbors probably do.

I have memories of sitting on the couch and waiting for whatever love interest I had at the time to get ready and me being like, "Are we going to fucking go?" I look back on that time so fondly because it's just the ritual of going out and playing certain music and listening to the stuff that you knew you would hear later. You would listen to "The Sparrows and Nightingales" by Wolfsheim at 8 p.m. and you would know that if it came on at 12:30 or 1 a.m., it's going to sound just that much better. Sometimes it was just as vital as being in the club … the anticipation of getting ready to go out, and ManRay was one of those clubs that demanded it. ManRay demanded a certain respect. It demanded a certain attitude and ManRay gave you the type of attitude that you had to give back.

A. Dominy Cusraque: I had a vision that just wouldn't quit. I had this picture in my head of what I wanted a night in the club to look like. It's just that I didn't get exactly there because in my head, we are fully developed freaky. The example I always use is if someone comes through the door and is wearing a banana yellow zoot suit with the hat and for me … I want that guy in my club

Aerial view of Central Square circa 1986
(Photograph courtesy of Cambridge Public Library Archive) Photograph: John Namian

Photo of Central Square
(Photograph courtesy of Cambridge Public Library Archive) Photograph John Namian

Top: Simeone's Restaurant--Circa 1950's

Bottom: Campus Nightclub, Circa 1984

(Photographs courtesy of Cambridge Historical Commission)

MANIFESTO

"The Art of Nightlife"

Our intentions and motives are simple:

We have built Man Ray because the creative act and creative people are nocturnal. They are at their best when they are nocturnal. Those who are mired in daylight activities must content themselves to dream.

We have built Man Ray because this great metropolis offers little more than the moon and a Seven Eleven after the late night news. Creative people need each other after dark.

We have built Man Ray because we believe in the Art of Nightlife. We are not a nightclub in the ordinary sense. We are a new crossroads on the map of the night. All nocturnal people are welcome here. We will challenge our own creative boundaries by our contact with each other.

Man Ray exists now to put people together--young and old, straight and gay. It has been built to provide a forum for new visual artists, performance artists, and those schooled in the art of revelry. It is a changing space made of color and human beings and the very best of the newest music.

It is an idea that invites us nightly to give it form.

ManRay Manifesto *(Photograph courtesy of the Bruce Jope Collection)*

• MAN RAY • THE ART OF NIGHTLIFE •
GRAND OPENING • THURSDAY, MARCH 21, 1985 •
8 P.M. • YOU'RE INVITED •
THIS INVITATION ADMITS ONE •
21A BROOKLINE ST. • CAMBRIDGE •
• 864-0400 •

ManRay Opening Night Invitation *(Photograph courtesy of the Bruce Jope Collection)*

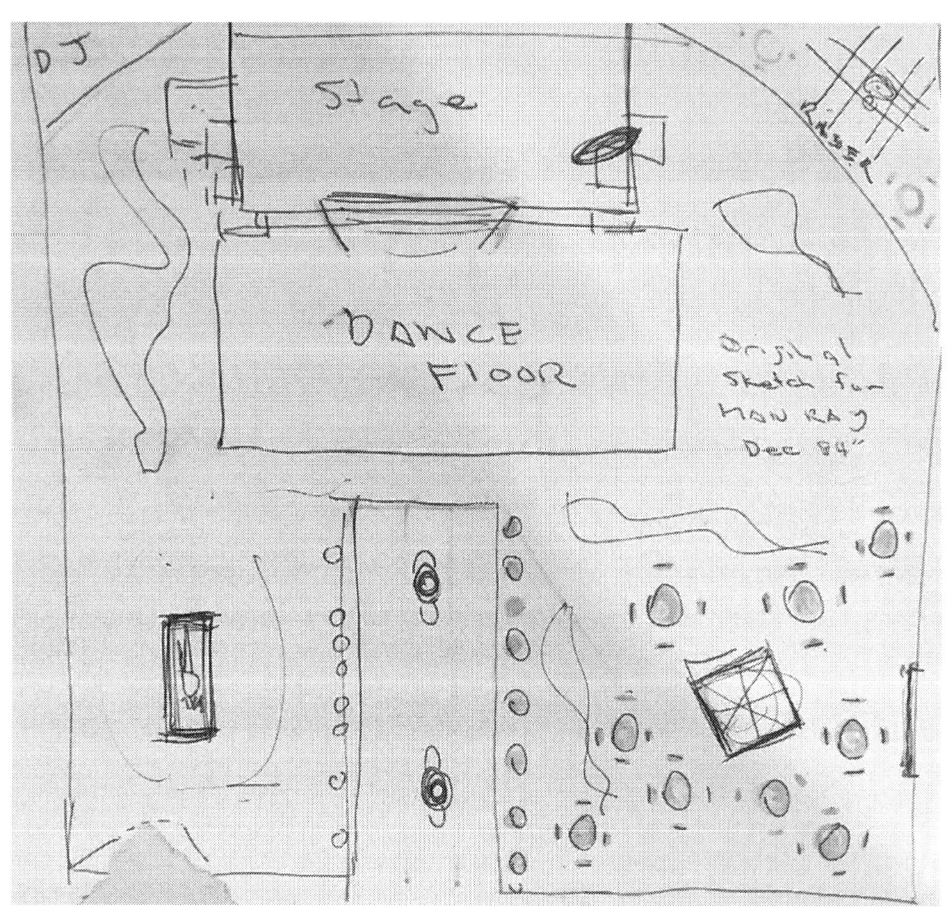

ManRay Floor Sketch (1985) *(Photograph courtesy of the Bruce Jope Collection)*

Top: Bruce Jope Francis Twohey, David "Daisy" Crowder, and Tom Yaz *(Photograph courtesy of the Bruce Jope Collection)*

Left: Paul Vitigliano (DJ Paul V) Circa 1985 *(Photograph courtesy of the Bruce Jope Collection)*

Bottom: Opening Night of ManRay, 1985 *(Photograph courtesy of the Bruce Jope Collection)*

You are cordially invited
to attend the Life Magazine
photo session
of the new "Astro Lounge" at
ManRay,
scheduled to appear in
the August Issue.

June 21 7 p.m. sharp

Invitation must be shown at door

Invitation to Astro Lounge Photo session Front and Back, Hosted by Life Magazine, June 21, 1985
(Courtesy of the Bruce Jope Collection)

Right: Bruce Jope and Divine, October 24, 1985 *(Photograph courtesy of the Bruce Jope Collection)*

Below: Flyer for Divine Show *(Photograph courtesy of the Bruce Jope Collection)*

Bottom Right: Divine Performing at ManRay, October 24, 1985 *(Photograph courtesy of David Schwartz)*

Right: Flyer for Halloween Ball, 1985 *(Photograph courtesy of the Bruce Jope Collection)*

Below: New Year Party flyer, Front and Back, 1985 *(Photograph courtesy of the Bruce Jope Collection)*

Terri Niedzwiecki and Chris Ewen, Circa 1990's, *(Photograph provided by Chris Ewen)*

Koren Bernardi (DJ Punketta Doilie) *(Photograph provided by Koren Bernardi)*

Above: Flyer for Alien Sex Fiend show, May 20, 1992, *(Photograpy and flyer provided by Adam Lewis)*

Left: Adam Lewis, *(Photograph provided by Adam Lewis)*

Flyer for Campus Dance night
*(Photograph provided by
Jenny Dahling)*

THURSDAYS
CAMPUS
GO!
Central Square,
Cambridge
(on the Red Line)

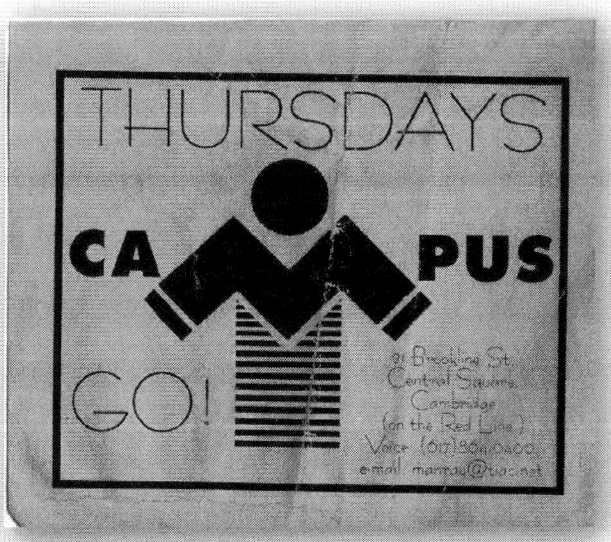

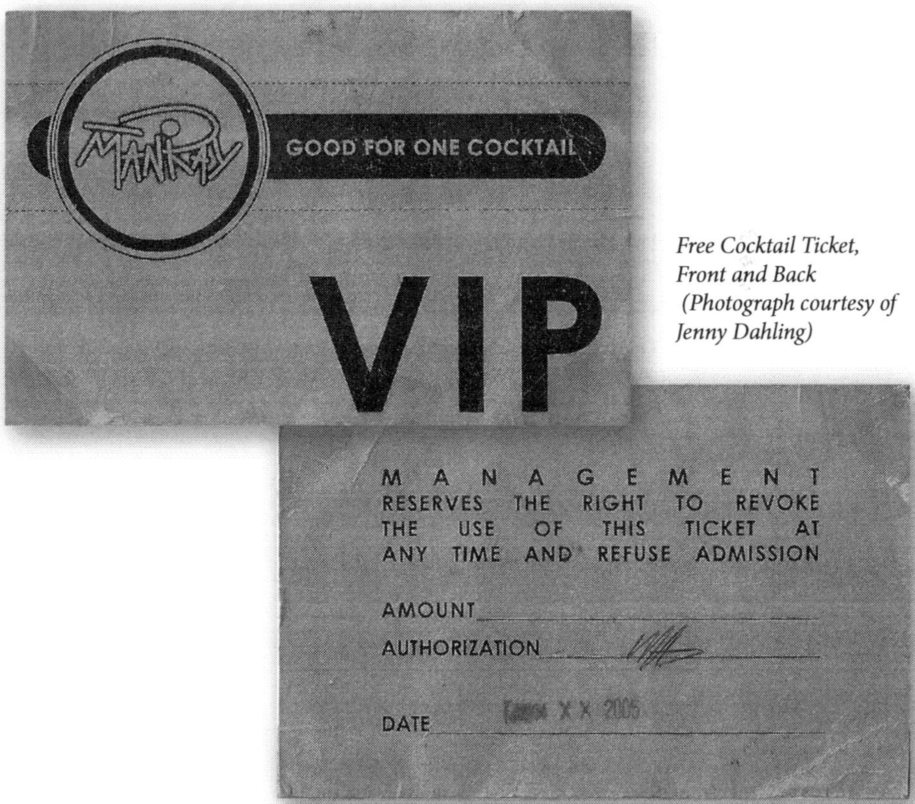
GOOD FOR ONE COCKTAIL
VIP
MANAGEMENT
RESERVES THE RIGHT TO REVOKE
THE USE OF THIS TICKET AT
ANY TIME AND REFUSE ADMISSION
AMOUNT
AUTHORIZATION
DATE

*Free Cocktail Ticket,
Front and Back
(Photograph courtesy of
Jenny Dahling)*

Emily Sweeney and Lauralee Summer, circa 1999. *(Photograph provided by Emily Sweeney)*

A. Dominy Cusraque and Koren Bernardi, circa 1990s.
(Photograph provided by Koren Bernardi)

Left: Julia Kilcoyne before a night at ManRay. *(Photograph provided by Julia Kilcoyne)*

Below: Jenny Dahling with Lewis Alves and Cookie Howard Inside ManRay. *(Photograph provided by Jenny Dahling)*

Left: First Annual Gothic Prom Save the Date Card. September 1998. *(Flyer provided by Lachesis/Sharon Rodda)*

Ladybee & Friends
present

Hong Kong Garden

The First Annual Gothic Prom

An Unforgettable Evening of Funereal Formality & Regal Romance
Liberally Laden With Cheese And Good Cheer!

Saturday, September 19th, 1998
7pm until Midnight
at the Cambridge Multicultural Arts Center
45 Second St., Cambridge, MA

For your dancing pleasure, music will be provided by
DJ Arcanus of Boston, MA,
DJ Fenris of Providence, RI,
& DJ Charlie the Slut of New York City, NY.
Your Invitation also guarantees you free admission to the
Post-Prom New Wave Party at Man Ray.

Formal dress is required.
Beer & wine will be served at a cash bar to those over 21 & possessing
valid legal ID.

Invitations may be purchased for $25 per couple or $15 stag,
& are available from Committee Members
on Wednesdays & at 'Scoundrels from Hell'
in the Lounge at Man Ray
or by appointment (email or call for more info).
There will be no admission at the door;
pre-obtained Invitations ONLY.
URL: http://www.apocalypse.org/pub/u/hilda/gothprom
Email: <rpollock@ici.net> & Vox: 617.787.5178

Right: First Annual Gothic Prom Staff Laminates. September 1998. Designed by Lachesis/Sharon Rodda.
(Flyer provided by Lachesis/Sharon Rodda)

Left: ManRay lounge LadyBee/Rachel Pollock, year unknown.
(Photograph provided by Lachesis/ Sharon Rodda)

Below: Sharon Rodda and Roland Rauch in the Manray lounge circa 2000.
(Photograph provided by Lachesis/ Sharon Rodda)

Left to Right: Deirdre Benson, Lizzy Angiello, Wyatt Birch, and Jeff Ferguson, circa 2000.
(Photograph provided by Lachesis/Sharon Rodda)

Sharon Rodda and Cat Barrett at Deli Haus, year unknown.
(Photograph provided by Lachesis/Sharon Rodda)

Eartha Harris performing as Project Sphere at ManRay's Summer Synthpop Invasion, May 2002. *(Photograph provided by Eartha Harris)*

ManRay in the throes of demolition, circa 2005. *(Photograph provided by Keith Ward)*

View inside ManRay in the throes of demolition, circa 2005. *(Photograph provided by Keith Ward)*

ManRay lives on. ManRay reunion at The Paradise. Boston, circa 2010s.
(Photograph provided by Shawn Driscoll)

Chapter 11

You Never Forget Your First Time

"We're all mad here. Please join us." — Gillian Cox

The resounding thump of music spills from the dark building and a collage of posters catch the eye while in line. The doors open to dim lighting and the smoke of clove cigarettes. The initial journey winds through the doors and bouncers, through the lounge, and down to the coat check before finally, truly arriving. A stop at the bar, where a drink is already poured and waiting, is key before making it out onto the heat of the dance floor as the music sweeps the crowd away.

A rather short and yet dark, imposing brick building, ManRay had a prime corner spot on Brookline Street whose outward aesthetic perfectly fit the crowd and atmosphere of the club. From the sounds to the sights, ManRay was a club that sought to reach out to all of your senses and engage you fully in the experience. Perhaps one of the best things about ManRay was its multiple rooms that allow patrons choice and variety during their night that other spaces could not provide. If the music and feel of one room wasn't doing it for you then you could try out the other. Similarly, the lounge or and multiple bars provided an escape where people could gather and socialize. The time, dedication, and creativity of the staff, performers, and patrons of ManRay created a truly artistic and open space.

S.L.

Kevin Farrington: When I was in high school and briefly in the Army, I played in several bands and I said to people that the experience of waiting to come on stage was very similar to what it felt like coming into ManRay, there was almost a performance element to it. It was kind of a question of do I belong here and where do I go? After I answered those two questions, I slotted into a previous experience, which is, "Hey, I'm in the middle of this and I feel like I'm performing for other people," which is interesting because, after all, I think that's a key element that drove a lot of us after we were there for a while, unconsciously or not. We were all performing for each other.

Lacey Prpic Hedtke: I just remember it feeling like anything goes. We're going to keep pushing the envelope, upping the ante into "How weird do you want to get?" It's like a community space. It was just a weird DIY space, but it had a little bit of "We'll get as weird as you want." I always have kind of felt like a weirdo, and, in going there, I was like, "Oh, shit!!!! These people are living their weirdness." It just felt like people were doubling down on their weirdness.

Anna Feder: I wasn't old enough to be there, and certainly not the person that I brought with me. It didn't seem like my sister thought that it was going to be a problem. It wasn't like, "Hey, we'll try to get in and sorry if it doesn't work out and make some other plans." It was just like, "We're gonna go to ManRay for New Year's Eve and it'll work out." I had a college student ID and people assumed I was 18. They used to put those big X's on your hands, which I vividly remember because they were kind of a mark of shame. You didn't really want them there, but you could be thrown out for trying to take them off. You didn't mess with those, but you did put very creative things on your hands like gloves or lace fingerless things, so it wasn't as obvious to people around you that you were a child.

Chris Ewen: I swear to God this is the truth, the DJ was playing Figures on A Beach, our most recent single, the first time I went in. We all kind of freaked out.

Norm: I remember that first night very, very well for many reasons. It was a Wednesday. We parked in the Green Street garage. The DJ booth was still on the ground floor. I was doing a lot of exploration of the place. The old Depeche Mode motif on the back of the coat room struck me very strongly. I was told by a wonderful young lady within about 10 minutes of the first time I ever went in there to use the girls bathroom if I needed to.

Tatiana Zimkus: You walked in and you weren't sure what you're getting yourself into because everything was black other than that neon sign outside. It's this mysterious club. I don't think I realized how big it was until I got inside because going to Ceremony was this tiny little space.

Going to ManRay, I immediately knew that I was in the right place. Everything was black and of course I was wearing black. I could see that they were very specific about allowing people to get in with a dress code.

I'm sure the first few times I must have felt very awkward about the idea of dancing. I might have gone dancing at Avalon or places like that, but it was people grinding up against you. I just kind of assumed that's what people were doing, but going to ManRay, walking in, and seeing all of these people in their own world swirling away to songs, most of which I recognized already. I can almost cry now thinking about it; I must have been really emotionally overwhelmed at knowing that I could do that for the first time in my life. I was able to let go and be in this moment. It was very meditative. It was very transformative.

Erika Spaulding: The first time I went there was on a Wednesday and I was 18, so I wasn't really going to any of the other nights. It was very dimly lit and felt dark and mysterious but also safe. I liked that people weren't up on each other. That was the thing that struck me immediately. I liked that people had their own self-expression right in the dance room. There were a lot of people with their own bubble of where they were at that moment and that struck me.

Lucretia X Machina: I went to Wednesday mostly first and then another boyfriend and I met there. I won't say his name. But yeah, we started going on Fridays. Because it's really cool, it's got a kick to it. You know, it's a little more adult. Because then Wednesdays felt like, oh, this is kid time and it's a little lower key and it's for newbies and you know we just wanted a little higher energy and older people. So, we started going on Friday nights much more regularly then.

Nate Roman: My first night at ManRay was Fantasy Factory. I was overwhelmed by what I was experiencing. I was so into the music in both rooms. I was really feeling it. The thing that struck me the most is that here's this group of people that are normally social outcasts all in one place. There was just that sense of belonging. This feels like a place that I can go and not feel like I'm pretending to be anything.

Kathryn Pollnac: I didn't really go out dancing that much until I started going to ManRay. It was like a drug. Once I started going, I just couldn't stop.

Mike (Farmboy): I had a friend who moved up to Cambridge and he was telling me about this club up there that was doing alternative music and that it wouldn't be a stereotypical nightclub. They were doing this record release party for a band we used to play on our college radio station called MDM. I recognized the name. I knew a couple of the songs. So I figured this should be fun. I'm kind of a shy and awkward guy. So, I kind of saw myself going in and being a wallflower. The first thing that hit me was the fact that it was a bit of a sensory overload. I had never seen so many black clothes in my entire life. I remember this one guy had short, short blond hair. I think it was February and this guy had shorts on and he's just dancing like a machine.

Michael Hsieh: It was almost overwhelming. It was one of Cusraque's monthly Hell nights in February, maybe Valentine's Day. I'm tromping through the slush and the cold in February to this club. I don't know what's gonna happen. You go through the door, walk up the stairs, and it was amazing. You see the Techno room on the right, the lounge in the back and then the hallway leads back into the main room. I just loved the decor. It was just a cozy space when you first walked in. It was lovely. The place was filled with people just dressed so beautifully and just having such a good time. It was just overwhelming. I kind of instantly felt like it was the most welcoming Goth club I'd ever been to. It was just so happy and warm and wonderful.

Brian Legault: The first of my very vivid memories is the bouncer at the door. I don't remember who it was, but I just remembered that he was enforcing a dress code. And I thought to myself, "Wow, I'm in the city where the Goth clubs actually are enforcing dress code." Montreal's a little bit hardcore, we dress up, but you don't always have to have to go all out. People do other scenes. There's a lot of techno-industrial crossover with the Goth scene, so people were dressed up in different things. A lot of people bounced from club to club. So, you might be going to a party, swing by the Goth club, and ultimately end up at a techno after party. So, the dress code isn't as rigidly enforced. I was standing in line at ManRay in all black clothes, but I think I was wearing sneakers. The guy made a comment, but they were black, so he allowed it. I remember walking through the door to see different groups sort of to the side. ManRay had a distinctive smell. My club in Montreal was actually rather small. It was maybe a quarter the size of ManRay.

Andrea Parros: Sight is a lot of people's primary sense. Dark in lighting and dark in color. Everything was black. I remember the boxes that people would dance on and the cages; that stuff was something I've never seen before growing up in a small town. I remember there was a bar. I'm sure there's a lot of people watching and talking with Cheryl. Then I also remember dancing too.

Becky D: You walk into ManRay and it's really an immediate change of your environment. It's dark. There was, if I remember correctly, a velvet couch. There was all this texture and color, but it was all dark color. You see all these people walking around and my first impression was "Oh my God, everyone's gorgeous and they look amazing, and they look so confident." The first time I was there was really just soaking in who the people were, what they were doing, what they were looking like, how they behaved and then soaking in the music that goes along with that and watching the waves of people coming on and off the dance floor, depending on which songs were playing.

My first time I sat there with a drink in my hand, probably a Red Death from Terri. I probably sat or stood on the edge of the dance floor and just stared and watched people dance. That was probably the most mesmerizing thing for me watching how they moved because it was so different. I think at that point I really fell in love with the movement of what the club had to offer along with the aesthetic and the sound of the music. I was just kind of immersing myself in the whole experience. I spent a lot of the first few times I went just watching how they danced, picking someone that I thought was a beautiful dancer, and trying to imitate them. Their movements were very different from what I was used to dancing.

The visuals … David hadn't done his mural at that point, but there was something else up on the back wall. I can't remember exactly what it was, but I remember being really impressed by the aesthetic of the design. ManRay felt like this underground basement thing, because it was dark and black and red and all that, but you look behind Terri's bar and she has these amazing lanterns. I just found it really beautiful right in this kind of Gothic way.

Cris Concepcion: I started college in Boston in 1993. I was a shy freshman kid who didn't know a lot of other people and was kind of getting used to being in America for the first time. I kept a lot to myself. I spied a couple of interesting kids hanging out in the cafeteria with wallet chains and Doc Martens, but I wasn't so sure how to approach them. I realized that these are club kids. I was really into the internet at the time, and I had joined an online community for ravers. They would publish a list of all the dance parties in New England for that weekend. I printed them out and with all my courage I went to these kids at this one table in the cafeteria and I dropped a stack of like dot matrix printed paper in front of them and said, "These are a bunch of parties, I have a car. I don't want to go there by myself. Do you want to go with me?" And they were like, "Where did you get this information?" I said, "Oh, the internet. Let me show you." And we basically hung out as a group of friends.

I'd been meaning to go to ManRay for a very long time, so in '95 we were at an MIT party that got busted and I suggested we go to ManRay. So, we just drove over. I remember the smell of clove smoke. It felt like an old place with this definite sort of weight to it. My friends went to the front room to dance to techno music, but I was making a beeline for the back. I'd always been curious about what a Goth night would look like because in Vancouver, where I grew up, we didn't have Goth nights. We had industrial nights. I had my first opportunity to see a bunch of people dressed in black with a lot of spikes and a lot of chains. The way they danced was fascinating because when you go to a rave club, dancers claim a lot of space. At ManRay you had these people doing these fairly elaborate, very dramatic postures and swooping and swirling. There was slow music where you could really think about what you could do with that. It was also really cool to see a bunch of people put a lot of thought into what they were going to wear that evening and I remember being really captivated by this scene. And imagine me having my earlier plans to go to MIT, I am wearing blue jeans and a white t-shirt with sneakers. Now I'm hanging out with a bunch of other Goth kids drinking it all in and having a lot of fun.

I turned to some guy who's 6 feet tall, towering over me and I asked him for a light. He's like, "I'm sorry, this is my last one" then turns and walks away. I'm like, "That's cool. That's fine" because I am the one who sticks out here and I'm going to come back next week and I'm going to ask somebody else here for light and I will be dressed correctly." That was the whole thing about that scene, it needs you to meet it where it was. But if you could do that there is a feeling that you could belong there as long as you're willing to put in that effort.

The kids I'd become friends with were a year ahead of me, so I knew that they were going to be leaving soon and I had to think about what I was going to do for socializing. These kids were business students, and they were doing this just to have fun. They were probably going to straighten up and stop going out afterwards. I wasn't ready to do that. After the first few times I really understood that I could be here by myself. Nobody was gonna stare at me and make me feel uncomfortable because I was here on my own. It really felt welcoming, whether you are by yourself or with your friends, and that was very different from any other club that I had been to.

Eloni Feliciano: Just walking up to the door I thought the two bouncers were kind of cooler than other bouncers. They were young and hip. A lot of times on Lansdowne they were monsters that you really didn't want to hang out with. They let me in no problem. It's bigger inside than it looks outside. The black light hits your eyes and you kind of get this weird white flash before your eyes adjust. Then you realize there's a whole bunch of sections of the clubs. It was smoky as hell in there and it always had this particular pungency, like the old building materials and carpet. Maybe years of old booze. I swear to God, I still have clothes with that smell.

I was 18 and it was a Saturday. For some reason it was not busy that night. There were a couple groups in different corners and a few people playing pool. It surprised me that clubs would have had a slow time. It was just so much prettier than a lot of the other clubs I'd seen in Boston, even in New York City. So, walking through there and not seeing that many people kind of surprised me. I remember the church pews they used to have. It was probably the thing that stood out to me the most, just the fact that it had that kind of very Gothic very churchy kind of an interior where the exterior just looks like this black wall.

Jennifer: The very first time I went I was still in high school because I was really underage. I think some friends just talked about it and it got stuck in my head as "the Goth club." I didn't really know much else. I was very inexperienced and young at the time. The first time I went to ManRay I went into Boston by myself. I got to the club and knew I was underage, so I was very nervous about getting it since it was a 21 plus night. I skipped the line and went right up to the front to the bouncer and said "Excuse me, sir. Can you help me? I left my license here last night. Can you see if they found it in the Lost and Found? I obviously don't have my license, I lost it. Can I get in?" And they let me in. For some reason the girl behind me vouched for me. After that first time they just recognized me, so it was no longer an issue. So, when I got in I was very relieved. I had no idea what

I was walking into, but I was excited. I loved that I could go in there and start dancing. It felt very comfortable.

Duane Bruce: From the outside it looked like something out of a horror movie. It could easily be a haunted house. The size and the girth of that building. How huge it was. When I went in the first time, I didn't know that they utilized basically the whole building as the club. I'm outside and it's like a Hollywood studio horror haunted house type of vibe. The building is painted black. It just reeked of what you were going to get when you went inside and that's perfect. There was no neon out front. That was appealing to me, the fact that it was almost generic, but in a sort of non-generic way. It stood out as something different than everything else around it. It was like the mothership that had landed.

I get inside and the first thing I see is the size of it. There's rooms off of rooms. I noticed the old wood floor. We had a three-story department store called Cranes in Maine that caught on fire in the basement and that thing went up like a tinderbox. My mom was on the third floor, but she got out. That's one of the things that I thought the first time — there's a lot of alcohol in here and a lot of people smoking cigarettes and a lot of things that could combust. It smells like sweat and leather. It smells like sex. It smells like Rock and roll. It had elements like The Rat and the downstairs of The Middle East. There weren't a lot of windows, per se, to air the place out.

Over time, I found the downstairs where the bands would go, which was kind of the green room. That smelled even more dank than the club did because everybody was really sweaty on stage. There was a pool table and a sweaty stinky old couch. It really looked like the basement of somebody's home that had never really been refinished with a grandmother's couch and maybe your dead uncle's pool table and all that stuff that had acquired over the years. I loved it because I found it to have a very different type of Rock and roll vibe. It was a much more honest vibe, just because of the whole layout and look and feel of the building itself before you even put a person into it.

Koren Bernardi: It was like a hard surface, but it would slide, so the front room had almost a gym floor kind of feel to it. It had this surface where I had these shoes that could kind of slide around like I had roller skates on so I could moonwalk.

Emily Taylor: I showed up and rang a bell because it was daytime still.

Someone let me and I felt like I'm the coolest person on the planet because I'd been admitted to a club before it even opened. I didn't have to pay, and the house lights were on. It was the front room where industrial stuff happened. There were pool tables. I noticed immediately that it smelled like clove cigarettes and mold and beer. There was a very strong smell, and this was before they redid the carpet. It had a very stale nightclub smell that I'm sure everyone you talked to will specifically be reminded of. I thought this place was cool. We went to the back room and there was the DJ booth up above, the phone booth in the corner where you could make requests, and Terri's bar.

Noel McKenna: I showed up with a bunch of Ground Zero people and we're all like, "Okay, we're going to change this place." I probably judged the crowd as being these college alternative types and turned my nose up at it. So probably the first thing that we did was head to the DJ booth, Chris was thrilled to see all of us, and we started making requests like Skinny Puppy, Ministry, and Front 242.

Me'lissa Nin: I want to say it was a Wednesday. We're standing in line. I was nervous as could be, but I figured, "Well, I'm here, I may as well just check it out." I remember fumbling through my wallet while in line to hand it to the doorman. I paid for the cover, I want to say it was $3 at the time. I remember seeing black lights. I remember the smell of clove cigarettes because you could still smoke inside at the time. I remember feeling the music. It was so loud there. It was definitely overwhelming all senses, but in the best possible way, I'm in this place I've never been. It's a sea of unfamiliar faces. I sat down just kind of observing everything. As I'm sitting there someone approached me and we started talking and this is the first friend I made. I felt a lot more comfortable at that point, like, "Okay, cool. I've got a guide. Show me the ManRay ropes if you will." I decided this is a good experience and I want to come back.

Greg Frisbee: Well, I had no idea what to think initially. I grew up as a really shy kid on the South Shore of Massachusetts and then attended Massasoit Community College, which would have been the fall of 1992. I started to come out of my shell and I met some friends who were in the alternative music scene who were the ones who initially had already gone to ManRay.

Emily Arkin: I remember it always being cold when I would go and you would be trying to be relatively undressed for nightclub life. Then there was gatekeeping, so you would kind of hear the music through the wall while freezing outside trying to get everyone carded. Every once in a while, they actually would enforce the dress code, which I don't think they did for women. I didn't drink a lot when I first went there because I wasn't over age, so I don't associate it with heading straight to the bar. I remember the different rooms where there'd be totally different music or different scenes and the people watching was almost like an anthropological zoo of subcultures.

Amy Butts: I went with my boyfriend and some friends. The moment I walked in I was hit in the face with a clove cigarette smell. It was dark and crowded and people were talking and dancing and drinking and smoking and everybody just looked so beautiful. I couldn't wait to be there, and I was finally there. I was so shy, so I didn't talk to anybody but my friends. But I soaked it all in. I couldn't believe it. I just was like "This is where I belong."

Liz Enthusiasm: The smell is very particular. I think it is probably the only place that smelled better before the smoking ban. You'd have that ManRay smell on your hair and your clothes, mostly Clove cigarettes and the smoke machine. I definitely remember there being the front room and the back room, and I thought that was really cool. It had a more divey and lived in feel. Lansdowne Street is always renovating every couple year. ManRay … I wouldn't call it neglected or anything, but it had sort of lived-in vibe to it. I also feel it was kind of less Gothy back in those days, even though we were going on Wednesdays.

Rebecca Corbett: I loved the smell, like a clove. There was that kind of excitement and you couldn't wait. I always went to the back room. The first time, I was a small-town girl that never saw anything like it. It was feeling like this is so freaking cool. I remember there was a skinny guy that had the longest hair with the hat with the feather that brought the pamphlets.

Tonya Sand: By the time we got there, it was pretty late, so we probably had like an hour there. I looked around and I just saw people in amazing outfits. I always listened to The Cure. I loved Nine Inch Nails. I loved all that stuff. I didn't understand that there was a concept called Goth, I just naturally gravitated to kind of hard things. I walked in and saw people actually dressed to the nines. It was an entire club full of people listening to music that I liked and just the pageantry of it all. Why didn't I know about this earlier? The smell is really interesting. It's something that I actually still miss because you could smoke inside places. People are smoking cloves and then you smell the smoke machine. It was an old space that was probably not the most sanitary when you think about it. It was musky. It was kind of like a basement.

Adam Lewis: It was definitely the first gay bar that I went to. I think it was everyone's first gay bar at that time because they were 18 plus. It had this chill front room where you could even hang out and the back room was not threatening at all. The music was fun and I knew it all. There was a comfort level. The front room would always be more abrasive house or techno with different DJs doing different things. There was definitely more real dancing. Whereas the back room was to grab a drink, twirl a little and have some fun. The music and the club fit each other. I felt completely comfortable there.

Sara S. Wendell: First off, you get the funky bass through your skeletal system. The music was more felt than heard when you first walked in because you couldn't really hear it clearly until you went into the back room. Lighting was fairly dim and very colorful, kind of what you would expect from any given nightclub. They never want the place to be too bright. You couldn't really smell anything over the smoke, other than the occasional tang of somebody who hadn't showered too recently. That was pretty much my first impression.

Jenny Dahling: It was good and bad mixed together. My very first thought upon walking in was it looks really cool. There is a big light fixture on the wall that says ManRay. There was a vibe that proved my art teacher was right, I do belong here. However, if I'm really telling you the gory honest truth, it was sort of a walk into a bathroom smell and liquor. Lights and kind of like, "What the hell is this place?" It's kind of down and dirty, not too ritzy and yet it is glamorous, and I dug that. I felt like it jived with my personality.

Xtine Santakas: Well, the very first time I walked in I was terrified. I had never been in a nightclub before in my life. I have been to bars, but they are a totally different experience. This was not a bar, in any stretch of the imagination. It was really utterly different, unique, and a new experiment.

I was terrified. I made my friend, Andy, go with me. The first thing that hit me was that smoking was still allowed inside and I had never smelled a clove cigarette before. I'm also severely asthmatic. The first person I saw was this very attractive woman in these huge Goth boots, which I immediately wanted, and she was wearing nothing but red saran wrap and some nipple tape. And I thought that was great, but I could never be that brave. You go girl.

Melanie Sharkey: I bumped into a pit acquaintance three steps into the door. Sheldon was kind of a nerd back when I knew him in the pit. He was awkward. He was really, really into the band Kiss. Fast forward to 2003 and he's got a feather boa, eyeliner, and he is living his best life. I'm like "Dude, what a transformation. Holy shit, you look amazing!" He had come out of his shell and was clearly in his element. He was like, "Oh my God! This place is great. We're going to dance. We're gonna have fun." I introduced him to my friend Mary Beth. I feel like there was red leather furniture in the lounge. Sort of a Twin Peaks vibe. I remember the music and dancing on rickety wooden boxes.

Prospero Eaton: I didn't really know what to expect. I seem to recall that it seemed pretty dark and mysterious to me, which was kind of appealing. I wasn't somebody before ManRay that really went to dance clubs, so I didn't really have a good frame of reference for it.

I think it was a pretty quiet night when I first went there. I don't remember there being a ton of people. I remember it being just very dark. There was a cage set up. The overall layout grabbed my attention because it was something unlike any that I have been to before. I felt a little awkward because I went by myself, so I didn't really know anybody. I was just there taking in the music. I think I was probably wearing latex pants so I fit in pretty well.

Patrick Fitzgerald: It was back when the air conditioning worked, that's for sure, because I remember it was pretty chilly there. We were there early. It was cold. It was dark. It was spooky. It smelled like smoke and cloves and perfume.

Christina Pearson: Walking into that club was like walking into my home. It was just an embrace, like this is where I belong. Then the music. You'd hope the music isn't too good while waiting to get in. Save my favorite songs for when I'm in there and I've got a drink and I'm ready to dance. As you're getting closer you can hear what they are playing. It's instantly too loud in a club when you first get in there, but you adjust to it pretty quickly.

Jamie DiBattista: As soon as you walk in there's a dance floor off to your right, then on your left there is a lounge area. It was very dark. The smell of beer and clove cigarettes and a smoke machine. It was very powerful. I still remember that smell to this day. We walked to the back room where they were playing New Wave. I was a sheltered kid, so it was like something out of a movie where they go to the Goth club. My jaw kind of hit the ground, but I also felt immediately at home, even though I didn't know anybody there. It was both strange and something I had never seen before, but also felt like I had been going there my entire life.

Gillian Cox: First thing that really comes to mind was that the air smells like clove cigarettes. At first, it's like I'm entering a "forbidden" place. There was some really excellent music. It was brilliant. I thought this is finally a place where I feel like I'm at home, and nobody's telling me you can't dance or you're weird. We're all weird. We're all mad here. Please join us.

Mark Clavet: I recall getting to see the dress code in action. I was in the back of line and this one guy was shouting at the bouncer who basically told them to get lost and the guy was drunk and wanted to start a fight. I didn't see what led to that, but I thought he went away yelling and threatening. I get a little bit further down the line and a couple of minutes later he returns with a couple buddies. These guys are fairly built up, probably college age and they were just looking to start stuff. I thought, "Uh-oh what's going to happen here?" Because going out to bars back then was a bit rougher than it is today. But ManRay was always known as a place that wouldn't tolerate that. This place is for all the alternatives — the Goth, punk, LGBT, anything else that doesn't go elsewhere, and this was your safe haven.

So I'm watching this thinking, "Can I make it back before these guys really start a big melee or do I stand in line? I've been waiting here and it's cold." They again approach and one guy pulls out a knife. The guy who was there before is yelling and swearing at the bouncer again. "We want to get in." The first one just laughed at him and then his two buddies approached as well and made their way towards the door. They went straight for the bouncer who wasn't laughing anymore. He turned around and with one knock on the door two other bouncers came out and these guys went to jump the bouncers. I thought, "Are you stupid?" I couldn't see exactly what took place, who threw a punch or a stab or a slice, but the next thing I see is the first bouncer had this gentleman, the one who was making the trouble, took him and actually threw him out through the air. Another one of the bouncers had the other two guys each by the seat of the pants, one in each arm, picked them up and shoved them out. He chucked them out and they were gone. The whole time that they were leaving they're still yelling and threatening. It was pretty amazing, and I thought, "Wow this really is a safe haven after all."

Emily Arkin: One time I got locked out because we didn't make the cut for the dress code. I brought a friend's boyfriend who was wearing jeans and they're like, "Uh-uh." I remember being in the freezing cold, going back to his car and him putting on her black jeans in the backseat of a car, which is very hard to do. They were way too small on him. They let us back in.

Arlene Guerrero-Watanabe: The line the first time was pretty short. It was cold and I was huddling with a few of my friends waiting at the door. We had no idea what to expect because none of us had actually been there, but we had heard really good things from our Boston friends. When we finally got in the first thing, I remember is that it wasn't cold anymore and I was trying to find the coat check because I wanted to show off my outfit. As I looked around, it was super crowded and full of Goths. I was so happy. We fought our way to the bar through these massive crowds of Goths. It was so amazing. It was like coming home.

Karla Clute: It smelled like cigarettes, which didn't bother me because I come from a home where my mom always smokes. I remember it being dark but not dark enough that you couldn't see anything. It meant that people, if they weren't looking at you, weren't getting a real good picture of you. It's not a huge club, but I think I was expecting this tiny ass-like room based on Ceremony. But it was three rooms. It was a lot bigger than I realized, especially from the outside.

I think going to Ceremony was a nice stepping off point because I wasn't completely overwhelmed going into ManRay. Maybe not the first night, but after a couple it definitely felt like home. It felt comfortable. I was with people that weren't judging me and that looked like me. Rocky was the same way, but it was nice to be somewhere where I felt more like an adult.

Jill Kempton: I got in line and I remember they turned someone away in blue jeans. I was like, "Yeah, that's cool. Alright. Put a little more into your look, dress up a little bit, even if you don't want to do the whole all black thing or look Victorian or something. You don't go out in blue jeans."

Chris Famulari: Reaching back into the memories of my brain I want to say it was dusk because it was still a little light out. I remember hearing the bumping music inside. Everybody was dressed in black. I was told to dress in black and not to wear sneakers. Very important. I needed something with a black sole, so I asked my dad and he gave me his dancing shoes, which I still own. They are imported Italian leather. He said the shoes were what he used to take my mom out dancing with. They actually had wooden soles, but they were painted black.

They kept the doors closed and then, after you've got admitted, the doors opened with this kind of whoosh. All of a sudden everything gets louder. You start to see the strobe lights. There are people hanging out in the vicinity of the door because they want to see who's coming in. You go up this little flight of steps, they stamped your hand, and then you're in. It's completely dark except for the strobe lights. There's just music pumping everywhere, there's people walking around, and there is so much to see, so much sensory input.

The first time that I went with Christine I bought a cape in Harvard Square which was like 88 bucks. I wore it like twice. Anyway, so I had a cape on. "Oh, look at me with my cape." Her son Andrew was tiny, and he was with us and we were swinging him and somebody said your family is cute and we were like, "Thank you." I had my cape on, and I walked in and I was in another world. It was like nothing I'd ever seen or felt before. I really didn't go to clubs or a lot of concerts. It was a lot to ingest.

Guari Desi-Ackerman: I remember the front room had red lights and was almost a more casual area. The main room where Chris would be spinning was definitely wider lights mixed with the blackness. At the time the whole stage area was much more open. The dancing caught my eye, for sure. I really enjoyed sort of getting into that, it just felt like aerobics to me. People were wearing makeup and hairstyles. It was like a whole new world for me.

Patrick Baldwin: One friend actually ran afoul of the dress code one night. I did not have a ton of sympathy for him because I was like, "Dude, you're in a white t-shirt with a frog on it and jeans and white sneakers and it may not get you in the door. I have clothes you can borrow." He's like, "Nope, I'm gonna wear what I want to." He was upset when they wouldn't let him in. And I was like, "You knew! I told you."

Kevin Farrington: There was a strange current that I noticed the very first time I was there with people almost moving like a school of fish through the door and into the chill room in the front, then back into the cage, then into the front room, then maybe a tour downstairs and up the back stairways. People were in constant motion. You could easily let go of reality and just kind of drift with the crowds as you went through it. If you choose, you could stop and talk, which wouldn't have happened the first night by any means, but later on that became something. When you watch schools of fish in the ocean, it's almost as if they all know what they're doing.

Lilly Moon: Sometimes when I went into ManRay and watched people dance on the dance floor it was like watching the ocean. People may not have been looking at each other or been on the same part of the dance floor, but it was almost as if their movements went together. It was like this connectedness between people in the energy there and it was really beautiful.

Jenn Sutkowski: I was with my friend across the hall, and we went to a club on Lansdowne Street. I was so excited to be an "adult" in the city and get to do stuff. We went and there were these guys who were just grinding up on us and it was so crowded. It was horrible. It was really awful. By contrast, the first time I went to ManRay I was like "Oh my God everybody allows each other space and people are moving like they mirror each other but not on each other unless they want to be" and I felt okay. Fuck Lansdowne Street, which I kind of knew anyway. I really loved that I could go and dance and not be assaulted and just have that freedom of movement. I just remember lots of stomping and big boots, which I loved. Everyone was in black, which I loved, dressed to the nines, and made up to the nines. There were lots of beautiful and interesting looking people. I remember going into the basement, which smelled like bleach, to the coatroom and the bathroom. The scent of cloves cigarettes. There was a feel to it that I really appreciated.

Kathryn Pollnac: I don't think I'd been to a club before that had separate rooms. You walk into ManRay and there's this room off to the right and the lounge area in the front with couches where you can sit down. There's this ManRay smell, maybe dry ice. I had clothes that I put away in '96 and then in '98 I came back, and I opened this box, and it was just like, whoa. Clove cigarettes and dry ice and the smoke machine and everything permeated these clothes. How is it possible that this box smells like ManRay?

When I went clubbing, I did not have my glasses on so visually I don't know, I guess I liked the way the light was in the club and the cage to the side of the stage back where the DJ booth was. When I first started going there, I didn't go up on the stage as much because I do have memories of being down on the floor, dancing. Pretty quickly a couple of friends and I would go up on the stage and dance. That corner of the stage over by Chris's booth, that was my spot. I had to get there first thing and that's where I was all night, except when I would run to get some water or down to the bathroom and hope that I could make it back upstairs before someone else. I wanted to dance to more than the song. I was skipping to go down to the bathroom because I was like the Energizer bunny. I'd get there and I couldn't stop.

Crayola Tidd: I think it was more of a very open crowd. I definitely had the sense that people were sexually open and very accepting of everybody. At the punk rock clubs, you really don't dance, you just jump around in a pit. So, it was fun and different and people would dance. They would either be very respectful and dance near you or they would dance very close to you and sexy. It was dark and there's this big spider web made of chains, which I loved. There are three different areas to dance and then the lounge area so you can move around. There was a much wider variety of people and I met so many interesting people. I love that people were free to dress very sexy and feel very safe. Sometimes going to Lansdowne Street, I remember I went to a Peter Murphy show when a baseball game got out. All these Goths went against the crowd to get to the Peter Murphy show. It's not a very accepting area, even though they're a bunch of nightclubs, but Cambridge is very accepting.

Krista Siren: It was before the smoking ban. It would settle on you over the course of the night, and I would come home, take a shower and still smell the smoke. Not the most pleasant experience, but it was a thing. I was so glad when they came up with a smoking ban.

I tried to get there really early because they usually offered a discount and I wanted to get settled. It was dark, but comfortable to the eye. I almost always went to the cage. Terri's bar over on the left. In the first hour or so of it being open there would be very few people around and Chris would be playing some low-key stuff. He definitely had a style shift from the first hour of things being open, to when he wanted to pick up the pace to get more people on the dance floor, to when he really wanted to crank it up with stuff that people were all familiar with.

Paul Calnan: I always remember the smell of clove cigarettes, which was always a really pleasant smell to me. Even now if I smell a clove cigarette it takes me back to ManRay. Visually, in all honesty, I was kind of taken aback by a lot of stuff. It was definitely something new for me, so I was just trying to take as much of it in as I could. I guess I was a little shocked at first. I felt a little out of my element. Not necessarily appearance-wise because I grew up playing in bands that were kind of really over the top image wise and I was kind of accustomed to looking or dressing the part. ManRay always gave off a very provocative, carnal kind of vibe to it, which I guess was exciting for me.

Patrick Baldwin: Getting there was pretty disorientating. I didn't really know Boston very well and I was picking up someone. I got lost a bunch, so it was a pretty overwhelming experience just getting there. I remember it being this giant black block with this astonishing cast of people in front of it. I remember going through and seeing the room for hanging out and thinking that's cool because I was used to little metal clubs that were like a cement box. I'd noticed the techno room; I heard it and saw the flashing lights. Erica and I wandered into the back Goth room where I saw that spider web. That was back when you could smoke inside and there was also a smoke machine, so there's this cloud, almost like something from old horror movies. There was a bunch of music I'd never heard before. Bauhaus and Peter Murphy were just not like anything else I'd ever heard. The Cure, Siouxsie. It introduced me to half the music I listen to. Another thing I noticed that was strikingly different from metal clubs was the dance floor. It was bigger than a lot of the ones I went to, and it was filled with people dancing in wildly different ways. Metal shows, there's mostly people standing or moshing, not so much dancing.

Lucretia X Machina: Black paint and black posters. I liked that it had multiple rooms. The first one on the right had a disco feel and felt like a roller-skating rink. The left was the lounge and then straight and then was obviously the main room with the warped floor and cage and the two bars. There was one in the center and one on the side. My feeling about it was just like, "Oh, this is funky and cool." I'm very open to all these things right now in my 20s and 30s. I'm meeting new people. I like creativity. People seem very respectful. They maintained their space, but they seemed friendly.

Athena Costa: We had already been going to dance nights for a while. There was a nice musty smell. I knew the room had murals on both sides of it. I had severe amounts of anxiety, so I would stand against the wall until I had enough willpower to run onto the dance floor when a certain song would come on, probably New Order. I would just stand there and soak in watching everybody dance from afar.

Mark Calvert: I was pretty excited and wasn't sure what to expect. I'm parked in the Green Street garage, thinking "Hey parking, that's one good reason to go anywhere here!" I got in line. Many bars at that time were still a little rough, so a few fistfights here and there were not uncommon, even standing in line in the freezing cold, but it was uneventful outdoors. I heard the music from outside and I thought, "What is this?" I couldn't quite make it out, of course now knowing that there were two dance floors makes a little more sense. I went in and was grateful that I brought earplugs.

On the doors and on the walls are poster advertisements for other events and different nights there. I'm trying to read and mentally make notes. I could finally find out which night is which because I kept getting conflicting information. I had the process of trying to decide which night would be my first. I ended up on a Saturday night. I walked into the entrance and to the left was what looked like it could have been a ballroom area at one time, I think there was a piano there. There were some people in the chaises, leather with buttons and pins in the upholstery, simply Victorian looking.

I had noticed a poster with a giant warning about the strict dress code, "You will not get in" with giant letters in Sharpie written out clearly and I thought, "Wow I'm glad that I wore all black." One thing that really blew me away the first several times was how many of the women going there were elaborately costumed and dressed up. They look like they had just walked out of a TARDIS with many in Victorian outfits, which kind of fits with the Goth and steampunk look. I have yet to see to this day any place with women dressed up that elaborately. It looked like they spent all damn week just getting dressed and that was amazing. I could never do that. Some even had the big hoop skirts and bustles and I thought that was not fun. How can anyone have the patience for that? I felt a bit lazy and sloppy at that point. I think I was in just a black t-shirt with a band or concert name, but it was newer, cleaner, and black jeans and I had my favorite studded black leather belt and some basic cheap combat boots.

I didn't realize that the coat check was in the basement, so I just followed people and stowed my coat away, discovered where the bathrooms were, always useful when you're out drinking, and totally got lost, like I was in an MC Escher painting. I made my way back up and found the first dance floor. I thought it was a neat arrangement with a recessed dance floor and everything neatly laid out. Tons of lighting. The back bar, even from the other side of the room, you could see shelves with lots of beautiful liquor all neatly lit up and a pair of bartenders back there storing drinks up. I didn't notice the DJ to the far right in the corner until I was drinking. I saw the first bar which is where Terri was. Of course, she was, as usual, wearing the witch's hat and dressed up appropriately and I thought that was the woman who would deliver into my hands my first drink from ManRay.

Richard LaDue: One of the things I remember was the bathrooms downstairs being confusing for some reason. I felt like there were two places I could go and I'm like "Am I going to the ladies room or the men's?" The doors had no signs. I remember being like, "Is this okay?" That would make me nervous, not having rules or structure. It may not be the worst thing, but definitely challenging at first.

I remember feeling like this is different from what I've known, but I'm really curious. I just remember all these people, they didn't seem dangerous, I mean the clothes are aggressive and the looks are aggressive, but their demeanor was really cool. So, it was just very interesting to be like "Wow, you guys have leather jackets on or big spikes in your hair, huge boots or a million piercings." But they were very, very cool.

Chris Manousaridis: Oh, I remember my first time. Absolutely. I got to the front door. The building is completely black. It is unlike any kind of nightclub that I've ever been to where it's usually dressed up. We went through the doors and paid. I've never seen anything like it because it was this room that had crushed velvet couches and a pool table. It looked like something out of the Addams Family. That was my first sort of thought:

I'm in the Addams family's parlor room. There was a room to the right, which I guess was the Campus room. I started going into what would be the main room. You could smell clove cigarettes and I was a smoker. The dance floor, stage, and cage. It was kind of overwhelming the first time, but all of a sudden, they started to play that fun 80s music and I was like, "Okay, I'm really digging this." People were dressed to the nines. You go to Vegas and they're all wearing party dresses. You go to ManRay and its leather and vinyl with the 80s. We got dancing and that was it. I had a blast. The DJ booth was right above us and you can see Chris up there spinning. We had a good time and I fell in love from day one.

Shane Blau: Well, the first exciting part was always waiting in line outside. The excitement was already building by then, being in a line of people where I felt comfortable and a little subversive. I was nervous. I was excited. I was anxious about how other people were reading me. I was very young. This was a group of people I didn't know. I had never been to a club before. I remember we got the big black X's on our hand because we were underage. I'd never had to go through a bouncer before.

It's really dark when you go in and it's immediately loud because the dance room was right off to the right. You get the beat right away and everything's already kind of vibrating. I am not someone who tends to enjoy crowds, but it never bothered me there. My general sensory memory of ManRay is that the floor is a tiny bit sticky. There's a little bit of a smell like old, spilled alcohol, but mostly bodies, people, sweat, excitement and pheromones. It was crowded. It's kind of like when you're a little kid and you're around a bunch of adults and you don't quite know what's going on, everything's just swirling around you. That's what my first night felt like. I felt very much like everything was just happening around me.

Constantine Valhouli: One of my first impressions of the club was the remarkable synergy between the setting and the people. Everything read as black and red, the recessed paneling in the front room, the massive balustrade and newel post which suggested that the building had a longer and richer history than a warehouse. Entering the main dance area, the low ceiling dramatically rises, and there were the raised dais with the wrap-around murals. A mix of classical motifs, columns, and black and white tiles like M.C. Escher, with some mythology thrown in there for good measure. All of this complemented the outfits of the guests — leather, torn dresses, fishnets, platform boots. It felt like an overlap of Renaissance fair,

Rocky Horror, and dystopian future. The space and people complemented each other. A space like this was where these people belonged, and it was all about belonging, finding a group of like-minded people.

Chapter 12

1997: The Year of the Goth

"It's funny because I didn't really understand Goth until I got there, and then I turned out to be a total Goth at heart." — Jennifer

Although it gained speed throughout the 90s and had some opportunities, 1997 was the year that Goth culture truly arrived on the scene. With schools like Harvard, Lesley, MIT, Cambridge College, Boston University, Boston College and many more, the city saw the coming and going of generations of young people. Each year, new creative young minds would pour into the city and leave their marks forever before they departed. For the Midwestern high school misfit that dressed head-to-toe in black and never quite fit in, stepping down off that bus into Cambridge during the 90s opened countless doors. From the School of Fine Arts to the Pit, there was a wide new world to explore. Where their hometowns had never so much as heard of a Goth night, suddenly they found a place and a crowd that eagerly brought them into the fold. Before long Boston-Cambridge was a darkly vibrant place that allowed the Goth culture options and a multitude of choices, encouraging them in their own pursuits and demands. To a crowd that had mostly been pushed to the wayside, nights like Crypt, Ceremony, and Hexx — each with their own slightly different blend — gave Goths and industrial enthusiasts alike multiple nights to find themselves the perfect fit and the place to call home S.L.

Mizery McRae: The rise of the Goth and S&M and all of that, for me, came out of nowhere and it got very, very strong. Maybe it was word of mouth. I think the reason why it got so strong was because it was so different, and everybody was texting "We have a place! This is where you need to come!"

Noel McKenna: 1990, at least in my view, was still transitioning from an alternative club into a more underground one. Saturday was one of the favorite nights of the week because of the music being heavier on the industrial side with some Goth. The crowd also shifted over time as well. So, unlike the earlier years, I think there was a stronger emphasis on industrial music and then it started to shift a little bit more into the Goth realm, maybe around 1993 to 1994.

Arlene Watanabe: I'm one of the people who thought the dress code was essential. The fact that was enforced rather strictly made a much better experience for those of us who really were lifestyle Goths. It was just the purity of the aesthetic. It prevented random normal off the street bros in sneakers from coming in and bothering people who are scantily clad. I could wear whatever I wanted to wear, and I was in really good shape. I didn't have to worry about anybody bothering me. I knew the guys at the front, and I could always go to them if I needed. I never had a problem at ManRay. Some of the Goth nights these days I don't go to because they allow people wearing jeans in.

Noel McKenna: Chris was exposing us to certain artists and record labels like Wax Trax. This was before the internet, so you'd have to write to the record label in order to get a catalog. We'd start researching what bands were on those labels and then we would start buying music. Maybe we planted the seeds of ManRay's evolution into more Goth music because of our requests.

Corey Reeves: The music was so significant. It would set the tone: so emotional, so emotive, got everybody moving. You have Covenant, Assemblage 23, and softcore industrial that was very palatable. People would be running to dance or just standing. You'd have a sea of black and people just doing their Goth moves or their dissociative leg movements. The music would inflame emotion and radiance because it really set the tone.

Constantine Valhouli: There was a robust crowd of people from all over New England. I remember when Anne Rice, at the peak of her celebrity, was signing books at the Barnes & Noble in Kenmore Square. The line of black-clad kids stretched for blocks, and one recognized familiar faces from ManRay throughout.

Me'lissa Nin: I compare it to every other Goth club I've ever been to. ManRay is my first love.

Mike (Farmboy): I started going generally on Friday nights. I remember there were Goth nights. There was Bound for Pleasure, which was like the last Friday of the month. I would go to a couple of the Friday ones, and occasionally a Saturday if I could crash at my friend's apartment. I started dyeing my hair and dressing like a bad vampire. That stereotypical awkward kid trying to be cool as a vampire.

Jen Lucky Cole: I was a freshman in high school in 1994 and I was a little advanced, so I skipped a year in science, and I wound up being with upperclassmen in my biology class. I ended up befriending somebody who was my introduction to teens and young adult Goth. She's also the one who introduced me to nightclubs. Going to Providence was almost like the junior leagues, if that makes sense, in the Goth world. They had a night called Communion that started up in '95 and we had heard of it and knew some kids that could get us in.

ManRay reminded me a little bit of this club in New York that was my favorite club called The Bank, which was an old bank that was haunted. I loved going there and I'm still friends with the DJ. I liked it because it was split like ManRay and you had two different dance floors. The main DJ's setlist was a lot like Chris' and you could kind of guarantee that the music was going to sound pretty similar. Once you went into the back room, you'd get a different aesthetic. Patrick would play very, very strict Goth.

Tatiana Zimkus: There was a biography that I had written for the Miss Gothic Massachusetts website and it was about my relationship with my grandfather. When I was growing up, he wanted me to be in pageants. I was aspiring to be that girl, that woman, very feminine. It's so ironic in retrospect. I never actually entered a pageant, but I did love being onstage. In my own weird warped ex-Catholic way this was my tribute to him. I'm never going to be a beauty queen. I'm never going to be Miss America, but maybe I'll be Miss Gothic Massachusetts. So, I was like, fuck it. Let's do this thing.

Koren Bernardi: Long story … I participated in the Miss Gothic Massachusetts contest.

Derek Kouyoumjian: I would never quite say I was entirely Goth, I just kind of floated above all these different scenes, but the Goth thing I definitely identified a lot with, and I appreciated.

Jen Lucky Cole: One thing that helped was the internet. You might have heard this brought up — the term net Goth. I became a part of that before I knew what the heck was going on. This was like 1991. I was kind of smart and I learned that stuff pretty quickly and I started learning about all kinds of different Usenet groups. I had these goals as I was getting older, that I really, really wanted to be a part of that because there all these different Gothic net communities out there and Sinister was based out of Cambridge. They literally had a three-story house right down the street from ManRay. It wasn't easy getting involved with Sinister, but once you did, they used to have a lot of really friggin cool parties, usually after ManRay.

Tony Lee: I think, historically, Goths have been treated by society as more of a counterculture, whether or not Goths actually view themselves as that. I definitely have friends who don't identify as Goth, but I feel like in a lot of ways, they are more Goth than a whole bunch of people I know who do identify as Goth because of their personality. I think there is enough room in the Gothic subculture for people to kind of figure out what is and isn't Goth for them. I have friends who have a list of things you need to be in order to be "Goth." But I think that's a bit limiting, and I think there are people who would disagree. I let people kind of figure it out for themselves.

Andrea Parros: I think that I definitely have Goth tendencies, but I think most people would look at me and they wouldn't think I'm Goth even though I definitely don't really wear color.

Constantine Valhouli: In the mid to late 90s, maybe later, there was a Gothic music and culture convention of some sort, and the first time I visited ManRay, that was going on in Boston. The club was packed, and it was my first visit, so I had no expectations. I assumed it was like this every week.

Brian Legault: I found that the Boston Goths were more friendly than Montreal Goths. There's a bit of a clique ethos here, but, in general, there's a different level of friendliness. I really enjoyed the scene and how people were friendly and took care of each other. In Montreal there is an English and French divide, the scene was actually stronger there but then there were egos involved. So, coming to Boston and seeing sort of a semi-unified scene where the promoters actually didn't sabotage each other was great.

Gauri Desai-Ackerman: I think from '95 to '97 the whole Goth scene kind of bloomed. So, there were a lot of different nights.

Hideki Watanabe: I thought that was a glorious summer. I went out five days out of seven to a Goth club which was amazing. I really wanted to; I probably could have gone to two more nights. There were so many different nights and I was going to go to all of them. I compare Boston's night life to other cities. Boston is very much a college town but also a city. It's a smaller city than most. The West Coast had a larger population to support a Goth scene. Boston was smaller and so I kind of wouldn't expect that we would have as many nights. So that was wonderful and I'm like "This is really great that summer" and then they went away. I'm like, "Yeah, we can't expect that to last."

Kevin Farrington: One of the differences in the early days between the front room and the cage was I thought the front room had more people having a lot of fun. Whereas I thought there was more of a Goth ethos in the cage and there were some serious swirling going on, but it was not grim, it was informed and had a purpose. Where I thought the front room, particularly on Thursdays, was hedonistic, it was just everybody in the pool and sometimes that's what it felt like. It was incredibly hot and humid and close in the summertime in that building.

Cris Concepcion: I think that music might have led to the culture, but the culture was what kept me there. Being somebody who lived in the suburbs and didn't really spend a lot of time in the city, hanging out with a bunch of people in my college years in the Boston Goth community was really important to establish relationships and friendships with people. The internet was my community within that community. It was through Net Goth that I knew Tony Lee who, in the spring of '96, said he needed a roommate. I was just starting to come out of my shell, and I was really ready to explore a whole bunch of opportunities and meet a whole ton of people. But the thing I really liked about having an online community was the fact that hanging out with people didn't have to stop when you left the club. You knew there were a bunch of people who were on the mailing list who could talk about what happened the previous night. There were other people who didn't go out as often because they were in Western Mass, but you could still have really deep conversations about music or history or politics or books. It's really easy to make friends there and I really liked to dive into interesting conversations that you can't really shout at each other in a club. So, for me, the people I am most bonded with and the people who are still my friends I became friends with in the 90s and 2000s through thc Boston Goth list.

Paul Vitagliano: Boston, being such a huge college town with sort of artistic types and the non-mainstream, (you have) people arriving in Boston from all over the country, all over the world. You have such a huge student population and young ideas and people coming into their own. They might have arrived from some bumpy small town feeling like a misfit then here they are in this great city and there's a nightlife, a scene that understands them. So, they're going to gravitate towards it and find it immediately.

Chris Ewen: Wednesdays were a gateway into the club. I noticed that a lot of younger people were coming in. People trying to figure out who they were and where they fit in. They would come in on Wednesday for a few weeks, meet some people, hang out, observe, and maybe dance. Maybe a couple weeks later, you'd also see them pop up on the weekend. It was really apparent that Wednesdays were something important. It drew a very, very diverse crowd. People would dress up to go out on a Wednesday night. They embraced their personas, and they went out now.

John O'Leary: I remember ManRay on Wednesday nights. You can't imagine doing a Goth night anywhere these days where you get three, four, or 500 people on a weekday. In the heyday of ManRay, there were so many people who were flocking there. You were an outsider because you're an artist. You're an outsider because you're weird. You're an outsider because you were gay. And nobody accepted you in your neighborhood.

Skot Kremen: Wednesday night was very exclusive to the people that were involved in the actual scene. Nobody went on Wednesdays who wasn't into the music and that was actually probably why I liked it so much. If I struck up a conversation with somebody about some weird Chameleon song, they would know it.

Koren Bernardi: I think it was a Wednesday, so it would be Crypt. That was in the beginning part of '99 which makes sense because I graduated at that point, so I didn't have to go to school the next day. I had a calendar that said, "Go to ManRay." At some point between going there the first time and the summer of '99, I was like, "Yep this is my social life now."

ML: It was interesting to watch Chris. I remember when he would do Wednesday once a month, and it was just cherry working because it wasn't enough business for everyone else, but I was watching it come into its own though. Gradually it really took off.

John O'Leary: I really liked Wednesdays. I remember hearing a lot of people be like, "Oh Wednesdays was for beginners until you graduate into a night like Fantasy Factory."

Adam Wolff: On Goth nights, you could smell the cloves from a block away. You'd get out of the garage and just follow the smell of clove cigarettes to the club. When you got into the club, everything hit you. Everything from the smell of the clove cigarettes and the occasional punch of marijuana to the colognes and the incense oils. If you were down in the basement, it always smelled a little damp. Then there was the sweat on the dance floor that just stayed on the dance floor. Visually it's just a little black box so when you walk up to it doesn't look like much. This black painted brick building with the gate and a bunch of very dressed up people.

Trent Stewart: I was part of the group that promoted Fantasy Factory. We used Wednesday before the club opened to do rehearsals. We were there anyway so that was a great night to just dance. We weren't entertainers. We weren't promoters, we just had fun that night. So, it's very relaxing.

Kathryn Pollnac: I liked going to the New Wave nights, but Wednesday's Crypt was really where it was for me. Just being able to go in there, especially if I got there early because the DJ would play slightly less completely dance floor-oriented stuff, so I knew that I could hear some of the songs that I personally maybe liked dancing to more than the general population who came to the club. I would be in line and, as soon as I got there, I'd go buy a drink then I'd plant myself on the stage. It was nice when the booth was over there because I can kind of lean over and see what's gonna be playing next.

Derek Kouyoumjian: It was a Wednesday night because it was cheap, it was easy to get it. I remembered Friday nights were more expensive.

Chris Ewen: There was a time when I first started playing Depeche Mode on a Goth night where I was really worried about how the crowd was going to accept it. They really wouldn't have been thought of in the same light as a Skinny Puppy or Siouxsie and the Banshees. They were a different animal altogether. But it turns out a lot of my Goth crowd were really closet Depeche Mode fans and they loved it.

Chris Manousaridis: Hands down it was Wednesday's Goth night. I started to really get into the music from the get-go. I knew some of it already because I loved the alternative 80s, so I was recognizing a lot of that and going, "Wow, this is really great." They don't play that on Saturday night, but they're playing stuff that I had been listening to, like Front 242 and others. I really ended up loving Wednesday night.

ML: There was a safe place to have a Goth night. It worked really well. My first experience working those nights … I thought I was a little bit of a happy person behind the bar and some of the Goth kids were offended, but they warmed up to me.

Trent Stewart: The issue with the Goth nights, and even Fantasy Factory to some extent, was there's a certain lack of maturity in the scene.

Adam Wolff: One of the sort of cardinal sins is you don't bring a drink on to the dance floor with you. You stand on the side with your drink, and you don't drink on the dance floor. In every other meat marketplace in the world, it's people holding beer while they dance, but that's not how Goths dance. We use our whole body.

We've got this little group of tourists, a couple of guys and a couple of girls, and they're just standing there in the middle of the fucking dance floor after making fun of the way that we danced and we're all kind of like, "Fuck this." The DJ put on "Blue Velvet" by Spit and it was just like a call to the dance floor. A bunch of us are pretty big guys. I'm a bit over six feet, and I would consider myself one of the smaller guys on the dance floor at that moment. All of a sudden, we're just dancing this tribal fucking industrial dancing circle around these tourists. "Don't you fucking look at me." It was a great feeling. Certainly, scared them off the dance floor.

Liz Lamanche: On the Goth night people were pretty regular and nice. Occasionally some boy would get excited about dancing close, and I would have to kind of fend them off. It's particularly wonderful how the Goth community developed consent culture quite nicely in the ensuing years. They were always on the forefront of that. It's more of a tribe and they have a sense of dignity and personal space.

Patrick Baldwin: Because of ManRay, I've gone to Goth clubs in a lot of states at this point. One of the things I found interesting is that Goth crowds are a really trouble-free crowd as these things go. The guy that ran the Metro, which is where Haven was first, we were his favorite night because there was almost never any issues. He'd have his club packed to capacity, not a bouncer had to do anything.

Maryellen Vega: I think I might have gone on Wednesday night one time and I wasn't really a Goth. I did listen to some Goth music, but I never wore makeup or clothes or anything like that. I was more into grunge punk, stuff like that.

Keith Ward: I stopped trying to go to Wednesday nights, even though I liked the music. The vibe was never the same.

Rachel E. Pollock: Cusraque made it his full-time job to promote that night and make sure that it ran smoothly. The performances happened in a timely fashion and the performers got paid. The same was true for Fantasy Factory. The same for Xmortis with Patrick and Eloni. There was always somebody who invested in the success of the night. For Crypt though, there really wasn't anything like it. The same way that Campus was the gay night, but nobody was the face of Campus unless maybe it was Daisy. That's why people became invested in the Friday and Saturday night programming because they could draw enough of a crowd to get paid a decent amount for their time and effort. Whereas Crypt, I got paid a flat rate to DJ. It didn't matter if I went out of my way to try and get people to come to it. I played the music. I got the money. That was that.

Tony Lee: Hexx was started by former ManRay employees. There was a pretty high turnover of security staff once in a while and a whole bunch of them decided that they wanted to start their own night. They got a space in the Theater District and wanted to continue doing something similar to ManRay because it had been done successfully for years. I was asked if

I wanted to spin a night on Saturday. I agreed to do it and it was a pretty amazing space. They wanted to have performances similar to Cusraque's Hell. They decided to just kind of make a whole parody of ManRay and Hell. ManRay got really, really pissed off about Hexx. Saturday was New Wave at ManRay, so we weren't competing Goth night to Goth night, but ManRay got really pissed off. I was told I was not welcome for quite a while.

Eloni Feliciano: I really did enjoy Hexx, unfortunately they kind of got pulled in a lot of different directions and there was definitely rivalry.

Tony Lee: They booked some sort of Indian lounge night in town in the space that was meant for like 30 people. It was just mind boggling because there were all these Goths crammed into that small lounge dining space. The night also didn't start until 10:45 or 11 o'clock, so it wasn't worth it for people who drove in from the suburbs and had to leave by midnight. I've never been able to figure out why they did that because we had several hundred people show up every single Saturday and they decided that they wanted to move us upstairs into this tiny space and give us less time.

Nate Roman: When Hexx came up I was psyched. Hexx was thinking of shutting down ManRay. I was like, "No!" I also saw that Hexx was operating right out of the gate at a scale that was going to be very difficult to maintain. It's a lot of work. It's really expensive and really complicated.

Patrick Fitzgerald: I wasn't as active in 1997, but I did go to Hexx a few times and Ceremony. I think Hexx was kind of weird in that I went a couple times, and it was really busy and then the last time I went over there most of the night was dead. I guess people just wouldn't show up until the last hour of that night.

Tony Lee: Originally, ManRay kind of had a monopoly. Before, if you were going to Goth events you had Friday night. Now there was Friday and Saturday night. You could either go to one or both. The weekend started to get loaded with nights and we had several hundred people per night on Saturday, just like ManRay did on Friday nights, so that was a real threat. That's a real concern for competition for a really small scene. There was just so much drama. At one point someone came over and told me "Look, ManRay and Ceremony are cool. But we are not cool with Hexx. So if you want to continue doing Hexx you will not be welcome at

ManRay."

Heather Morgan: I graduated from BU in '96. After I graduated, I stuck around and was living in a loft on Melter Street in the Summer Street loft area. I lived in this really great space with windows on both sides, so I had a really great view of the Fort Point channel. I was going to Hex and ManRay.

Tony Lee: I just wanted to play music. I understand that I'm working with the staff at Hexx who definitely do not like ManRay and ManRay fired them. So, I can understand that ManRay sees me working with them and was like, "That's not cool," but I'm doing it because I have an opportunity to play music to people and I don't really care about the politics of it.

I'm not holding a grudge against ManRay for doing that. It's a business decision on their part if they don't want me there because I'm DJ and competing. But at some point, I got a call that everything was cool, and I started going back to ManRay. Eventually, everything blew over and people in Boston saw that you could have different nights and different DJs, and everything would work out.

Nate Roman: I decided to just launch my own night and just go for it. I found a club in Worcester called The Penitentiary that offered to let me do a night. I had no idea how to promote an event. It was the worst possible night in the worst possible place. It was an absolute complete disaster, and I gave everyone's money back. Later, being a DJ at ManRay and hearing that I tried to do something got this guy's attention and he approached me about starting a night over pancakes at Deli Haus. He had the idea to call it Ceremony after the Joy Division song. Somehow, we convinced the Paradise Cafe to give us a shot there. I just stepped up and took it over after the organizer left. I felt passionately about it. I thought I had a very clear vision for what I thought I wanted it to be.

Obviously, there is a financial side of this stuff. Goth nights are notorious for not making a lot of money. When I first approached Vinny, he wasn't feeling it at all. I told him my plan. I don't want to step on anybody's toes or take anything away from ManRay, I just wanted to add and prove that it's going to be fine. So, we did our thing and we didn't try to bad mouth ManRay. We didn't work against them; we made a real intention not to compete with ManRay. I recall many people telling me that, with a club like ManRay in Boston, you just can't compete with that. I never competed with them and I quite intentionally kept Ceremony on the small side. Ceremony could thrive with 100 people a night. We wanted anyone to feel like they could just show up without getting super dressed but also feel comfortable if they did. It quickly became clear that we actually reached some people.

Rachel E. Pollock: I did Ceremony longer than I did ManRay. I started as an equal partner. When I DJed at Ceremony, I would split the night with Nate 50/50. Also, I would get a stack of flyers, even on the weeks that I wasn't DJ.

Tony Lee: In October '96 I was asked if I wanted to come on board for Ceremony at the Paradise Cafe and I was like, "Hell yeah!" We did our night, which was really successful and ManRay saw that it had zero impact on the number of people who showed up on Wednesday night.

Rachel E. Pollock: I perceived there to be an anti-ManRay sentiment inherent in some of the rise of other competing nights.

Chris Ewen: Ceremony, when it started, wanted to be the anti-ManRay. Despite the fact that ManRay was very underground and not in the mainstream at all, there were a lot of people that thought that ManRay was the commercial side of it. They wanted to go deeper, be more obscure, and darker and cooler than ManRay.

Julia Kilcoyne: Ceremony. That was the night for people who worked in restaurants. If your job has you working on the weekends, a hairdresser or waitstaff, then that's your night. I thought it was kind of cool that they had that.

Matt Gleason: I went to Ceremony, not every week, but I did like it a lot. I never got a chance to go to ManRay because I was working. That's the downfall of working in nightclubs. You don't get to really go out that much on the weekends. If you're going to go, Ceremony is a perfect opportunity because it's on a Monday. ManRay was Wednesday and Friday and I was always working those nights.

Brian Legault: The easiest way of describing Ceremony is that Ceremony was where everyone went, and Crypt was where people actually dressed up a little bit. It's not often that you see someone with their shirt off at a Ceremony to dance, but half of the guys had their shirts off at Crypt.

Eloni Feliciano: Ceremony was two blocks away from my house, so that was not a hard choice for me at all because I could literally get dressed up in the most ridiculous outfit and go and, if I got tired, I could go home. Ceremony was no problem. There also was not really direct competition. First of all, it was a Monday night which was a dead night. Like ManRay was its own Cheers, Ceremony was its own Cheers in a different way, where people would mostly go to socialize for a couple of hours. You don't need to be crazy bananas.

It was probably their biggest competition because it was on the same night as other nights that were going on at ManRay and they were mad. I know that ManRay was very mad about them breaking off. They were all people who decided they no longer wanted to work with the club. I actually ended up going to their fetish night first, before I went to the one at ManRay, only because they are 19 plus while ManRay was 21 plus.

Chris Manousaridis: We had fun at Ceremony. Wednesday wasn't enough for me. Usually, nobody did anything on Monday, it was a dead night, but he would bring a crowd. It was me and Nate and Adam spinning, and it was just so much fun. I could do a lot of different things there and add different things. The atmosphere was different.

John O'Leary: Ceremony has done an unbelievable job. I love the fact that those guys have been able to do that for 25 years. I remember when they first did it at the Paradise. I was at the very first one and I used to go to all of them.

Nate Roman: The thing about ManRay is it's all about consistency, in a sense. If you went on a Wednesday night or Friday night, you have a very clear idea of what music to expect. I wanted to do something that had more variety to it. I wanted Ceremony to be a place where more people could be involved. I wanted to give people the opportunity to try things out and a lot of people did. I tried all kinds of stuff. Some of it was huge and very successful and some of it was a complete and utterly colossal failure. But I had the freedom to experiment, which was really important to me.

Eventually it got to a point where people were starting to get picky. Like if you start giving your customers a variety, they start getting very picky about what they like and don't like. There are people that really want industrial stuff while others want slower down tempo stuff. So I turned it into recurring monthly events. There's Down with Tempo, which was the first Monday and then Thud, which was on the third Monday to cater to those more specific audiences.

Emily Taylor: I went to Ceremony a lot because they were doing down tempo nights and I really liked down tempo because it was like rolling around and enjoying. I liked how Ceremony would differentiate itself by having these different styles of music throughout the month. I went to The Pill a couple times, but that was more my sister's scene. At that point in our lives, we were trying to differentiate from each other a lot because we're identical twins. She wanted to have her own thing and I wanted to have my own thing and my thing was ManRay and her thing was The Pill, but we would sometimes go to each other's thing.

Mark Clavet: That's what I enjoyed about ManRay, that you could find mixed people there any time. Regardless if it was Goth night or something else there would always be some spillover no matter which evening you went to it. Take your pick of any particular night. It wasn't really rigid.

Mike Hsieh: Everybody can just kind of mix. Most nights you'd have some of the gay boys coming into the Goth room because they loved it and then Goths were going to the techno room because we love techno too. It was just a riot. It was just fun because nobody thought that there was anywhere that you shouldn't go, or you shouldn't enjoy. We were just all just there and loving it.

Skot Kremen: It was sort of almost like going to a Goth version of Cheers. It was a place where literally everybody knew my name.

Tatiana Zimkus: I'm there three times a week. It would be Monday night Ceremony, Wednesday night Crypt, Friday night whatever Goth night was happening, and then occasionally I'd go to Heroes.

Adam Wolff: There was always something going on in the lounge, like art shows and vendors, especially on Friday nights.

David Winthrop: I felt like a fish out of water on Thursday, but it's only because I wasn't gay, not that I felt unwelcomed by any means. So many of the people that were regulars at any of those nights went a lot of the other nights. No matter what night I was there, I would see people I knew. That was guaranteed between the bartenders, the staff, and just regular patrons as well. There was always somebody there to say "Hey, hi how are you"? It was a family, and it was a pretty amazing one full of some really incredibly eccentric, incredibly amazing people.

Michael Hsieh: What was just so special and so unique was the fact that the Goth community and the gay community and the fetish community were all there and just having a good time. At other Goth clubs I've been to, there can be some pretentiousness or standoffishness. But they are also just the loveliest bunch of weirdos. I think it probably has something to do with all the schools here. It just brings in new people who just celebrate being themselves and dressing how they want to.

Eloni Feliciano: There's something about them that society would not necessarily be comfortable with, whether it be Goth kids because we want to dress in black or fetish people because you don't understand sexuality then again with gay people and trans people. It's all different types of people that are there. They don't actually pose a threat to the world by wanting to express themselves in certain ways.

Michael Marotta: I was on a Wednesday and Saturday schedule. It was really two different moods but a welcoming community. That was the one thing that I always appreciated.

Gene Dante: During its heyday it was packed every time. That was a lot of fun. We would go on occasion to Heroes which is a fusion of old top and alternative and some modern stuff, mostly a dance night, very eclectic. There was a night on Wednesdays that was strictly Goth. I had to work a job, so it was hard to go out late on a weeknight.

Sara S. Wendell: When I first started going, I didn't know anybody other than the two or three people I went with. Then slowly getting to know the people who ran it and eventually getting to know the regulars. I called it "Goth-mosis." After a while you've been around somebody in the same places in the same parties for long enough that you just know each other, even if you've never been formally introduced.

Matt Gleason: As a customer it was great to have this variety of places to go on any given night.

Me'lissa Nin: I went pretty much every night. I really loved every night because it was different each night that you went — Wednesday, Thursday, Friday, and Saturday. Saturdays had the New Wave crowd, Thursdays you had Campus. One thing that I really loved was that there was such a crossover. You had people who went to ManRay on Wednesdays and who also went on Saturdays, people who went on Fridays but also went on Thursdays. So, it was this nice melting pot. Everyone treated everyone else with respect. It was really nice because, think about high school and how cliquey high schools can be, but this wasn't like that at all, everyone was so friendly, and people embraced. It didn't matter what night you went to; it didn't matter how you dressed or didn't dress, people were just really nice and accepting. So that was something that really stands out in my mind.

Athena Costa: It wasn't just a Goth club. It was a very accepting club. You didn't have to be a Goth person or gay person to go there. They didn't judge you; you could just go and have fun.

Kyle Blaisdell: It was the most inclusive environment, even though the dress code was all black and the people range from all walks of life. We just had to have some things in common. You didn't have to have everything in common. As long as you conducted yourself accordingly you were welcome.

Emily Arkin: I don't know if I was like that critical consumer of that culture. I was sort of a punk Goth light. If I went somewhere and there were people dressed in black and it wouldn't be bro-y or jock-y, I would say this is my scene and these are my people. But I don't know if I knew enough to know all the nuances. I always think of that NPR story where she talks about being an "advanced Goth." She said at some point you get to wear pink and white if you are really advanced Goth. I was not there. I liked to wear black.

Anna Feder: Goth nights felt really comfortable to me, the dressing up. I really loved music, not industrial, that was never my thing, but the more poppy stuff was certainly a crossover with what Chris would play like Sisters of Mercy and Siouxsie and The Cure and The Envy Nation. That stuff I really fell in love with. The Goth nights, the Friday nights, Xmortis, and then Chris' night really stick out.

Liz Lamanche: I wasn't a lifestyle Goth, but I could dress up and go enjoy the party and the people.

Jennifer: I don't think I knew what I was walking into the first time. The very first time I went I never really understood what Goth was. I was trying to sample and do my makeup for the first night. I thought I'd try the big black rings around my eyes and I'm so glad I decided at the last minute not to go that route. I didn't really understand Goth until I got there and then I turned out to be a total goth at heart. I kind of always had my own distinct look. I think I just finally found it and just fit in.

Taylor Vecchio: I think with ManRay I would have more fun with it. I would wear a fun outfit because I feel like people would dress fucking crazy. You're like, "This is an opportunity for me to play a little." At ManRay there's a certain style and aesthetic that people have there. It's not one that I would like to wear all the time when I go out, so let me use this as an opportunity to wear something that's a little darker and more playful. Or more makeup than I normally would, or something like that.

Emily Taylor: I didn't have a lot of money and I was just kind of a sad Goth kid. I had a lot of fishnets and things like that. I wouldn't often have time to get ready at home, so I would be in the car, and that means that I would have on like a tape with some Goth music that some boyfriend, or boy who wanted to be my boyfriend, probably made for me.

Jon Whitney: Tolerance. Everybody's human underneath whatever clothing they're wearing, whatever style they have, and just respect. ManRay wasn't — and maybe this is just a Hollywood misnomer where you see Goth clubs in movies, and everybody's just mean — but at ManRay people went there to have a good time and be around people that they could be comfortable around. They could dress up, they could dress down, they could be what they want to be.

Andrea Parros: First and foremost, black. You can't wear something other than black. It would be different black shirts to choose from or different black tights or dresses. It had to be black. It's a chance to wear night gear. It's a chance to wear something you wouldn't wear during the day. It can be a little bit more revealing, a little more risqué. It could be something almost like a character. It could be something you wouldn't ever really wear in your day-to-day life, but it kind of allowed you to be in character. Maybe you always wanted to look like a goth princess.

I definitely remember watching people dance in cages and the pedestals or podiums because I remember being really drawn to how competent all those people seemed. Everybody was really comfortable and confident and some of it might be exhibitionism. It was just always something that I wanted. At the time, I really was still kind of an awkward college kid still working on confidence. I used to really enjoy watching people because that would be like, "Wow, what's it like to be that confident?"

Chris Manousaridis: You had the Cybergoths, you had the more Victorian, and the 50s pinups. All these different styles are kind of brought together as one, but everybody still had their individuality.

Cris Concepcion: I'm not a big fan of the sort of elitist point of view that if you don't wear a lot of black, you're not really worth our time or you're in some ways inferior to other folks. Everyone has an interesting story to tell. Everyone has a challenge. I like the idea of a shared weirdness as a way of flipping that lens.

Koren Bernardi: At first, I had to be prepared because we're going to go to this club and it has a dress code. At that time, I was kind of not super into fashion. The look I had was very black — black boots and probably worn jeans or fish nets with some sort of layered rippy kind of top. I felt pretty comfortable in that I didn't feel like I was putting on a new skin, but it was new to be able to walk into a place and be completely surrounded by people in that scene. I wasn't the weird kid that was in black going to a funeral. Everybody was wearing black. Everybody had makeup, some was precise or some kind of smeary Cyberpunk Blade Runner. Everybody looked cool. It wasn't like one person out of a mall full of people. It was so freeing. Visually, I was in love. It's dark. It's creepy. It's got red, it's got black lights and it's got cool art. I love the sound of the music that was playing.

Emily Arkin: I actually want to credit one place that I think really influenced my style, which was Gypsy Moon. It was in North Cambridge so near my neighborhood where I was growing up. It was definitely bohemian, but it was also very Goth and had lots of chokers and long black velvet cloaks and whatnot.

Emily Taylor: At that stage of my life, I was mostly Gothy and I dressed like that every day unless I was at work. I dyed my hair. I had burgundy colored hair with Bettie Page bangs for a long time. That was me.

Keith Ward: Everybody in the hardcore scene kind of dressed the same, not the same, but the same. Same with Goths. They all had their own little bit of style, but they all dressed kind of the same. Same with our group and same with a lot of scenes like that. Back then you could be different, but you couldn't be that different or you catch shit in the scene.

Lily Moonstorm: I had prepared by doing a ritual, so I was already really energetically charged. I felt kind of like déjà vu and like coming home at the same time. I grew up in New Hampshire, where, in the 90s, there were not a lot of Goths and you got a lot of crap for it. When you could find each other, it was really rare and hopefully you got along. So, coming to a place with music and people that have similar tastes that you could bond over was really cool.

Tonya Sand: Wednesday was more of the Gothy night. The music was definitely a lot elder school kind of Goth. Wednesday is kind of like, I would never say casual because people dressed up a lot and I did too. It was definitely more elegant going out on a super impressive night like Hell for example. On Wednesdays you're still super dressed up, but it wasn't on the scale of a Friday or a Fantasy Factory.

Sara S. Wendell: When they started doing the Goth night on Wednesdays, I figured I would check that out. I loved that one. I checked out both Thursdays and Saturdays. The crowd for each night was definitely somewhat different although there were a bunch of people that you could see on any given night. Wednesday and Friday, I think had the most overlap in the crowds that would come to both. Thursdays you would see a few of the Goth people, but there was a much different vibe for Campus. The overall feel of the club was much more lighthearted, I guess would be a good word for it. Whereas the Goths took themselves a little more seriously, or at least it's kind of the atmosphere. Saturdays were fun, mainly because I am a child of the 80s, so I love the music. Saturdays I found, overall, to be more friendly toward your average slob on the street who would come in figuring he could pick up some hot vampire chick and that was kind of obnoxious. You got a lot less of that on the other nights, I think.

Kathryn Pollnac: I think I was Goth by default. I didn't set out to be Goth. It was the late 80s, early 90s, I was a college radio DJ, I was an art student, and I was living in southern Rhode Island where there was no scene there. Suddenly I found my people. I think, for me, it centered more on art and music and less on clothes. When I started going out there, I always wore black and had fun with thrift store clothes and making costumes. My mom could probably tell you that when I was a little kid I was running around in costumes because it's just what I do.

When I first started going to ManRay I really didn't have a lot of club-appropriate clothes. All my money was going to art supplies and buying rccords. So, it's like, "Well, what do I have at hand? What can I get at Salvation Army or some thrift store on a clearance rack that's really cheap that I can throw together and look good?" I had all this black lace that I whipped up a dress from. One of the first things I wore was this long floor length black velvet skirt. I kind of salvaged some stuff from my mom. Her mom had made her a black velvet dress when she was younger, so I kind of took that and turned it into a skirt and I remember safely pinning it at the waist because it didn't have a zipper. I had a pair of fishnet hose that I put on with a sleeveless tight tank top and whatever necklace. I started getting more clothes when I found out about the Garment District.

Emily Taylor: After Marilyn Manson started happening and the subculture of the Goth industry started becoming more mainstream, you started seeing people coming in that were clearly different from the kind of Goth that I was when I started going to ManRay and the Goths that existed before me. I was actually a little younger than a lot of people there and I almost felt that, in a lot of ways, the prime time had passed of my people being at ManRay … I was at the tail end of my own subculture there.

Chapter 13

SPECIAL CONNECTIONS

"I always tell other people that ManRay starts as being the craziest, wildest place you could ever imagine when you first get there and six months later it's your living room" — Norm

Nightclubs, at their most basic, are social places. ManRay understood that and encouraged it. One of the building's greatest features was its multiple rooms. If the music in one room wasn't doing it, you could migrate to the other, meeting new people on your way. If you needed a quiet moment to escape or just wanted to hang with friends, the basement and the lounge were perfect areas for that. If you needed a break from the dance floor the bartenders were there to welcome, you. Friends would meet up, get ready, and hit the club together. Even if you went solo, there were many opportunities to find yourself a group to dance the night away with.

When 1 a.m. rolled around and the last song was played many were not quite ready for the night to be over. People spilled out onto Brookline Street while the staff desperately tried to keep everyone quiet. Post night activities ranged far and wide from continuing the night at an after party to hitting up Hi-Fi, Deli Haus, or IHOP for much needed sustenance to the long drive home to western Mass. The club drew in a pretty steady regular crowd. For those who came week after week, faces that began as strangers soon morphed into some of the closest friends anyone could hope to have. For many, their time at ManRay created the foundation of lasting relationships that continue on into today. S.L.

Paul Vitagliano: When you go to a place that everybody goes to that is the most popular, the most known, the most advertised or the most packed, then you're just a number. And, even though you might have the best time of your life, it doesn't have that special connection. When you kind of live a little bit on the fringes and you're not a mainstream person, you have maybe an artistic bend, then you find a place that immediately feels expressive and artistic and wants you to be different and "Oh my God there's five people that look just like me who I've never seen in a nightclub before!"

The best clubs don't necessarily have to have the most people filling the room. They have to have the right people. A room full of 50 people that really want to be there and really want to add to the energy is more exciting and better than 1000 people who fill the room and don't add shit to the energy. They're just taking up space.

Chris Ewen: I think one of the reasons that ManRay succeeded as a venue was that it was a space where people knew they would find like-minded souls; where they could gather and dance and drink, but also meet each other. I know tons and tons of people who met at ManRay through that social scene and are still very close. When the nightclub closed they continued to socialize and hang out. ManRay was the basis for people who wouldn't necessarily have met otherwise.

Mizery McRae: The one thing I told everybody I brought there was just to be open minded, see what it is because you don't want anybody telling you that you can't be gay, or you can't do that. Everybody that I brought loved it.

Rebecca Griffin: I think it's almost like a sixth sense with ManRay because it was unlike anything I'd ever felt or experienced in my life. It was different at ManRay because it was that instant welcoming feeling that gave me that initial pull. I found connections with work but going into ManRay … it was instantaneous.

Don is there to greet you. He learned your name off the bat. I think I probably just went back the next day. So, it was an incident like "Oh, were you here yesterday?" That camaraderie between the staff. I ended up dating and hanging out with half the staff while I was there. I think that also helped to inundate me to learning and meeting a lot of people probably a lot faster. Even though it was a short time for me, it was the relationships that I developed during that time that were important. You'll see these kinds of relationships and friendships in people that went to sororities.

Emily Taylor: I was constantly meeting new people. I was at that stage of my life where I was not very snobby. I was really friendly so people would talk to me all the time, mostly male people. One thing I will say about dating at ManRay was that it felt very safe at the time because creepy people, you could get them away from you very quickly. All you had to do was talk to a security guard and they'd be out. It was a lot of power for a person like me to have. I worked there. I had a lot of friends there. I had my posse. I had security. I had the power of youth and sexuality. It was a very powerful feeling for me at that stage in my life where I was a young person who didn't have a lot of power. With that in mind, I became very aggressive as far as dating people. If I saw someone, and I thought they were really cute, I would be the one that was like, "YOU!!!!" and it worked great. I probably met every single boyfriend I had from 17 to 25 at ManRay.

One thing I will say is that this place was such a family for me, a dysfunctional family in a lot of ways. I once had a dream that my own family showed up to have Thanksgiving dinner at ManRay and they were serving peas and mashed potatoes and all this stuff and I was just like, "Oh shit! My actual family is so weird." My mom actually showed art once at ManRay. So, my world kind of blends a little bit.

Gauri Desai-Ackerman: It was horrible at other clubs. But at ManRay there was sort of an unwritten law … it was just really looked down upon for anybody to really harass anyone at ManRay. One thing I really loved about ManRay was that you had all types of people. There was a guy there, I remember seeing him dancing, who was an amputee. He'd get out there on his crutches and he would dance up a storm on one leg and two crutches. It was phenomenal. There was a guy that came in a wheelchair who would come in and pop around in his wheelchair and hang out. I just thought that was fantastic. That's a place for me.

I can't go to other places. I can't be bothered with that. Get me to a place where people are just having fun, relaxing, enjoying each other, meeting new people. A place where you don't have to be scared that you're going to get into a situation. Of course, there were bad people who went there and people who had bad experiences. That's true for anywhere in the city, but you kept your head up and you kept your eyes out for those sketchy people and if you kept your distance, you'd be fine. The thing that was really unique about ManRay was that if you felt scared, if you felt you were next to someone sketchy, you could go to anyone and say

"Hey, I'm being bothered" and they would all look out for you. That was a community you really didn't see anywhere else.

Gibby Miller: I certainly met friends at ManRay, but I don't think that I met the majority of the people that I met through romance. That was at other clubs.

Adam Wolff: Community and ManRay are practically synonymous. It's hard to separate one from the other and that's why so many of us are so nostalgic about ManRay. ManRay was a family. For the most part it was a very accepting scene. We had our occasional problems with tourists which was bound to happen. We were a freak show, but it was such an incredibly safe place for us to express ourselves in such a dramatic and wild and sexy way.

Gene Dante: It was a place where people were encouraged to express themselves. It did become a hangout for a group of people who otherwise might have been misfits. I felt ManRay fostered a sense of community because we had much more of a routine than the rock clubs. The routine definitely made it possible to foster community because, whether it's your book club or your meeting, it's going to happen on the same night of the week. Human beings are social creatures.

Julia Kilcoyne: Everybody was really nice, that's what surprised me the most about ManRay. ManRay was definitely out of the norm, but at the same time, the people that you met there were not what you thought. You had everyone from your Goths to your fetish to your New Wavers. A good example, many people may remember "sweater man." I don't know who he is. He was a skinny white dude, middle aged, and used to dance with a sweater wrapped around his shoulders. That was his thing, and nobody cared.

Emily Sweeney: You knew right away that you were good because you were being greeted by friendly faces. From the first time I walked in, I didn't know anybody, but people actually smiled and seemed friendly. It was unlike any other nightclub I had been to before. Usually, the first stop would be Daisy's bar to get a drink.

Erin Falkell: No matter who I was with, whether I was in a relationship or not, especially at Campus, I wanted to dance. I would dance with my friends. I remember people just digging a song and having, not necessarily sexual, but intimate hanging on each other looking at each other's eyes and just experiencing that moment.

Nate Roman: I was there for the music. I was there just for the experience of the night. I loved to dance, and it just threw me right in. It didn't take me long to build up some kind of social network.

Abigail Taylor: When I first started going there, I met so many people. I just wanted to know everybody. We all became very, very close. There was a constant flux of people coming in and coming out all the time, but there were the core people there as well.

It was always difficult watching people break up. There was one summer where everybody broke up with everybody and then everybody started dating other people. It was a chaotic shift. So, in one way, it was easy to meet people, but in another way, there were people who were kind of off limits, like you couldn't date certain people because certain people had dated them before.

Norm: It's important, if you're going to be going back to a place time and time again, to become a mirror. You order the same thing all the time if you can help it. It became a game later on to see how fast it would take, how quickly I can become a regular somewhere. Terri kind of took me in early on and stuck up for me.

Jennifer: I was very comfortable right away, except for the fact that I thought I was gonna get in trouble because I was underage. I didn't really know anybody, but I quickly got to meet some people. By the second or third time I went there, Trent came up to me and told me I was a good dancer and from there on, I started getting integrated into the scene. Then I started working at the nightclub. My only regret would be that I was always a little bit shy when it came to meeting new people and I wish I was a little bit more open with that because all these people are great friends now. I'm thankful that they stayed in our lives.

Norm: There was a camaraderie with being there. You protected people when you were there, which was a very important part of the club.

Mizery McRae: Being a drag queen and being an entertainer, you meet so many people. A lot of people become acquaintances and then friends. I became friends with the management and most of the bartenders.

Tatiana Zimkus: I have always been someone that's felt the need to connect with other people in one way or another, so being in a place in my life where I can finally truly connect with people on a deeper level, people that I felt understood me and vice versa, it really just became such a part of my life and so important to me and still is.

Abigail Taylor: When I think of ManRay it feels like family. It felt like home. In fact, there was a Depeche Mode song called "Home" and there's a line that says "Finally, I feel that I belong here." It was a song that Chris would close the night out with a lot. When I hear that song now it makes me cry, even though it sounds kind of cheesy. I miss those days and I miss that family. There's a lot of parts of my relationships with those people that would not fit into the 2021 world. There were things that we did, and places we went to that don't fit now that I would never engage in now. It just felt like a sense of belonging that I've never felt anywhere else. It was specific to that time. If I tried to go back in time and be who I am now, it wouldn't feel the same.

Becky D: When I'm in a new space and I don't know a lot of people, I tend to be very shy. I was introduced to a lot of people like Trent and Michael which helped me meet more people. As I became a regular, and then became part of the working crew for ManRay, it was much easier to meet people because I felt more confident. I felt like it was more my space. So, I had the confidence that, if I wanted to meet someone, I would walk up and say hello.

Jen Lucky Cole: Don would come by and just talk to you and go "Hey, you want to drink? I think I know the guy who owns this place." He was king of the dad joke before that was a thing. He was just so funny.

Norm: There was an anonymity that went on there that allowed people to exist outside of society. Maybe it's a reflection of the camaraderie we were talking about. There was an inside and outside, and there were enough people who went there to be anonymous.

Rebecca Griffin: Initially it was people that were interested in coming up to me in a romantic way. One of my really good male friends now, we met there, and he used to hit on me, week after week, and he was disabled. I know he wasn't there for a while and it's because he was in the hospital. He already gave me his number, so I called to check on him, "Why haven't you been at the club?" He told me that he couldn't drive. I picked him up and took him to ManRay. He comes to every one of my holidays and now he's uncle to my kids. It definitely started with him hitting on me and we were able to segue into that and to now understand respect and long-term friendship.

Jennifer: There was definitely a year or two where I felt very appreciated. They wanted me to be in this photo shoot. They wanted me to be in this performance. So you just feel very comfortable and welcomed.

Jennifer Chandler: At ManRay you never knew who you were going to run into when you were there.

Jen Lucky Cole: We were lucky because they had a former state trooper, Michael Cafferty, who was a very, very, very good security guy. People try to fight him … it wouldn't last very long. He knew how to get people to leave so they wouldn't even want to fight. Cambridge police were always at least in front of Hi-Fi, if not over by The Middle East on the side, just waiting for something.

Koren Bernardi: I don't know how it came up, but I was working in a call center somewhere for my day job and I mentioned ManRay, kind of in passing, not knowing that most people didn't, and my boss at the time was like "ManRay in Central Square? I used to go there." At the time I was 20-year-old and she was 40. I was like, "Old lady, go to bed."

Athena Costa: In general, when you read comics, you have customers and then you have friend customers and then new friends. So, you'd have these friend customers, people you're super familiar with that you may eventually hang out with. I would see some people around, I would go out and kind of spot them from afar or they would approach me and say, "You work at Newbury Comics," because I was always on the register. That was how I met people, from going out to dance nights and clubs to some of them being my customers.

Alyssa Hassan: I could go to Campus by myself and I knew I was going to see a bunch of people I knew and can dance with and we'd have a great time. It meant a lot to be able to find this community that kind of understood or accepted you for all the crap that happened to you in life.

Elizabeth Galbraith: It's a totally different atmosphere, as a young woman walking into clubs like The Roxy or Avalon. Sometimes they'd make comments as you walk in and tell you what number you are on a scale of beauty. I would never get that at ManRay. I never felt like I was ugly there, I felt awesome. I can't say from others' experience, but the group of people I was with, we always looked out for each other.

Emily Arkin: I was a little bit of a dilettante or a dabbler. I would usually recruit different friends to go. I didn't have a regular crew, but it was something we could do. I felt more like I was learning about other subcultures by going there rather than being among them. I think I was a little standoffish meeting new people. Maybe I was being jaded and a little guarded as a person, but I never went in as a meat market. I usually went with someone I knew and left with that person.

Erika Spaulding: Pretty quickly I made a lot of friends and realized how nice everybody was and how artistic everybody was, and everybody had something to contribute or something they were making, and it became more about the people for me then. I saw it as a creative expression, but the happy surprise was how many great people were there and the lifelong friendships that I made.

Jennifer Chandler: Totally different vibe. It almost felt like a second home because everybody I knew or was in love with was there. I remember singing our way to the parking lot in the garage. I definitely felt safe, but I think it was because of the company we kept. I don't think it was necessarily the club itself.

Constantine Valhouli: The decor worked — it evoked the tattered grandeur, faded aristocrat, Brahmin-gone-naughty vibe of Boston — but above all it was the people. Truly, as long as one could assemble that crowd, or any crowd of similarly minded strangers really, you'd get a microcosm of demi-monde society much like that. If the music and the décor worked too, then you'd have a place that could endure for a while. But then the next generation should reinvent it and make it their own. Now that we are the older generation, we'd be delighted to visit a place like that and maybe become regulars again.

It was flirtatious, sexy, fun, eccentric, unexpected. It was, long before we had such language available to us, a safe space. A place that was beyond judgment. You could go there with friends to celebrate, but it was just as much fun to go there alone and have incredible conversations. It had the Boston reserve, where people needed to be there a while before others would open up to them, but if architecture, as some architect said, is a machine for living, then the club scene is a machine for empathy. It really was about a sense of belonging for people whose interests diverged from that of mainstream society in some way.

Me'lissa Nin: For me, it was if it happened, it happened. I didn't go there with the intention of trying to meet someone to date. For me it was going there, seeing my friends dancing, listening to music, and having those connections.

Jen Lucky Cole: Once I started working at ManRay in 1999, I was in a position to be able to help grow the community. I noticed that, in the last hour of the night, we would go through an insane amount of receipt paper and lose all our pencils and pens because people would be exchanging numbers. The owner would get a little angry because the wasted receipt paper would cost them money. So, I came up with these little annotated things at the table by the ATM machine, which said your name, your phone number, email, and then the date so you can remember when you met the person. A neat little idea because I thought it would help grow the community. When people stopped smoking, we didn't have matchbooks so that's when they started bugging the piss out of all the bartenders who would be trying to cash out.

Jenny Dahling: I can't say that was a primary reason for going. I guess it seemed just so natural there. I would be out having a cigarette and I would strike up a conversation with someone outside and it didn't even occur to me that they would rebuff me, or they'd be a dick. It just felt I had found my tribe. There's no reason to be self-conscious or doubt myself. Looking back, it's like "God damn, I have it." If I could have harnessed that feeling.

Paul Calnan: For the most part, it was always the type of place that I didn't have to necessarily worry about, as a guy, leaving your girlfriend or your wife alone for five minutes and you come back and there is a swarm of guys around her. At ManRay that didn't really happen very much which was a big part of the reason why my wife and a lot of her friends enjoyed going so much because they could let loose and be themselves and dance and not have to worry about the night at the Roxbury guys. I very rarely ever saw trouble there. There were never any incidents of me having problems, like the potential for a fight, or anything like that. Even if you're on the dance floor going crazy and you bump into somebody you'd turn around and kind of shake hands or high five and just go about your business.

Greg Frisbee: I felt that everybody was friendly. It was and still is probably the most non-judgmental club I've ever been to in my life. Nobody cared how you looked, nobody cared how you danced. As long as you were cool with everybody doing everything, they cared about then they were cool with you doing everything you wanted to do. Even though it's this underground club that's supposed to be edgy and underground, I always felt very safe at ManRay. There was always that sense of "I'm home. I'm with friends. I'm safe. I'm here to have fun and nobody's gonna judge or say anything." You could always talk to people.

Steve Friedrich: At first, I'd meet a group of four or five people and hang out with them. Then some of them just stopped going or moved away and I'd have to find another group that didn't hang out by the bar because I didn't drink at the time. I was definitely straight edge.

Jenn Sutkowski: I definitely cared about meeting people for potential relationships. This is dorky, but I remember dragging my friend Shannon to Berklee College of Music, standing in the door hoping that some guy would see me and like me. Going to a club was a far more viable option. At the same time, there were always missed connections. I remember being asked out a few times by people that I was totally not attracted to while one of the people that I really liked had a girlfriend who went to a different school. I felt like he kind of liked me too but nothing inappropriate ever happened.

Russ Carter: So, we showed up at ManRay and literally just sat there. All these people are kind of standing in the dark corners just staring because everybody is so anti-social. They're just kind of watching us and we are listening to Alien Sex Fiend and eating mushrooms. That was one of my first memories and it was kind of uneventful, to be honest, but just the fact that I was surrounded, even though everybody was so antisocial, it was a camaraderie. All these people, they all look very different from each other, but it was clear that you're cut from the same cloth.

Emily Arkin: ManRay was one of the few places I felt comfortable. I would go to Lansdowne Street and just be like, "I don't belong here. I feel weird, pick me up and take me home." There is a funny thing with nightlife where you want to create familiarity. You want to be with your people, but you also want something different to happen and you want to meet someone.

Michael Marotta: You were in there for a reason. It's not as if you're walking down the middle of Faneuil Hall trying to find someone that has a similar interest, you're already on that same playing field with someone. I would kind of meet people through the dance floor. I would know a lot of the music that was being played and I would try to use that to my advantage. If "Once in a Lifetime" by Wolfsheim came on you knew the material, which I think gave you a certain confidence to be able to dance a certain way and to act a certain way. I definitely have fond memories of making eye contact with someone across the room on the dance floor and then you slowly gravitate closer and closer to that person. Sometimes you hit it off and sometimes you don't. Maybe you follow up that at the bar and Terri helps get you drunk. You have a good time with that person.

Rebecca Corbett: I felt like I did have people there that I absolutely loved and chatted with. Every time I saw them it was super exciting. It was a way of life. It wasn't just a club. ManRay was a part of who you really were in your identity. I loved it.

Melanie Sharkey: Mostly it was me just admiring people from afar and being a little too shy to go up to them and be like, "Hey, I love you. Who are you?"

Jamie DiBattista: I met quite a few new people yet none of them are in my life now. It was all very brief. I definitely, probably less than some others, hooked up a bunch of people there. Which is a lot of fun, but nothing ever turned into a real relationship.

Chris Famulari: Believe it or not, I'm pretty shy. I'm pretty open in a group setting. Let's just say I'm making jokes with a table full of people and maybe two of them or three of them agree. I don't mind being the jokey joke person and talking to them, but I would never have the gusto to go up to them and be like, "Hey, I like you." Yet, I met a ton of people. A lot of gentlemen would come over and offer to buy me a drink, and I would always say to them, "I will gladly accept the drink. I am straight. I have no problem sitting with you and talking, though, if you want." Sometimes they would forget it and sometimes they would sit down. For the most part I just wanted to go there, get a buzz and dance. If I was with somebody that's great and, if not, that's fine too.

Christina Pearson: I remember there was a girl at Simmons that I had a huge crush on. I'd pass her in the hallways. I knew where she was going to be. I wasn't stalking her or anything crazy like that, but I just always kept an eye out. I would not have tried to talk to her in school; it would never even occur to me. I was just like "Oh my God, she's so cute. She's so cute. I'm gonna die." Then one night she showed up at ManRay and I'm like, "Oh, well that's it. She's mine now."

Hyson Concepcion: I didn't really date at ManRay. The funny thing was it often felt like there were sort of missed opportunities because I didn't have a car and a lot of other people didn't have cars. So, if I met someone who lived in Charlestown how were we going to hang out? It was one of those things.

Gauri Desai-Ackerman: I would say from '94 to '95 I was kind of alone. I just went in and people would recognize that. I would make friends and sometimes we'd hang out outside. There was one friend in particular, Brian, who I used to hang out with a lot. He was more into EDM, so he introduced me to a lot more the darker electronic stuff that was out there at the time. He was sort of my dance partner, for lack of a better word, my clubbing partner for pretty much all of the Boston scene. We used to meet up and go together. Then after '97 I met a few people on New York's Goth list who went to the same school I was at. I really enjoy meeting different people and hanging out in different scenes.

Liz Enthusiasm: I would generally go with a couple of my friends. We would walk because nobody had a car. It's freezing cold. It showed just how totally dedicated we were. I liked going with my group of friends, so we weren't necessarily wanting to meet other people. We weren't actively searching, it just happened very organically. After we had been there for a few years we kind of started branching out and meeting other people. Every once in a while, there would be some cheesy pickup attempts. I feel like everybody just kind of wanted to dance by themselves and do their own thing. Lansdowne Street is clearly a meat market, but I don't think it's why people went to ManRay, people went there for the music.

Amy Butts: It was not easy for me. I am terrified of people. Eventually, if you see the same person over and over and over you tend to get comfortable. If you happen to be getting a drink at the same time you might shoot a comment over to this person that you've seen a million times but never talked to. Or I would be introduced. That's how I met a lot of people. I would meet somebody that would know other people and I would get introduced because I was terrible at waking up being like "Hey!!!"

Heather Morgan: It was just a parade of people, a buffet of people. One night, I didn't really have anybody that I knew with me and I was kind of bummed out because it was my birthday, but I ended up talking to some guy and then we ended up just walking all around the city together and celebrating my birthday and then hooking up in a playground slide. A total stranger that I just ran into at ManRay. I definitely made friends with people there that I stayed friends with for a long time. I met people there who were just acquaintances that I might even get into some pretty big arguments with. I had quite a few frenemies.

Susanne Boitano: When I got there, I was happy to float around. You could talk to anybody. You could also not talk to anybody. There was that wonderful way you could be anonymous in a crowd. Being on the dance floor is a community, just sort of being in the embrace of great music and great company. It's a tribal thing. Y'all get out there and jump around to Nine Inch Nails and it fixes you and gets out everything that's poisonous, stops the blues.

New York is a big place where everybody's got their own niche. Whereas Cambridge in this area, and also Lansdowne Street, where there's more of a tourist flow. You've got to know where you're going when you show up at that low slung building, it didn't really announce itself particularly. It seemed to me it was a magnet, there was a need for people who wanted to go to a place that was utterly non-judgmental, to the degree that they demanded the best of you in terms of your appearance, which I love.

Shane Blau: Mostly I let my friend Anne Z take the lead in terms of introducing us to people, finding us crowds to get involved with. It was really good for me to be a sidekick. It was really good for me to have this outgoing silly funny person that I could hang with. She loved to pick on me, like, if we were riding the T together all of a sudden, she would just stand up and yell "I can't believe you slept with her!" right in my face just to see what would happen. She forced me to get involved with people to a certain extent. I met people at ManRay, but mostly I was meeting people that were already connected to the crowd I was with. I don't remember ever meeting someone random and being like, "Come with us for food afterwards." Pretty much who I went with is also who I left with.

Brian Legault: I was always traveling and eventually the Marriott at Kendall Square started upgrading me to suites because I was there so much. There were a couple of times where I had made enough friends at ManRay that I actually said, "Anyone want to come over and pre-party at my suite?" and I had a mini pre-party on a Wednesday night after dinner before going to ManRay.

Patrick Baldwin: I'd say it was hard for me to meet new people at ManRay but that might give the wrong impression. I am not by nature a terribly active social person. I wasn't really going to ManRay specifically to meet new people. It wasn't a thing I was putting a lot of energy towards. I was mostly going to ManRay to hang out with my friends, to watch the people, have a cigarette and listen to music.

Niki Nevulis: Despite the fact that I seemed really outgoing, at times I wasn't really interested in meeting a lot of new people. If somebody was brought into our circle of friends it was by somebody else, it wasn't because I was outwardly seeking it. From a romantic perspective, there might have been people that I was dating at the time that were part of our circle. I wasn't going there to seek out romance. I really went to hang out with my friends. We had a really great group of friends. I loved hanging out. I loved dancing. We had that common thread. There was the after party at Bickfords. That camaraderie. I remember my dad always saying, "Enjoy it, it's gonna be the best time of your life, kid."

David Winthrop: I never had any trouble meeting people. People would want to introduce me to others, saying "This is David, he's taking the pictures." Other people that are interested in photography would obviously want to talk to me about it or wanted to get their photos taken.

Paul Calnan: I did meet my wife at ManRay, and we've been together for

24 years now. We met through mutual friends. Ironically, at the time, she was dating a friend of mine, but it was nothing serious and I was just coming out of another relationship myself. This was in '97. I'll have to admit both of us were pretty inebriated then so it made things a little awkward, but we just hit it off and obviously one thing led to another.

Anastasia Taslis: I'm not really a go out and make friends kind of person. I'm kind of a wait-and-see-who-comes- to-me person. It took a long time for me to start meeting people, branching out more than just my little core group.

Kevin Farrington: It didn't take too many trips before all of a sudden you were "best friends" with a lot of different people fairly quickly and fairly deeply. I think the combination of transitioning from somebody who's just standing alone in a corner watching what other people are doing, once you begin to do it, it kind of envelopes you very quickly into that same physical wave of emotion and energy and awareness and colors and sound.

I was 50 when we started going, and by the time the club closed I'm 57 and the choice for me was either to do the rational thing and take care of myself and sleep or do this or do that, but hell, the life I was living away from the club was crazy anyway. The draw to be part of ManRay and to connect with all those people on a regular basis, sometimes that's what got me through the work week when I'm sitting out there in the middle of Western Massachusetts saying to myself, I don't know how many more times I can start this thing. The thought of being able to be safe, and that's an interesting choice of words, or to be part of what was supplying the energy for the parts of life that I loved was what drove me forward. ManRay was a choice that I made freely and willingly, and I've never looked back. It was one of the best experiences of my life.

Mark Calvert: I didn't really know anyone who had been living in the area or anyone who attended regularly. The one friend I had who had been there didn't really go out much, so I ended up there on my own. I kept asking people, inviting friends but some were too busy, and some weren't interested in the club. I eventually dragged a couple of friends there and a co-worker who was curious. Of course, I started chatting with Terri, which was a great way to meet people, chatting with the bartender. Eventually I would meet people there, but they would come and go, not always regulars. I might see the different two or three people that I know just randomly, without even planning.

Terri Niedzwiecki: Oh, I'm sure that people coming out at the end of the night still scare a lot of people. But I never got any complaints about catcalling like what happened with Red Sox people. No one had any problem walking around Central Square. Back in the day, when I told people I worked in Central Square, they were horrified.

Susanne Boitano: My favorite expression is "You don't have to go home, but you can't stay here." A lot of time I went down to Hi-Fi pizza and risked murder and mayhem to get a slice because that place was a little dicey. Definitely a snack. If I was with my boyfriend, we lived in Dorchester, we would go to M&M Barbecue or the Barbecue Pit, which was this palace that was basically on fire on the corner that makes delicious ribs. It had weird hours. It was the kind of place you could pull up to at 2:30 in the morning and get some food. The problem was it's Boston and everything shut up tight like a clam.

Emily Taylor: When I first started going, I was living in Marshfield and I wasn't drinking so I would just drive home. Sometimes I would crash at a friend's for a little bit then get on the road and go home. My parents still wanted me to wake up there.

Sunday is a day of rest. The Lord wants us to rest. We would go do ManRay stuff and then we'd go out to Deli Haus afterward for food. I was often out until 5 in the morning. Sometimes we would go to the South Street Diner which is open 24 hours in the South Station area. Sometimes we would go to a friend's house and crash. Sometimes we would go to Hi-Fi and get a couple slices and then figure out what we were doing after that. Or sometimes I would go home with someone. I would be waiting all night to figure out if I was going to go with that person. And then once the lights would come on, I'd be like, let's go. So then yeah, that was pretty much my ritual.

Kyle Blaisdell: There was almost always an after party and, if there wasn't, I would wind up hosting one at whatever living accommodations I was in at the time. There was never a worry about what to do. The immediate group of friends of ours were taking that lifestyle right out into the streets and then to the next day while trying to hold on to whatever day jobs we could manage. There we were gathering in the streets of Boston looking like a bunch of rejects.

Alyssa Hassan: Hi-Fi, we would often go there to get some pizza and sometimes figure out where we were going after. The first couple years I would always go home. With my non-grad school friends, we would find a party a lot of times. Rise, that was a place that we went to quite a bit. My best friend Jimmy and I went back to his place and would just hang out and continue the party.

Prospero Eaton: I didn't really like after parties. Occasionally, some friends might have something going on. I remember going over to Hi-Fi pizza which was a pretty popular hang out.

Elizabeth Galbraith: I'd usually go to eat, like IHOP or something that was open late. Sometimes I'd go to the Deli Haus and of course Hi-Fi.

Wendy Austin: Again, I don't care how drunk, I always got that pizza.

Emily Taylor: The lights would come on and we were told to start saying goodbye to each other. It was nice because you can actually hear people's voices at that point. We're all a little bit deaf from the music but you can see people's actual faces and we were trying to figure out where we're going to go. We would stay there until they kicked us out, which we were kicked out last because we worked there. Usually, there would be some kind of food situation. Deli Haus was great because everybody went there so it was like the club part two but you actually have to socialize. I kind of always felt bad for the people who work there, but they loved us!

Heather Morgan: Usually my outfits for ManRay were purchased after ManRay by staying up all night and going to Dollar a Pound. So it would be ManRay, Deli Haus, hanging out at somebody's house, and then going to Dollar a Pound at five in the morning. Then it was buying all these clothes, going back to the dorm, treating people to breakfast, trying on clothes with my friends in my room, and then finally going to sleep at like 11 or noon.

Kara Nemergut: When I was going with Keith we would pretty regularly go to gross Hi-Fi and then back to his house on Brookline Street. Hi-Fi was so gross except for after ManRay. We went to South Street Diner a lot after the clubs. Or we went to people's houses. Occasionally I would just go home.

Brian Legault: I might grab a slice of Hi-Fi pizza on the way back to the hotel. It was not usually a social thing for me because I needed to get my ass to the bed and get going the next day.

Jill Kempton: I didn't want you to see me after sweating dancing, even though I still look pretty good. I wanted to get out of there. I don't care if you saw me beforehand, where I'm stunning, but I'm out of there before the lights come on. No after party. Honestly, I was too shy. It's like that Seinfeld episode ... leave on a high note, I'm out of here. A couple times I stopped for food. Not only did I just work all day Friday, I worked Saturdays. I worked in a salon. I got to go home and go to bed.

Adam Lewis: When I was working there, you would have your shift drink and hang out and shoot the shit for a while. Often it depended on if Don was there and what type of mood Don was in that night. Or Terri, for that matter. If people are in a shitty mood and they didn't make much money or they had a bad night, then there was no hanging out there. But if people are in a good mood, you're hanging out and you're always guaranteed one shift drink afterwards.

Krista Siren: I kind of wish that I had a community where I could have gone out and hung out with folks at Hi-Fi or IHOP. I really didn't except for when I was dating somebody. I wasn't really as connected. There were folks that I saw and would say hello to each week, and we complemented each other on our outfits. I knew those folks' faces, but I didn't really hang out afterwards. I usually went home and popped on online and sat in the chat room while I was either still in club wear or having just rinsed off from disrobing.

Mark Clavet: I rarely went to after parties because the hour was late, and I was drained by then from dancing and drinking. I lived in the suburbs, so there's the ride home. Sometimes I would be the designated driver, so I would have to leave immediately. There were some nights I recalled going to places in Central Square to eat, especially Hi-Fi. Even in the winter, you could stumble your way drunkenly over there and get a slice of questionable pizza. They were open until maybe 4 a.m. and you would often encounter other people from the club. You'd see little pockets of people coming out of The Middle East and from all over. You'd hear them talking about, "Oh, I just saw this band or this thing here or this club is pretty neat." You'd find out even more about what's in the surrounding area and then get a slice of pizza and be on your way.

Richard LaDue: If it was a Thursday we would roll over to The Paradise as soon as we could. If it was a Saturday, we'd probably grab pizza on the corner. You didn't want the night to end, but a part of it was "How the fuck am I getting home?" I lived in Newton at this dorm. I hardly have any money left because I bought a drink. "Are we going to pool our money for a taxi? Does a friend have a car?" Getting home was never easy with the MBTA.

Shane Blau: We would take the T there, but the T was closed by the time the club was done so we would walk home most nights, unless it was so cold or so raining that we could convince my friends to all chip in for a cab. The walk was really fun, actually, because you walked by the Necco factory, so it always smelled like candy. Then you had the long walk over the river, and we were all still hyper and we all still had tons of energy. We'd walk back to Kenmore Square to this little dive. We went to Deli Haus and would get knishes. There was a waffle place somewhere in Kenmore Square that we would go to. We almost always went out for food afterwards, our night kept going. We didn't ever go back anywhere and keep partying. The dorms at BU were pretty strict and you couldn't get into dorms that weren't your own, so we stayed out for our continuing enjoyment.

Chris Famulari: I always ended up going outside and smoking a couple of cigarettes while people mulled around and talked. Eventually the cops would tell us to go home. We would either go back to the parking lot or decide where we were going next. I remember one night me, and Jamie went back to the garage and I was supposed to drive home and I was like, "I can't drive right now dude. I'm just going to take a little nap." He's like, "Yeah, no problem." Well, he left because I woke up and it was morning, I talked to him the next day, he said, "Well, I tried to wake you up four or five times and you didn't. I figured you really needed to sleep. So, I just left." That was a very interesting night.

Jenn Sutkowski: Most often Deli Haus. I would get a cheese omelet or a burger.

Sara S. Wendell: Frequently, it's two o'clock, so I thought I should put something in my stomach other than booze. Hi-Fi has really disgusting pizza, which at two in the morning when you're drunk, wasn't that disgusting. There's usually a fair crowd of people from ManRay doing exactly the same thing so they got used to the black clad influx at two in the morning. Once in a while, I would hit an after party, but not often.

Usually, I was fried, and I just wanted to go home and crash.

Hideki Watanabe: Sometimes we went to Deli Haus and had the Atomic Fire Rings. We wanted the experience. Near the beginning they warned us, "You can't get your money back. They are very hot. This is not just a word or description, it's really hot." So, we did it. We didn't stop eating. We finished it all. It was painful. The waitress was bringing us shots of milk that were left over when someone would order a milkshake just to help us out. My college friend had gone to Deli Haus on a separate occasion and ate the Atomic Fire Rings, and one of them was like "I have to go to the bathroom." Someone else was like "Yeah I'll go too." They came back after a few minutes and one was like "My balls are burning." Everyone else was like "What the fuck is wrong with you guys?" and then they realized that they didn't wash their hands.

Paul Vitagliano: There would be a scene outside of ManRay and Campus for a good half hour, just people milling about, having cigarettes, cruising, chatting, whatever. That tended to happen often at the end of the night. Then you might head over to Hi-Fi and continue the night.

Jon Whitney: I think I've only ever been to one or two after parties, and it was just never things that I was into. I was like "Okay, well this is nice but I just kind of feel uncomfortable because I only know one or two people." It wasn't my scene, so most of the time I would just go home. I worked.

Maryellen Vega: Bickfords in Braintree. I would have French fries with butter. It was always hopping and when I ordered my French fries with butter they were like "You are the weird one who gets that." I remember once I was with Jim and Fam and Darren, the guys used to curl the brims of their hats back in the 90s, and a group of older people, probably 30 maybe 40, started going "You curled brims in there like flat hats!" and we were in Bickfords yelling back and forth at each other.

Kathy Landes: I really probably drank too much and had to trek down in the freezing cold to Green Street where we parked. You were running as fast as you could to get the car. I probably shouldn't have been driving. I should repent. We would make the mad dash down Mass Ave to get to the Braintree Bickfords.

Greg Frisbee: I remember a lot of times we would, because my car was parked at the Braintree T, get rides back with people. We would cram ourselves into a car or even take a taxi and try to get to Bickford's in Braintree so we could stay out later. Even if we left early to catch the last train, we would go to Bickford's to reserve a table for people so that, when they did arrive, we would still be able to hang out with our friends.

Me'lissa Nin: There were times when a bunch of us would pile into a car together and go over to Deli Haus. Boy those were some good times there. I wanted to do everything because I wanted to extend the night for as long as humanly possible. Who wants the night to end?

Emily Taylor: I would come home with my friend Jill and just lay there listening to music all night. We would barely sleep because we were just young.

Keith Ward: That was the convenience of it — when I was living on Brookline Street, I could stumble down the street at the end of the night and there was no driving home. There was no worry about, "Oh, is my designated driver drunk?" There was no worrying about any of that shit. I was also single.

Trent Stewart: Well, we didn't eat a lot before the club because you don't want to be bloated. So we wanted food. I didn't want Hi-Fi, I wanted fruit. When you come out of the club scene in Lansdowne there was Sausage Scott.

Jennifer: We just finished ManRay, and I was bored and I drove around. I saw my now husband talking to someone. We had talked a few times at the club and I was like, "Hey, you want to go get coffee somewhere?" and he brought me to Deli Haus. I'd never been to Deli Haus. That's where I met my husband.

Becky D: It depends on which group I was hanging out with. In the beginning it was a mad rush to Deli Haus to try to get in line and get a table before they closed. If you don't make it then you drive to IHOP. Towards the late 90s, early 2000s it was a house party. There was a point where I was partying a little bit too much. You start on Friday. You go to the club in the morning. "Who's having the party?" A lot of times it was a friend that lived in Newtonville. It would be like 11 a.m. and we would still be up and we'd be like, "Okay, what are we doing tonight? Let's go take a quick nap before we do it."

Heather Morgan: From ManRay, we would spill out into the street dizzy. I was a smoker so I would immediately be smoking. I always went to Deli Haus, but often we would stop at Christy's first. I was out for the night. My ManRay nights went until the next day without fail. There was a period of time where we would all go to this abandoned incinerator on Albany Street that they just called "The Building." I was a "The Building" person. I just wanted to go wherever there were going to be a lot of people.

Noel McKenna: Off Route 93 there's a prison. There used to be an incinerator so there were three big smokestacks. One time after ManRay we went and explored the building. We're lucky we didn't get killed. We snuck into the building. It was like something out of Blade Runner.

Tatiana Zimkus: The nights that I'm at ManRay or Ceremony I would still be ready and willing to go somewhere else afterward. I know everybody went to Hi-Fi afterwards. I didn't have a car, so I was like, "Where do you guys want to take me?" I ended up in a lot of crazy places with a lot of crazy people.

Julia Kilcoyne: We'd go to after parties and that's when the harder drinking started. Some of those parties took interesting turns and not in good ways. We'd be getting home at 4:30 and crash. There were many nights that I fell asleep with false eyelashes and makeup on which is a really bad idea. Usually, the biggest thing coming out of ManRay was, "Oh my God. I gotta go to the bathroom." You're wearing tights or you have to undo your corset, which you can't do without help, and then you'll never get it back on.

Lacey Prpic Hedtke: I remember leaving ManRay and being like, "Ha-ha … no one knows what kind of night we just had because everyone's like, 'Oh, we went to the Red Sox game or whatever.'"

Chapter 14

Turn of the Century: The Years 1997-2001

"As clubs started to disappear and keep unfortunately disappearing, there's less places to go, and again, with that the scene changed as well. There weren't as many people out there supporting those clubs." — Julie Kramer

Many changes in Boston arrived with the 21st century. Larger ideas about urban renewal and gentrification began to sweep the nation, and Boston was no exception. Having always been a nightclub surrounded by residential buildings, ManRay was in a pressured situation. The area of Central Square, which certainly had questionable times in its life, also found itself under pressure to change. Was it for the better or did it lose some of its character?

The dawn of a new century also saw a dramatic change in the nation's growing digital imprint. ManRay had its very first website and email address. Advertisements and ways of disseminating information about the club changed rapidly. The ability to make friends and keep in closer contact became easier. Music and crowds began changing with the growth of electronic music and the Cyberpunk subculture. The footprint that ManRay and its patrons were leaving now had a different form, perhaps a wider and larger form. Did this put ManRay on a map greater than just the Boston area? Did it help the club grow and expand? Did the club lose some of its original identity?

With the events of September 11, 2001 many questions began filling the air space: What is the future of nightlife? What is the prevailing idea of what people want to do in a post-9/11 world? How could people be kept safe? How would the problems now facing American culture graft itself onto nightlife? Whatever the answers, life had changed irrevocably. S.L.

Derek Kouyoumjian: When I was younger, I remember being introduced to tarot cards. Up until that point in my life, I always kept thinking of the stereotypical horror movie elements, like "Oh no tarot cards, something bad's gonna go down." Sure enough the death card comes up and that means someone's going to die. However, it doesn't mean someone's gonna die. It just means change. I didn't quite understand that concept. I didn't quite grasp it. I'm like, "Change? That's kind of weird." But as I grew older, I began to understand that concept more as the world I knew as a child, teenager, and young adult began to change. The city changed drastically. Whole neighborhoods were gone, leveled, turned.

Richard LaDue: I was working at Rise on Sunday nights going into Monday mornings. After '91 to '92, a lot of my going out would almost be research related. "What are the kids listening to? What are they responding to? What's working well? What's not?" Rise, during this time period, was an after-hours club scene. It was removed from the ManRay world. I would go to New York City and chase music and go to nightclubs and do the Satellite Record routine.

A lot of the music that came out of New York at that time I thought was kind of like a cartoon. It's total candy. It just felt like there wasn't a lot of art in it. It was the drum roll, the pitch bend, the whole creating that enormous explosion and then it comes back down. There were just these waves of sound. This might be my age. I'd be curious if there's someone like, "Oh my God, remember the music of the 2000s?" I don't know if it sinks in, that music. I think American music got a little bit more cartoonish and sillier and less interesting and more predictable. At that point for me, I was mostly into dance music. A lot of the gay kids wanted to hear a lot of this New York House music that was fun and effective and, if they're dancing on drugs, it sounds amazing, but there's really not much there. It really felt like it was made by a computer.

Rachel E. Pollock: In the 90s, a lot of music that would fit in at a club like ManRay, a lot of the bands were basically trying to mimic Sisters of Mercy or Bauhaus or Siouxsie and the Banshees or Switchblade Symphony. There's a shift really at the millennium when electronica bands like Interpol start gaining traction.

Emily Arkin: Cambridge was a town with so many record stores. It was a place where there were a lot of cross currents of different music scenes influencing each other.

Mark Clavet: I attended Nine Inch Nails at the Boston Garden just before it was torn up, so that was pretty memorable. There were a lot of industrial scenes in Boston. At the time, there was a constant stream of bands touring and stopping and playing many different nights at different venues. I used to go to Axis and Avalon down the street and ManRay.

Eileen Dover: I think after the year 2000 to 2001 there were fewer people that put effort into their looks.

Erin Falkell: When I was a kid, Central Square scared the shit out of me. I remember there was a lot happening and I felt like it was out of control. But what was so amazing to me is that, once I moved on to Ellery Street and started really getting more engaged with Central Square, it was this incredibly amazing place.

Taylor Vecchio: I always wanted to live in Central Square. In 2003 I was finally able to find an apartment on Prospect Street, which is a pretty major thoroughfare. I wanted to live there because there was all this nightlife and all these cool places to hang out. Specifically, The Middle East and T.T. the Bear's, which was close to where ManRay was. There were always people just hanging out around all the cool bars and restaurants. Also, it was grimy. I don't know if it's still grimy, but I remember people having this t-shirt that said, "Central Square is for lovers." It was a picture of a bum passed out on a bench with a bottle in his hand because that was a big thing. Every bench was occupied by homeless people and we would even get to know them personally.

Rachel E. Pollock: It is admittedly hard for me to recollect what else was going on at that time, but I have a general sense that there was gentrification of Central Square. There were two Starbucks where there had been locally owned coffee shops. It had a very bohemian atmosphere to it when I moved to Boston around '97. It was a turning point around the millennium when you started to see more chain restaurants and more corporate businesses start to take over the street level storefront that had previously been occupied by local places.

Liz Enthusiasm: It hasn't really gotten as gentrified as other parts of Cambridge, Somerville, or Allston. It still definitely has that grubby sort of character to it. Just the fact that The Middle East is still there and it's still pretty similar. Of all the areas of this city that I used to go to and still occasionally go to I would say Central Square is probably the most similar from back in the day, for better or for worse.

John Whitney: I think it really started to change in the late 90s. More construction was going on. Things were changing. Things were cleaning up. People were making a bigger effort to make sure the streets were cleaner, and they have the fancy square names around.

Emily Arkin: One thing that changed a lot in my lifetime was Cambridge. It was a place where a lot of students lived. It was very bohemian and had a lot of cafes. And it had rent control, which I think made it a very socio-economic and racially diverse city. Then, when I was a teen or slightly older, rent control was abolished statewide and I felt like Cambridge changed rapidly after that. A lot of places went through this gentrification and everyone moved one town out or two towns out who couldn't afford to live there without rent control.

I think it's Central Square or a similar area where there's the urban legend, or maybe it's true, that Kennedy was preparing Massachusetts to be the home of NASA, but after he was assassinated it moved to Texas. So sometimes people say that's how you ended up with the industrial wasteland of East Cambridge, even though the city has, ironically, one of the richest places. Brattle Street has always been mansions galore. Even now there are no houses for under $2 million in Cambridge.

Norm: There was definitely a movement where a lot of the younger patrons from the early to mid-90s became the dominant people at the club itself, in terms of being partially involved with the entertainment, what nights were going to happen, and what nights weren't going to happen. It was a very interesting thing to watch as people were not just going but now were definitely involved with the events. There is a very interesting bubbling up of talent being brought in — people coming and dancing, having a good time, getting used to it, becoming regulars and then, two or three years later, they are the ones involved in the club's actual structure and performances. There were a good amount of art students, a good amount of music students, and there were a good number of dancers. There definitely was creativity there. People who have that creative mindset were drawn to the place.

Chris Ewen: There were a lot of people who did work at MIT and Harvard that came to the venue. People who did really innovative stuff with the internet and starting email, people who were really connected with technology. Really smart people. It's amazing and it congregates around ManRay.

Wendy Austin: I remember Lansdowne was more like douchebag central.

Chris Manousaridis: From Central Square to Harvard Square you went down to the Pit. To an outsider you think of Harvard College, but Harvard Square was a bunch of squatters. Your punks were all right there in the Pit going down to the train. You had the Garage, Newbury Comics, and all these little, tiny boutiques that weren't your everyday stores. You had a silver shop that sold chain jewelry and the little restaurants and the record stores and the thrift stores. It was sort of its own entity within Harvard Square. Central Square, if you didn't know it was there, you kind of walked by and ignored it. But as time progressed, you saw less and less of it. When more of the bigger retail stores or franchises were coming in then you started seeing less and less of the squatters.

Norm: ManRay existed outside the real world in many ways. We were a group of outsiders who wanted to be outsiders. People who had a very similar mindset because we were outsiders from the rest of the world. We were still, to some degree, lemmings within our own little world. We swam a different way, but once you were swimming, it was in the same direction.

Julie Kramer: As clubs started to disappear and kept unfortunately disappearing, there's less places to go, and again, with that the scene changed as well. There weren't as many people out there supporting those clubs after 2000. If people were out like they were back in the late 80s, early 90s five nights a week then those clubs wouldn't have to sell out. As things changed, there were plenty of times I went out to see a band and there were only 15 people there. As people stopped going out as much in support of nightlife then those clubs started disappearing. The people who wanted to go out, thank goodness, created those nights so they could keep doing what they love doing, it was just that there were just less places to do it.

Emily Arkin: I would call it fairly eclectic. There was a room for lots of different kinds of bands. There was like a large college going audience for a lot of music, so you could kind of peacefully coexist with other bands. We would go on tour and see other bands where they were the one big act in town so they would play with anything that came through. Boston wasn't like that but there wasn't a ton of jockeying. We were also maybe not trying to be in any kind of hyper competitive space. We were indie rockers.

Liz Lamanche: I got more involved in the burner scene and there was a lot happening there at the time. There were some groups of people and DJs, like the Gnome Fatty Collective and Circle, who would have parties at the Marsh Post outdoors on the banks of the Charles in the summer. It was EDM music and a lot of people in the spin jam flow arts community. Everyone just come, be yourself, and be fabulous.

Maryellen Vega: I went into the rave room one time because I was mad at Ian. He didn't want me to go in there alone, so I went there with my sister-in-law and there was a guy in there dancing with a pot on his head and I thought "He's a real pot head!"

Koren Bernardi: I have repeated mentions of ManRay in my journal all the way through 1999 and in 2000. Leading up to the big year 2000, I started hanging out with folks from Angeldustrial. There were a bunch of folks that were from Rocky Horror that we knew also. We started doing our own kind of events and started going to ManRay on a regular basis because people were doing stuff. So either people were performing in bands that were playing there or somebody was DJing, or somebody was dancing at one of the nights.

Becky D: By '99 I felt like it was my second home because, at that point, I kind of understood that this was the subculture that I wanted to be a part of. I felt more like myself than I had ever before. It was also a time at which I knew enough people that, if I hadn't talked to anyone that Wednesday and decided I wanted to go to Crypt, I knew that I would see friends. I wouldn't be there by myself.

We felt awkward and uncomfortable in our own skin, especially when we were in high school. We were quirky or we had different personalities from the rest of the world. So finding an environment where that quirkiness was not only accepted, but almost celebrated was kind of a boost.

Chris Ewen: It's weird … 9/11 … I remember waking up and turning on the TV. It was a lot for me to wrap my head around. As far as I remember, we just kind of pushed forward and did what we thought was necessary to keep our people safe. One of the things about club life, in general, is that there can be catharsis. When you go out and dance you are able to take something bad that's happened and either forget it or express yourself and deal with tragedy, especially a tragedy like that. In some ways, New York and D.C. weren't necessarily close in terms of, "Oh my God, they're going to target the Hancock building or something in Boston." I don't think we thought we were in imminent danger. I don't think that we felt there was necessarily a risk in us being open in any kind of tangible way. Our job was to make people feel happy. I saw my role as to continue on and not pretend like it didn't happen, but to make sure that things had the veneer of normalcy despite what happened. We couldn't let these people win.

John O'Leary: The Tuesday before 9/11 was 600 people. On the Tuesday of 9/11 they shut down. Then the Tuesday afterwards was 60 people and it never recovered.

Patrick Fitzgerald: You can't really talk about the early 2000s, and any scene, without addressing 9/11 because that made a huge impact on everybody. I distinctly remember being at ManRay that week on a Wednesday and it was something like an Irish Wake.

Norm: There were obviously changes in security and security protocol but that was the biggest thing I could say about the difference before and after 9/11. I never saw it affecting me because, by that point, I was so embedded in there.

Rachel E. Pollock: I had a friend online from Chicago and she and her partner were thinking about moving to Boston. I told her to come out, visit and crash with me. We could go to ManRay and she could see what the town was like. She was slated to fly on September 11. It was an early flight and she got in touch with me saying "My plane is not going anywhere, there's something going on." By then I already knew what was going on and I was like, "You are not going to be flying anytime soon." Whenever flights resumed, she went into, I think, New York City and drove up. We went to ManRay and I also did the wedding of a couple who were ManRay goers while she was there.

The event that does stand out for me as a marker of things changing was Columbine. It immediately got pinned on Goth kids and everybody that worked at ManRay was fielding all sorts of inquiries from the press to give statements about whether Goths were murderous crazy shooters or not. I remember us having a meeting to talk about how we were going to approach it as a group, or as an institution, so we had a united message that can totally condemn the actions of these people and completely deflects it away from us because our people are not going to shoot up your schools. We had a benefit show called 15 Lilies for the 15 victims of the Columbine shooting and it was all local bands and DJs who donated their time.

That was the dividing event in terms of there being a ManRay pre-Columbine and post-Columbine. Right after that shooting I remember one of Terri's bar backs got the shit beat out of him just for wearing eyeliner. I felt like we had gotten to the point where there was a certain amount of tolerance, but it really became kind of dangerous to be freaky in the aftermath of Columbine.

Mizery McRae: There was a huge shift. Before, everybody was carefree and enjoying themselves. After 9/11, when people went out, everybody was looking at everybody and their surroundings. It was like "Okay, who's behind me? Who's in front of me? Where are the exits?" Everybody was really apprehensive and scared, but they still wanted to go out and try to have a good time, but it didn't do its purpose because they were so guarded. When you go to a nightclub it is to let go, be free, and enjoy the music. After 9/11, everybody was so guarded. They weren't enjoying the music, but they felt they had to be out. It's a major shift from being free and then coming back and being guarded. It was almost like coming out of the closet, looking out, and saying, "Oh shit" and then going back in and closing the door.

Chapter 15

Exactly What It Is Supposed To Be: Fantasy Factory

"You could be whatever fantasy you want to be ... Everybody was exactly who they wanted to be, nobody shamed them, and they just had fun for the four or five hours they were at the club." — Trent Stewart

Friday nights at ManRay were truly revolutionary. The kink and BDSM lifestyles had long been ignored or ridiculed by mainstream culture, thrust into the dark corners as if too shameful to be acknowledged. For ManRay, providing nights specifically dedicated to these crowds was certainly a risk, but one that paid off tenfold. ManRay gave these communities a voice and a platform to speak from; the club stood up to say that these lifestyles were both vital and viable. With a place to discover finally and freely who they were or where they could be their already authentic selves, Friday nights drew in a hugely popular and dedicated crowd. Fridays proved to be equal parts fun but also equal parts business. People long denied an outlet, people who wanted and needed a place to be themselves, were finally able to do that with freedom and revelry. Fantasy Factory quickly rose up to develop themes that suited and allowed for expressions of their crowds desires. It also drew in a creative mindset that wanted to do more. Many nights at Fantasy Factory contained performances to catch the eye, courtesy of the Delicious Dancers who took time out of their own schedules to plan, create, and rehearse before gracing ManRay's stage. While fun was certainly had, again, harkening back to its birth as a gay club, ManRay understood the importance of privacy and consent culture for those who attended these nights. The club already had firmly established ideas about privacy, with its no photo, no video policy and the security who watched out for and took care of problems that arose, making it a haven where many felt safe. The community that was ManRay's patrons did just as much work as the staff to make the club something that deeply valued safety, privacy, and consent. S.L.

Trent Stewart: A group of friends were going out dancing and I thought it sounded good. They said, "I don't think this is for you." As they got dressed, I got a little confused because not only are they wearing black, but they put on makeup to make themselves a little paler, which was kind of interesting considering they were already Caucasian. I figured they may know something I didn't and left it alone. About two years later I was dating someone who wanted to go dancing and I started naming clubs and she said, "No, I want to take you to this place in Cambridge." I said no at first because I remembered what my other friends said but she convinced me by mentioning that I would like the music because I just saw this movie *Tank Girl* and really liked the soundtrack. She said, "This is where you'd find that kind of music" so I wcnt, and it was a Fantasy Factory night.

Terri Niedzwiecki: I would say Diana brought more of the kinks people with the real fetishes. They were just basically going to other people's basements. I don't even think there was any kind of business that was catering to them. John was horrified when I approached him about it. He didn't understand anything about it. He's thinking that people are going to be running around showing off their bits and I'm like, "No, no, no, no, no, it's nothing illegal." He was always very open as long as nothing was illegal, and everyone kept their clothes on because he did get a lot of flak from neighbors who complained when people walked down the street in latex and this and that. The first night we did it there were 500 people.

Andrea Parros: That was a place where people could express themselves. It was a safe space for that type of stuff, and it was a way to meet other people that were into that. As a small-town kid all that stuff was just like, "Whoa, what is all this?" and kind of learning more about that. It was cool to have a place where you could learn a little more about that side of life.

Terri Niedzwiecki: Some people were a little scared when the fetish thing started and, to be honest, that was my feeling as well. But we all know that worked out well.

Rebecca Griffin: I think it really wasn't until stepping in on Friday night that I was really like, "Oh my God … there are other people like me in the world! Holy crap." And then just falling and learning all the different nights.

Trent Stewart: We were the promoters for the night. We have to be the welcoming body of the night. If you aren't making people who are new feel welcome, then you're not doing your job.

Trent Stewart: Fantasy Factory picked the traditional dime store romance fantasies like mile high night where we were basically all dressed as stewardesses or pilots. We'd do a wild west night where everyone's a cowboy. We would actually decorate the club that way and we would dress in that theme.

Eloni Feliciano: You have people that want to match the interior of the club and it definitely helps with the atmosphere. We felt like we were transported somewhere else.

Emily Taylor: Occasionally I would go to Eros Boutique. There were a couple of shops in the Garage in Harvard Square. I would go there, especially if it was a theme night because we'd need costumes for the night. Dorothy's Boutique had a wig shop, makeup, stockings, and all kinds of shit. That place was great.

Wendy Austin: Hubba Hubba was around the corner and that was one of the only fetish stores in Cambridge.

Jen Lucky Cole: I felt really cool the day that we got in there to go shopping. I went there frequently because you got a discount if you said you went to Fantasy Factory.

A. Dominy Cusraque: It was an incredibly moneyed crowd, except for certain people in the fetish world. Yeah, they definitely had some money.

Krista Siren: I'd be going on Fridays or Wednesdays and for those they have some kind of dress code with an all-black minimum. The first time I went I was not confident enough to dress in femme mode, but I did go for something semi kinky on one of the Friday nights. I had gotten some latex-colored block shirts and black PVC pants. I walked in and did my thing.

Rebecca Griffin: I would eat the cheapest but healthiest food so I could spend all my money on fetish clothes. I will tell you; vinyl does not hold up my friend. It does not hold out for 20 years. It disintegrated. It was a poor investment in the long run.

Krista Siren: If you wore latex at ManRay you wanted to make a point of finding out where the air conditioning vents were. That was a key thing, especially if it was very crowded. I'd make a point to plant myself under one of those.

Terri Niedzwiecki: There was a sign on the side door saying, "Do not open," but it would get hot in there, of course, so people would open the door to get fresh air and blast out the neighbors. The neighbors would call the police. Police would come and just basically shut down live music.

Emily Arkin: It was definitely where we learned a lot about a lot about kink culture before the internet. I'd see people like, "Oh I know this person is the clerk from a local store, and now they're being led on a dog collar around ManRay." In a way, it was such a way to see people in a different element and it brought out different things and people you might already know in different contexts.

Matt Richard: I was hanging out in the lounge on the sofa with a friend of mine who is a dominatrix. There was a guy like "Oh man. Oh, you're so beautiful" and she brushes them off. People would ask me for permission and I'm like "We're just friends." We're shooting a shit one night watching some folks play pool when somebody hit the ball that they didn't want to hit. It started going into the pocket and they tried to retrieve it out of the pocket and their arm got stuck in the pool pocket. She and I, we're getting the entertainment of the night. It's not fetish related, it's actually just a pool game gone wrong. Sure enough this person now has their arm fully stuck in the pocket. You have folks running downstairs to the dressing rooms and coming back with all kinds of sample packets of lube to try and squirt down there. I think somebody came out with some ice to try and make the guy relax and have his arm shrink. The funny thing was, since it was a fetish night, you have people wearing EMT uniforms or police uniforms, and you're not sure if they are actually on duty or if they were just wearing fetish stuff. So we got to watch the scene unfold for a little bit and then we got up and we left. I think we agreed to let somebody else have our seats for the show. I came back the next week and, sure enough, there was a large piece of plywood over the pool table.

Matt Richard: There was one time where I actually got stuck working my day job at Salem Hospital on a Friday night until 11 o'clock and I didn't know what to wear. My friends hit me up at the last minute so I'm kind of in a pinch. I'd have to go back to mom and dad's house and pack up a bag. It was a Friday night and I just basically changed out of my scrubs at work. I put on a clean set of scrubs and wore those into the club. When I got to ManRay I'm standing at the steps and they weren't gonna let me in and I looked at him like, "Are you kidding? This is a uniform. This is a fetish night. The dress code is fetish, PVC, black, uniform, and this is a medical uniform and there are folks in there with medical fetishes."

Susanne Boitano: I love it because I love the costume. I love latex. I love see-through. I love that hyper-sexual. If I've got to be looking at people, they better be dressed up pretty darn crazy, and it was the only place doing it. Again, I came from New York where it just was just sort of in the background. I was happy to see it. I was glad it was something different. Those people tend to be dolls. They look like they will unwillingly tattoo or pierce you, but they really are just some of the nicest people. I loved it when I would see somebody that I know normally would be sitting home by themselves not able to go out because they would not be wanted or felt that they could dress in their fullest and maybe they weren't the most glamorous person, but they go out and sit and be in their outfit. I love that you could just really show up extremely beautiful all the way around. It was a wonderful mix. Also, it demands costumes. It's not a place you can show up. I had handmade corsets and I had vinyl gloves up past the elbows in two or three different colors and I had the black tutus and long velvet coats. It was great to be outlandish.

David Winthrop: What I remember the most about Fantasy Factory night was that it was the night people really dressed up. That was the night the girls were dolled up and really outrageous and a lot of the guys too. That was the night they went all out, like Industrial Steve with his two-foot mohawk. He was just someone that always stood out. There was an old guy in his 50s and he looked like Daddy Warbucks. People really took that night seriously. It was a time to shine, it was a time they're really dressed up, and it was a time to show off whatever new outfit they had. Then the dancers downstairs, I mean those outfits are always pretty amazing and definitely really brought it.

Becky D: I was working at this insurance company in the late 90s, so it was still a button up super conservative kind of work environment. It was a fetish night and I looked across the front room and saw a co-worker of mine. It was like a clash of my worlds. I was like "Crap! Someone from work is here. Oh, wait … that means we're both kind of ...” Then there was one experience where I was in business school and I brought a friend with her boyfriend. Hindsight being what it is, I should have known that she was too conservative for this. She stopped hanging out with me after that.

Lacey Prpic Hedtke: I think it gave me permission, I don't even know what the word is, not be so uptight or not feel ashamed of things that I might even just be slightly interested in, especially with the kink nights. I remember being slightly embarrassed for people because they were so on display but then also being like “I don't even know if I would ever have the bravery or courage to do that” and I respected them a lot.

Eloni Feliciano: It didn't take long before I ended up becoming part of a Fantasy Factory. I remember just looking at the people on the stage and being like, “I want to do that today. It looks so glamorous.” I kind of laugh about it now because I know how messy things were. God, we cover ourselves in blood and peanut butter.

Elizabeth Galbraith: I became quite involved with Fantasy Factory after a while because my friends were already doing some stuff on the stage. I wasn't a regular onstage, but every once in a while, I would help out. I was finding myself sexually back then, being in that period of time where one does that.

Jennifer: I love dancing. I love the people. I love the excitement of the nights and to be able to go do that and to be accepted, it was very exciting. I miss that.

Chris Ewen: Fantasy Factory's performances revolved around a certain theme and they showed that off throughout the entire night. The dancers would dress up in a medical theme or a school theme. They were very together as far as putting together an entire package. We all tried to make everything flow smoothly and make the whole night a really immersive experience for the people who came. I definitely would play some songs with a sci-fi theme or a school theme. There are definitely songs that I would fit in to enhance the overall atmosphere and mood of it, things that I would never play on any other night.

Maryellen Vega: I went Friday night one time. I was almost taken back because I've never been to a club with an S&M night and that was more of a shocker.

Mike (Farmboy): I started dating my girlfriend and I started meeting people through her. I was one of the promoters for one of the nights. They asked me if I would actually dance and be one of the dancers. That is how I joined Fantasy Factory. For my awkward self it was the best of all worlds. I'm on the block which is a whole different set of dance skills that I had to learn. People would come up and talk to me which did make it easier for me to start interacting with new people. Because this became people's home for however short or long of a period of time you would see them again.

Michael Hsieh: One of the things that made ManRay so special was all the performances. First it was pretty much always Cusraque. It was really great to all sort of have a structure to the night. Fantasy Factory was maybe more of a dancey sort of fetish. Themes let us do something with a little bit more variety.

Becky D: The people who were running the fetish nights were the Goth industrial kids. They had a kink side to them, but they weren't first and foremost kinky people, they were first and foremost Goth industrial people who went to ManRay. Where I don't think that was necessarily the case for other cities.

Norm: There was a lot of creativity and love poured into these things.

Julia Kilcoyne: I could be chastised for this probably, but in my mind, I never saw that much distinction between the Friday nights.

Emily Taylor: There was definitely some shit that was way different from anything I was into. There was definitely a guy that used to stand in the corner on fetish night and wear a French maid outfit and smack himself in the dick all night … and that was how he wanted to live his life at ManRay.

Michael Hsieh: There's so many other clubs that don't have performances. You could just dance all night. We broke it up to put on this show which just feels fun. I know it's a big goofy kind of thing. Even if you're not into it, at the very least, it's funny. It's just something fun to do.

Liz Lamanche: Well, one standout, of course, is the fetish nights. It is so dark and full of people being fun and uninhibited and sexy. It was not brand new or shocking to me, but it was amazing to have all of these people being themselves, being free exploring and having so much fun. It was just incredibly liberating to me to step into that environment and realize that this kind of fun can be had, and people are all around doing this.

Mike (Farmboy): Though I had done a few performances beforehand for Hell, Fantasy Factory became my performance outlet. I went from dancer to performer to dance master organizing the dancers that were going on the blocks at night. The morning I joined Fantasy Factory was probably the single most important event in my ManRay. I never would have had that experience were it not for Fantasy Factory. I love theatre, but I was never in any sort of theater. I wasn't really a part of Rocky. This was it for me and it was marvelous. We were just kind of happy to have it be what it was.

Becky D: There was a lot of structure to performances because it's blocked out and choreographed. I think I built up a lot of my project management skills with these performances.

Mike (Farmboy): I know there are some people who will refer to it as "resource problem," where people want to do things for all the nights, but it becomes a reliability issue. Some people would be like, "Oh, I'm doing this" and then forgot that they also volunteered for something else. I don't know if this existed in any other nightclub in my entire life, but I think we had the largest number of people volunteering to work in a club in some capacity. At one point Fantasy Factory had somewhere between 30 and 40 people working for it. Multiple dancers, multiple performances. X Mortis used to do two performances a night plus supply dancers for the night. I think X Mortis ended up picking up dancers and then eventually Sin too.

Becky D: For actually being a Delicious Dancer, someone up on the blocks or for Fantasy Factory, other than figuring out what your outfit was there wasn't a lot of prep. There would usually be a Fantasy Factory meeting to plot out what the themes were for the coming months, so you had a heads up, but you wouldn't necessarily know you're going to dance until a week or two before.

Michael Hsieh: We had a lot of artists as members of Fantasy Factory. They certainly helped out making props and backdrops. We definitely had plenty of people with artistic sensibilities.

Gene Dante: When I say dark it wasn't like walking into a room with a single bulb hanging on a string. It was lit correctly. I'd never been to a place like this before. It was new. I had my own experiences in rock clubs, and it's supposed to be dark in the rock club except for the stage or the bar. That's what I first noticed. The second thing I noticed was the decor and the way the patrons would dress. We went on a night that was called Fantasy Night. Everybody was in some form of fetish which was new to me.

Chris Ewen: The "challenge" of Fantasy Factory was finding that nice balance between playing some down tempo things and then playing some up tempo and mixing it all up into a new format. It was finding all the right elements to create a night. I think Fantasy Factory helped in some ways with that because we had the Delicious Dancers and they wanted to be flowing and sexy. I always had a request list from the dancers that they wanted to hear. That helped me expand my music a little bit.

Terri Niedzwiecki: Fantasy Factory came about to get the aesthetic from the younger folk. They were sexy, they were titillating. Everyone was always very, very sweet.

Michael Hsieh: As far as the fetish community … I'm sure they probably thought of us as not being serious about it because you can't put on any serious bondage stuff on the live stage in Massachusetts. They probably just thought we were those kids playing.

Julia Kilcoyne: ManRay became the place that made you feel like you could be who you truly are. It's the whole superhero thing: Clark Kent or Superman. We're allowed as human beings to wear many, many hats. I struggle with that a lot. Here I am in a hoodie and my favorite job was working in the woods. I am kind of a tomboy. And then here I just became this creature and is this creature me? This creature is me, this person who's the real me, and then to be able to absorb and understand that all of those things are me and that's okay.

Charles Bandes: Generally speaking, I would pretty much only go to ManRay when I had a choice. When I was elsewhere visiting friends, I would go to Goth or fetish nights in their town, but I was always disappointed. A lot of the other places I would go for fetish nights were much cruder, showing actual porn on the TVs or having strippers dancing. I don't mind it but I kind of liked that ManRay kept it more to the imagination. I didn't want to feel like I was going to a strip club. I wanted to feel like I was going to a dance club that happened to cater to people like me. ManRay sort of trod that line very well. It kept things pretty sexy, but not vulgar, and that was kind of important to me and I think that was a pretty rare combination.

Trent Stewart: I realized that what was special about ManRay, but especially the Fantasy Factory night, is that you could be whatever fantasy you wanted to be. Nobody was going to tell you that you don't look good. Everybody was exactly who they wanted to be, nobody shamed them, and they just had fun for the four or five hours they were at the club.

Lacey Prpic Hedtke: I think one of the special things about ManRay was that it felt secret in some ways. It was this place you could go and really let your freak flag fly and do whatever and no one was going to judge you. You could try on parts of yourself that maybe you're ready to show to the world a little bit more. It's like a lab where other people are going to be supportive.

Erika Spaulding: The thing that struck me most in the very beginning, and is the one that still continues, is that people were there to support each other. People were there to have a kinship in things that they liked. They wanted to share that with other people, and it was done in a way that made you feel safe. You felt safe being weird. The only thing that was not cool is if you pressed your kink upon somebody else.

Rebecca Griffin: I think that's also what made it a sanctuary was the fact that you could walk in there and there was freedom. You left your shit out the door, you came in with pasties and a thong, and nobody gave a shit.

Abigail Taylor: Any bad thing that ever happened to me in ManRay always happened on a Friday night because it was just crazy. There would be random people trying to get in all the time. Sometimes they'd be able to sneak in wearing black and they end up being jocks and then they try to grab me while I was dancing.

Rachel E. Pollock: One time I was at Terri's bar and a fight broke out between a regular patron and a tourist townie guy who had dressed in black and gotten in and felt like he had the permission to grope women.

He made the mistake of groping the girlfriend of this Goth guy who was there, and they got in an all-out fist fight. The Goth guy jammed the townie guy into the DJ booth request phone booth. He slammed the guy in there and started cracking his head against the glass of the phone booth. I think there was a sort of a blanket policy on behalf of security that you always believed the regular over the outsider and that you always believed the person who is at a physical disadvantage. So if it's a woman wearing basically a bikini and she says this dude groped her, you get rid of the guy. We don't care what his excuses are. Once in a blue moon somebody could abuse that privilege, but from ManRay's perspective, that was collateral damage. I always felt extremely safe there, no matter what I was wearing or not wearing, and I always knew that the security guys would have my back instantaneously.

Terri Niedzwiecki: We had a guy who was head of security, because, let's face it, pretty girls have very little to no clothes on. You know these guys could lose their marbles but, for the most part, everybody took care of each other and it really wasn't a problem.

Becky D: Mike was focused on making sure everyone was staying safe and watching out for random Lansdowne Street dudes that were going to cause trouble. The people that worked there were super supportive. The bouncers loved us. If you went up to them and said you needed help with something, they were there in a heartbeat. They were watching out for you. We would go into practice for performances or to get ready and everyone was always really pleasant, even though we were all kind of hanging out eating pizza on the dance floor and they're trying to get ready to open up. Managing the dancers and then doing performances was always a relatively positive experience.

Chris Ewen: ManRay developed into a safe spot. In a lot of ways that sprung from our real enforcement of a no camera policy. The regulars respected that policy because they knew it was for them. If someone tried to take pictures in the club then someone would go to a security person and that person would be either removed or their camera would be taken until the end of the night. Everyone who worked at ManRay tried to enforce that boundary and the customers also tried to help because they viewed their privacy as seriously as we did.

Terri Niedzwiecki: When we started doing fetish nights there were plenty of cops.

Chris Manousaridis: It really all depends, because you had Thursday night, which was a night you never knew what to expect. That was one of those nights when you're not sure how that night's gonna go. You know everyone's going to have a good time, but, at the same time, you don't know what can go down. There were only a few times that we had real major issues, everybody else was usually so cool. Most of the time it was me going in the bathroom because our bathrooms were coed.

I'd say the most fights we had were on Friday nights, on fetish nights and it was all due to tourists who get drunk and stupid and tried to molest the dancers. The regulars were all cool. To the people being stupid they would say "Knock it off" or they would move and go to a different box to dance on to kind of diffuse the situation, hoping people would get the hint. But when you get idiots who are drunk, who don't care about the rules and don't care about people's personal space, that's when we sort of had to end it. We had one that was pretty bad where I threw him and his buddy out. He swung on us. There was a cop car right in the front and the cops knew us. He asked me what happened, and I said, "He reached up under one of my dancers skirts and tried to molest her and he wouldn't stop so we're throwing them out. He took a swing on me." We had that respect with the police because they knew that we were strict. That was John's code, "You guys need to be strict, there's no leeway." I remember the cop putting this guy in the cop car and missing the door several times which I knew was on purpose. He's like, "Oops, you didn't sit down low enough," because this guy was fighting and resisting arrest.

Trent Stewart: I took it upon myself to make sure that it was safe. For the number of people that love me, there's probably an equal number of people who are annoyed at how seriously I took the job. One of my main rules, especially on the nights that I worked, was that every dancer and performer had to tell me how they were getting home. I would actually walk people to their cars or drive them home.

There were a lot of rules that had to be in place, and it was told to me a couple of times that I was taking the fun out of this. Someone said this is our playground and I said "Yes. But your playground is someone else's place of business. We have to remember that as well."

Gibby Miller: I feel like ManRay did a great job in its time making sure that people felt safe. They kept the bullshit to a minimum. If there were problems, then they handled it respectfully and quickly.

Jennifer: I would say I didn't feel like ManRay protected us. I felt like our community protected us. Not saying that there were many people you couldn't count on, but it was kind of like Fantasy Factory looked out for Fantasy Factory. When you're a woman there by yourself, half undressed and dancing, you have to be very careful of who you're talking to. It's normally the creepier people who try to make friends with you first. There were only a few people that you ever really had to worry about. It wasn't the regulars. It wasn't the guy heavily into his fetish. It was the college kids coming for a laugh or the people thinking they could touch us. Usually you would either go put your arm around somebody and or you would whisper to one of the people who are keeping an eye on things and they make them go away.

Abigail Taylor: I'd only been to a few other nightclubs before ManRay. I went with some college kids to Axis and ended up getting groped many times and getting grinded with and just put through the fucking ringer and being followed around by dudes. I was like "This is not for me." So going to ManRay was very, very refreshing in the sense that, when I was there as a patron, I always felt safe. I never felt like anyone was trying to hit on me. I felt safe when I was dancing because there was always a security guard near us watching and there were actual signs that said "Do not touch the dancers. Do not touch them, you will be thrown out if you try."

Terri Niedzwiecki: Everyone was polite and behaved themselves.

Emily Sweeney: ManRay ensures a safe space for a lot of people.

Trent Stewart: There were only a couple of people that really seemed apprehensive of my existence. At first, I thought it was about color, to be completely honest. But the more I looked into it, it was about being a stranger. I found out later that frat boys basically do their initiation by sending the newbies to the club. ManRay was very small and protective, and I was an outsider. There was one person who warned people against me. Later, I met the promoter for Fantasy Factory Fridays, and we hit it off and she had me up on stage a month later.

Derek Kouyoumjian: They allowed me to go in with my camera, but that was because I was usually there on official business. I was always very respectful to people. Something that I attribute my success to as a nightclub photographer is that I always keep a level of respect to people and how they felt about being photographed. Whenever I would photograph people I would either directly ask them or say "Hi I'm Derek, I'm taking pictures, would you mind if I took a picture of you dancing?" Which usually messes me up because something that they were doing is really intriguing me and I want to capture that, but now I can't because I just introduced myself and ruined the moment. However, I'd rather that than offend and get someone really upset.

Rachel E. Pollock: Somebody took a photograph of a performance and put it on the ManRay website with the caption "Somebody needs to get a bigger tampon." I went through the roof because I was not consulted about photography. There were two photographers that were sanctioned to take pictures, like Derek, and they had very strict policies.

Eileen Dover: I know for me I didn't care. I wanted to be photographed every five minutes. I really love the camera, but I know that there were other people who didn't.

Kathryn Pollnac: When I moved to Atlanta, we tried a couple times to go to the Chamber and there were people with cameras. This is 2002 or 2003 and Goth and fetish are kind of rolling around together into this big mass. They were letting anybody into this club and there were people with cameras and there were people harassing us. I went and I talked to someone and said, "Hey this person is harassing me and my friends," and they are looking at you like "Yeah whatever." I never set foot in that place again because my club experience was ManRay. ManRay always felt so safe to me, like everybody was watching out for you and, if somebody was causing trouble, they were out and that was that.

Charles Bandes: I think that it would be pretty hard to maintain as strict a no photo or video policy now that everybody had two or three cameras on them at any given point in time. But by the same token, I don't think that ManRay would have worked if everybody felt like they were being surveilled. I think that it's much harder to feel safe, especially on a fetish night. It's harder to feel safe and anonymous when everybody can be taking a picture of you and whatever you're doing. I'm a photographer and I was always kind of disappointed that I couldn't bring my camera, but at the same time, I really understand why they had that rule.

Patrick Baldwin People prized personal space and I really appreciated that. I liked that you could move around freely, even when the place was really full, because people have some respect for personal space. I think that some of that comes from the really strong presence of the kink community at ManRay.

Emily Arkin: I would dance with strangers and I talked to strangers. One of my worst ManRay experiences was when I got asked to dance and they were like, "Would you like to dance in the cage?" I was like, "Yes, that sounds great," but very quickly I was uncomfortable with how many of my physical boundaries were being pushed in the cage and I was like, "never again."

Crayola Tidd: The fetish nights. It's a great community and it's very safe. After a while, the thought of going to other clubs that weren't like that felt not safe. I remember when I went to this club and it was a nightmare. We got so harassed. People were following us around and we even asked a bouncer to tell someone to leave us alone and the bouncer kind of followed us around. I definitely wanted to leave. It convinced me that there was no place equal or similar to ManRay where you could feel totally comfortable.

Only once did something that made me uncomfortable, and the bouncers jumped right in. A guy that worked up the street at Hi-Fi pizza, where we often went after the club closed, got chummy with a lot of people. We used to always joke and say "You should take a day off" and "You need to go see ManRay, so fun. It's terrible that you have to work. One day, come see what the club's like." One New Year, he was at ManRay. I recognized him and said "Oh look, you finally get a day off. That's great. Happy New Year." "Happy New Year," and he gave me a hug and then he started dragging me, like he was going to drag me out of the club. I'm screaming "Let me go!" and in seconds the bouncers were like "This guy's got to go."

Erika Spaulding: It became really clear to me really quickly, once I could go to other places like Axis or Avalon or any of the Lansdowne stuff, that it felt like women were commodities there. I think it's kind of ironic, because the assumption is, that if I get dolled up in liquid latex and I'll let people see, I'm trying to make myself a commodity, but it was not that way. For me, it felt like it was a fun, creative thing to do. It was different and I liked being a part of that. What I noticed right away at ManRay was that people had a sense of autonomy and it seemed to be the first place I've ever been where it felt like people were respecting boundaries and there was no chance of anybody else approaching or touching another person. I felt like I was in an environment that, if somebody were to do that, several other people would have intervened. It was more about the clientele that went there, as opposed to what they were wearing or the way that we're dancing or the type of music. That stuff didn't matter. It was more the people that were there that made it feel safe.

Sara S. Wendell: ManRay had a vibe. I would say it was much, much safer than I felt at any other club in the greater Boston area. Part of it was because we were a tight knit community and most of us knew each other. So if it was a matter of somebody getting in your face and any of your friends spotting that they were going to come back at you. I watched it happen time and time again. I didn't tend to get unwanted attention I think as often as a lot of women did because I didn't fit the standard ManRay Goth type, and I have a fairly powerful personality. I'm not somebody who would put up with it. We were all looking out for each other, especially on Fridays when there were people running around in next to nothing and you would get the predatory types who would come in and expected that meant that they were going to get laid because obviously if she's not wearing anything that means she wants to sleep with me.

I watched many times somebody tried to start harassing someone and they got shut down by a wall of men almost immediately. "Is this guy bothering you?" And if she said yes, they'd be like, "All right, you need to leave now." On the flip side, I have been to clubs on Lansdowne Street where it's nothing but a bloody meat market. I had no problem going to ManRay by myself, I did that all the time, whereas at a place on Lansdowne I would never go by myself. For me as a woman, it's asking for trouble.

Avril dePagter: I probably didn't even notice it until we were talking about it now, the difference in vibes of different places. ManRay was not a place where I was going to be groped by men. I don't think I hardcore identified it at that time, but, if I look back now, it was such a gift. ManRay was a place where I felt like I could completely control and be in charge of my own body and that's why I miss it very, very deeply. It almost makes me emotional and miss that feeling of going out and just being totally in control.

Corey Reeves: If people were to ask what Thursday was about or what Wednesday was about, I would say, "Hey, we're here, number one. Number two, you should come and explore for yourself and see what you enjoy." Some Goths love hip hop. It would expand people's horizons to try something. If they don't like it, they don't like it. People would come to the door on a Friday night and not come back because they would be too mortified or traumatized or saw their priest there. The concept was very, very dark, but the thing was that black brought out the colors of people. It was an educational experience. It was wonderful to see people stepping outside their element. It was enlightenment, despite the darkness.

Becky D: About a month before ManRay closed Chris actually called me up and asked me to run Fantasy Factory. To be honest, I had mixed feelings. Two years prior to that, I would have been ecstatic at the idea of running the group. But, by that time, I was not going out as much. Maybe I should have said no and I should have kind of let someone else who was more invested do it. It was mixed. I was excited and happy to take it over, but I also didn't know if I was the best person for it. Then there's also the conflict of the club's closing. I asked the bigger question of whether Fantasy Factory should continue at that point because that was about when the Goth industrial scene was taking a little bit of a slump as far as attendance was concerned.

We hit a big peak around when the Matrix was really popular. We started seeing people who weren't really part of the underground scene poke their head in and like what they saw or who were just checking it out for thrills. Then there was something shiny and new in the burner scene, so people are gravitating to that. At the same time, people who were kind of Goth kids in the 80s and 90s were adults who had careers and who were getting married and having kids. There wasn't that incoming group of Goth industrial kids to keep the momentum. In Boston, we tied the Gothic industrial scene very closely to the fetish scene, which is not necessarily the case in other cities. So when the Goth industrial scene started going down in attendance that meant that the fetish nights were going to take a hit too.

Eileen Dover: There's nothing really important about the building, it was the people and the ideas and the freedoms that that building afforded the people who went into it. It was the collective. It was the attitude. It was the idea. It was empathy. It was the unity. It was the freedom that you'd have, maybe on a Saturday or Friday night, for two or three hours and then you go back to the rest of your week and you deal with all these fucking assholes who would scoff at you if they saw you on a Friday or Saturday night. When you go into that building you don't get scoffed out, you get embraced.

Becky D: Michael, especially towards the end, was helping me with a lot of performances. It was exhausting and we spent a lot of time on it, but it was really rewarding to create these performances. It's hard work but then you're like spending a lot of time with these people who were friends. You're sharing this experience together and that brings you closer. You're putting together something new that's never been done. You have this creative outlet. You're doing the performance and getting that energy with the audience.

Who gets to do this when you're 20 and right out of school? Who gets the opportunity to be creative with all their friends in this really cool environment? It was a unique once in a lifetime experience and it is something I will treasure always.

Chapter 16

These Are My People

"One of the principles of happiness, and finding happiness as a human being, is having a community that could be your church. For some people it might be church but, for a lot of people, it's something like ManRay." — Tatiana Zimkus

Drawing in a regular and varied crowd, ManRay was a social place. The club saw the making, strengthening, and breaking of friendships, love found and lost, new discoveries about life, the first introductions and the sad goodbyes. Some groups had dedicated pre-club rituals where they met up, got dressed, and descended on the club en masse. For others, they arrived at the door solo to meet up with their crowd or find new faces. ManRay was unquestionably a close-knit community united by their shared weirdness and shared love. After a few visits the staff knew you, the regulars became recognizable faces and friends, everyone looked out for each other. It provided a place to celebrate the things you loved — music, dancing, aesthetic, performance — and find those who shared those loves. You had found your people and the night quickly became your own. S.L.

Eileen Dover: ManRay was the intersection for everyone.

Mizery McRae: It's a spectrum of people that made that bar what it was.

Kyle Blaisdell: Usually little tribes of us would gather beforehand because we lived communally often anyway. It wasn't uncommon for 10 people to be in a house or an apartment. Some of those houses would develop nicknames. One place was the Messiah village, one house might be hackers and club kids or transvestites and drag queens. We would all gather. We'd trek out together. There'd be a few stragglers depending on who's working that day or whatnot, but it was usually a group event. We had really tight knit friends; we lived, played, and fought together constantly.

Greg Frisbee: There was definitely that sense of camaraderie. There was a sense of "I belong here because I know so many people here." It was like an extension of our own party. There were times that I remember going to ManRay and I knew every single person on that dance floor. If I happened to show up late, because I didn't get there until 10 or 10:30, people would be like "Frisbee!" and tackle me on the dance floor. They'd be like "You're late and where have you been?"

Emily Taylor: I would often go to ManRay by myself. Part of the reason why I liked it was that all my friends were there, so I would show up by myself maybe, but I would walk in and be like "Oh hey! Oh hey! Oh hey!" I rarely went to ManRay in a group. In fact, I never waited in line at ManRay because I had a badge, and I would just go inside because I'm a snob. [laughs] I'm one of those people, sorry! I had a gigantic friend circle there. I couldn't walk through the door without people saying hello so much that sometimes it would take me 15 to 20 minutes to get to the stairs to go downstairs to the dressing room. I worked with all the promoters, so Cusraque, Jack, Jen, Chris, Terri, Daisy, all the people who worked there were my buddies. The security guards too. Don, the owner.

Every single one of my boyfriends that I ever had, from that time, I got them because of that community, which was good in a lot of ways and not great in others. It was very incestuous. There were a lot of poly people there. It was just fun … we were all fun sexy people. Similarly, all my living arrangements were usually ManRay people. If I got a new apartment, it was because someone else had a roommate that was moving out. Pretty much every friend I had, aside from my high school friends, was a ManRay person for years.

Paul Calnan: We'd meet up in a big group and go in together. We'd go in like 15 to 20 people together, that's typically how we did it.

Shane Blau: I always went with my crew. There were six of us, give or take, sometimes four or eight. It was always the crew from Boston University. We would gather together, get ready together, and go together. It grew and shrunk over time, but there was always a core of us. I don't think I would have gone by myself because going with them was a really important part of it for me. I loved getting ready with them and then going to the club with them. Afterwards we'd go to eat in Kenmore Square.

Eloni Feliciano: I felt like I had a crew. There are more of us that would either meet up to go there or we'd end up taking the same transportation back.

Me'lissa Nin: There were times that I hung out in Harvard Square at the Pit and, oftentimes, I would go with a group of friends. Other times, I would walk in the door by myself. In the beginning, I would go with a friend or two, just as a moral support kind of thing. "You're going to be my social crutch because I'm not good at talking to people." But eventually I grew out of that. I remember how I felt nervous and intimidated walking in there for the first time and I didn't want anybody else to feel that way so I thought, "I'm going to be an ambassador and I'm going to make it a point to introduce myself to new faces." I'm still friends with a lot of folks that I met at ManRay, which is nice.

Erin Falkell: Typically it was meeting people beforehand and doing the bar crawl up Central Square to make it to ManRay. So we'd go see little Joe Cook performing, we'd go to the Phoenix Landing, and then we'd get everyone together and wind up at ManRay.

Michael Hsieh: I think I almost always went with a crew of people just because we all knew each other, and we all lived close to each other. For two years, my girlfriend lived a couple blocks away. For ManRay, we'd plan to go over a couple hours early. Her roommates would have their friends over, we'd all be getting ready while listening to music and just we'd walk over to the club later.

John O'Leary: You felt more at home in a club like ManRay then you did in your own living room.

Kathryn Pollnac: I lived in Rhode Island so there were a few people from Providence that I went with. Sometimes I would go up with a friend of mine who I went to the University with who was also the DJ there. I'd go with boyfriends sometimes. A lot of times I would also just go up by myself because I really liked to get there early. I had to wait for other people that wanted to get there at midnight, but I wanted to be able to have longer at the club. Coming from southern Rhode Island, it was probably an hour and a half, an hour and 45-minute drive depending on traffic. I'm not going to spend almost four hours in the car to be there for only an hour and a half.

Athena Costa: There are some people I know that moved here from out of state a few years ago. At some point they came up to me to have a conversation. "I'm familiar with you and I've been staring at you from across the room for four years now."

Jill Kempton: I went singularly because I always lived in the suburbs. Every once in a while, I would maybe meet up with a friend beforehand, but usually I went by myself. I was young and a little anxious about doing that, but I was gonna go no matter what and just assumed that everyone you knew was going to be there. I was shy and young and I just kind of went to dance. You meet a lot of people banging into them on the dance floor, not even always purposely, and now you're their friend.

Patrick Baldwin: On Wednesdays, we'd often go in a group while on Fridays we'd often meet people there. There were three or four people that I went regularly with on Wednesdays. Fridays were a little more random. I was more likely to be able to convince some random friend who'd never been before to go on a Friday for some reason. There were a lot of folks I knew well enough to say hello to and maybe have a drink with.

David Winthrop: In the early days, I was living in a frat house scenario. I would usually go in by myself because those guys, that wasn't something they were interested in. I had this whole series of friends that I grew up with, and all of them did go to ManRay a few times here and there, but for the most part, I would meet my club friends at the club.

Michael Hsieh: It was very easy and very engaging. Everybody seemed to be having a great time because everybody kind of knew each other. Once you meet one person, they're going to introduce you to everybody and you're going to be having a good time. If you click with somebody, then you would end up making out or maybe go on a date. It was a social scene. Cusraque may have been the first or second person I met at the club and many people will probably say the same thing because, as a promoter, that's his job and he's just very good at it. He was always introducing people.

Abigail Taylor: When I walked in there, I would know everyone. It was just a given. I would go there alone. I would go there with friends. I knew if I went there alone that everyone would be there. We were a part of a family and we all cared about each other. We all had drama with each other. We all dated each other in one way or another.

Tatiana Zimkus: It was kind of an incestuous group. Everyone kind of dated each other. I definitely kind of did my rounds, I guess.

Jon Whitney: I think there were nights that I went alone and there were nights I went with other friends. I went there for the music, whether my friends would join me, or I was going alone. Either way, nothing really stops me from going. I wouldn't be like "Oh well, someone says they're not going so I guess I'm not going to go tonight." I just went because I wanted to go.

Paul Vitagliano: On a much deeper level we're just as much misfits and outcasts and freaks as everybody that's in the room with us. We're all together. Obviously, if people stuck with the club for years and years and years, they felt some form of a similar bond and similar trust.

Chris Ewen: A guy named Craig Mellow would come every Wednesday night; he was a regular who would always come in and dance. He was really cool, and he had great requests. One day, in the mid-80s, he told me he was going to have to stop coming because he was going to focus on his work. I was sad to see him go. When you lose someone who is part of the fabric, the structure of any night, it is sad. Years later, in 2006, I found out that he won the Nobel Prize for physiology or medicine.

Tatiana Zimkus: Whether it was naive or not, I did put a lot of trust and faith in that community. And I have to say that they repaid me. It was a community of people that, for the most part, had common interests. If there's someone in that community that is suffering, people come to your aid. That's something that I haven't experienced since.

Becky D: There are Goth people that would go to raves, so I started getting to know them. Those are probably my closest friends, even today. I have friendships, even still, that span back to that original group of people that I hung out with. I wasn't someone who just stuck with the same group of people through the 10 years I was going to ManRay. I kind of moved around depending on what I was doing and what my interests were and what other people were doing.

Rachel E. Pollock: Once I wanted to fuck with people. I had a goatee and mustache and eyebrows bigger than my female eyebrows that I put on. I had a mohawk at the time, but I put it up in a bun. I put on eyeliner and men's Goth clothes. I bound my chest. So I went to ManRay and I looked like a man. I told my cab driver where to take me and he was like, "Man, I heard there's naked vampire chicks at that club." And I was like, "I don't know about that."

Emily Taylor: It was the home of my youth. I lived there. I had to do a lot of processing about that because I basically grew up in a fetish club. I got exposed to a lot of stuff as a kid that I probably shouldn't have been exposed to and I turned out fine [laughs]. When I find out that my friends went to ManRay, or they were part of ManRay, I get elated. I'm very pleased to have that connection because I know they understand something about me, and I understand something about them. It was the first place in my life where I ever felt powerful and beautiful and sexy and mysterious and cool. I was not cool in high school; I was a weirdo. But I go to this place and I'm like the coolest bitch ever. It was amazing.

Jennifer: Looking back, the people who are my closest friends right now are from ManRay. I met my husband at ManRay, and we've been together for over 20 years. A lot of bad came out of ManRay, but there was also a lot of good. Relationships — our friends got married and divorced and all kinds of stuff over the years. It was a huge part of a lot of our lives for a while. I might have only gone a short window compared to other people, but we would eat, sleep, and breathe the club. We'd have a party at our house. We'd be at rehearsals a few nights a week for Fantasy Factory. We stayed up all night. We lived at ManRay.

Trent Stewart: My wife. My dad. My daughters, godparents, lawyer, chiropractor … All produced from the club.

Niki Nevulis: I did feel safe, but I felt safe for a couple of reasons. I had a lot of guy friends that were there, and we went with a bunch of us, so there's always somebody there to look out for you. I did not feel objectified. You're always careful and on alert, but I felt that level of safety there because people weren't there to go find somebody to be nefarious with or be their fuck buddy for the night. Everybody was going because it was a safe zone, for us non-cookie cutters, LGBTQ, if you're into weird shit, fetish night, and stuff like that. You were not judged.

Greg Frisbee: ManRay had become a second home for us. It holds a very nostalgic place in my heart in terms of my youth. ManRay was the place that we would go to be young and carefree, and all get together. It was this glue, even when people moved on to different colleges or jobs or cities. When we could, it's like "Let's meet up at ManRay. Let's go to ManRay, there's a New Wave night, there's Darkwave night." ManRay was the meeting spot. "Let's go out and grab a slice of Hi-Fi or grab some food."

Jenn Sutkowski: I had a small group that I would go with. I would also see the same people and I definitely met people there. I remember there was this girl who didn't really like me but gave me a ride home. So people kind of looked out for each other. Most of the time was spent dancing. I didn't like to talk to many people outside of my small group. I sort of had my sights set on one of the people in my group, it was an unrequited love, so I wasn't really that concerned with everybody else. But I appreciated how diverse the crowd was Goths and there was a bigger LGBTQ population there.

Anna Feder: I was somebody who went with my boyfriend pretty much exclusively, so I think that prevented me, in some ways, from really getting to know people there. We had a codependent relationship. We would dance and we would socialize here and there and say hello to people we remembered. Part of it is on me. It may have been really easy if I had tried. A lot of people that we knew from Western Mass that had moved to Boston went there. I had a whole lot of people who were friends before ManRay that went to ManRay. Some I had brought and some who discovered it on their own. A bunch of my friends from high school found their way there. At the same time there was a really cool exciting city life vibe that we didn't really know. We were living in Amherst and then Northampton, so we had kind of a different experience of ManRay, and we weren't really part of the community, so to speak.

Prospero Eaton: I tended to go on my own and meet up with people once I was there. If I had a girlfriend at the time she might have gone with me.

Tatiana Zimkus: It wasn't just the place or the music. It was the people. It's a combination. It's the trifecta. The word that keeps coming to my mind is community. One of the principles of happiness and finding happiness as a human being is having a community that could be your church. For some people it might be church, but for a lot of people it's something like ManRay or it can be your D&D group. I think we all strive to have that in our lives. This group, these people, and my experience was what I had been longing for for so long.

Tonya Sand: At the very beginning, when I was going to college, I went by myself. There's nobody at school. I was the only Gothy person on the entire campus. I knew a couple people who were kind of weird and understood it, but nobody came with me.

Keith Ward: As people kind of faded away from it for a little bit it wasn't as fun. We had that huge group. There were nights where our core group was like 25 to 30 deep.

Xtine Santakas: I married very young, and he had cheated on me and I was absolutely devastated. A big mistake. Love is blind, especially when you're young. But one night, my ex-husband showed up. I didn't want to cause a scene, so I went into the front room. I didn't say anything to anybody. Tashi came up to me and said, "What the hell are you doing?" And I said, "I'm just hanging out here tonight." "Why?" I said, "Because my ex is in the corner." And he goes, "Oh, for the love of Christ" and he grabs my wrist, pulls me back into the corner right up to him and gets in his face. "You don't belong here. This is Christine's corner; you need to leave now."

Mayellen Vega: I got into a fight. Well, I didn't get into a fight. I pushed this girl because she was getting flirty with Darren, and Darren had a thing for her. All of the guys I was with, they were madly in love with her. Darren was dancing with her and I went, "No!" and pushed her away. "Get out of here! You shouldn't be dancing with her."

Eartha Harris: I was always half a part of some particular social group at any given time, but perhaps due to some sort of avoidant tendencies in me, I would always keep one foot out of whatever circle I was in. I can count at least five distinctly different social circles I was a part of during those years, and those five different social circles really define different eras in my life during my 20s.

Shane Blau: My friend Anne Z can fall asleep anywhere, so she got kicked out a good handful of times just by falling asleep head down on the table. Not because of how much she drank, it was just because she really could fall asleep anywhere.

Patrick Baldwin: It was wildly different taking new people there. I had some friends that were like, "This is basically the best place ever" and they took off on their own and I had to corral them at the end of the night. I had a few friends who were not quite sure what to make of the place.

Keith Ward: We went with a core group of friends and that group grew exponentially over the years. Now it's friends, friends of friends, and friends of friends of friends. I don't think I met any friends there. Any friends I made there were kind of already friends of friends.

ML: It was interesting to watch people come into their own on those nights, because they went from waiting in the Wednesday crowd as young college kids just discovering the glossy, to being married with kids and moving on with their lives. It was a 14-year span I saw a generation grow up

ML: It started with a very young crowd and then, as time went on, that's not the young crowd anymore. There was still a new young crowd coming in. It's a way of life. It was fun and there was nowhere else you could really get that at that time.

Taylor Vecchio: ManRay is definitely a place you would go to with people you're already friends with. You'd have a fucking blast and dance and just feel really welcomed and feel really cool. I also feel like if I kind of knew some guy, and I saw that he was a ManRay, I would think he was cool.

Jenny Dahling: I would go initially with one to three friends at the most. After I got to know people there, going alone wasn't really a big deal because I knew I would see people I knew there. A sense of community absolutely was hugely important to me, especially at the age I was at. It was post-high school and college. I kind of fumbled through or failed, so I only made a smattering of friends. All of a sudden, I'm on the doorstep of young adulthood and who do you hang out with? It would seem weird to only hang out with your high school friends. You want to branch out and do adult things and begin drinking. So it felt liberating to be able to go by myself. It felt really great just to be with my fellow weirdos.

Christina Pearson: It was definitely a collective experience. It was a crucial piece. Going into ManRay was like going home and meeting up with the people that were family. Being with close friends that you went with and actually had experiences there with was so crucial, absolutely crucial, and also contributed to why I always felt completely safe. I had lost my religion. I was no longer a good Christian girl. That family was gone, and then with them gone, I went from that to having a new group of people that were going to accept me. Even the people who were in the club that didn't know me accepted me.

Jamie DiBattista: At its height we were 30 people. But it didn't get to that point until about the mid-90s. I didn't go to New Wave night in a singular sense, but I would go to Goth night by myself. It was definitely a more interesting thing when you're not 30 people deep. It was fun to do it by yourself.

Liz Lamanche: When you start going solo you sort of see who's there and get a feel of the room and then wind-up having conversations, at least at the bar, with whoever's around and looks friendly. Gradually, those people turned into friends and then you met their friends. You get to know who the tribe is. I was never the core of the group, but there were the friendly faces that I would see. Now, a whole bunch of them are my longtime core group of friends. Boston is, as everyone will tell you, small enough that the freaks and weirdos all know each other. It's not like San Francisco where the Goths never meet the burners. There's tremendous crossover between different flavors of freaks and weirdos. I sort of inhabit that ecosystem.

Susanne Boitano: It's one of those places as Robert Frost said: "Home is the place where, when you have to go there, they have to take you in" ... provided you have the right clothing for the dress code. And, if you went home and put on the right clothing, they'll let you right in. It was a place that was accepting. We're all in this mosaic together. There were just so many permutations of people there. It was extraordinary. ManRay was just the encapsulation of a further generation of unique thinkers and unique dressers that could come to a place and enjoy themselves. Nowadays I'm glad people don't understand what it means to be a fashion outcast or a sexual outcast or any manner of deviant because I think the lids are off what would be now acceptable things. I never heard a cross word there. In all honesty, I've seen people be shittier in church. It was a wonderful feeling to go and engage or be left alone. You are not expected to do more than just be part of the fun.

Kathy Landes: I definitely felt like we belong to some sort of subculture, for sure. You went to that club and really felt just a sense of belonging. We may not have known everybody there, but I felt like there were certain key people that we just saw all the time. It wasn't like that when I started going to other clubs. Nothing could match what was at ManRay. There wasn't the feeling like I could be weird and just be myself.

Charles Bandes: I would usually go by myself or with one or two friends or a girlfriend. I definitely felt like I was surrounded by my people when I was there and I definitely identified as part of both the Goth community and the fetish community, but I never really had a particularly social experience at ManRay.

Becky D: I tended to weave my way through different groups. When I first started going, I was hanging out with one group of people and then a lot of who I hung out with regularly changed as I joined Fantasy Factory and did other stuff.

Emily Taylor: I felt like we were all just a family in that there were Goths that were more industrial or more squirrely and there were full on fetish people and we were all just there together. This is where all the weirdos hang out. It wasn't cliquey in like "Oh, you're gay so we don't we hang out" It's like never like that.

Corey Reeves: ManRay had a true feeling of care. There was a true feeling of identity.

Becky D: I felt I was becoming a part of the ManRay scene. Feeling like I had an identity and belonging really helped me figure out who I was and built confidence. Being a part of that subculture was almost part of my identity. I needed to hold on to something like that to figure out who I was because I was kind of lost in the larger world at that point. I was in this no man's land of understanding who I was.

Trent Stewart: I would comfortably fit into so many different groups. I never really cared about belonging to a culture.

Lucretia X Machina: I identify myself as a pagan and Goth. Kind of independent but wanting to find a few solid friendships, which I did get out of ManRay.

Erika Spaulding: I felt like I was a single bee in a hive of bees, and it felt happy and productive and not like a subculture. It felt like it was big enough to be its own culture. It was different.

Lily Moonstorm: I've always just identified as an individual. But I guess that after all these years, and my tastes not really changing that much, you'd probably lump me in the Goth subculture.

Adam Wolff: ManRay was this very mixed club. It was the center of alternative culture in Boston. It was the gay club and the Goth club and that kind of anything goes clubs.

Prospero Eaton: As far as subculture, I definitely identified with a lot of the industrial music at the time. It also kind of had a lot of overlap with the Gothic subculture, so I identified with that one quite a bit as well. I've never been somebody that fit completely into one subculture. I'm just kind of my own person and in a lot of ways. Beyond that, it was just really inspiring to see how other people dressed and the wild things that people would wear would kind of inspire me. I think that there's almost like a subculture within ManRay itself really.

Crayola Tidd: I definitely consider myself Goth and I used to joke and say, "Well, I'm happy and I'm blonde." I always wanted dark hair, but it doesn't look good on me. So I joke and say I'm that "happy blonde Goth." Not typical.

Athena Costa: I always thought of myself as part of a subculture. In the alternative scene there are always subcultures to a degree. In the 90s, we were all growing up listening to classic rock. Then in high school, there was just so much more music. Ever since I was in middle school, I always thought "I'm different and I belong with those people and that's who I am."

Arlene Guerrero-Watanabe: One of my best friends from Miami was a flight attendant. His name is Armando, and he was very, very gay. He and his partner would come up to visit me because he could travel for free, and I would take him to ManRay. The first time I took them, he wasn't super Goth. A little bit Goth is more like a New Wave type person. I dressed them up in our clothes and put them all in black and they loved it. They were so smitten with it.

Trent Stewart: Just because you dress a particular way, doesn't mean that you're into a certain subculture.

Emily Taylor: I think that shared weirdness was so important there. For example in my high school there might have been one other Goth, so I hung out with all the guys who were into metal and grunge. The alternative people all kind of hung out together because we were the weirdos. Then, when I started going to ManRay, it's like we all just kind of accepted each other's weirdness. There was a guy that used to show up before anyone would was dancing, when it was just the house music on, and he would just twirl around on the dance floor with a little fanny pack on, wearing a unitard and a beret, and he would just close his eyes and spin around like a little figure skater. I loved him because he was doing his own things and feeling it. I just thought "Thank God for this guy. He's keeping it weird. What would we do without a place where we could go to just be ourselves and be where no one would beat us up?" I got the shit kicked out to me a couple times for dressing the way that I did. Some guy attacked my boyfriend and I in Kenmore Square one night, and just kicked the shit out of us because we looked weird. ManRay was a place where you can go to be safe.

Julie Kramer: It was a home for a certain sect of people, and you could make it yours.

Emily Arkin: I would see some alternative lifestyles. I think people wouldn't, unless you really specifically went to gay bars, have come into contact with all these subcultures. You'd already have to be a member, or you'd have to date someone who is already in that scene to enter it. I think it sort of made Cambridge a more multifaceted cultural place, and I don't mean that just in the sense of speaking different languages. I'm not sure that night clubbing worked that way in a lot of other cities.

Marcia Post: ManRay was such a place to just be outside the norm and be who you are. In the 90s I think it split off into all the subcultures with different nights where you're welcome, not that anyone else was excluded.

Derek Kouyoumjian: They all converge on ManRay, all these different communities, all these different scenes and people. It was them just coming in and having a good time together.

Richard LaDue: I think there's an Avalon gay guy who's like, "Give me some glitz, give me some lights, this is my shit." I think every club actually has its own kind of tribe or family. I'll just throw this up there: I think the person that goes to ManRay probably, in that time period, had fewer places to have those feelings, then the person who went to Avalon. I think you could get into gay culture and like Barbra Streisand and Liza Minnelli in the early, late 90s, 2000s. Whereas ManRay was just kind of different and more subversive or alternative.

Emily Arkin: There were other places I went dancing. Some hotels would have a dance night, or I would go to Mod Night a lot. That might also be where I went other than ManRay. I think there was some overlap. But with all of those I am always conscious that I was gravitating to one DJ and not a whole scene or a whole culture. ManRay felt like a complete experience, even if you went to different nights that were totally different.

Arlene Guerrero-Watanabe: It was really cool because there were so many different people. There were these crazy tall drag queen types. It seemed like everybody was Goth but there were different subcultures of Gothness. I personally love the back room because I was more of a Goth. I like wearing a black. I was in grad school, so I didn't have to work yet. I looked however I wanted to look.

Koren Bernardi: I feel like I was able to cross over to different cliques. I think working there, you get to know people in a professional kind of sense.

Athena Costa: Subcultures in America have become so normalized with different sub genres. But being a Goth is not about being depressed. I think being Goth is really just macabre. You really like wearing black to stick it to the man. You're just doing it because it's what makes you happy, and you're portraying how you feel in your own way. At the time it wasn't like you could just go to the store and buy a bunch black clothes or club clothes, instead you had to seek it out. Whatever your thing was, whether you were a raver kid or punk kid or Goth kid, there wasn't like a prefabricated store you could go to and just buy things. I would create my attire from what I had access to, which meant a load of thrift stores or your grandparents old sweater. You would Frankenstein it together.

Jennifer Chandler: I think it would have been the most amazing place for the amateur photographer to take photos of the culture.

Skot Kremen: There are alternative ways of living. There's a couple of places that are hubs of that sort of lifestyle. I think that without ManRay, Boston/Cambridge would not have even been on the map.

Heather Morgan: I gravitated to a couple of different groups. One was all the alternative kids at BU that turned up at ManRay. There were a lot of us and we would see each other in other places too, like the dining hall and the School of Fine Arts. The Goth kids, or ManRay kids, at BU were easy to pick out walking down the street. Even if you didn't have people's phone numbers, you'd be walking up and down Comm Ave seeing people that you knew from ManRay and chatting with them. The others that I identified with and hung around with were the people at ManRay who were in bands and all knew each other, like DDT and You Shriek, and their friends and followers.

Abigail Taylor: I never really identified with a subculture. I never really thought of myself as Goth or punk or anything. I didn't ever really feel like I could identify myself as something. I wasn't even totally straight. I was just sort of me. So it was nice because there were a lot of people there that were the same. I think that we are part of the ManRay culture. The thing that connected us was ManRay, it wasn't being Goth, it wasn't being punk, it wasn't being gay, it was just part of ManRay.

David Winthrop: In the subculture of youth and that subculture of the forgotten youth, ManRay was a gathering place for all the kids that got made fun of in high school and all the kids that didn't quite fit in. They were at home at ManRay. There was the kid that finally felt comfortable in his own skin because they were surrounded by like-minded people who were non-judgmental. They all gathered together and intermingled. I think that allowed so many people the freedom of expression that kids from suburban towns in Massachusetts just couldn't find in their hometown. In the city you get exposed to all these people who think like you, act like you, are like you. That's the biggest gift that the club gave to so many lost souls.

Chapter 17

Time Marches On: The Years 2001-2005

"It's funny when you're a certain age in life and you know something that's very profound, but then all of a sudden your life shifts and changes." — Derek Kouyoumjian

Having been open for nearly twenty years, ManRay had an entire generation that grew up at the club. But those who had danced the night away in their twenties were growing older alongside their happy place. Things change. People began having families and kids of their own, some were settling down into careers, some were moving away from the area, and others were too tired to make the long nights. Many patrons had to think about where their lives were now versus ten years prior and they had to ask themselves how ManRay fit into their lives. The smoking ban came to public buildings in Boston and the first rumblings of closure began cropping up. This is the last year. ManRay is going to close soon. Our days at the club are over. For the next four years these whispers abounded, not only about ManRay but other surrounding clubs as well as questions about nightlife and its legitimacy in the new world were being voiced. Nevertheless, even at the end of its life, ManRay was still cranking out amazing dance nights and nocturnal joy. The new dance night, Xmortis, in particular seemed to have everything's that the wider audience of the club was looking for; it was an amalgamation of all ManRay's famous nights - queer friendly, Gothy, New Wave, performance pieces. It was a night that could have birthed the new generation of ManRay, had the club survived in physicality. Even still, with the building lost and maybe the death of nightclubs over dance nights, nights like Xmortis live on for those still looking for that place they belong. --- SL

Kyle Blaisdell: At the end of the 90s, we could see it happening. We were all Gen Xers, and all the Millennials were coming of age. As they were coming of age, we were seeing more of the Cybergoth crowd, the Day-Glo Goth crowd moving in and, of course, they're already wired. I really couldn't see the two crossing over. The world was changing. I guess we all saw it coming and we knew we had to adapt and that the lifestyle for us wasn't going to be sustainable a whole lot longer. We saw the casualties.

Marcia Post: I love that it provided the space, but it became less. It started to have more kink nights and Goth nights and I just remember the lesbian night was gone.

Becky D: Things like burners and burning nights were kind of popping up, so there were other alternative club nights that people were gravitating to and it was a little different. There weren't as many of the people who would have been going to the fetish nights. We were kind of moving away from that.

Tony Lee: Since Wednesday was a weeknight there were definitely fewer people there than Fridays and Saturdays. Attendance had definitely tapered off and people were going off and doing other things or only going to one night. I know the last few years at ManRay, there were fewer people going to clubs in general, whether it was Wednesday, Friday, or Saturday night in the very early 2000s versus in the 90s. There were still a good number of people who went, but sometimes, Wednesdays might only have 50 people when before there might be 150.

Nate Roman: There were definitely aspects of the last couple years, and I don't want to imply that there wasn't a lot of love and a lot of care and what went into it, but it definitely felt like some things were just kind of being let go. There wasn't quite as much attention and passion for some of the things. It was so overdue for renovation. I remember Wednesday nights, towards the end, were just dead. We were having a harder time drawing in the newer younger crowd toward the end.

Constantine Valhouli: Towards the end, the club felt like it had seen its better days a while back. The energy wasn't there. It was continuing on for the moment but there hadn't been new faces in the scene. The music and space didn't feel as relevant as they had five, ten, or fifteen years earlier. That's fine. These spaces aren't meant to be permanent but are meant to coalesce and find their moment and then dissipate. But the last week of the club … hot damn it was packed like that Gothic convention in Boston from the early 1990s. It was one of the liveliest, sweatiest dancefloors I have ever seen, bar none. It was like a reunion of people from two decades of one's life, friends, former lovers, everything.

Matt Gleason: I did not like what nightclubs were turning into. We had a lot of problems. There were a few things in play. The Station nightclub fire and what happened with that was horrible and it could have absolutely been prevented. They strengthened the fire code in Massachusetts because of it. A lot of nightclubs had heat sensors and now you had to have smoke detectors. Cigarette smoking was only outside now. It took away the ability to use a smoke machine almost completely. You go to the nightclub for sound and lights. There is definitely an energy with seeing the light and the sound of the music. They took that away.

Additionally, dance music generally was starting to become less popular, probably because Generation X was starting to get older and hip hop was becoming the primary popular music. I like rap and hip hop, but sometimes those nights can get very violent. The music's good, but people act differently. It's very weird how music will affect your perception, attitude, and how you treat others. For some reason hip hop music makes people act like assholes. While all through the 90s there were raves but ravers all about love, happiness and taking ecstasy. You never heard about a fight.

Chris Ewen: The smoking ban happened in Boston before it happened in Cambridge. In a way, when it first started, it gave ManRay an advantage. You can't smoke in clubs and bars in Boston, but you can cross the river and do what you want. Things took a dip for a while, but I also noticed that there were people who didn't want to be around smokers who started coming out. It's like, "Oh my lord, finally, I can go out and not smell of cloves and tobacco!"

Chris Ewen: Because of the smoking ban, it became really apparent to us just what the air in the club was masking, as far as the carpet smells.

Constantine Valhouli: I never realized how much the smell of clove cigarettes and regular cigarettes and patchouli covered up the fact that the building was in terrible shape and smelled of mildew. Many of us supported the smoking ban, but then were almost willing to make an exception after sniffing the club without a protective layer of burnt nicotine.

Chris Manousaridis: I was doing a small tour in Florida where I had my residency then I was in North Carolina doing a show with the Crüxshadows. Later I did a night at ManRay and then Ceremony over Thanksgiving weekend. I went back and there was no smoking allowed in the club which freaked me out. I showed up and people were outside smoking in the cold. I was like "What's going on here?" Because I've literally walked into the club with a cigarette in my mouth and music cases in my hand. Suddenly you can't smoke. I had to run outside to take a few puffs and go back to spinning in Ceremony.

Eloni Feliciano: Xmortis is a little bit complicated because it sort of springs from the absence of Hell. The original way I put my foot in the door was because I did the Miss Gothic Pageant.

Norm: Xmortis began because there needs to be new blood sometimes. Performances and the nights were much less organized, much less professional and a lot more seat-of-your-pants. When I first got there, I remember being thrown up on stage with about 30 seconds worth of instructions. There was a lot of that amateur energy going on. But as time went on, the nights got more and more choreographed and themed.

Eloni Feliciano: I started thinking about it most of the year before everything kind of came to fruition. I had to create, I had to get contestants, create a website, and all of these things I've never done before. It was also more than what other people were doing at the time. Nobody really had a website for the individual nights; people would kind of just promote by mouth to mouth or give people flyers.

Patrick and I, when we went into Xmortis we did it more as partners. We were approached by the club without ever having thought that we wanted to do a monthly event. They called us downstairs and were like, "We want to offer you the second night of the month to do a Goth event." We had a concept, so they gave us an offer. They can offer whatever the heck they want but we weren't going to do it if they didn't give us what we wanted. They thought that we just really wanted to take over the Hell spot, which is lucrative because it's a huge Goth day basically once a month.

We accepted. They wanted us to just mirror and be a mimic of

Hell and we didn't want to be a mimic obviously for various reasons. They wanted us to produce food and we did because they asked us to. They were trying to name it for us. They want us to call it "Voodoo." Nope. I think after the second month, they were like, "You guys got it down." We ended up having a decent relationship with the club and the manager.

It was one of those experimental experiences and we changed it throughout the years. We wanted to change it up and make it a little bit different from what music was doing because we didn't want to be a mirror of work that others worked so hard on for years. So we didn't want to do those large performances like Cusraque did, but we wanted to hire people from within the community to do Xmortis for us. Occasionally, we'd have burlesque dancers or circus acts and even full dance troupes. Each time we tried to keep it a little bit fresher, a little bit different. We even had Mexican wrestlers.

The second part of it was that we wanted to have a guest DJ every single time. We wanted a third DJ just to change up the music a little bit. Sometimes they tag teamed with Chris or they would just play the first hour or two, but that was another little experimental part and that extended into when we moved to T.T the Bear's.

Eloni Feliciano: A lot of misinformation was going on. Some people were spreading rumors and sometimes the catty ones said we had stolen the night from Cusraque, which is absolutely not the case. We were approached, and we didn't really have a chance to talk to Cusraque. Another night started somewhere in Union Square with Cusraque, I believe it was Toast. We went to it and he gave us his blessing. He said, "Hey, I totally understand." So, we were friends throughout with Cusraque. At no point did we have any problems. Eventually people became more used to what we were doing, and we would sort of be experimental about it and we were open to people giving us suggestions. We actually got a lot of feedback. You want to have dancers, but the concept of dancers for Xmortis was very different from dancers at Fantasy Factory. We wanted people to just get there and dance. Sometimes when you arrive in the club and you don't see anybody on the dance floor you might feel a little shy so they would just start dancing so people could feel a little bit loose a little bit earlier. Our dancers were supposed to meld with the crowd versus stand out on the boxes.

Patrick Fitzgerald In 2004, Eloni and I were very content doing what we were doing. We kind of fancied ourselves more into the fetish scene during that time and certainly still the club scene aspect of it. I think Cusraque had a night called Sin. Hell was kind of starting to falter a little bit. When Cusraque and the club parted ways, the club needed somebody to fill that spot. Eloni and I were very conflicted about that because Cusraque was our friend. Eloni and I were people that worked with him closely, that he trained and was essentially grooming to take over another slot. Eventually we agreed. We had a pretty good idea of what we were doing and, in the very beginning, we kind of wanted there to be as little disruption in people's routines as possible.

Eloni Feliciano: We had never done a monthly. The first couple of months were exhausting because usually we had a lot more time to prepare, but now we had to think about the following month while we were preparing for the month that was coming up. A lot of the promotion had to happen much quicker. Patrick had to design the flyer from scratch. We had to promote it at that club. We created the website and we had to put it all over Myspace and promote it that way.

We wanted to do theme nights next month. Originally, we wanted to focus on music instead of other things so that's where we came up with the concept of "old school." In September is the replay of the older hits of Goth. Sisters of Mercy and Bauhaus and stuff like that. That was definitely one of the ideas from the original Xmortis lineup that we had. We also did a beach party night, a little bit sillier, in June or August and which eventually turned into Tiki night. The themes we will recycle are ones that we know people are interested in or that are interesting at a certain time, for example, Steam Punk was really popular for a while. We also created a prom night just so people could dress sort of fancy. We had other music events, for example, we tried to put a little bit more heavy metal into our Viking night.

Chris Ewen: When Xmortis started, it was a great way to marry the overtly Goth and more overtly industrial styles into one complete picture. Xmortis was a Goth-industrial-fetish night which allowed me the freedom to pick the best of all of them and create a new hybrid. Xmortis established itself really quickly as something that was fantastic and reliably great in every way. With a different personality than Hell, it was able to stand on its own two legs very early.

Eloni Feliciano: This is where I give Patrick a lot of credit. He did a lot of research on what would be the best way to reach out to people. You can pay for ads. I don't think they offered it for Myspace, but they did for Facebook. He made sure the website was up to date and didn't look crappy even though the website did not get as much attention as the Myspace and Facebook pages. That became a major focus, especially as we were realizing that we knew about events in other cities. It's much easier for people who may not go to the city to know about an event. You don't necessarily have the people coming from the last event or going to any other events where you had a flyer. It was really one of the best ways to reach more people. We realized that we've got a good amount of people from other states, even as far as New York City, but we figured we got people from the surrounding New England area because of it.

Norm: One of the things that was nice was that Xmortis was allowed to do more. We're a little bit different. We're not bound by the history of a night here or by Hell. So, we know we can be creative.

Terri Niedzwiecki: I'll say this for Xmortis, the younger girls started dressing up a little bit more.

Patrick Fitzgerald: Probably a lot of it. I know how to do it. And also probably have a bit more social anxiety or did at the time than Eloni. She kind of would deal more face time with people, and I would focus on electronic presence. We're talking about live journal posts. That was the big thing. And Myspace. God, I can remember the muscle memory of, like, click, click, click. I mean I think the Xmortis account had like 3,500 people by the time Myspace became obsolete. And it took that to build that event and rebuild that event, particularly in the aftermath of the club closing. And at that time, it's not like there was a book on it and now there are literally many books on how to promote things online now. No one had any idea how to do it. I just kind of went and did it.

Mark Clavet: I moved upstate, and it was sad. ManRay was one of the things I was going to miss. Fortunately, I found a similar club where I'd moved to that was a smaller version with one and a half dance floors and multiple bars. It was a little reminder, a little piece of home. They didn't have Mistress Mimi, but they did have the dancing cages. In place of Mistress Mimi was a guy dressed head-to-toe like a Viking around a stone fire pit named Thor who would welcome you outdoors into the club. It's in Austin, Texas. It was called Atomic Cafe at the time, now it's called

Elysium.

Keith Ward: I think it had to do with less people going. It wasn't as fun and it wasn't fun going by myself. There was less of the core group. Everybody kind of spread out and did their own things. I was still in the city, but I wasn't going as much. I was going to do other things.

Heather Morgan: I moved away because I got into Yale. I wasn't looking to leave Boston, and I definitely didn't want to go to grad school just to go to any grad school, but I was like, "If I get into Yale I will go." Their painting program is amazing.

Abigail Taylor: I stopped working there after I broke up with a guy. ManRay was our place and I started dating another guy who wasn't really into ManRay. He would go with me sometimes. It wasn't written down anywhere but there was sort of an unwritten rule: "Okay you had ManRay first, so I will let you have it and I won't go there with my new boyfriend." We dated for almost five years. We grew up together, so it was a really hard breakup. I sort of had to back away from ManRay a little bit because of that.

Koren Bernardi: Towards the end, I was going less often because I was DJing at other places. When you DJ someplace two nights a week, then going out to party that third night, it's like "I'm not even going to get paid for this and I'm not getting free drinks." Although Daisy was awesome. I kind of went if there was a DJ playing that I hadn't heard before. I love Chris, but if you've seen him play a million times then going another time that week wouldn't be necessarily top of my list.

Chris Manousaridis: I stopped going about six months before 2001. I started doing a lot more weddings and corporate events. Any DJ will tell you that clubs are great and fun, but there's no money in it. I had plans to move to North Carolina. And James died, that was another big thing. When James passed away that sort of hit me and put me in a bad spot. I didn't want to be in the state anymore. I definitely wanted to stay away from ManRay because for all that time, James and I were two peas in a pod. His death really shocked me. His office was across the street from mine, so we would meet up for a liquid lunch three times a week. I saw him on a Friday, we had our shot and beer, and then on Monday morning I had gotten to my office early and Lori called me from Lucretia's Daggers and said, "Are you going to the funeral?" And I said, "What funeral?" And she said, "Your best friend James." I'm like "What are you talking about? I'm supposed to meet him for lunch at noon." She's like, "No, you're not. Here's the info." So I flipped out. I had no vehicle tags. Mine was broken down so I called Greg Frisbee and told him what was going on. He took a day off, came and picked me up, and we went to the funeral. I buried him that day. Putting him in the ground sort of killed my ManRay experience where I really didn't want to go back there. I said, "I don't want to be here. I can't." It was just way too much and I kind of blamed myself a little bit for his death. James worked the front door with me almost every night. Blue flames tattooed on his neck. He had a drug addiction, and, at the time, he was having issues with his roommate. He and I made a deal that I would spend three days a week in his apartment. So I was paying for two apartments. I was trying to help him out. I would stay there, and our deal was that if he talks about it, looks at it, or even thinks about it I'm going to punch him in the face. After that point I decided I would move to North Carolina.

Liz Lamanche: I got married and moved further out of town. I would still go on specifically planned nights with friends, but I could no longer just bounce over without a care in the world. I would have to plan to spend 40 minutes driving there. I would still enjoy going for date nights, but it wasn't the habitual thing anymore. My spouse is not much of a dancer, so we started going to more Burning Man stuff. The burner dance nights were a different flavor of thing and it was easy for him to go off and have conversations with friends about building things or whatever; they were more of a heterogeneous environment. So I would be on the dance floor and hula hooping and he could crawl up into a loft and talk about engineering with old school friends.

Kathy Landes: I would go, but not as much as I had in the past, and that was because I got out of school.

Noel McKenna: Jim was a very visible figure at ManRay. Everybody knew him. He was friends with everybody. He was one of my best friends too. He killed himself and that kind of changed the experience of ManRay, for me at least. At the same time, I started hanging out a little bit more in the gay scene at Axis and Avalon. My social interest was changing. In the mid to late 90s I just became less interested in the ManRay scene. It's not like I disliked it, I was just becoming more interested in other things.

Maryellen Vega: I got married in '97 and I was expecting my second child. Maybe I would go back once in a great while to try and spark some old feelings, but it was never like it used to be. We had two children, so we had to get a babysitter. You also stop hanging out with those people because you had children and they didn't. They were doing their own thing and we were parents.

Niki Nevulis: My going to ManRay probably started to whittle down towards the late 90s, maybe a little bit later. I was just too tired to go out and I became an adult. I had an adult job and school, which I was putting myself through. I just couldn't balance going out at night, I was exhausted. I would have loved to have gone but it just wasn't an option.

Andrea Parros: Probably a lot of it was around my personal life at the time. When I graduated in 2004, I moved home back to Hanson, because apartments were expensive getting out of school. We didn't have school-based apartments anymore. I remember moving home for at least that summer because I was having this quarter life crisis of "Okay school is over."

Alyssa Hassan: Leading up to ManRay's closure, it felt like it had been going downhill. It didn't feel as alive as it used to be. A lot of people had stopped going.

Emily Arkin: The more my friends had significant others the less people wanted to just go dancing. It wasn't because we were trolling to meet people there, but I think we had more dumb double dates. Around the same time I started to be in a band. It's true you have practice at least once a week and you're probably playing a lot of weird night shows.

Jennifer: I was already starting to pull away from the club a little bit. I only danced occasionally. Then we moved out to Framingham and bought our house. In some ways I was kind of relieved because I felt like, for my husband and I, our professional life was starting to get very busy. We were moving up the corporate ladder and it was very hard to juggle both. So in some ways I was thankful because it gave us the ability to push that aside a little bit and focus on where we thought we needed to go. But looking back, I wish I spent more time there. I think my priorities were all screwed up. I should have been in the club dancing.

Adam Lewis: It was sad because I don't think anyone likes change, especially when it's your history and youth that's going away. It was a bummer. It wasn't my place anymore, yet it was still a place that always felt like home. Terri would be there, Chris would be spinning, Don would be there, and Daisy would be behind the bar. That never changed. Even though there were other people coming and going there was always a core group of people there forever. I don't think I really believed that it would truly close because Don kind of had 19 lives. I always just thought he would be able to pull it off. Even after they closed there was all this talk of other locations. It was sad to see a place go away, as our society becomes self-homogenized, and everything's all mixed together. It was sad to see something that was so specific for one kind of scene to go away.

Emily Taylor: Well, I started to go less that last year. I definitely wasn't performing anymore, and I just felt like I was moving on. I had a real job and I just sort of felt like I was growing out of it.

Eartha Harris: I was technically there till the bitter end, but my attendance did diminish over the last few years. Working full time as a Boston newspaper graphic designer meant the weeknights were out. Additionally, as I began to take my music career more seriously, I started funneling my free time into production more and more. I also felt some personal changes happening in me that made me crave social environments more positive for my creative pursuits. Which is not to say that ManRay itself wasn't supportive, but any Goth industrial scene (at least back in the day) would naturally have its fair share of depression and judgmental energy. I guess I just got to a point where I started seeking out communities that had a greater focus on mental and physical health, wellbeing, and creative positivity, which led me to Burning Man and it's various subcultures. I needed a change — more happiness, sunshine, different art. For about 15 years after ManRay closed, I didn't even listen to any music from that time. Only recently have I been reconnecting with music and friends from the ManRay days, and now it feels very comforting.

Emily Sweeney: I feel like ManRay and Machine were both ahead of their times and they also weren't just a typical club. There's obviously different nights, but they also had performances and they were big enough spaces where you could get a huge swath of different people to come in. ManRay and Machine were also able to have multiple DJs play at the same time.

Emily Taylor: I used to have tons of fun at Heroes when it was at T.T. the Bear's. I definitely was so glad that it was still there, and I was going constantly. I didn't necessarily feel like the fetish scene had anywhere to go after that. I just stopped going out as much because of the stage I was in in my life. I still went to Love Night a lot, still went to T.T.'s a lot. I started going to rock shows and more actual music nights.

Jenny Dahling: I think they could have maintained the no photo, no video policy only because of Sin-O-Matic, which was an offshoot of a night that ended up at Machine. They maintained the same policy. I even remember trying to take a selfie once and there wasn't even anyone around me, but someone nicely said "Hey, you really can't do that." I also think the bouncers were a little judicious in who they let in.

Corey Reeves: I would think, because of the regulations and what had gone on there, which would continue through to this day, that there would still be no phones, just like at school. The policy on Friday nights is a no brainer. If you want to get in, you have to abide by it. There would be a special place where people would be able to pick up their phones, a phone attendant that would give the phone back to the person at the end of the night or if the person had to use the phone to call for Uber or Lyft. Like a coat check. There's always imaginative ways to solve something. If you don't like the policy, you don't have to come in. And if people were found with phones then they would be asked to leave or go to the phone check.

Heather Morgan: I think ManRay would have had their little Instagram spots. They already had these areas that were sort of backdrops for no reason other than the aesthetic of it and to make for a good hangout. Now I feel like they would be using those same areas as your spot to IG. Downstairs, they had a photo booth. They're not against you having fun.

Prospero Eaton: I would like to think that the rules would live on and be respected because it was really good. Some people might not have felt comfortable coming out and expressing themselves if they knew they could be caught on video or camera. It wasn't a concern of mine, but I'm sure that some people were concerned. Some people had very different lives during the daytime versus during the nighttime. So I would hope that would have been in place still, but I feel like it would have been really hard to keep because I feel like the culture would almost demand it.

Kevin Farrington: I think one of the things that enabled or enhanced the community, the journey, the experience that people that have been going there had, was the fact that there was anonymity and privacy. I'm not so sure that would have been possible in this day and age, simply because of the constant high-definition photography or living your selfie life.

One time, I took a ton of pictures, but those pictures were either taken in parking lots and parking garages or after parties. They weren't taken in the club and I think that, for a lot of people, maybe myself as well, I wouldn't have been as experimental, I wouldn't have been as open, I wouldn't have been as interested in trying different things in different ways if I'd known that everything, I did on the Friday night was going to be visible to everybody that worked within the hospital. So I'm not sure that ManRay could have been the same in this day and age. Part of me, the romantic, would like to say they would have held onto the ban, but that's a different generation. Whereas privacy and anonymity might have been important 15 years ago, I'm not so sure that if you introduced it to an audience today … I hate to do this, but younger generations would have been as happy or as comfortable not being able to exhibit what they were doing. For some people, that would have been the reason for them to come, and they might have gotten a larger crowd, but, on the other hand, a lot of people would have been put off by the loss of privacy.

Krista Siren: You start to see some of this happen after ManRay at some comparable event. Sin-O-Matic, which was basically comparable to the fetish nights at ManRay, had a thing where they did let folks take pictures, but they were very policed about consent on photos. I don't know how easy it is to make sure that everybody in frame is consenting to it and to make sure that there's nobody surreptitiously taking non-consensual pics.

I think that having the no pics policy was very important to making it feel like a comfortable homey place. I've got these memories with no documentation and I kind of want some pictures of me and some of the folks that I used to talk with. On the old ManRay website they had a collection of pictures, most of which were taken during the last month of operation, and I found one that's got me in it. I'm walking to one side in the cage. I'm in a latex Wonder Woman outfit that I had made myself, that I still have and that I just tried on again … and it still fits.

Liz Lamanche: I think they would have been able to enforce the photo video policy anyway because the subsequent Goth nights did the same. I used to go to Ceremony and Down with Tempo, and I was never actually particularly conscious of it, but I think they did have the same policy. The burner nights that I was part of from the mid-90s and beyond became a consent conversation and they went from "yes" photos to "no" photos over the years. It's more about culture than it is about technology. I've been involved with science fiction conventions and the local Burning Man group and there's been a popular meme "costume is not to consent." Just because someone is wearing a cute thing doesn't mean you have permission to take their photo. You need to ask.

Patrick Baldwin: Well, for one, I would provide staff photographers so you could have pictures of you and your friends if you wanted to, but it would be in a designated place that wouldn't catch people who didn't want to be out there. I'm not sure of the legality of confiscating phones in Massachusetts. If that was on the table, it would certainly be a thing that I would consider, or just ejecting people who do it. I'm an IT person by trade so one of my thoughts is that I would probably also suppress wireless access.

Emily Arkin: I'm not aware of anywhere that still has that policy. I've been to rock shows where they take away your phone or chase you down if you try to take pictures but it's pretty rare. I think ManRay's culture would have stood up to that indefinitely. I definitely think something is lost because then people do things in a much more performative way. Of course it's performative, it's all theatrical to go out and literally dress in a Halloween costume, but it was sort of for yourself at the moment and a little less for my Instagram profile.

Me'lissa Nin: I think even if ManRay were still up and running strong, even if there was still the strict no video, no photo policy, people, especially non-regular people, would get sneaky. They'd still take photos and shoot videos. I don't doubt that.

Matt Richard: Today I think they would have video cameras in the corners just as a security aspect. But for social reasons, I think that because they had the dress code and because of how good we were policing our own, I think that for the most part, we would be respectful about that. I remember someone saying "We don't want photography. That isn't allowed because you don't want to have a certain local congressman or businessperson in the background who is seeking privacy get picked up on somebody's picture." We all kind of respected that and we looked out for it.

Jon Whitney: It's hard for me to postulate on that because, in some respects, I think ManRay would want to be protective of people. They were very protective of their patrons. I think they might have tried to encourage people to dress a little bit more conservatively, not to show off as much. I don't think they really would, though. Keep in mind that, when smartphones started coming out, that's when places like the Improper Bostonian had people who would put pictures from every nightclub. That's when most places were dying out. People weren't really posting things on Facebook and Instagram all over the place until probably after 2010, so I don't think that they would have had some time to acclimate to it.

Susanne Boitano: I can see one thing where they would perhaps have a ManRay "photo area," which places often do. You could pose next to the ManRay sign and they would make a couple bucks off of it. I think that they might ask their patrons what they think. Now, people taking pictures of themselves is ubiquitous. If you show up at ManRay I think you would have, in this day and age, full knowledge that you might wind up in the background of some kind of a picture, in which case wear a mask or don't go. For the fetish fairs, where they really wanted people to take photos, you would get a little fluorescent patch that meant don't take a photo of me.

Jen Lucky Cole: I can tell you how this would have happened because I used to have to deal with people as technology started advancing and people started trying to get clever about it. If it was an analog camera, we let them keep their camera. We would take the film and they wouldn't get it back. A lot of venues would be collecting almost like a coat check.

Adam Lewis: In today's time, only Hell would even be able to try to get away with it. It would be really hard because every single person has a cell phone and they're not going to want to leave their cell phone behind. So I don't think we would be telling people not to bring their cell phones. I do think that maybe the community would respect the request. I think it might be a little bit of self-policing going on. The two would have to learn to live with each other a little bit. We would have club photographers. I would like to believe that, with the times changing, people would be a little less sensitive about it.

Lucretia X Machina: I would think that because there's so many older

Goths now ManRay would have adapted to it. It's really impossible to get away from people and their phones. If there was a complaint, then they would have to take it as they went. It's also good publicity. ManRay would have been all over the internet all the time for free.

Chapter 18

The Last Goodbye

"I found out that the end date was just two or three weeks after I arrived ... I thought, 'Wow, this is sad, I'm definitely dressing in black for this.'" — Mark Clavet

When it became official that ManRay would be closing its doors for good, the club went out with a bang. It was celebrated with a seemingly endless week-long party. People from all over the Boston-Cambridge area, New England, and even the country came to pay their respects to the place that had been a home for them. Some came for the night that meant the most to them during their tenure as a club patron, others spent every second they possibly could behind those dark brick walls that week. The club was packed well beyond capacity. The drinks were poured in rivers. The music blared a comforting soundtrack. The dancing was nonstop. The memories were forever. While untold tears were shed that week, it also provided moments of love, community, catharsis, and closure. S.L.

Daisy Crowder: Starting around the turn of the century, it was mainly a rumor that ManRay wasn't going to last much longer. Of course that was really nothing other than speculation. As time progressed it became clear that it may not last more than a few years. It turned out to be true.

Jen Lucky Cole: Don knew it was going to close in 2001. He was doing everything he could with his lawyers to try to get it turned into a historical landmark. The owner of that property was this older lady named Mrs. Joe. We'd be in Boston in February on Friday morning when all of a sudden, the phone's ringing off the hook. Don comes in. It's about noon and it's Mrs. Joe calling from Florida bitching about the trash in the parking lot. Just stupid crap. Don would literally run out of the building and pretend he wasn't there. He didn't want to deal with her.

Gene Dante: I can neither confirm nor deny that I know that we, the staff, never had any issues with the lease. Residential buildings surrounded ManRay, so if there was an issue I'm sure we would have heard about it pretty quickly. As a business owner, it's a pretty good idea to be friendly with the local police department and your local fire department.

Emily Sweeney: I got hired at *The Globe* in 2001 while I was still going to ManRay on the weekends. A few years into my journalism career I started looking at ManRay thinking, "You know what, this isn't really going to last," not that I had any inside info. I knew there were so many cool stories, so I just started pitching to my editors like, "Look, I go to this club all the time … "

Emily Sweeney: When I first started going, it was mostly just to meet people or go with a couple good friends. By the early 2000s, I could walk in on any night and somebody I know would be there. Everybody seemed to be online at the time, and we'd all be like "It's gone." We were all shooting back and forth messages, so you'd have an idea of who's going to be there or if you want to eat before you go.

Gene Dante: The sad fact about city living is that whenever there's something cool, the greedy move in pretty quickly. ManRay was cool, but it was also in a very cool neighborhood that was rapidly becoming completely unaffordable for anyone.

Emily Sweeney: Obviously, leading up to the closure, people were talking about it. There were whispers about it moving and a lot of talk about it reopening. I used to contribute to the nightlife blog at *The Globe,* so I was constantly following every tidbit of news about it. It was such a cool nightclub. Where else can you find a space like that? People were talking about all these different places and in my head, I was thinking "You can never get that cool setup that ManRay had with those three unique rooms." The promise of it reopening kind of softens the blow.

Tony Lee: There were rumors for years about ManRay closing. After a while we all just kind of joke about it. Then it was like "This is actually for real." Chris gave me a call saying he was going to be out of town playing with the Magnetic Fields in New York. So he asked me "Do you want to play on Wednesday?" I was like, "Yeah, of course." It was a huge honor even to be asked to play that last night.

Matt Richard: First off, it was "Oh it's closing, well that sucks, but the owner is still retaining a liquor license and is looking for a new venue." So there was hope, the venue will be closed, but the embodiment will carry on and it's going to be up in three months. There was that hope and expectation that it was just a matter of finding a new location.

Richard LaDue: I was 35. I was teaching. Honestly, I don't remember feeling any kind of way. When I look back, I just think about how this was a thing that people, even pre-COVID, didn't do as much. At least in Boston, and especially in New York City, you wouldn't have these super clubs or places that can do programming four or five nights a week and be busy. A nightclub is a hard thing to do. It gets increasingly hard. It reminds me of a time where you had to go out to see people and you didn't have Instagram. You just saw that person at the club, who had the outfit that you liked or the song you wanted. It was harder to find your tribe or your people.

Terri Niedzwiecki: Well, I'm sure there were a certain number of neighbors that were like, "Oh, thank God."

David Winthrop: My initial thoughts were sort of a sigh of relief for personal reasons. I had partied a lot in that club and I thought it was sort of going to wind me down from my party days, it did not, but that was my initial thought. I was also looking forward to it moving and there being a new place because I thought a new venue could be really interesting.

Susanne Boitano: I was super sad. I was just like, "No, you can't take ManRay from me." It was one of the first of the closings of things. I came to Boston in my early 20s, so I didn't have a relationship with The Rat, but ManRay … I had been there since the inception.

It was like a community center. It was a church. It was a hangout. It was a refugee. It was a sanctuary. So it was sad. I couldn't understand what happened, necessarily. Did we really need more condos? I didn't see why they didn't have money to save it. I just felt like "Why? Why this of all the things?" What I love about ManRay, and it's everlasting soul, is that it was a club that would not die, it reincarnated itself across the street and then over someplace else. The vampire of clubs. It's extraordinary, this club and the people, it's little dark denizens that will not let it go.

Nate Roman: I was the first or second person to make an announcement to the crowd that ManRay was closing. Part of that announcement was saying that a new location was in the works.

Anna Feder: It was so upsetting when they announced they were closing because I was like, "I finally made it here to live in Boston. I can finally be part of this community." I remember the fucking website, for years it was like "Rising from the ashes" and it just never did. There would be news here and there, it was supposed to move into where the Blockbuster was and then nothing ever happened. Maybe it would have been better to be able to feel that was it, and then you could say a proper goodbye to it. I didn't like the fact that it was potentially going to reopen and then it just didn't.

Becky D: When I first heard the news it was pretty shocking. We heard the rumors back and forth. We always figured Don would have a plan and the rug wouldn't be pulled out from under him, but that's what happened. So it was a bit of a shock to hear that it was closing, especially because I think it was within a month of hearing the news. First there was sadness, right, because I was losing the space where I just needed to get out of the house and go dancing. I wasn't going to have that anymore. I guess Ceremony was still going, but it was different. The space itself wasn't ours. I had noticed that attendance had been going down. There weren't as many new people coming in because Goth was kind of fading out as a popular underground thing to do. I think it would have been more heartbreaking to see ManRay die because people were not interested anymore. I think that would have been a harder thing to see than to have an abrupt end like we did. So there was a part of me that felt a little bittersweet. I'd rather see it go like this.

Chris Manousaridis: I was shocked at first, and then I was mad. I literally got angry, like, "How can you just destroy this building? This has been a staple in the community since the 80s." The two staples were ManRay and the pizza place on the corner. It's like taking a national monument and destroying it for condos.

In 2005 I started going through my horrible divorce and we had two hurricanes destroy the house. My wife and my daughter lived in Animal Kingdoms at Walt Disney World for three and a half months while we were rebuilding the house. I wanted to come down for the end, but there was no money because I was going through this really expensive crazy divorce. So I couldn't make it to the end.

Koren Bernardi: It had been rumored for so many years. Now that I look at it in the context of that whole thing, I realized that in 2005 everything was getting bigger and bigger and bigger and bigger. We'd always thought that spot was going to get condos because there were other housing things going on and that was the hip new spot. It's kind of one of my first experiences of loss. That always had been there, whenever I wanted or needed it … I didn't realize what it was going to mean because I'd never had a place like that before to lose. When I couldn't go there anymore, I was like, "Oh, shit!! I saw all these people and don't even know what their names are. I never thought to get their phone numbers or their email addresses!"

Derek Kouyoumjian: I've always been very averse to change. Everything dies and changes and I was always very much against that. For me, ManRay honestly didn't change very much in all the time I was there. It looked very much the same when I first stepped foot in there all the way up to the very end. It was a second home to me. It was somewhere that was always around and always a part of my life. Suddenly now it wasn't going to be. Getting turned into condos … I always kind of felt like the city was our CEO. The rich gentry gave it up and they were like, "Fine you take the town. It's yours." Now they were like "Oh no, we want it back." It's like, "Fuck you, you abandoned it. We nurtured it and kept it together. Now you want it back, fuck you."

Me'lissa Nin: It felt like the seven stages of grief. The last stage is acceptance. At first, I thought, "No, this is just a rumor." So talking with Don and then talking with Terri and Chris, I was like," No, this can't be. Why?" I would say everybody was really bummed out about it, especially people who had been going for a while. I was really depressed because here's this place that I called home and it's almost like your house is burning down. You know there will be other places, but anything that comes after that just won't be the same. I was pretty devastated.

Chris Ewen: There was a lot of denial on my part that it was actually going to happen. I didn't think it was possible. I thought the rumor mills were just swirling. It's just another one of the many storms that ManRay had beaten, and there had been plenty. There would be a Hail Mary situation, like "It's going to close, but the lease will be renegotiated and ManRay would be saved." As we moved closer, I still really wasn't that worried. It's like, "Yes ManRay is going to close," but Don had talked a lot about "Don't worry, we're going to find a space and reopen." I think Don felt very proprietary over his employees. He was never like "I'm just going to give up the fight and go home." He was seriously looking into other situations.

A. Dominy Cusraque: I heard that it was closing, and, on the one hand, I knew that it was a huge thing. ManRay was a huge part of my life, the best years of my life, so it was sad.

Tony Lee: Over the years, I made lots and lots of friends. We would have huge parties at our place before ManRay closed. I still knew most of the people who went and, when I saw them, we would have deep, meaningful conversations in public spaces, but we never made plans to hang out outside of those public gatherings. There are a lot of people who I never saw anymore. I've lost contact with a good number of them. Social media does still give us a connection.

Michael Hsieh: It was certainly very upsetting and depressing. Everybody was so upset, asking themselves, "What are we going to do?" Everybody was just in this sort of bizarre state. It was our lives for 10 years. It's how we met. It's how we kept in touch with people, how we built relationships with people. Because it was so valuable, we've all tried to keep that sense of community. We try to keep in touch with each other. I'm happy that we have such a strong group that supports these scenes, but they're smaller.

Terri Niedzwiecki: I made it quite clear that, "Oh no, we're not gonna have any sobbing in front of me because if I lose my marbles, then we're all done."

Matt Gleason: Even though we were out for a while and Don was afforded enough time to look for a place, when it was time to close it was time to close. Don gave me a look and told me two or three weeks before we closed. One of the city councilors, I forget his name, but he was trying to help find a place. We wanted to go out tastefully.

Emily Taylor: Honestly, I was happy to see it go and the reason why is because it was like closing a door on that chapter of my life. It felt like I was free to move on from that scene and those people and all the drama. I was ready to evolve into something else. I felt like I was putting the last nail in the coffin of that place and I didn't ever have to go there and not know anybody and feel weird about it. I know I can't ever go back and I can't feel like an outsider there because it's gone. There was something really relieving about that. I didn't want to go in there and feel like a stranger.

Mizery McRae: Just like with Machine, I was told a month before it actually closed. Nobody knew when, but we knew it was coming. So we just went there and enjoyed ourselves and did what we had to do. I went there to work as if it was last night. I just kept working. I kept doing my thing. I kept booking the girls and that was it.

Saturday was my last night. I've worked at a lot of clubs that have closed and it is the same feeling. It's a conglomerate of feelings. It's sadness, anger, joy. Joy to be part of it for such a long time and anger because it was such a great bar. You meet so many people and you build so many relationships. It was like the matriarch of the family died.

Matt Gleason: It was definitely a certain sadness. I had never closed a place before. What really stuck out was that there were 75 to 100 people that came by during the day. Some of them were older, some of them went to the club in the early 90s, some had met their spouse there and they were still with them. People were coming by because they just wanted to see the place during the day.

There was a serial robber going around robbing bars happening around that time. He was hitting places in Cambridge, Somerville, and Brookline. He was breaking into these bars for the safes because a lot of people don't make deposits on weekends. That was a concern, so we thought that there was a group of people checking our place out at that time as well. It was a little nerve wracking at first when people started coming by during the day. Mostly it was people who probably went there before, and they just really wanted to take one last look at the place. A lot of them said they had never seen the place with the lights on, so they were curious. It was cool to see that. If we were able to do it, I would let them in and give them a walk around.

Michael Marotta: It was a shock. If ManRay was able to survive for 20 years. Why wouldn't it survive? I'm definitely more experienced in the world of clubs closing than I was back in 2005. We've all fucking seen it now and we've all experienced it. It's kind of like a rite of passage. It just doesn't end. Venues are disappearing yearly and there's no real end in sight. But in 2005 I was not sure I necessarily saw the writing on the wall. I viewed the Goth subculture as a pretty dedicated one, but we were living in a time where subcultures do not make up the majority by the very definition, so it's difficult to maintain. I mean the place was fucking massive. ManRay was not so much a nightclub as it was a complex. There were multiple rooms downstairs and the DJ booth upstairs. Most venues are single rooms.

I do remember kind of feeling a little homelessness. But Chris Ewen is a trooper who battled through and now he's brought Heroes and his other nights to other venues. He's weathered the storm multiple times over.

A. Dorian Rose: I mean, you can't do anything about it. So there's a certain part of me that just had to accept it. You have to kind of make peace with it and it's definitely the ending of a chapter.

Arlene Guerrero-Watanabe: It was home. I cried so much when it closed. It was traumatic. We did not want it to close. We wanted it to keep going because it was our club.

Xtine Santakas: It was sad. It was almost devastating really. But I felt that it was also a new beginning. There were a lot of people there who fought with each other a lot, and there were a couple of people that tried to really assert themselves like "It's my way or the highway. These are my roles. This is my club." But ManRay was really everyone's club. So, in a way, I was kind of looking forward to that attitude going away.

Athena Costa: I was really upset. Everything else except for The Pill had ended. The last three days I went were really chaotic, super packed, super-hot, and everyone was like, "I don't give a fuck."

Crayola Tidd: One thing I had a true belief that it was going to open some around. Because Don, the owner had told me he's just going to find another place, probably in Central Square and I held on to that belief for a number of years. I was very sad because I felt like it was so much of my social life, you know, like a lot of people, I only see there.

Jenny Dahling: I was heartbroken, of course, because I was in this wonderful world that I was enjoying immensely and then all of a sudden it was getting the kibosh. So obviously I wasn't very happy about it.

Amy Butts: I was not happy. I was very distraught. At the same time, I didn't believe it was actually going to close. I really thought that we were going to have a new space — we'd jump right into a nice new place and we would just continue on doing what we had been doing. So it was kind of a slap in the face that never happened.

Kevin Farrington: I was "well connected" with a lot of different people and I heard the rumors that it was going to close. Once the stories about the condos being built came in I think there was a finality to it.

Mark Clavet: I just happened to be visiting the area and heard the impending news but didn't know there was a date set. Then I found out that the end date was just two or three weeks after I arrived. I thought, "Oh man, I've got to go out." But I was staying with relatives about an hour's drive away, so it wasn't as easy to make it. I thought, "Wow, this is sad, I'm definitely dressing in black for this." I just went, I didn't bother scooping anyone else up. I didn't give a damn if anyone else went or not. I went and the first thing was to get a drink and speak with Terri for a bit and just take it all in. There were not as many people, of course. I wasn't able to go the following weeks.

Niki Nevulis: When I heard it was closing for good, I was extremely sad … devastated would be the right word. I talked to my friend Steve that I worked with and we were going every goddamn night, on the weekends, until the place closed down. I was definitely there last night. I'm sure that the club was packed illegally full of people. It was like a combination of all of the crowds that would hang out there.

Julia Kilcoyne: I think we went on Wednesday and Friday. I remember it was hot as hell. I was wearing my hair in ponytails because I absolutely could not wear a wig that night. There was only one air conditioner that was still working, and I remember standing under that while trying not to die. I had enough conversations with Don Holland and Cheryl to understand the gravity of the situation and the reality. There was a pervasive sadness and non-reality to it. In some ways, I was grateful to be out of that space because it was falling apart so badly.

Niki Nevulis: In the last few weeks that it was closing, I was going pretty much every weekend. Everybody was going. You saw New Wave kids and Hell or fetish night people. I wasn't shocked, but of course, I was much older and a little bit more worldly at that point. I was just very comfortable with that. It felt very serene there because no airs were getting put on and everybody was comfortable in their own skin.

Susanne Boitano: I was like, "No, you can't. No no no no no no no no no." So I tried to fit in as much ManRay as humanly possible. I went to almost every last night there was. I remember the last night and just that feeling of trying to squeeze every little moment into it. Not even moving, but just sucking it all in and, when they turn those lights on, just shuffling like the slowest shuffling shuffle. It's like the last day of the beach in the summer.

Gene Dante: Well, we knew that it was going to be off the hook, because this is people's last chance. We knew it was gonna be crazy. It did not disappoint.

Eileen Dover: My last time there, I was sober. I was not dressed up. It was a weird feeling. We all had this identity which ManRay was a huge part of, where you got to be a certain way, and now that was being taken, but nothing was replacing it other than these online sad versions of chat rooms. I just remember being sad and just being hopeful that it would come back.

Tony Lee: Once people found out the club was closing all the nights were pretty well attended. Every single night was so packed, like sardines. I made sure that every time I went to the bar, I got at least two drinks for myself so I wouldn't have to go back for another one because it would take almost an hour to get a drink.

Matt Gleason: It was last week; we weren't really that busy because there's no more advertising to do. We got all our final orders. There was no maintenance to be done. It was kind of nice to see how many people came by. There was definitely a lot of sadness. It was all the regulars, obviously, and there were people that hadn't been in a long time, but we recognized them. I heard a lot of people traveled from California that just came back to Boston to go to this last night. I was impressed that they still paid attention to the advertisements or maybe they just knew through the grapevine of friends talking.

Jen Lucky Cole: I'll be honest, it didn't feel like it was really it. I didn't think it was gonna be torn down. I didn't really believe it. I wasn't gonna believe it until it happened. I was in denial. I did the whole week. I brought my mother actually. That last week, if the bartenders knew you at all, they were just giving you a whole bottle of fucking liquor because they had to get rid of it. Their legal capacity was 303. Wednesday they had over 1000 people. I want to say it was 1,600 on Friday. I didn't have to wait in line, obviously. The line was a friggin parking lot and I was laughing about that. We walked past everybody and I wasn't rude, saying "Hi" to friends. At the front Michael pulls back the velvet rope and I thank him. That Friday night was unreal. There were so many people. It was like a tuna can because it was in the summer, so it was hot and they had a horrible HVAC system.

Amy Butts: It was so crowded because people literally came out of the woodwork, regulars that I hadn't seen in years and people that didn't come out often. Everybody came out for that last week and people were dancing like it was some kind of dance off. The music was great. The dance floor was packed. People were dancing on everything they could dance on. It was just crazy.

I was on crutches, so I was at the bar. It was an interesting thing though because everybody came to get a drink from Terri. So I was visited by everybody as they came to get drinks. I went so often, and these people were always constants in my life for 10 years. They were always around and then all of a sudden, the club closed and it's like, "Where did all the people go?" I really never got in touch with them again. It was just such a strange feeling.

Jenny Dahling: What I remember most about the last week was every Johnny-come-lately showed up, which really pissed me off, especially the very last night if memory serves. I went to the last gay night and then Saturday. The last gay night was certainly busier than usual, but there wasn't much of a vibe of the last hurrah. That Saturday, though … Holy shit. I knew that it was going to be an extraordinarily busy night, so I got there early enough to get in the parking lot in the back. I must have shown up around nine. I remember drinking champagne in my car as a kind of toast to ManRay. Later, I went out for a cigarette and the line was down the block. I had never seen anything like that before. What really made me mad, though, was I befriended people who had been going there for years and years and years, but there were all these people who had literally never been there before, at least I'd never seen them there, and they got in. I remember feeling so angry about that and almost feeling like maybe I should leave, grabbing one of those people and saying, "I'm leaving. So let this person in." I also remember there being no place to sit. I also have the distinct memory of it being so stinking hot. I'd steal someone's drink so I could dump it over my head, no lie, I was so overheated.

Gene Dante: I worked. It was all hands on deck. It was out of control. We were running out of liquor because you were not going to place the liquor order and we can't have anything left over.

Trent Stewart: Do you remember your last day of high school? The last week of high school, the last week of college, I wanted no regrets. That last week … I didn't enjoy it as much as I could have because I was making sure I had the contact information to anyone who was important to me. I feared the out of sight, out of mind mentality that some people have. I was kind of one of the catalysts for the first ManRay reunions. Other people ran with it, but it was a conversation I was having. I personally am the type of person that will say "Hey I'm just thinking of you or is everything okay? I don't want to trouble you if you're busy, but I want to basically let you know that I'm still here if you need anything."

Tatiana Zimkus: As far as last week goes, I was one of the dancers. The last Goth night there was the latex movie *Night of the Dolls*. I danced that last Friday night on stage in a latex catsuit and eight-inch platforms with red and black hair extensions. I was a sweaty emotional mess by the end of the night. I went to Heroes the next night too, but the last night for me felt like that Friday night because I performed for the last time there. It was like the last day of high school where you want everyone to sign your yearbook.

Skot Kremen: In July I knew that ManRay was closing. The last night I went was sad. It did feel like a homecoming because everybody was there to see the last hurrah. There were so many people there and everybody was saying goodbye. I remember one of the things that we were thinking, "Where the fuck are, we going to go?"

Becky D: That last week was pretty surreal. I didn't go to the last night, which I think was technically a New Wave night. I went to the last Goth night. A lot of my energy was spent looking for people I wanted to see one last time in the club. The last song that Chris played was "Home" by Depeche Mode. I was up on the blocks dancing and one of my closest friends at the time jumped up and danced with me. It was just a perfect ending to the club for me because I love the song. It was such a perfect song to play as the last song for that night. So to be up on the blocks dancing to one of my favorite songs with one of my favorite people and seeing a sea of familiar faces that I care deeply about and associated with ManRay was the perfect ending for me.

Abigail Taylor: I remember being there and feeling sad that it wasn't ending on a Wednesday. It was packed. I didn't even recognize half the people that night. I was like "Who are these people? Why are they here? I want this for myself. I want it for my family. I want to say goodbye to it. I want to have a funeral for it." I wanted it to be that core group of people and that's it. "Who are you? Go away. This is sad for me and you're all cheering and having fun and I am losing a part of my history and you're dancing." I also felt pissed that it was turning into condos and being bulldozed to the ground. It was really painful to lose, but there was also a part of me that knew it was time for it to go.

Anastasia Taslis: We believed them at the time that it was only going to be three months, so we were hopeful. I went Wednesday, Thursday, Friday, Saturday … we were going to everything. I remember it was summer and it was like 8 million degrees.

Matt Gleason: There was definitely a lot of sadness, but people were also just trying to have a good time. Wednesday was kind of sad. We always had a pre-shift meeting around Terri's bar and talked because nobody was there. But we had a line on Wednesday nights, so we didn't really get to that. Wednesday night was packed. I saw kids come from all over New England. People would make a trip for Wednesday night, but it was never really that busy. That night though, we were packed. We were a little understaffed. We did put on a couple extra bartenders. We didn't realize it was going to be so big. It was Wednesday so we didn't really have much security concerns anyway, but that was a very manageable night.

Thursday came around. Don had raised the cover and I knew that was going to hurt us really badly because we had a competing night on Lansdowne Street. So Thursday hadn't been going very well. But we didn't drop our staff levels and it ended up being packed. Even the promoters from the other nights came down.

Friday was really the heart and soul of the club. On Friday and Saturday all the employees were there. It was kind of weird to think that was the last Friday. It was the last time. That's when it really hit me because that was my favorite night. I just told everybody to really think about how we act to our customers tonight because this is the way that they're going to remember us forever. The look on everybody's face … it was the right thing to say, and it was the realest thing that I could think of at the time. My employees were all like, "Oh my God, you're so right." Everybody had such a good time and people were hugging at the end of the night. Saturday night came around and it was fun, but once it was quiet it was kind of deafening to know that it was never going to be loud in there again.

Sara S. Wendell: The final weekend, I went the entire time. Every night. I'm really glad I did because it was amazing. The line was covering the sidewalk on both sides of Brookline. People who never even came into the club showed up and it was 105 degrees there. You could barely move. I never made so many friends as I did when I got a couple ice cubes from Terri and ran around pressing it on people. We knew this was the last hurrah so we gotta make the most of it while we can.

Of course there were going to be people who would try to pick up the slack and take over for a space for some of these nights and some of this crowd, but it was never going to be the same. I did have hopes that maybe they could find another space and I knew Don was looking. But I think I knew that it wasn't coming back. It was an incredibly depressing thought because this was the place that had been my social home for years. Losing that just was like graduating from high school. There are people you're never going to see again no matter how much you say you will. Maybe you're going to stay in touch but life's going to get in the way and they're going to fall to the wayside and that's pretty much what happened.

Emily Taylor: That last week we went every single night. We danced and we really lived it up. I remember dancing on top of the bar at one point. I think some friends of mine peed on the stage as a way to mark their territory. It was great. It was really hot and super sweaty. It was summertime. It felt very cathartic to finally just say goodbye to this old friend and this person that I used to be. I really didn't feel like that person anymore though. It was really nice to see a lot of friends who I hadn't seen in a while. It was also sad, and I was worried about what Chris and Terri were going to do and all the people who work there. I was worried about what it meant for our scene. "Where are we going to go? Where were all the girls going?" I haven't really felt that same sense of home for weirdos in the Cambridge-Boston area since then. I think we've splintered off into little groups.

Kevin Farrington: We did go Friday night and we chose not to go on Saturday. The reason we did was because one, we kind of left everything we had there on a Friday night rather than be there for the absolutely last night. We were here in Watertown, so the commuting wasn't an issue, but it was a question of not wanting to go for that final time that they turn the lights up. Emotionally, it was difficult to say that you can't turn around and show up again on Friday night because it's been such a regular pattern and time. On the other hand, it was madness there on the Friday night and barely habitable and barely danceable. All the people that we knew, in large part, were there and we made connections and promised to always connect and all the things that people say. In some cases, those connections have been true and wouldn't have been altered by going on Saturday or not. In other cases, I think it probably would have been harder to do Saturday night. So it was kind of a joint decision we made driving away from it on a Friday night, that sometimes it's better to leave it alive and vibrant in your mind as opposed to worrying about being the person wandering the empty streets of a ghost town which I find daunting.

Eloni Feliciano: Once I heard it was closing, I started going Wednesday, Thursday, Friday, Saturday, any day that I possibly could just to fill my senses with it so that I could remember it better and to connect with the people that I might lose. Many people would cross over. Some of the Thursday night people would cross over into Saturday night, so I wanted to make sure that I kept in contact with them afterward and also with the bartenders. You don't realize that you are friends with people at work someplace, but then it ends up being a significant loss. I think that people forget that these workers are also part of our social scene.

Lucretia X Machina: I went every night. I think last night was Heroes. I was crying my eyes out and some girl who'd never been there before, said to me, "Why are you crying, what's the big deal?" I'm like, "Are you fucking kidding me? It's shutting down forever. Fuck off."

Karla Clute: Oh God … that last week. I went on Wednesday and Friday. Wednesday was probably the busiest I'd ever seen, and Friday was just straight out insane. There were lines of people down the street around the block. There were people who were drawing stamps on other people. One of the girls I met through Rocky Horror was outside and she traced the stamp from someone's hand, licked it and then transferred it to somebody else's hand and then redrew it on their hand because you couldn't get in otherwise.

Cris Concepcion: From my point of view, there was this recognition of an era coming to an end. We still believe that there would be some sequel to this, partially informed by my own involvement with Ceremony and Hexx. I don't think I appreciated just how special ManRay was as a venue, at the time. In college my freshman year, I was part of a social club, the Asian Student Association, who did a lot of dance parties and social gatherings. The following year our membership turned over a bunch of people who were really involved in my freshman year and we had to rebuild our group again. One of the seniors in the club said that was okay because the people you met your freshman year found their friends. They got their group, and they don't need us anymore, so we've kind of done our job. That's what comes to mind when thinking about ManRay. I had a very solid community that transcended ManRay but was very much of that place. We were moving on with our lives. We were getting married and having kids. We didn't think that losing ManRay was going to deplete that community in a meaningful way. We were kind of almost selfishly thinking that we were glad we had it. It was too bad that others won't get to enjoy it, but it's probably going to revive itself in some other form and we'll get to enjoy it. It was definitely a loss for the overall Boston-Cambridge scene that has never come back.

Adam Wolff: I played the last Crypt night there as the DJ. Chris gave us that night so that we could get our one last hurrah in the booth. That was pretty awesome. Here's a little personal note — the first time that I ever went to ManRay was for a Halloween party in 1992, and the first song that I ever danced to was "Bela Lugosi's Dead," which was my jam. That was the first song that I ever danced to on the floor at ManRay and the last song I ever played at ManRay on that Crypt night. I closed the night with "Bela Lugosi's Dead." Then I ran down to my spot on the catwalk where I was always dancing, and I cried the whole song and it's like eight and a half minutes long.

Paul Calnan: We definitely went right up until they closed. I will say that my last time at ManRay probably was one of my least favorite nights. I don't know if they were closing and they just didn't care anymore, but I remember — ManRay was always very strict with their dress code because you want it to create a vibe, you want to create that atmosphere — but one of the last nights we went I remember walking in there and looking around going "What is going on?" It almost didn't feel like ManRay because there were guys walking around in Patriots shirts and baseball hats. "Am I at a sports bar?" I don't know whether it was just so close to the end that security didn't care anymore. That was one of the only nights that we went there, in all the years, where the girls that were with us had problems. The girls that were with me would say "I was just harassed, a guy just tried to grab me." That was probably the last night, unfortunately, and it kind of stinks in a way that it has to end on a sour note.

Emily Sweeney: The last playlist of Crypt, Wednesday July 27, 2005.

DJ Arcanus
The Wake -- "Sideshow", 1993
The Sisterhood -- "Giving Ground", 1986
Corpus Delicti -- "Saraband", 1996
X-Mal Deutschland -- "Incubus Succubus II", 1983
Sunshine Blind -- "Regodless", 1995
Fields of the Nephilim -- "Moonchild", 1988
Virgin Prunes -- "Baby Turns Blue", 1982
Specimen -- "Kiss Kiss Bang Bang", 1983
Ministry -- "Revenge", 1983
Cruxshadows -- "Monsters", 1996
Peter Murphy -- "Cuts You Up", 1989
Chameleons UK -- "Tears", 1986
Switchblade Symphony -- "Wallflower", 1995
The Swans -- "Love Will Tear Us Apart ",1988
Sisters of Mercy -- "Floorshow", 1983
Rosetta Stone -- "Adrenaline", 1992
DJ Addam
KMFDM -- "Juke Joint Jezebel", 1995
DJ Javier
Dronning Maud Land -- "Hallow Eyes", 1992

Siouxsie & the Banshees -- Monitor", 1981
Joy Division -- "A Means To An End", 1980
Iggy Pop -- "The Passenger", 1990
The Cure -- "The Hanging Garden", 1982
Diamanda Galas -- "Double-"Barrel Prayer", 1988
DJ Addam
You Shriek -- "Everything In Colors", 1992
Nine Inch Nails -- "Down In It (Shred)", 1989
Depeche Mode -- "Never Let Me Down Again", 1989
Wolfsheim -- "Kunstliche Welten", 1999
New Order -- "Bizarre Love Triangle", 1986
Addambombb -- "Kill By Numbers", 2005
Queen & David Bowie -- "Under Pressure", 1981
DJ Arcanus
Prick -- "Animal", 1995
Pop Will Eat Itself -- "Ich Bin Ein Auslander", 1994
My Life With the Thrill Kill Kult -- "Sex on Wheelz", 1991
London After Midnight -- "Sacrifice", 1995
Current 93 -- "Happy Birthday Pigface Christus", 1993
Death In June -- "Little Black Angel", 1992
Tear Garden -- "In Search of My Rose", 1996
Nick Cave & the Bad Seeds -- "The Weeping Song", 1990
BiGod 20 -- "Like a Prayer", 1992
DJ Javier
Soft Cell -- "Martin", 1983
Suspiria -- "Behind the Wheel", 1995
Wolfsheim -- "A Look Into Your Heart", 1992
Project Pitchfork -- "Souls", 1994
Death In June -- "The Calling (MKII)", 1985
Mephisto Walz -- "Painted Black", 1994
DJ Addam
The Cure -- "Never Enough", 1990
Siouxsie & the Banshees -- "Peek-A-Book", 1988
Concrete Blonde -- "Bloodletting (The Vampire Song)", 1990
Cruxshadowns -- "Marilyn, My Bitterness v2.0", 1996/2004
Apoptygma Berzerk -- "In This Together (Club)", 2005
Covenant -- "Dead Stars", 2000
Shriekback -- "Nemesis", 1985
Bauhaus -- "Bela Lugosi's Dead", 1979

Chris Ewen: That whole last week my vantage point was upstairs in my DJ booth looking down on people. So I just saw a rising sea of people. Everyone who went to all the different nights of ManRay were there. The attitude was "Do what we can." It was a free-for-all, in the sense that we can relive all our memories throughout all the years in one week. If I saw somebody that I knew I'd run downstairs and say, "Come up to the booth I want to take pictures with you." So I spent time that week, and especially that last night, bringing people up to the booth and snapping photos. I just tried to create some kind of archive of the experience.

I recorded the music for each of the nights and I looked at it as "Let's go out with a bang if this is really happening." I guess there wasn't time to be emotional because I had a job to do and that was to make everybody love every minute of their last time they could be in that building.

David Winthrop: I knew it was going to be an emotional night for a lot of people. That club meant the world to me at a time, but that time had kind of passed for me and I was okay with it moving forward. When it was gone, it was just gone.

Skot Kremen: In July I knew that ManRay was closing. The last night I went was sad. It did feel like a homecoming because everybody was there to see the last hurrah. There were so many people there and everybody's saying goodbye. I remember one of the things that we were thinking, "Where the fuck are, we going to go?"

Patrick Baldwin: It is almost impossible for me to describe it because it was this kaleidoscopic blur for me because there were so many people and so many who I knew. It was just so packed, and I was fairly altered. The combination, it was almost like an even trippier version of that scene from Labyrinth, like the whole ballroom just kind of whirling around. It was also like a roller coaster of all my friends and these people I haven't seen in years. This is so great, but it is also the last time. How is this really true? It was deeply surreal. One thing I will say — I hate what they put up in place of it so much. Not just condos, but giant beige boxes.

Matt Richard: I went to the last Friday night. I know some people were religious and went three or four nights that week, but I had the 45-minute commute and my day job. It was sad to see part of my social life gone, but at that point in my life, I wasn't going every night of the week.

I got there and parked the car and got in the really, really long line and made a friend or two. I guess I got there at the right time. It was the longest line I've been in since I started going there, but I was only in line for about 20 minutes. There were maybe three or four people ahead of me and I heard this woman say, "Is there anybody around that knows how to lace a corset?" "Oh, I'll help you out" and I kind of skipped the line a little bit, helped her lace it, and made two new friends. "Nice to meet you. It's the last night so we're not gonna be able to hang out." Thankfully, Myspace started around then so there was a network that, outside of ManRay, crowds or connections could meet. When you go to a show or to see live bands you might see two or three people that you remember from that last night at ManRay and make those connections; the groundwork was there for some of the connections with other community members, which is kind of cool.

John O'Leary: It was so packed and hot most of the night. I remember the Dandy Warhols and Brian Jonestown Massacre were playing across the street. The last song I remember hearing was "Home" by Depeche Mode. It wasn't a big emotional crying thing for me. It's weird, the sadness about losing ManRay didn't really seep in for me until a couple years later. We didn't know what we had when we had it and didn't really see it until nothing replaced it.

Jamie DiBattista: We went to the last Heroes, which I believe was the very last night. Holy shit it was a fucking crazy. It was awesome. It was amazing. They didn't care about their capacity. I think they were just lubing people up and shoving them in. We were just drenched in sweat, all of us. I don't remember what time they stopped, but they didn't stop at two. They just kept going and they didn't give a shit if you smoked in there. It was such a joyous experience. It was just jam-packed, and everyone was just celebrating. Probably one of the best dance nights ever. Certainly, the best in Boston.

Tony Lee: That last night I celebrated with everybody. We played hits that reminded everybody song after song why they loved going to the club and all the stuff that they had heard throughout the years. We were pretty much playing through an entire catalog. My job was to make that night a celebration of the club. It was not about challenging people or playing new things. That night was not about me. I'm one of three people standing in that DJ booth to give people a particular experience one last time.

Eartha Harris: I was there on the last night. Part of me was really sad, but a bigger part of me was relieved since I knew I was already transitioning to a different trajectory and ManRay no longer existing would relieve me of the FOMO I had been dreading (or the chance of returning).

Gene Dante: It was packed. We were at capacity at least the last two nights. Friday and Saturday were off the hook and bars were packed all night long. We were exhausted. It was crazy. It was a lot of work, but it was fun and you know the end is in sight, the finish line is there. You don't give up. You take it all the way to the end. I was proud to work there. I was so excited to be part of the team last night.

Terri Niedzwiecki: How I envisioned it was exactly how it turned out. There was no time to think. No time to do anything. It was incredible and exhausting, emotionally exhausting. I couldn't even go out and sneak a cigarette and I'm pretty good at that. That's how chaotic it was. Then, all of a sudden, I smelled smoke and there was Eloni at the end of my bar waving a cigarette around. I looked at her and she looked at me and she went "What the hell are they going to do, close us down?" And I'm like, "Ok," and I lit up right then and there. Then I remember then Don came by and looked at me like "What the hell are you doing?" I pointed at her kidding around and said, "We started it." By that time half the club was smoking.

Jon Whitney: My last night was the Death in June concert. The people that I used to go with moved on, left town, things like that, so it was different for me. I was sad that it was going away because that was another example of Cambridge losing its identity. It really had culture. It had these places and was very colorful.

Chris Ewen The last song I played was by Cristina. She had recorded a scandalous version of the Peggy Lee song "Is That All There Is." Leading up to that I had played some Killing Joke and Gang of Four songs and some up-tempo punk stuff to a full dance floor. Then I decided the last song should be "Is That All There Is" by Christina, which has really dark and really funny lyrics. It just seemed like the perfect ending moment that also wouldn't get people so worked up that they would tear the building down before the night was over. It was very emotional and very apt as far as its message. It also allowed people a little bit of cool off time although you know obviously people dance their butts off to it. When the song was over, I made the goodbye announcement and good night announcement.

The lights came on, there was a champagne toast, and everyone just hung out. There was no "Okay it's quarter after two, you got to go." We just kept it going.

Chapter 19

Where Do We Go From Here?

"It was the end of an era because there's no place else that's ever going to come close to that. It reminds me of the Kinks song, "Come Dancing." I hear that song and there's that sense of sadness when he thinks about his sister crying when they knock the place down." — Niki Nevulis

Rumors circulated for months: ManRay is closing. It is going to happen this year. The end is near. The venue is just going to move to a different location. In 2005, the rumors became reality. After a week of revelry and tears, the club officially closed its doors on July 30, 2005. For many, it still hurts to walk through a Central Square bereft of ManRay. It is perhaps even more heartbreaking to gaze upon 21 Brookline Street and see what has become of the ominous black building that had welcomed countless patrons. But those very people refused to let ManRay die. The question that was immediately on everyone's mind following that last night was "What do we do now?" With the changing landscape, were nightclubs, themselves, even viable anymore? Quickly, various reincarnations of ManRay popped up all over the Boston-Cambridge area with dance nights like Heroes and Xmortis. While the club may have been the home, it is the people who are truly the soul and spirit of ManRay, and they continue to help it live on into the 21st century, continuing the legacy. S.L.

Chris Ewen: In 2004 to 2005 all of us at ManRay thought that we were invincible. I don't think any of us thought ManRay was gonna really close until that last month. It seemed that ManRay had a life of its own. I know that Xmortis was a part of that cohesiveness. It was really telling that after ManRay closed, Xmortis was the first event to find a home in another venue. It just goes to show you the strength of the night.

Matt Gleason: Just about everybody knew the day was going to come where it would either close or move. The lease was going to go up and we were pretty sure that the owner was most likely going to develop the land and not renew the lease. I don't remember the exact date, but we actually operated out of lease for quite some time. Definitely over a year. We were just sitting around wondering what was going to happen. We were looking at places, there was no rush. The owner didn't really have any set plans right away. I think that he even offered to sell the place back to Don because Don was the owner of the property years ago. But, with the way the property was acquired and the market value at the time, Don knew he was getting a bad deal. So he didn't go for the inflated price. I was a little sad about it because we weren't really finding good locations to move to. We did find one place that I really wish we got because it would have been hilarious as it was Lansdowne Street. Everything was really promising, and it was the right size, but they did not want to give us a big lease.

Jen Lucky Cole: I walked down the street and it was just wide open. I walked in and there was nobody there, but they had pulled the mirrors down from the Campus room. They had been doing some remodeling all morning and afternoon so, by the time I went down there, there was a lot of stuff. I remember sitting across the stage. Everything from the office was up top and a lot of stuff had been stripped away. I thought, "Well, I'm never going to be in this building again so I'm going to walk through the whole thing, including the basement." The basement was always sketchy because they had an open sewer. There was about six inches of water down there. I went in and found some old strobe lights and disco lights and I grabbed a couple of things. Four days later I started getting a fever. I had the worst frickin' pneumonia after I had walked around in there and I literally got possessed temporarily by the spirit of ManRay. It was awful. I was crying. I was getting all emotional in different areas at different moments. Then it was really real. It felt like someone was crushing my dreams.

Bruce Jope: I'm really sad that I missed all this because it's like having a child and giving it up for adoption … every now and then you'll sort of sneak by and drive by the house, but you don't want to interfere with the child's life.

Elizabeth Galbraith: I remember being upset. The biggest impact for me was just walking by it and it being a parking lot.

Benny Blanco: I moved to New York in 2003 so I physically couldn't be there. It was sad to hear about it, but it was sadder when the venue was lost. I think that crushed me more, the loss of the original space. That was more of a bummer for me to hear than if they just had to switch spots. The building itself is really where the sentiment lies for me. The venue itself was just special: waiting in line to get in, get the ID check, go in and be in my haven for four hours.

Koren Bernardi: I did feel like it was still a huge loss because that was where I went every night. I felt comfortable and knew people and knew the staff. For me personally, the ability to feel the comfort of my tribe and how people at ManRay could be different from who they are in the outside world or not. That awareness kind of translates into my outside of ManRay life right now.

Trent Stewart: ManRay was definitely the glue that held it all together. I felt sad. I felt as if it was an end but that gave me resolve. Those people that were important to me were going to remain important to me. I wasn't going to let proximity, or lack of physical place to meet, change anything. We just had to be more proactive.

Greg Frisbee: It was an experience. You can go and experience ManRay and maybe you embrace it and you find yourself becoming part of that community or you go and you have the experience once. In that way, it's like skydiving. I've had the experience of skydiving. I don't know if I want to go skydiving again, but I had the experience and I enjoyed it. It was thrilling. It was exhilarating. Everything I thought it would be, but I don't ever want to do it again.

Kara Nemergut: ManRay closing made me a lot more aware of the idea of developers really taking over spaces that people had considered iconic. I wasn't very old, I was 21 when it closed, and it hadn't really occurred to me that there could be these spaces that people love, that had been there for decades which wouldn't get a fair shake. Up until that point, I never really realized that someone could take a pretty beloved thing and just be like "Screw you, I want more money if there's condos here. You're booted out."

Avril dePagter: I felt like everything was closed. ManRay closed, Paradise closed, which, admittedly, we didn't go to a lot because Paradise was intense if you are a woman. I thought it was devastating, especially when I knew it was going to be condos or apartments. A lot of places closed that were interesting or spaces for people of LGBTQIA+ community.

Chris Ewen: The next day I was crushed, I spent the next couple months depressed about it. I was very proud of what I had done, but I kind of didn't see a path forward. I felt really devastated. I had heard from folks that thought that my position at ManRay wasn't really earned, that I had just kind of gotten it by default, that I wasn't a great DJ, that I was just there. I hadn't really earned my place. So that was devastating. It wasn't until we started doing Heroes and bringing back Wednesday's Crypt that I began to revive.

We approached a couple places and Terri and I tried to figure out what we wanted to do. Because of Xmortis, we thought that maybe Heroes would be good and it would have attraction. It would be a good starting point and good rallying point. It was the start of something, but we also thought that this was a temporary fix until the next ManRay happened. Still being a part of Xmortis was kind of convincing myself that I was deserving of that legacy and getting out there and doing it and still having a draw.

Terri Niedzwiecki: We didn't realize at the time how difficult it was going to be to get a space. Chris and I were like "Oh hell. We have to do something. We've got to pay the bills."

Nate Roman: It's funny that skepticism that I had about ManRay closing. People saying it was going to open in a few months … I just didn't see how that's possible. It's not that I didn't want it to happen. I thought that would be the best thing for ManRay, to reinvent itself and come back better than it was before. I did think it was going to happen. I just thought it was going to take a long time. I was excited to be a part of ManRay 2.0, but after a while it became clear that wasn't going to happen. It was a real bummer. Nightclubs don't really close though. People keep doing events in the name of that nightclub. Some of the best things that ManRay had to offer got preserved and went forward.

Noel McKenna: Following the close, ManRay reincarnated in different ways.

Matt Richard: As far as long term goes, I would have to say that ManRay was the nexus for my Goth, industrial, fetish scene. When the nexus closed, a vacuum also appeared and the people who were either DJing or promoting at that venue, the community kind of asked them "What next?" They took the initiative, and they went and found homes for the nights that they were doing. We had Patrick and Eloni with Chris Ewen. They all combined efforts and started doing Xmortis. Then Michael de Carlo took the fetish theme folks and scored connections at Ramrod and Machine where we were welcomed. So I brought that crew there. It was different incarnations, but the same minds behind it. Those were the main pillars that set up shop in Boston.

Krista Siren: I missed the space. I definitely wanted to keep that community and they were all about promises of coming back and I believed that. I thought that the community could probably mostly continue, and it turned out that there were successor nights at other nearby venues. The fetish stuff went over to Machine. Then Chris's New Wave night and the occasional Xmortis went across the street.

I went to the 2019 ManRay anniversary and I was kind of sad at that one because I was the only one wearing this blue latex outfit that I had worn at ManRay and I was definitely the only one wearing something not black latex. Back in the day, I was trying to make a point of dressing to dress code, but not in all black. It was just disappointing. All the Xmortis and Heroes nights that I've been to since, the creative costuming has not been present on those nights that I've been there like it was back in the day.

Xtine Santakas: For a little while after ManRay closed Heroes had moved to Lansdowne. Now it was terrifying, not just the clubs, but being outside on Lansdowne street dressed as a Goth. I do remember the early days of going to Machine back when we were taking taxis. I remember getting out of the taxi and running for our lives to the door of Machine. I didn't like it at all.

Terri Niedzwiecki: At the time it was the epitome of what a Boston nightclub was supposed to be. I said to myself, "My God, the place is a circus. I don't want to work on Lansdowne Street. I didn't even want to go."

Eloni Feliciano They had been talking about closing for a couple of months. We actually got told at the last Xmortis, when we were setting up, that it would be closed before the next event. We already had a prefix for the following Xmortis and we had to create new flyers for it. The first thing that happened was we panicked. We were a little bit unsure of what to make of it. That got me really depressed, but I was also kind of in a go, go, go mode. I started hitting a list of all the different clubs in the area and speaking to their managers just to see if we could get in. That's how we ended up at T.T the Bear's. The good thing about that is people don't have to totally change their routine for going out. It's just a little bit just across the street. I think it was a little sad because it was so much smaller so we wouldn't really be able to grow with it, which is why I went to The Middle East, but T.T.'s was at least an opportunity. We didn't have to stop. The next thought was, "Who's going to DJ for us?" I was speaking to Terri about it and Terri said, "Well, why don't you just ask Chris?" For some reason we hadn't thought of the possibility that we could ask Chris. So we asked Chris and then Terri was like, "Bring me along." Terri is friends with Bonnie, the owner of T.T.'s, so it wasn't hard to negotiate. It worked out really well. We could bring our family with us.

Eloni Feliciano: Unfortunately, it was a little depressing. I think a lot of people really wanted that ManRay feel. So I think we had maybe 100 people that first night. We were disheartened by it. But the people that showed up had a good time and they found that their friends were there. I think that's what kept people coming out. At first they were depressed and didn't want to go see Chris and all of us and have to look across the street at ManRay. Meanwhile, you're in this far smaller club without the magical pews and all that, but after a while people realized they could find each other there. Our numbers definitely increased that first night. It was slow and I was sad but it definitely built up from there.

Eloni Feliciano: We look upon the time that we had at ManRay as being beautiful. It was beautiful because we have this world, this space that we could experiment with. With T.T's, we kind of had to become a little bit savvier with how we spaced things. That was another thing that started becoming an issue — if it stays crowded every single time, people are going to stop coming out because they're going to be like, "I can't even dance at Xmorits." So it was always trying to balance having too many people against having just enough people.

Jennifer: Well, let's start with Cambridge. So much of its identity has been wiped away, part of the history and the soul of the city. It was things like ManRay that made Cambridge what it was. It brought out the art scene, it brought out a lot of the music scenes and since that's been gone a lot of that other stuff is gone.

Once ManRay closed we would try to go to some of the other nights but we never really felt part of the other nights. Ceremony wasn't so bad at first, but then Ceremony moved and I never went again. I felt like I was old and there was this whole new group of Goth kids that I didn't even know, little baby bats flying around. I started losing interest after we tried a few nights here and there. None of these other nights seem to have that same connection to people. You still go out and you still do a little dancing, but it's not quite the same.

Chris Ewen: Heroes can be a lot of different things to a lot of different people. It makes them happy in different ways.

Xtine Santakas: I'll tell you it was exhilarating. It's been one of the best rides in my life and I hope it doesn't end anytime soon. Knock on wood. It was great. It was something I didn't know I had in me. It was something I didn't expect. There were three people, not including Chris and Terri, and they said, "Well, we're going to move over to T.T.'s" and I was like, "Oh, thank God!" They said, "We want you to help us set it up and host the night." And I was like, "Oh my God!" I have to decorate differently because it's not a Goth night and I think that really broke me until I started thinking a lot about Campus, which was the night that I never got to experience. How do I attract those people and how do I attract Goths too?

Honestly, it was a real collaboration between Chris, Terri, and I. It was really about the music, about the drinking, and then it all came together bringing that feeling of home and safety across the street. It's really about inclusion and friendship and feeling safe and being welcomed. There's a reason why, at the end of the night, I stand at the door and I say goodnight to you. I'm looking you dead in the eye making sure that you're okay when you leave and that you're happy. There have been people that I have actually pulled aside at the end of the night and said, "Are you okay with the people that you're with?" and things like that. I've gotten to know my patrons. It's not so much going to a club night to get drunk. I'm going to a club night. I'm going to have a couple of drinks. I'm going to dance to some great music. I'm going to meet up with my friends and I might even meet a new friend. I know that I'm going to have a good time and that's what really makes the night successful.

Becky D: Delicious Dancers kept doing a lot of stuff for a couple of years after that. Chris would run at night and he would ask us to come dance, especially the stuff in Machine upstairs. I tried to find a new venue, but it didn't pan out. It's hard to find a venue for a fetish night, right, because you need a little bit of privacy, you need a place where people can have a dressing room of some sort where they can change, and you need someplace where the people who work there are going to be supportive and helpful and tolerant.

You really didn't have an official Fantasy Factory night after ManRay closed. There were fits and starts of parts of Fantasy Factory, but having a Fantasy Factory night … I don't think it ever happened again. It would have been nice to have a couple of months before the club closed because then we would have been able to do a couple of interesting things. I had a meeting with some Fantasy Factory people about new things we wanted to try out.

Patrick Fitzgerald: There were hundreds if not thousands of people who thought the Goth scene was over. I still encounter people and they're somehow surprised to hear that there's been a Goth scene this whole time. When we first had Xmortis post-ManRay at T.T. 's. We had only about 70 fucking people show up. We were doing close to 400 at ManRay. Things were kind of down across the board in general. Still we were doing okay for a relatively new night.

Mizery McRae: I loved when Heroes was at Machine more than anything because the dance floor was sunken in just like it was at ManRay. Machine was such a bigger space that could accommodate more people and teach more people about the lifestyle.

Andrea Parros: I think it's really sad to think that it doesn't exist anymore, but I do know that it lives on in the nights that still go on with Chris Ewen and Heroes and all that. I think for a while Ceremony was happening, and there were different little nights, so that same culture lives on.

Anna Feder: That was my consolation, that Heroes was still going. I could still listen to music that I liked and see some of the same people, even though I didn't really know them very well. It wasn't like I was integrated into the community at all. I love the ManRay reunions because you see the same people in the same outfits and I don't know what formaldehyde they were sleeping in but they look the same.

Paul Calnan: I never felt the same going to other places after ManRay, that's one of the significant impacts that it had. Going to other clubs after ManRay was gone never felt the same. We tried, we started going to Sin-O-Matic and Xmortis and other places, but it was never the same. I'm not saying those places were bad, we did have some fun nights at those clubs, but nothing ever captured that overall ManRay experience and that overall ManRay vibe.

Mark Clavet: We had the chance to heal. I thought, "Wow, this is sad." I was constantly wondering "Will it reopen, will it just relocate, what's going to happen?" At the same time, I thought, "Well, I wasn't living here at the time, so … " But to be able to follow along with what was happening and attend several dozen times before closing would have been nice. Then some years later, I had returned to the area and then Heroes opened and I was just overjoyed to hear this.

Nate Roman: I spun Xmortis at The Middle East with Chris. We played all this music we remembered playing at ManRay. It was so fun to do that. For me, it was just like memories all night, playing the songs and seeing the kids dance. Those are the best memories.

Chris Ewen: When we were eventually closing, we took things like all of the panels of the cage and some of David Dukakis' artwork that we could remove. We put them in storage for an eventual ManRay resurrection. There was no thought that this was the final end. But what happened in that building made that space legendary to us.

I didn't take a lot from the building, surprisingly. In my booth I had a lot of posters, like Alien Sex Fiend autographed posters to me. I have bricks from the building that I snuck in and stole after demolition. I had boxes of gifts people brought me, stuffed animals, and toys. So I had all those mementos and a piece of the building, and that was enough for me.

Constantine Valhouli: I was at the furniture and fixtures auction of ManRay. It was so odd to see the club in almost clinical bright light being dissected and dismantled. On one hand, it made one want to bring back a piece of the club as a memento of those wonderful years. I ended up with the antique wooden door to one of the DJ booths that I cleaned up and used as a kitchen door. It always made me smile.

At the auction, someone bought the exterior neon ManRay sign. I think that was the prize item for the whole auction. We all joked it would be like the Bat signal, we'd see it in different places throughout Boston and Cambridge, and know that the party would re-appear, for one night, there. People were also joking that constructing an apartment on the site of ManRay itself was like building on haunted ground, that the residents of this building would, from time to time, maybe on a full moon, on some Wednesday nights, feel an urge to put on black leather trousers and listen to Depeche Mode.

Greg Frisbee It was one of those things where it's like sending out the signal. You put out the ManRay signal and you'd see the giant M in the sky … ManRay kids unite.

Amy Butts: We have bricks from the building. We went through the rubble on a rainy night to get them.

Terri Niedzwiecki: I still have the iron lanterns with the hands. I have one of those on my front porch.

Anastasia Taslis: I still have one good black brick somewhere. It has moved with me multiple times and people are like, "Why are you moving this thing around?" and I'm like "Because I need it." I have a bottle opener from Terri's bar.

Abigail Taylor: There were little offshoots, like Ceremony. Once ManRay closed there were a bunch of different segments of ManRay and DJs that would create their own nights. It was the only place you could go that had this kind of subculture. There were lots of different bars in New York playing that music, yet they were not the same as in Cambridge. I think of Chris Ewen. He's still spinning the same music. He's still bringing in new artists and influencing a lot of people. He's the core of that culture. I just looked at a Facebook memory today. I went and saw Future Bible Heroes on this day several years ago and that was one of his bands. He is still incredibly influential to several generations of people.

Matt Gleason: I don't really think that it needed to close or like it was the right time for it to close. The only thing that I kind of wish is that the scenes still survived because I don't think that there's that much of a scene in the city anymore. All the old customers might come out if ManRay reopened tomorrow. But I kind of felt like it didn't carry on.

Emily Arkin: I definitely thought it was a loss and now it pales compared to how many things are closing all at once right now. It felt like anything that had so many different scenes and people was a cultural thing that disappeared. So it was very sad when I heard about it. I did not think it was not good for Cambridge.

There aren't a lot of nightclubs. I always found the Boston scene to be not my thing at all the few times I got dragged there. I had this almost Waiting for Godot thing with Rise, where people always told me about it. One friend, who was really a raver, would always be like, "I'm going to take you to Rise, but you have to party first, you can't just go to Rise." I was like, "But I really don't want to." If ManRay had still been around then, I would have wanted to just go there, but instead it was Lansdowne Street, which was horrible. The night would be ruined and you'd be like, "Never mind. I don't even want to go to Rise anymore." So I never went.

Bruce Jope: You move on. Your life becomes a different life and you develop different interests. Since ManRay, I went into manufacturing museum reproductions, I went into the clock business, I opened another club down the Cape. I've done many, many things since then, and none of them would have happened if I'd stayed at ManRay. I'm not the kind of person who wants to stay and do something for a long time. I'm never going to be the kind of person who puts 20 years in on anything. So after I left, I walked away and I thought it was going to be a disaster. I was very proud it stayed open after I left. Twenty years without a name change. We were always proud that it kept the name and the logo for all those years.

I had a magazine called Hit Parade which I had run for five years before I did ManRay. It made a living, but it never lived up to the creative vision we had for it. It was never a great success. When we did ManRay it was this phenomenon and it was a huge success creatively for Francis and myself, and it gave me a level of confidence that I could create with the magic that Francis and I had in our heads and our minds and our hands and we did. ManRay, in a way, made me fearless and gave me confidence that I could risk everything I had.

Eileen Dover: I hope we have more ManRay reunion nights or an event again. You want to see faces that you haven't seen. That was more important to me. I wasn't accepted in high school so the ManRay reunions were more important than my high school reunion.

John O'Leary: You never think that's going to go away. You think that's the way it's going to be forever, right, it's always going to be like this. We took advantage of ManRay so much. We loved it.

Emily Sweeney: It's a huge loss. I wish ManRay still existed. I think it would contribute a lot to the local and even national music, art, and fashion scenes. The place was such a fountain of creativity in so many different forms of media. The fashion shows, the live stage performances, the dancing, and the music. It's a shame that it's still not there. The cool thing about ManRay was you didn't know everybody that was going to be there. You never knew who you were going to meet.

Tatiana Zimkus: My partner and I, who went to Boston with me for the first time a few years ago, he'd hear me reminisce and talk about it and didn't really get why I was having so many issues with people out here and the culture out here and all that until he went back and saw things through my eyes and met those people and went to Ceremony.

Rebecca Griffin: It's special here and that's what I learned about Bostonians and that's what ManRay taught me about Bostonians. The culture here and the social circles, they may be off putting at first, but once you make that connection, there's loyalty in the city like I've never experienced. Once you make those connections, they are lifelong and I think ManRay was the embodiment of that and it's still proving that now. I mean, how many different spaces have we all moved to and danced in since ManRay closed?

MJ Pullins: The real challenge right now is that Cambridge is losing its core value of people who have grown up in the city. My parents grew up in Cambridge, I grew up in Cambridge, but the working class can't afford to live in Cambridge anymore. It will become a bedroom community. One of the beauties of Cambridge is its character and its character comes down to its people. Nobody cares what you do. The working man is just as important as the Harvard professor and they drink together at the bar and they have beautiful conversations.

Arlene Guerrero-Watanabe: Today, it's different. People are more embracing of multiple aesthetics these days. People still identify as Goth but they don't dress Goth all the time. Today it's more fluid and you can be all of these things. But back in the 90s we had a certain pride in that we were whatever aesthetic we were. At least it was the case for Goths.

Heather Morgan: History says that we are going to have a boom in nightlife. What format it takes, because of real estate greed, malignant capitalism, and if a club is profitable enough to use a building, is hard to say. I don't know if devoting big buildings to elaborate spaces is something that is going to come back into vogue, but nightlife will come back in some form and I think it'll come back big. You're definitely going to have places where people need to meet and drink and stand really close together and dance. People are gonna want to do that.

Adam Lewis: Music was exploding everywhere. So I'm not sure I would give ManRay as much credit on the music side because alternative and all these things were just exploding throughout the 90s everywhere. But in terms of having a safe place, a place where you could go and feel normal on any night, not just one night a week. Not just gay night on Sundays at Avalon or whatever. At ManRay, you could go four nights a week and feel at home and comfortable.

I think that for an entire generation, especially because Boston and Cambridge are college cities, and because ManRay is situated right by Harvard, MIT, and right across the river to Boston University and Northeastern, it was all college kids. As kids discovered ManRay, it became an oasis for them. It was the one place you could go at that time to find community. There wasn't the internet yet, so you couldn't find like minded people. I think that is its greatest impact and greatest legacy in terms of having a community and finding your own and making you feel like you're not alone.

Jamie DiBattista: I feel like there wasn't anything else like it. I don't think there could be. I think millennials and younger kids are so homogenized when it comes to music. I mean, I work with Millennials all the time. I think, since the mid-90s, corporate America has worked really hard to produce cookie cutter consumers and that's Millennials. And it's definitely Gen Z. As much as I love ManRay, and will always love ManRay, I don't think it could exist these days, at least not with the young crowd. It would all be old, old geezers like us, which I'd be fine with.

Niki Nevulis: It was the end of an era because there's no place else that's ever going to come close to that. It reminds me of the Kinks song, "Come Dancing." It reminds me exactly of that; I hear that song and there's that sense of sadness when he thinks about his sister crying when they knock the place down and that was the feeling. That song just kind of says that all; that was that sanctuary, that safe place where you didn't worry about whether you look good dancing or not. You just danced without judgment.

It was probably the last place in Boston without judgment and it didn't matter how old we were going there. That was the beauty of it all.

I was in New Orleans, probably nine years ago, down in the French Quarter with some colleagues when we walked into this club that was playing the same kind of music that we used to hear at ManRay. I sat down next to this woman and started talking. She said she was from Boston and I asked if she ever went to ManRay and her face just lit up. She's like "You've been to ManRay?!" We just started reminiscing. Here we are in New Orleans, just two people that didn't know each other, but absolutely bonding over this club that we had gone to and sharing in the joy and then the sadness of it having been closed down and turned into condos. There was this shared experience and sentimentalism, like the Barbra Streisand song "Memories", where you look back and there's this line about not remembering the bad times and just remembering the good times. It was really about that celebration of the good times. It was like family, and when you find somebody, it's like finding that long lost family member that you didn't even know you had, which is so critically important.

After dark, I am plagued by restlessness The thrum of dirges and anthems is still in my bones and gin's become gauze in my skull.

There's perfumes on me of peacocks and swans; the musk of sharks and wolves too. But it's the memories of happy coincidence that stick: Mood and music in synchronicity; gazes met in mutual humor, or hunger, or simple pleasure. An unexpected friend, unexpected beauty.

I am restless with a temporary confusion of fantasy and truth. From that streamlined demimonde of people made into icons-From having *myself* pared down to an icon--I am slow in returning to my messy and variegated reality. I am slow in remembering that the characters I met are not characters; that the night in which I bloomed is not the world. Having reveled in a powerful sensation of *being alive*, I am slow in coming back to my life. Quang Pho (ManRay Attendee)

Chapter 20

Legacy: Endings and Beginnings

"My time at ManRay really encapsulated the whole spectrum of human emotions, and in the end, I definitely feel I am a better person for getting to experience it." — Eartha Harris

The words "safe" and "home" are not traditionally associated with nightclubs, but for countless patrons of ManRay that is exactly what the club was. When Campus first opened its doors in 1983, it welcomed the LGBTQ+ community and provided them with a place to be themselves and discover the possibilities. As it morphed into ManRay, the club continued to provide a place for people, cultures, and communities that were often on the outskirts of mainstream society, the people that society did not always know to value. No matter the night a person called their own, from Crypt to New Wave to Fantasy Factory, the club welcomed all. When ManRay closed its doors on July 30, 2005, after an amazing 20-year run, it was heartbreaking. Nevertheless, the memories and impact that the club had on its patrons continues to live on, from discovering their own style to falling in love with music to mixing with ManRay's wonderfully unique crowd. For many, their time at ManRay, whether long or short, was truly transformative. Although the building is no longer standing, the legacy of ManRay lives on. S.L.

Chris Ewen: It's weird. I think people tend to think of ManRay as something that was static. Like we did this and that was the way it always was. But ManRay changed a lot. All the time.

Chris Ewen: As far as ManRay having an impact … we were very welcoming of all. People started coming when they were 18,19, 20, 21. We gave them a space where they could find out for themselves who they were, and what made them happy. We helped people find their true selves just by being a place where people knew that they didn't have to be alone. There were lots of like-minded people no matter what you are into. Whether you are gay or lesbian or trans, whether your into the kink scene or Goth culture.

Terri Niedzwiecki: I can honestly say with 100 percent sincerity that ManRay was the first club that I've ever seen, I probably ever will see, that just accepted anyone in everything.

Michael Hsieh: I think it's terrible that the kids today, 18 and 19-year-olds who just got to college in Boston, who don't have anywhere to go. It breaks my heart to think that the kids today don't have what we did. They don't have the opportunity for that community, for that gluc. Maybe it is there and I'm just not aware of it because I'm not a 19-year-old anymore, new to the city. I hope that little Goths now have somewhere to go. I'm sure they do, but it's not ManRay.

Paul Vitagliano: The fact that ManRay was able to maintain a pretty dedicated devoted fan base and crowd of people, that says a lot in the nightlife world. That is success. You're lucky if you have two to three to five years of a good consistent crowd because a lot of people are very onto the next thing, or they only want to go to the new hip thing. The luster fades on the newness.

Adam Wolff: If they've been to ManRay it's like you have to be tall enough to ride the ride. I think that's part of why you feel that comfort immediately when somebody says, "I was at ManRay." Well then, they can't be too much of a douchebag.

Steve Friedrich: It did obviously make me more accepting, whether it's seeing friends transition to genders, or "Hey, I can wear a skirt and it's okay." In the early 90s you would get stuff yelled at you as a guy wearing a skirt walking down the road. It helped you just be more friendly and cool.

Tony Lee: That just opened the doors for a lot of people to play music and a whole bunch of them are still playing now. It's definitely a reason why there is just this massive number of DJs in Boston. Nights were being run by more than one person. Many included guest DJs from everywhere to cross promote and build a better scene. It has made the New England scene really strong and tight knit, because we all know each other's nights over the past 20 years or so.

Julia Kilcoyne: In large measure, I've had to keep that part of my life pretty pocketed because not everybody is open to discussing that I used to hang out at this fetish club. It validated a premise that I've always had, and that is that everyone has a secret life. Whether that is internal or external, people have more facets than you ever know. That leads me to be tolerant and understanding in my everyday life. Trying to understand that what we see is maybe not what's there. Alternately, people are more vulnerable and more open than you would ever know. I think ManRay really helped me just get a better understanding of humanity, as corny as that sounds.

Lily Moonstorm: It was a place to go that was not only safe to be who you were but also to celebrate who you were.

Eartha Harris: ManRay was a time in my life that I yearn to relive, yet simultaneously would never want to live again. It was the joys of being accepted and feeling beautiful and popular, the pain of betrayal and heartbreak, the euphoria of being young and narcissistic and not caring about the future, mixed with the confusion of not knowing really who I was or how to be an adult yet. I had a lot of beautiful moments. I had some ugly ones too. My time at ManRay really encapsulated the whole spectrum of human emotions, and in the end, I definitely feel I am a better person for getting to experience it. The only drawback is that, because of having an experience like that, deep down inside me there has remained a little piece of me still searching for it again. But I know that's impossible because I'm different now — better, healthier, wiser — but still different, and I'm just not sure there is any reliving the mysteries and drama and excitement of being in such an amazing place at such an amazing time in our culture and at such a young age, even if I were to walk through those doors again.

Rachel E. Pollock: The fact that somebody spent three, four, or five years of their life going out to ManRay is equivalent to four years at a university. It functions in a way that it becomes like a facet of your identity and it seems like many people saw themselves as part of the ManRay community.

Eileen Dover: The folks that went to ManRay saw drag queens and transvestites and transsexuals, and now they have kids and they're teaching their kids not to be homophobic, not to be transphobic. There was the diversity of people of color. Boston has a history of being quite racist, but there was every color of the rainbow at ManRay. Those people who are parents now are raising a generation of people that don't have that hatred in their heart that we had to face. It was an evolutionary thing.

Andrea Parros: I think that seeing a lot of different types of people and walks of life and being exposed to a different area of culture was really enriching as a person. Being able to hear a lot of different types of music … I got really into all that music and now it's almost like ManRay lives on through a club I go to in Rochester called Vertex. They were started independently; they were open around the same time. I went to this club and went, "Oh, I recognize this! This is ManRay. This is the same thing." I always kind of feel like an ally to people that are different. That's definitely ManRay, a safe space for people that are different.

Skot Kremen: ManRay saw me at my best when I was on top of the world and I felt great. It also saw me at my worst. There were times when I would go and cry in the girl's bathroom. People would come there and make me feel better or worse, depending on what I did that made me cry in the bathroom. My professional life, in part, revolved around ManRay and my social life did too.

Emily Sweeney: I really miss dancing. It was so great having so many different places on the dance floor to dance. You could jump up on the stage and be in the cage, which was really cool. I discovered so much music that I'd never heard before like Assemblage 23, VNV Nation, Wolfsheim. ManRay, the friends that I met, the DJs that I met there, introduced me too so much.

Derek Kouyoumjian: Well for me, quite honestly, it was good to be a photographer at ManRay. That to me was a massive achievement. The first thing you saw when you came in there: No cameras. And here I was welcomed with my camera. I felt very comfortable and safe and easy to direct people. I always felt at home at ManRay and I always felt very honored and privileged to be allowed my camera in there.

Jennifer: I still think a lot of what made Boston what it was has deteriorated since ManRay closed. All the record shops are gone, Deli Haus is gone, a lot of the music venues are gone. There doesn't seem to be any heart left in the city. It makes it more depressing. I feel like our society as a whole, people are more comfortable being who they are. It's okay if you're gay. It's okay if you're Goth. Our society is much more accepting these days, but all the things that we had there to support us are gone. So it's like, "Okay, great. You can be more open, but you can't do any of the fun stuff anymore."

Nate Roman: I was a part of ManRay. Being a regular member of the ManRay staff feels like you're part of a secret society. It translated toward how I aspired to do some other things. I wouldn't say it applies a lot in my professional life, except for projects like Ceremony. Lessons Cusraque taught me about promoting always stuck with me. Lessons like how much time you should lead up to an event. Those are things I've learned and I've even brought that to work.

Gene Dante: I think there are several marriages that happened because of relationships at ManRay, even some children produced from that. So there's a nice long-lasting effect.

Terri Niedzwiecki: You thought everything was going to last forever and you always think you have more time.

Chris Ewen: A couple of years ago the band Cold Cave came to town. They're just very cool. I went to see them and I posted about it on my Facebook page. I said how fantastic they were and Wesley from Cold Cave actually responded. He apparently went to school in Boston and came to ManRay back in the day and absorbed all of that culture and it played a part in what he became professionally and what he's done musically. He's brilliant. I read that and almost fell off my chair.

Me'lissa Nin: ManRay was a social experiment. ManRay was family and self-discovery. Every time I set foot in ManRay; it was like coming home after a very long journey. That feeling of having a hole in your heart and having it filled with all of these wonderful memories and feelings. That's what ManRay is to me.

Erika Spaulding: It is its own creature that develops and matures with people. It pulls new people. It's not just this one little phenomenon that had its little pop-up and then was gone. It was something that changed with the people and it brought new people. Who I am and who I became.

It's a steppingstone. Unfortunately that path ended way too soon, but I love that I was a part of that time and that will be in my heart forever, along with anybody that ever went there.

Eileen Dover: I don't really know how to say how I felt because I was one person going in the 90s. The first time I went in I snuck in underage, then I became a veteran ManRay fixture who worked there for years and was close to my ManRay family. But I was a sober person and I had changed my values in the end. I didn't have as much to prove or didn't have as much to say. I wanted to become more of a serious artist. I was a better person for having ManRay as a part of my journey.

Emily Taylor: Heroes is a huge community too. It was a different community than the one I was mostly involved in, but since then, it has evolved into its own subculture of Heroes people. That community is way more diverse than the ManRay one. I do think it had a seismic effect and it gave us a place to go that wasn't fucking Lansdowne Street where you would get beat up.

Trent Stewart: ManRay taught me that there are new adventures to be had. You think your personality is set, you think your tastes are set, etc. This was an entirely different world for me. There are people that are important to me. I learned about a lot of different music that I didn't know about, different literature, and different art. I wasn't closed minded. I'm not as set in my ways as I thought I was.

Mizery McRae: ManRay taught me a lot of things, but the most important thing is my work ethic. It taught me to be on time for work and, if you're on time, you're still late. I'm always there 20 minutes before I'm supposed to be there. It taught me that being on time, you will never get fired or get spoken to or let go. You're there before people are supposed to be there and you're sitting looking flawless.

Jen Lucky Cole: It's funny because that's my ambition now — to create a safe space that's focused on art and music. That was my dream when I found out about ManRay: to work there. I really didn't think it was ever going to close. If I consolidate everything I've done and everything I've learned, ManRay is such a huge chunk of it. Don was kind of putting it in the back of my head that it was a good thing to learn. He was teaching me when I was working there — what he was doing and how he kept the club open. That's always kind of in the back of my mind. He literally would have teaching moments where he told me "Listen, pay attention, this will matter in the business world, if you want to be good and successful and let people like you, and that's what I want to do." Don taught me more about being an adult than my parents did. I wasn't prepared to leave the house when I was 18. Don is amazing. He is always moving on to the next business, the next idea, the next thing. What I actually took away from him, to sum it all up, is that when you get in a position to have employees treat them well, treat them like family, treat them like humans. Giving them chances for forgiveness is a gift that you can give them and you can always talk it out.

Jennifer: It definitely took confidence to go out there and be who I am and not try to conform to what others think I should be. I learned it was okay to take risks, getting up there in latex or doing some photo shoots. It seems funny but it makes you comfortable. I'm totally comfortable getting up in front of a boardroom with all these high-end execs and saying whatever I need to say without being nervous because I used to dance in freakin' latex in front of them. It definitely gives you confidence in yourself.

Keith Ward: I think it gave to disenfranchised people, people that didn't fit in, the local rock scene, or people that didn't go to Narcissus or Lansdowne Street for club nights. It gave people somewhere to go that didn't necessarily fit in elsewhere.

Rebecca Griffin: I think it helped develop me as a more well-rounded person. That was a profound thing for me. Coming to ManRay was seeing all these people who have different capabilities in that one space. It was a comfort seeing that people can coexist in that way. It didn't have to be these various segregated groups if you will. It broadened my understanding of music as well as tolerance. ManRay really did help expand my mind, my relation, and my viewpoints of other people. I think it helped me as far as breaking down stereotypes of people and understanding that people are so multifaceted, people evolve and they change. I really try to look at everyone as an individual versus a group and to see things through their eyes.

Koren Bernardi: For me it was a safe place to be around people like me and learn about ways that you could be weird and still be successful. That's the thing that is amazing about it. The people I still know from ManRay are such smart people. They're doing amazing work. They're in education, science, and tech. People do brilliant stuff. They just live life and laugh with friends. I still feel that kind of kinship.

Emily Arkin: I think there's an amount of openness to being willing to go into a space where you don't know anyone and you know there's gonna be a culture that you're not already indoctrinated in. Something's going to happen that's going to change your point of view. It's almost like traveling. I think of what I've done since then, things that seemed scary and then weren't, like going into a hammam, a religious one, a Turkish bath, and not being able to speak the language and having people kind of yell at you and be like, "No cold before hot." ManRay was like that, it's a way to travel at home.

Hyson Concepcion: Community. The relationships, the friendships, and other connections that go back. I'm still astonished. The way that people who did have drama, like great breakups, many of those people are fine and we were still really good friends.

A. Dorian Rose: ManRay was home. It was the most beautiful club I have ever stepped foot in and that's after being in many clubs and bars. I might sound like such a jetsetter but clubs in Paris, Berlin, Brussels, London, and Glasgow ... ManRay was singular and there's nothing like it. It truly was a home. You had your rooms and your different relationships and the different things than you did.

Lacey Prpic Hedtke: It didn't make me wear anything different or listen to anything different. It was a lot more about being accepting and cool with the parts of myself that I might have thought were too freaky, too out there, too taboo, too sexual, too queer, too weird. It's seeing people experiment with their identity, with their look, with their sexuality, and with how they're expressing their sexuality.

Michael Marotta: It was a kaleidoscope of artistic creativity and expression and I think that it was reflected in the music. I think that it was also reflected in the people and their colorful personalities. The fact that it was a nightclub and not a bar. The fact that it appreciated that type of patron. It did not let the bro off the street come into gawk at someone or make someone feel uncomfortable. If you wanted to be half naked you could be half naked and no one would be sexually inappropriate toward you. People respected other people's boundaries. Four nights out of the week you could go there and be amongst other like-minded people and feel calm knowing that the people around you probably had a similar story to yours, whether it was growing up listening to the Smiths by yourself in your bedroom or having a weird taste for just this fucked up music that no one you ever met ever also really liked. You could be yourself and I think spaces like that are so limited and don't really exist too much anymore.

Anna Feder: The number one is probably embracing my queerness, and queer wouldn't have been a word I used at the time. I was someone who probably identified as bisexual, and I mean not just about sexuality, I mean all of the facets of my personality that are outside of gender and sexuality norms. It took me a long time to get there, but I'm sure the seeds were planted at ManRay, and now I'm a drag king. The performative side of me took a very long time to get to. It started with karaoke when I was living in Western Mass, but I feel the seeds of it were started at ManRay dancing in the cage and having that experience of people watching you. I was a teenager. My brain was still forming. It was a time when I needed to see what was possible for me, for society. ManRay was a place without judgment. This all may sound really grand, but it was important at that time of my life to see a space where, even if I wasn't part of that community in all the ways that lots of other people were, it still felt like my space. It still felt like a space where I was welcome and I was valued however I presented myself, whether I was just observing or whether I was participating. I was part of the mill. I was part of the environment. It definitely had a lot of influence on my personality and my outlook. I feel like, before that time, I didn't know what to look for. I didn't know what I wanted or needed. I didn't know how to look for a community.

Finding those spaces were so important for my soul. After ManRay it was like "Where else can I find this?" It was a matter of realizing what that did for me and gave me and then trying to find other spaces that did that. It really set the bar high because nothing else is quite measured up. I'm sad that I didn't necessarily appreciate it as much when it was around. I didn't understand how important it would be, how rare, how unique. I was not as comfortable in my own skin as I am now. I think that it'd be really nice to experience it now in my 40s when I have all of the confidence in the world and know myself well. I would be really at home with myself in that space. I'm kind of sad that I wasn't even 30 when it closed.

That space was really sacred and we were lucky to have it. There really isn't anything else that came along that compares. When it went under, I figured there would be some other space, not realizing how precious and how fragile that space was. But these are all down to some developer or decision of somebody who doesn't understand or care, somebody for whom profit is the only motive. We're constantly fighting that in Boston.

Prospero Eaton: It helped me feel more comfortable really and it opened up how I expressed myself. ManRay opened up doors for me. It made me a little more open minded and a little more adventurous and daring knowing that I can put what I want out there. I don't have to worry that some "mainstream society" person is going to tell me that I can't do it. It definitely liberated me.

Taylor Vecchio: I didn't realize how I was living that dream that I wanted at that time, which was going out on Wednesday night, getting drunk, meeting people and having fun while still going to school. That would be a lesson that I would learn because even though now I'm an adult with responsibilities, I still think that you can make time to go and see your friends and enjoy your passions.

Skot Kremen: It's almost like this ghost that haunts Boston. The new venues? ... it's not that you don't have fun, but it is not ManRay. None of those places feel like home.

Rick Webb: I mean it is 2021 and a large number of those people are still some of my closest friends. People say that about college. I've got about three friends from college. I've got like 30 friends from ManRay. It is such a part of our lives. We still listen to that music. I choose to remember the good days more than the bad obviously

Sara S. Wendell: There is still a core of what I call a "ManRay crowd" that I'm still in touch with. Occasionally somebody will pop back into my life that I haven't seen since and just it all snaps back. Part of what it had created was the realization that it's possible. I don't know of any other place that ever had that kind of a feel to it.

Xtine Santaks: Those people that I met at ManRay have been a big part of my life and continue to be, and I hope that they always will be. I hope that I will always be a big part of theirs. ManRay was an anchor, it was the epicenter is the only way I could describe it.

Prospero Eaton: ManRay had that long term effect on me. It opened up my mind and that, in turn, influenced me to take art seriously.

Melanie Sharkey: I will always remember the vibe of people who are way cooler than me dancing, way better than me dressed, way cooler than me, but not being snobby about it. I still felt included, which is something that I struggled with a lot as a teenager. For example, being in high school in the 90s as a teenager, I was pretty awkward and always looking for inclusion. I kind of danced around different subcultures. I always just felt happy at ManRay, like I was part of the crowd that I had always wanted to find as a wayward teenager and young adult. The clothes, the hair, the shoes, the culture, the music and it really made a lasting impression on me.

Kathy Landes: I feel like it was honestly a very foundational experience for me. It brought me a sense of that fact that you could be who you wanted to be and it was okay. Let people just do what they want to do.

Patrick Fitzgerald: So young people, particularly at that age, particularly the weird ones kind of tend to think they're alone in the world, are not necessarily going to find people that are just as weird as they are. I've seen a lot of them die, kill themselves, or just abuse themselves to death because they don't necessarily connect with the community that they relate to the way I remember relating to the community. I found that at ManRay when I was that age. I still remember the magic of belonging that I experienced at ManRay when I was teenager. I thought I found fucking wonderland. I felt like one of the cool kids and I had people that cared about me and that I cared about. We were all watching out for each other and that was magic. That's very close to my heart when it comes to doing Xmortis and a lot of why I want to be able to continue to do it.

Kathy Landes: It was an establishment in Cambridge and Central Square in particular. I walked through there before the pandemic every day and I feel as though it was a part of the culture of that neighborhood and Central Square.

Lucretia X Machina: Nothing compares to ManRay. That was my church. That was the place for all versions of an open-minded society that you might not get outside of that building.

Jenn Sutkowski: It kind of made me excited to have this club where people, who would be considered freaks, were all dressed up. The visibility of people in the community and seeing that these are people who are just like us doing their thing and having a good time. I think the visibility of super artistic people who are going about life is probably a little bit different than regular people. I think it is really important for the rest of the community to see, whether or not they think anything of it. It has positive effects for the community and beyond Cambridge when people are allowed to be out, free, and dressing however they want. That's really powerful. It's powerful for other people who consider themselves or are called freaks at other places.

Christina Pearson: Oh God I miss it so much. It was like a home. It's some of the best memories I have. It's like remembering your favorite Christmas. Even though I was going to college and doing other things the best times were always going to be had there. And sometimes the worst. There'd be crazy drama and the fights and all that, but it will always work out.

Liz Enthusiasm: In terms of the physical building, I was like, "That's fine," because it was smelly and had gotten kind of disgusting with all the sewage issues and none of the bathroom doors closing. All the smoke kind of hid all the other terrible odors. I definitely was sad about it closing, but they had so many false alarms about it that it seemed sort of surreal. Still I was just kind of like, "Well, I'll follow Chris wherever he ends up." We lost a good location but that stuff happens.

Christina Pearson: I had a feeling of acceptance. We needed a place in the Boston area that would do that. I feel like I didn't see as much of a Goth presence in the area. When I first started in '91, it just seemed like people were able to go out and be that every day and I think that a club like ManRay is what made that possible.

Jenny Dahling: I'm not sure how well known it is outside of the relative microcosm of Boston nightlife, but I can tell you that I have been to many nightclubs all over the place and, in my opinion, there is nothing even remotely close to ManRay. I don't know if it was just the age I was or the world was different or maybe it really was that everything clicked in the place from how the club was laid out, to the clientele, to the music but the vibe there was awesome. I think it had a profound effect on my life. I couldn't imagine how my adult life would have looked if it had not been around. We're still going to the nights that began at ManRay and people still ask about ManRay. It's still in peoples' minds 15 years later, so that's saying something.

Jenn Sutkowski: I feel I have very fond memories of it, having gone through some kind of shitty things in high school, trauma and having my identity questioned. At ManRay I was just very accepted. If I ran into someone else who happened to go there, I definitely would feel a sense of familiarity for having this shared space and I would definitely want to know more about what their experience was like.

Hideki Watanabe: In high school I was a Goth, but I didn't know what Goth was. I didn't know anyone that was like that either. Later on, I was like "Oh yeah, that explains everything." Meeting people like me definitely helped me formalize everything. I came into myself. I was weird in high school for many different reasons. A lot of us are weird, but my parents were Japanese. They're classical musicians. That's kind of weird, rather than just a regular existence in America. I was Japanese in the Midwest where there weren't that many Japanese people. It really allowed me to figure out who I was in that one aspect and definitely feels like a formative period in my life.

Kevin Farrington: The opportunity to interact with all the different sorts of people and all the different elements of experience made me a more complete person, somebody that wasn't just narrowly defined by things I did for work or things I had done before or things that I learned in school. It allowed me to experience a much wider spectrum of life, my own and those of people around me. After seven years of ManRay I was not the person, thank God, that I was when I walked in the door. It was a transformative element; it was a healing element. The experience, in many cases, allowed me to put my time in Vietnam to bed, my use of anger or rage as a negotiating or an interactive tool away. It allowed me to enjoy the freedom of physical expression. It allowed me to sample and enjoy a less masculine side of my personality. All these things that I never would have come upon, experienced, sampled, or expressed if I'd never experienced that seven years of ManRay. In some ways, I had no idea what lay in store for me when I first walked through the doors, but in other ways, I like to think that, regardless of what I didn't know, I made the right decision and would walk through those same doors again.

I came to ManRay knowing that time and life and community are precious, because I had risked all that unwillingly, and not of my own free will and volition, overseas in Vietnam. Then I risked it again every time I jumped in that silly ass helicopter in Worcester and went out to deal with somebody's stupid human trick. So knowing that there were absolutely no guarantees that you would have another 5 minutes, another 10 minutes, another day, another night, another month … I walked in the door knowing, what probably most of the people there did not know, that they were young and they expected a full life. I was not young and I knew it could stop at any instance. So, for me, it was desperately important that I squeeze every possible sequence of life out of the time I spent there. What I gave to the club, the club returned to me tenfold, and it's that energy that's allowed me to live with a certain degree of relaxed satisfaction that, when the moment came, I didn't walk away from it and say, no, that's too high. That's too far. That's too long. Something about me realized that it was a moment in my life that I would always think highly of and always look back upon and always value, but I had to seize it. That seizing came with a great deal of price, whether it's physical exhaustion, whether it's the complications that happen, who knows. But I think all those things kind of tie together.

Jennifer Chandler: I know it's different. The hope is there, but you're never going to find a group like that. A couple Saturdays ago I was watching *Almost Famous* by myself and, even in that generation, you had the six good solid friends that you hang around with, the group. We had ours, it was a little bit more than six, but you had that solid group of people that you hung out with that you hoped for your children. That's not the way it is. These days people don't hang out in groups anymore. They know they are more isolated than our generation and the generation before us. You don't have the Big Chill of the 2020's.

Gillian Cox: Cambridge has always been a beacon in terms of acceptance and tolerance. ManRay amplified that. ManRay sort of made the statement "We are here. We're not going away." Basically, all of those cultures were in that building. There was a safe space. You're not just tolerated. You're accepted, you're loved. If you're going through something with your identity then here's a nice weekend and here's a place where you can go and be with people who are like you. You're not alone.

Guari Desi-Ackerman: It's pretty much my coming-of-age place. I'm 48 now so, whenever they have the ManRay get togethers, it's actually a little depressing because I look around and go, "Oh my God, we are all so old." But it's definitely a place where I got to work out a lot of my own thoughts about what I wanted to be as an adult, how I wanted to live my own life, and how I wanted to express myself. Do I think it was all good? No, I think that in some ways, it did hinder me, that I could have succeeded more professionally or even socially. But it was a nice place to come home to for a little while.

Crayola Tidd: I think Central Square Cambridge has always been, and probably still is, a very nice mix of people, but I feel like ManRay just made it that much more of an interesting mix. I'm worried that it's going to become less and less of that nice mix. I feel like a lot of clubs are turning into condos. Places are more about making money and not making a scene. We've lost all the punk clubs and now the Goths and even the gay clubs are dwindling. These were all a huge part of people's social life.

Kyle Blaisdell: One thing I took away from ManRay was just being absolutely fearless. I overcame a lot of self-consciousness just being there and then involving myself and becoming such an exhibitionist about the whole situation. It was a huge social step for me, even though nobody around me knew what was going on. The character I created was an alter ego and I got to live vicariously through him, and he was hard to turn off. He spilled offstage and it was fun.

Patrick Baldwin: Appreciating dancing, hearing a song, and having that kinesthetic feeling. A lot of my memories of ManRay are kinesthetic honestly, the way that it felt to be dancing on the dance floor. If you were doing it right it was a little like flying.

Amy Butts: Before I went to ManRay, I liked to dance, but I was too shy to really do it. I love to dance and I kind of found my dancing voice at ManRay. I also learned how to have all different types of people in my life and all different kinds of friends.

Amy Butts: Chris really encouraged so much music love and people really ate it up in the Boston area. There's a lot of bands that are very, very Boston. It's not like we made them big, but I think that we helped move them along. So many major relationships that happened back in ManRay still have an effect on the community and the people now. Just think about all the things that are still tied in together.

Matt Richard: I think that some of the folks who went to ManRay wanted to make a name for themselves. As for myself, I've been doing Darq now in Salem since 2008, almost 14 years now, and I did it just by answering an ad on Myspace for somebody doing a night in Somerville. I was at a party with Chris Ewen and Patrick Fitzgerald, who do Xmortis, and they're the ones that, after my first club night I inherited ran its course, said "What are you going to do next?" I figured I would take my local Boston resources to Salem and create Darq. If I hadn't gone to ManRay I probably would not have met some of the folks, I would not have made the connections, I would not have been going into Boston frequently to hear that music and this wouldn't have happened. So, if not for ManRay, I would have gone to college and gotten into music, not had somewhere to hear the music, and then it might have dried up. But ManRay was that segue and it kept the industrial promoters in Boston and allowed me to meet them.

Heather Morgan: Heartbreaking, just the end of an institution. Unbelievable. That is where I first tried out the ability that we all have to change, to consider ourselves completely free to be one person one day and something else another. Costume and ritual and music all factor into the performance of being yourself. ManRay was the first stage for my identity. That was my first theater for who to be and how to be as a person. At that time, I really thought that there was some immutable kernel of myself that had to be in this certain dark aesthetic because of the way I grew up. But as time went on, and I studied more literature and art, I learned that wasn't necessarily true. I think there is a lot more freedom to what you can be. The performance aspect of the self that I picked up to flash around at ManRay, you realize you have more freedom with it, but that's still what you want to do. You want to play with the possibilities and then realize that you have more of them. Now I can dress with more color and I don't have to describe myself with one word like "Goth." I'm still looking at life as theater. I got hooked on that at ManRay and that's what my work is all about. That's what my whole life is all about. What the paintings are all about. Things have opened up for me a lot more aesthetically, there are a lot more different brushes in the box.

Shane Blau: Losing that whole crowd in general. It was a super formative part of my early queer identity, so leaving that was sad. ManRay made me feel almost like I was being subversive just by going, just by being out and queer, letting myself look queer and going with my friends. All of that was part of me, forcing the area to be okay with who I was. It felt so good to have this crowd of people and to be able to push back with other people was such a good feeling for me. It was so empowering in terms of figuring out who I was. I think it was that insistence on getting to be as loud and queer as I wanted to be and getting to be proud of it. I was always proud of my queer identity, I never felt like it was something I needed to hide, but to feel hot, to be in a crowd where I didn't feel ugly or where I didn't feel like I was constantly being judged by people around me in a negative way, was incredibly important for me being able to date people, for me being able to have any sense of myself. I didn't have to agonize about what the right thing to wear was because it was okay. When I got to San Francisco, I discovered there were different ways to be queer and that was important for me too, but I wouldn't have been able to step into it if I hadn't already spent the time getting to be proud, being with a group of proud people, and getting to be young and stupid together. When you're a queer teenager, you get your teenage experience in these little moments, instead of getting them all in one; it's not your high school years that give you your queer teenagerhood, instead you get your adolescence in these little moments where you have your community around you. You get to define your identity in that moment and then you put it all away during the rest of the time because you're not getting that reflected back to you. ManRay was one of those places that was my queer youth, it was my queer high school. It's one of the places that made me understand myself and made me know how to take action. In the queer community, especially at the time, there was such a sense of needing to find the queer elders who would kind of pass it down to you because there was nowhere else to get cultural information. That was sort of what ManRay was for me, for sure. I started going with a couple of upperclassmen who literally were like "Come on we're going to queer club tonight" and it felt like an after school special moment. Then I was the elder. I was the junior and senior and we had little freshmen coming along with us for the first time who were all excited. So I felt like I was contributing to the community and building it.

Jenny Dahling: I've known a lot of people who aren't in the scene. They don't understand. They say, "Oh, you're well into your 30s and you're going to a nightclub?" And I said, "Yes!!"

Kara Nemergut: I was pretty bummed because it was right after I graduated college, so I was kind of freer to do things. I was waiting tables, so I had a pretty flexible schedule, and I was like "Oh great I have more time to hang out with people and go to these nights that they all go to," and then it closed.

Niki Nevulis: I think there was acceptance because what we saw there was not the same as what was suburban. While we were aware of different lifestyles, ManRay actually mixed into and normalized the elements of different cultures. The best way to say it is like when you go to another country and you start to appreciate the value of looking at things through different perspectives or living in a different way. That, I'm able to bring into the workplace, I'm able to bring to my life. I'm able to advocate for and be a voice for those people, and I think that it impacts the political mindset. A great example of that is what the current tyrant in office has done, making statements that disenfranchises and puts many Americans at risk. When I have friends that flee the state of Texas because they're married but they're afraid because they are same sex and they can't hold hands on the beach … yeah, that's the problem. I probably would not have had as much appreciation for that if it wasn't for ManRay.

Avril dePagter: That idea of dressing yourself and presenting how you want to, the idea that I can put things on and that's an expression of my interiority is really interesting to me and something I still like to play around with even though I'm about to be 40.

I always think of humility with ManRay. As awesome, as wild, and as ridiculous as it was sometimes, there is something about it that always felt like mine, but also other people's. It was something that I was allowed to experience and be a part of. It wasn't just mine. That feeling of appreciating other people and taking people for how they are, getting to be a person that reacts and responds to that, is something that I am eternally grateful for and that I use every day in my work. I get to do that every single day. I get to go into a place and feel it out and interact with people. Sometimes it's awesome and sometimes it's terrible. But it's always new.

Corey Reeves: It was a place where my inner freak, my inner creativity could come out. I'm very grateful to have been a part of that because, aside from the black and aside from the skulls, which I love, there was a ton of warmth and collective love. People wanted to have a connection with people of their ilk. You would have seen all kinds of things, either turned your head in dismay and walked out the door, or you could have been like

"Wow, this is really great." So my feeling is that I was in a cool badass place that, in turn, was a very creative warm situation. The people that I worked with, the people that came to my bar, the people that I became acquainted with, and friends I hold truly dear are all because I was hired at ManRay.

David Winthrop: I learned how to talk to people when I was taking their pictures there. The way I communicate with a subject I'm photographing is very similar to ways I did then, it was very straightforward, very direct. I learned that, as much as a person might be an exhibitionist, there were many people who were very shy and needed someone to direct them in posing and body placement. My attitude towards anyone different, I carried that from those days. I like to think I was always pretty open and accepting of people of all different types. ManRay and its people just made me realize that there's so many different types of people and there's so many great people and there's so many assholes too. I learned to not judge people at ManRay very quickly. If you did, you'd be surprised because the weirdest person there you think "Oh God I don't want to talk to him" and he'd wind up being one of your greatest friends and the most interesting person you can talk to, and I think that still carries through my life today for sure.

Liz Lamanche: I think it was a really formative part of my exploring and realizing that people can be themselves in a really fun way; finding that freedom, possibility, and just experimenting and enjoying what you enjoy and meeting other people who are also experiencing that freedom. There are plenty of varied and valid ways of having fun and being in the world.

Anna Feder: In the short term, we're going to lose a lot of spaces because our fucking government isn't bailing anybody out, not people or spaces that matter, or communities. I think there's gonna be a lot more underground spaces. I wouldn't obviously go to any of them because it's not safe, but I think there's going to be a real renaissance of basement spaces which, in some ways, is exciting and, in some ways, is scary. When you end up with these spaces out of necessity because they can't be above ground or because those spaces don't exist or they're inaccessible, then you then end up in spaces where safety isn't the top priority. I worry about that. But I think that, even if it isn't in the same kinds of spaces, there is going to be an explosion of people. At first it's going to take a little while, but, once they get going again, it's going to be like the Roaring 20s. It's gonna be Party Central. There definitely will be a real renaissance of these spaces. I think people took them for granted in some ways, believing they would always be accessible and always be there, which ManRay showed us. That space was really sacred and we were lucky to have it. There really isn't anything else that came along that compares. When it went under, I thought there would be some other space, not realizing how precious and how fragile that space actually was. But these are all down to some developer or decision of somebody who doesn't understand or care, somebody for whom profit is the only motive and we're constantly fighting that.

Emily Arkin: It's hard to know about dance nights. I feel like I haven't supported them myself. I did until my late 30s. At some point, I was just like, "I don't want to be so old that it's creeping the younger people out." But I do love dancing. Now I get my dancing fix because I volunteer at Girls Rock Camp in Boston. We have dance parties and karaoke all the time. I do think karaoke became accepted as a way for grownups to get drunk and be silly too. But in some ways, I do miss dancing, because it's a way of interacting with people. For me, the most important thing about both dance and live music is there's so few things we're experiencing at the same time as other people. Your experience of time is shaped by the music you're hearing. I feel like people really get into sync with each other and you really get these sort of peak religious life experiences. A lot of people are all grooving on the same thing. I think people miss that really badly. I miss that communal experience. I miss that communal bond.

Becky D: ManRay is the physical manifestation of my coming of age in my community. I don't know who I would be today. I don't know where I would be in my life. All the closest friends that I have, with the exception of a handful, are because I met them at ManRay and these are relationships that I've had for 20 plus years. I don't know if I would have the confidence that I do now about myself. I don't know if I would be as comfortable in my own skin without ManRay. It was such a core part of my identity and such an important part of my coming of age. It was learning who I was as an adult and as an individual, separate from my family.

ML: It was definitely the place for subcultures in all respects. The fetish community faced and was stigmatized. If you weren't there on a Goth night then you would see only how Goths were portrayed on TV. In so many ways it influenced other clubs. It was not a place for people to experience the typical Boston nightclub.

A. Dominy Cusraque: If ManRay could be a witness to all the cultural and technological changes.

Chris Ewen: We knew ManRay was something good. We knew that we had done something very worthwhile as far as nightlife. We were very proud of it and still are. We were a scrappy bunch of people trying to do things that no one else was doing. We had built ourselves into something that no one else was really doing and felt really good.

EPILOGUE

September 2005. I am once again standing on the corner of Green St and Brookline. It's strangely chilly and raw for September. Yet, the weather brings back memories of that evening thirteen years past. That evening where I am standing on the same corner, looking at the club, a world of possibility in front of me.

The club, once standing in full, is now in what can only be described as in the throes of destruction. Gutted and with at least one wall gone, It is hard to imagine that a few months before, the club was alive and vibrant. It was one thing to make your peace with ManRay's closing. It was another to witness the physical destruction of the building. For myself, living on Brookline Street and having to walk past the crumbling and decaying former building, a sense of sadness and melancholy was pervasive inside me.

Nostalgia, in my estimation, is never a bad thing. If used properly, it can be a great tool. For this moment in time, I was always bringing it back, in my mind, to that first night. How much had changed since then. Relationships, a child, jobs, the realization that I needed to go back to school and doing so. I was no longer the youthful 19-year-old. Time, life and experience had changed me. Yet part of that change was deeply rooted in my time at ManRay

I walked through the doors of ManRay that night in 1992 and in the following thirteen years, I walked through them again and again, and again. I showed my ID, paid my entrance fee, got my stamp (later my wristband), ordered my drink (thank you Terri) and took in every night and experience I could.

Nightclub experiences for most are fleeting. You go, dance, congregate, have as much fun as the night provides, and you allow yourself to have. Maybe you go again in a few months, maybe a year, maybe never again. However, ManRay was different. The dance nights were built for repetition but never ever repetitive. You had the same cast of characters in your friends who also joined you at the club. Yet, this cast was always rotating. Adding new, while losing veterans. For the longtime ManRay attendee, as weeks turned to months and months turned to years, you settled into a happy path. Sometimes emotionally bumpy, fueled at times with Red Deaths and Mind erasers, but it's your path. Good or bad, you own it. It is a path for each of us to walk down. Leisurely or at a sprint. We all wish at times "I wish I was older", it is natural to want this. ManRay in ways both quantifiable and unquantifiable helped to nurture that youthfulness in us.

I am an adult, but still a child. A child born from my experiences here. The friends I entered the door with are still in my life. New people, born from my time at ManRay, are now friends. We all share a deeply connective bond. Not with a building, now long gone. But with a moment, a song, a libation, a kiss, a dance move. We are bonded by music, by our shared weirdness.

In its twenty years of existence, ManRay gave birth to many, not just the active adolescence of its patrons, but to openness, inclusion, creativity, a sense of community, a reverence for who and what came before and a hopefulness for what lies on the road ahead. It is in our memory now. To be called on when we need it. And there will always be a need for it.

SCD

Appendix 1 (The Music of ManRay)
(Curated from our interview contributors)

Absolutely Fabulous - Pet Shop Boys
Headhunter - Front 242
Set You Free - Planet Soul
Safety Dance - Men Without Hats
Common People - Pulp
It's Not Right, But It's Okay - Whitney Houston
Unspeakable Joy - Kim English
Maryland My Bitterness - Cruxshadows
Sex Dwarf - Leather Strip cover
Sex Dwarf - Soft Cell
Ziggy Stardust - David Bowie
Beautiful People - Marilyn Manson
Love Cats - The Cure
Head Like a Hole - Nine Inch Nails
Freaks and Animals - Rishloo
Cut You Up - Peter Murphy
Warm Weather - Pieces of a Dream
O Fortuna
Spellbound - Siouxsie and the Banshees
Silence - Sarah McLachlan
Pale Shelter - Tears for Fears
Ubiquitous Mr. Lovegrove - Dead Can Dance
Dead Stars - Covenant
Cities in Dust - Siouxsie and the Banshees
Killing Moon - Echo and the Bunnymen
The Chauffer - Duran Duran
Blue Monday - Orgy
Stigmata - Ministry
Red Right Hand - Nick Cave & The Bad Seeds
Blue Monday - New Order
Obsession - Animotion
Spin Me Right Round - Dead or Alive
Kamikaze Dove - O Positive
Lies - The Thompson Twins
Deutchmaschine - And One
Once in a Lifetime - Wolfsheim

Hokey Pokey - Annette Funicello
Tears - The Chameleons
Monitor - Siouxsie and the Banshees
Haus der Lüge - Einstürzende Neubauten
Is That All There Is - Christina
Friday, I'm In Love - The Cure
Come On Eileen - Dexy's Midnight Runners
Major Tom - Peter Schilling
Sunday Girl - Blondie
Tainted Love - Soft Cell
Cotton Eye Joe - Rednex
Hallelujah - Happy Mondays
Cuts You Up - Peter Murphy
Getting Closer - Nitzer Ebb
Rock Lobster - The B-52s
The New Zero - Rasputina
The Days of Swine and Roses - My Life With the Thrill Kill Kult
I'm a Vampire - Future Bible Heroes
Home - Depeche Mode
Sex On Wheels - My Life With the Kill Thrill Kult
I'm Afraid of Americans - David Bowie
Take On Me - Aha
Isn't She Pretty in Pink - The Psychedelic Furs
Teardrop - Massive Attack
Dominion - Sisters of Mercy
Down in the Park - Gary Numan
Send Me an Angel - Real Life
Seventeen - Ladytron
Swamp Thing - The Chameleons
Slut - Velvet Acid Christ
Like Cockatoos - The Cure
Hey Yeah - Outkast
Toxic - Brittany Spears
Fuck the Pain Away - Peaches
Deception - Cruxshadows
How Soon Is Now - The Smiths
Bloodletting - Concrete Blonde
Love Will Tear Us Apart - Joy Division
Elyria - Faith in the Muse

Love Buzz - Nirvana
La Isla Bonita - Madonna
Choke - Skinny Puppy
This Corrosion - Sisters of Mercy
Bela Lugosi's Dead - Bauhaus
Heresy - Nine Inch Nails
Scorched Blood - Xorcist
Behind the Wheel - Depeche Mode
Pussy - Lords of Acid
Warlock - Skinny Puppy
One Hundred Years - The Cure
Rippin Kitten - Golden Boy & Miss Kitten
Suedehead - Morrissey
The Sky's Gone Out - Bauhaus
I'll Melt With You - Modern English

Appendix 2
(Partial list of shows performed)

OCT 24, 1985---Divine at ManRay, Cambridge, MA, USA
OCT 26, 1989---Mudhoney at ManRay, Cambridge, MA, USA
AUG 8, 1990---Revolting Cocks at ManRay, Cambridge, MA, USA
APR 18, 1990---Nirvana at ManRay, Cambridge, MA, USA
OCT 16, 1990---MC 900 Ft Jesus at ManRay, Cambridge, MA, USA
NOV 27, 1990---Breadwinner at ManRay, Cambridge, MA, USA
NOV 27, 1990---The Jesus Lizard at ManRay, Cambridge, MA, USA
APR 29, 1991---Pigface at ManRay, Cambridge, MA, USA
JUN 28, 1991---Consolidated at ManRay, Cambridge, MA, USA
JUN 28, 1991---Meat Beat Manifesto at ManRay, Cambridge, MA, USA
JUL 19, 1991---Funeral Party at ManRay, Cambridge, MA, USA
JUL 19, 1991---Holy Cow at ManRay, Cambridge, MA, USA
SEP 27, 1991---New Model Army at ManRay, Cambridge, MA, USA
APR 4, 1992---Wrecking Crew at ManRay, Cambridge, MA, USA
APR 4, 1992---Agnostic Front at ManRay, Cambridge, MA, USA
APR 4, 1992---The Bruisers at ManRay, Cambridge, MA, USA
JUN 14, 1992---Die Krupps at ManRay, Cambridge, MA, USA
JUL 10, 1992---Laibach at ManRay, Cambridge, MA, USA
JUL 17. 1992---Suicide at ManRay, Cambridge, MA, USA
OCT 2, 1992---The Neighborhoods at ManRay, Cambridge, MA, USA
OCT 23, 1992---KMFDM at ManRay, Cambridge, MA, USA
FEB 26, 1993---Women of the SS at ManRay, Cambridge, MA, USA
JUN 11, 1994---Opium Den at ManRay, Cambridge, MA, USA
JUL 9, 1994---Skrew at ManRay, Cambridge, MA, USA
AUG 13, 1994---Sleep Chamber at ManRay, Cambridge, MA, USA
DEC 31, 1995---Sleep Chamber at ManRay, Cambridge, MA, USA
APR 17, 2000--VNV Nation at ManRay, Cambridge, MA, USA
NOV 9, 2000---Apoptygma Berzerk at ManRay, Cambridge, MA, USA
JUN 20, 2001---ohGr at ManRay, Cambridge, MA, USA
APR 17, 2002---Haujobb at ManRay, Cambridge, MA, USA
APR 17, 2002---VNV Nation at ManRay, Cambridge, MA, USA
MAY 12,2002---Apoptygma Berzerk at ManRay, Cambridge, MA, USA
MAR 26, 2004---Wolfsheim at ManRay, Cambridge, MA, USA
(Source: Setlist.fm)

ACKNOWLEDGEMENTS

We would like to give special thanks and acknowledgements to the following, without whose help and guidance, this book would not be what it is.

The Cambridge Public Library, The Cambridge Public Library Archive and Alyssa Pacy. Eric Hall and the Cambridge Historical Commission. Marc Levy and Cambridge Day. MJ Pullins and Hubba Hubba. The Boston Public Library, Riley Driscoll, Elizabeth Wahlman-White, Linda Hixon, Chris Ewen, Terri Niedźwiecki, Eve Costarelli, Shaula Clark. David Schwartz, Steve Shook, Joanne Kaliontzis, Tom Yaz, Erika Briesacher, Ahenbah Lane, Brian Volk. Indebted thanks to Charlene Henry and Curry Printing, and we are grateful to Melissa Maerz for all the helpful guidance.

And a special acknowledgement to ManRay owner Don Holland for guiding ManRay through the better part of three decades, promoting creativity, inclusion, and revelry. For the last 16 years we've lived in a world bereft of ManRay. We live in hope that, through the ideas and work of Don Holland, the club will once again rise and court a new generation of those seeking their crowd. We hope a new generation will be able to find creativity, nightlife....and possibly home.

ABOUT THE AUTHOR

Shawn Driscoll is a historian, writer and adjunct professor in History and Political Science. He is the co-author of The Grip-The 1918 Pandemic and a City Under Siege. He has published work in books that cover topics ranging from World War I (They Ventured Far, Dutcher & Ellsworth) to Women in Hollywood (Hollywood Heroines--ABC-Clio) Shawn, a native of the Massachusetts South Shore, resides in Worcester Massachusetts with his wife, and two children.